European Charter for Solar Energy in Architecture and Urban Planning

Europäische Charta für Solarenergie in Architektur und Stadtplanung
Carta europea per l'Energia solare in architettura e pianificazione urbana

Preamble

Roughly half of the energy consumed in Europe is used to run buildings. A further 25% is accounted for by traffic. Large quantities of non-renewable fossil fuel are used to generate this energy, fuel that will not be available to future generations. The processes involved in the conversion of fuel into energy also have a lasting negative effect on the environment through the emissions they cause. In addition to this, unscrupulous, intensive cultivation, a destructive exploitation of raw materials, and a worldwide reduction in the areas of land devoted to agriculture are leading to a progressive diminution of natural habitats.

This situation calls for a rapid and fundamental reorientation in our thinking, particularly on the part of planners and institutions involved in the process of construction. The form of our future built environment must be based on a responsible approach to nature and the use of the inexhaustible energy potential of the sun.

The role of architecture as a responsible profession is of far-reaching significance in this respect. In future, architects must exert a far more decisive influence on the conception and layout of urban structures and buildings on the use of materials and construction components, and thus on the use of energy, than they have in the past.

The aim of our work in the future must, therefore, be to design buildings and urban spaces in such a way that natural resources will be conserved and renewable forms of energy – especially solar energy – will be used as extensively as possible, thus avoiding many of these undesirable developments.

In order to attain these goals, it will be necessary to modify existing courses of instruction and training, as well as energy supply systems, funding and distribution models, standards, statutory regulations and laws in accordance with the new objectives.

Präambel

Rund die Hälfte der in Europa verbrauchten Energie dient dem Betrieb von Gebäuden, hinzu kommt der für den Verkehr aufgewendete Anteil in Höhe von über 25 %. Für die Bereitstellung dieser Energie werden in großem Umfang nicht wiederbringbare, fossile Brennstoffe verbraucht, die künftigen Generationen fehlen werden. Zu ihrer Erzeugung sind Umwandlungsprozesse erforderlich, deren Emissionen sich nachhaltig negativ auf die Umwelt auswirken. Zudem verursachen rücksichtslose Intensivbewirtschaftung und zerstörerische Rohstoffausbeute sowie ein weltweiter Rückgang der Agrarflächen eine zunehmende Verringerung der natürlichen Lebensräume.

Diese Situation erfordert ein rasches und grundlegendes Umdenken, besonders für die am Bauprozeß beteiligten Planer und Institutionen. Ein verantwortlicher Umgang mit der Natur und die Nutzung des unerschöpflichen Energiepotentials der Sonne müssen Grundvoraussetzung für die Gestaltung der gebauten Umwelt werden.

In diesem Zusammenhang ist die Rolle der Architektenschaft als verantwortlicher Profession von weitreichender Bedeutung. Sie muß erheblich mehr als bisher entscheidenden Einfluß auf die Konzeption und die Disposition von Stadtstrukturen, Gebäuden, die Verwendung der Materialien und Systemkomponenten und damit auch auf den Energieverbrauch nehmen.

Das Ziel künftiger Arbeit muß deshalb sein, Stadträume und Gebäude so zu gestalten, daß sowohl Ressourcen geschont als auch erneuerbare Energien – speziell Solarenergie – möglichst umfassend genutzt werden, wodurch die Fortsetzung der genannten Fehlentwicklungen vermieden werden kann.

Zur Durchführung dieser Forderungen sind die derzeit bestehenden Ausbildungsgänge, Energieversorgungssysteme, Finanzierungs- und Verteilungsmodelle, Normen und Gesetze den neuen Zielsetzungen anzupassen.

Preambolo

Attualmente il consumo della metà dell'energia in Europa è impiegato per la gestione degli insediamenti umani. In aggiunta un 25 % si deve stimare per il traffico. Per sopperire a questo fabbisogno di energia vengono impiegate ingenti quantità di combustibile fossile non rinnovabile, una risorsa, questa, che non sarà più disponibile per le generazioni future. I processi impiegati nella conversione dei combustibili in energia, inoltre, causano emissioni che hanno un permanente effetto negativo sull'ambiente. Oltre a ciò, coltivazioni intensive senza scrupoli, uno sfruttamento distruttivo di materiali grezzi e una riduzione in tutto il mondo di superfici di terreno a destinazione agricola, ci stanno conducendo verso una progressiva diminuzione degli habitats naturali.

Questa situazione esige un rapido e fondamentale riorientamento del nostro modo di pensare, progettare, costruire, prerogativa essenziale degli architetti e delle istituzioni coinvolte nello sviluppo degli insediamenti umani. Le forme e i caratteri del nostro futuro ambiente costruito devono basarsi su un approccio che comporta l'assunzione di responsabilità nei confronti dell'ambiente, e l'uso della potenziale ed inesauribile energia del sole.

Il ruolo dell'architettura quale professione responsabile è quello di dare espressione a questa forma di rispetto. In futuro gli architetti dovranno esercitare un'influenza più decisiva di quanto essi ne abbiano avuta in passato nella concezione e pianificazione di strutture urbane ed edilizie, nell'utilizzazione di materiali e sistemi complessi, e di conseguenza nell'impiego di energia.

Lo scopo del nostro lavoro in futuro deve quindi essere quello di progettare edifici e spazi urbani in maniera tale da salvaguardare le riserve naturali ed impiegare quanto più ampiamente possibile forme rinnovabili di energia per evitare molti dei possibili indesiderabili sviluppi.

Per il conseguimento di questi risultati, sarà necessario da un lato modificare le strutture esistenti per l'istruzione e la formazione professionale, dall'altro individuare sistemi di energia innovativi e formularne i relativi modelli di distribuzione, gli standars, le norme statutarie e le leggi.

Planners

Architects and engineers must design their projects with a knowledge of local conditions, existing resources, and the main criteria governing the use of renewable forms of energy and materials. In view of the responsibility they are thus required to assume, their role in society must be strengthened in relation to that of non-independent planning companies and commercial undertakings. New design concepts must be developed that will increase awareness of the sun as a source of light and heat; for an acceptance of solar technology in construction by the general public can only be achieved by means of convincing visual ideas and examples.

This means:
– cities, buildings and their various elements must be interpreted as a complex system of material and energy flows;
– the use of environmentally friendly forms of energy must be planned from a holistic point of view. A professional knowledge of all functional, technical and design relationships, conditions and possibilities is a precondition for the creation of modern architecture;
– the extensive and constantly expanding body of knowledge about the conditions governing the internal climate of buildings, the development of solar technology, and the scope for simulation, calculation and measurement must be systematically represented and made available in a clear, comprehensible and extendible form;
– the training and further education of architects and engineers must be related to future needs and should take place within mutually related systems on various levels, using the facilities afforded by the new media. Schools, universities, and professional associations are called upon to develop relevant options.

Die Planer

Architekten und Ingenieure müssen in Kenntnis der lokalen Gegebenheiten, der bestehenden Ressourcen und der maßgeblichen Kriterien für die Verwendung von erneuerbaren Energien und Materialien ihre Projekte entwerfen. Ihre gesellschaftliche Rolle muß angesichts der hier zu übernehmenden Verantwortung gegenüber der nicht unabhängigen Planung von Firmen gestärkt werden. Neue Gestaltungskonzepte sind zu entwickeln, welche die Sonne als Licht- und Wärmequelle bewußt machen, weil allgemeine öffentliche Akzeptanz nur mit bildhaften Vorstellungen vom solaren Bauen zu erreichen ist.

Dies bedeutet:
– Städte, Bauten und ihre Teile müssen als komplexes System von Stoff- und Energieflüssen interpretiert werden.
– Der Einsatz von Umweltenergien muß aus ganzheitlicher Sicht geplant werden. Professionelle Kenntnis aller funktionalen, technischen und gestalterischen Zusammenhänge, Bedingungen und Möglichkeiten ist Voraussetzung für das Entstehen von zeitgemäßer Architektur.
– Das umfangreiche, sich ständig erweiternde Wissen über die Bedingungen des Gebäudeklimas, über die technologische Entwicklung der Solartechnik, über die Möglichkeiten der Simulation, Berechnung und Messung muß in übersichtlicher, verständlicher und erweiterbarer Form systematisch dargestellt und verfügbar gemacht werden.
– Schulung und Weiterbildung von Architekten und Ingenieuren müssen in aufeinander abgestimmten Systemen auf unterschiedlichem Niveau unter Einsatz neuer Medien bedarfsbezogen erfolgen. Hochschulen und Berufsverbände sind aufgefordert, entsprechende Angebote zu entwickeln.

Le figure professionali

Architetti ed ingegneri devono concepire i loro progetti sulla base di una conoscenza delle condizioni locali, delle risorse esistenti e dei principali criteri che regolano l'impiego di forme diverse di energia rinnovabili e di componenti e tecniche eco-compatibili.
In vista della responsabilità che essi sono chiamati ad assumere, il loro ruolo nella società deve essere potenziato nell'indirizzare un approccio in armonia con la natura delle compagnie di progettazione non indipendenti e delle imprese di sviluppo.
Nuove filosofie progettuali devono essere sviluppate in maniera tale da incrementare la consapevolezza che il sole è fonte di calore e di luce; perchè il consenso per l'applicabilità dell'energia solare nell'edilizia da parte del grande pubblico può essere solamente ottenuto attraverso convincenti idee rese visibili ed esempi realizzati.

Ciò significa che:
– città, edilizia e loro componenti devono essere interpretati come un sistema complesso di flussi di materiali e d'energia;
– la pianificazione dell'impiego di forme d'energia con un sereno impatto ambientale deve partire da un punto di vista olistico. La conoscenza professionale di tutte le relazioni, condizioni e possibilità funzionali, tecniche e progettuali, è condizione preliminare per la creazione di un'architettura moderna;
– l'ampio corpo della conoscenza delle condizioni che governano il clima interno degli edifici, costantemente in via di espansione, lo sviluppo dell'impiego di energia solare, e la capacità di simulazione, calcolo e misurazione, devono essere sistematicamente rappresentate e rese disponibili in una forma chiara, comprensibile ed ampliabile;
– l'esperienza pratica e in generale il completamento della formazione degli architetti e degli ingegneri deve essere messo in relazione con le esigenze future; ciò potrebbe avvenire con sistemi relazionati mutuamente tra loro su vari livelli, usando le facilitazioni offerte dai nuovi media. Scuole, università ed associazioni professionali sono oggi chiamate ad esercitare importanti scelte.

Building sites

The specific local situation, the existing vegetation and building fabric, climatic and topographical factors, and the range and availability of ecologically sustainable forms of energy seen in relation to the duration and intensity of their use, as well as local constraints, all have to be analysed and evaluated as the basis for each individual planning project.

The natural resources available in a given location, especially sun, wind and geothermal heat, should be harnessed for the climatic conditioning of buildings and should be reflected in the design of their layout and form.

Depending on the geographical situation, the physical form, the material composition and the use to which a structure is put, the various existing or emerging patterns of building development will enter into a reciprocal relationship with the following local factors:

– climatic data (elevation of the sun, seasonal and regional range of sunlight, air temperatures, wind force and direction, periods when winds occur, quantities of precipitation, etc.);
– the degree of exposure and aspect of open spaces and the surface of the ground (angle of slope, form, contour, proportion, scale, etc.);
– the location, geometry, dimensions and volume of surrounding buildings, topographical formations, areas of water and vegetation (changing patterns of shade, reflection, volume, emissions, etc.);
– the suitability of existing earth masses as thermal storage bodies;
– human and mechanical patterns of movement;
– existing building conventions and the architectural heritage.

Der Bauplatz

Die spezifische lokale Situation, die vorhandene Vegetation und Bausubstanz, die klimatischen und topographischen Gegebenheiten, das Angebot an Umweltenergien, bezogen auf den Zeitraum und die Intensität ihres Wirkens, sowie die örtlich gegebenen Einschränkungen müssen als Grundlage der Planung in jedem Einzelfall analysiert und bewertet werden.

Die vor Ort verfügbaren natürlichen Ressourcen, insbesondere Sonne, Wind und Erdwärme, sind für die Konditionierung der Gebäude und die Ausprägung ihrer Gestalt wirksam zu machen. Die unterschiedlichen vorhandenen oder entstehenden Bebauungsmuster stehen je nach geographischer Lage, physischer Form und materieller Beschaffenheit sowie je nach Nutzungsart in Wechselwirkung mit unterschiedlichen lokalen Gegebenheiten wie:

– Klimadaten (Sonnenstand, Sonnenverteilung, Lufttemperaturen, Windrichtungen, Windstärken, Zeiträume des Windanfalls, Niederschlagsmengen ...)
– Exposition und Ausrichtung von Freiräumen und von Geländeoberflächen (Neigung, Form, Relief, Proportion und Maß ...)
– Lage, Geometrie, Dimensionen und Masse umgebender Gebäude, Geländeformation, Gewässer und Vegetation (wechselnde Verschattung, Reflexion, Volumen, Emissionen ...)
– Thermische Speicher vorhandener Bodenmassen
– Bewegungsabläufe von Menschen und Maschinen
– Vorhandene Baukultur und architektonisches Erbe

Gli insediamenti umani

La specifica situazione locale, la vegetazione esistente e il tessuto edificato, i fattori climatici e topografici e la vasta gamma di forme d'energia disponibili ed ecologicamente sostenibili, viste in relazione alla durata e all'intensità del loro uso devono, tanto quanto i vincoli locali, essere tutti analizzati e valutati come il substrato di riferimento per ogni singolo progetto di pianificazione.

Le risorse naturali disponibili in un certo luogo, specialmente sole, vento e calore geotermico, potrebbero essere utilizzate per la climatizzazione degli edifici e potrebbero riflettersi nella stessa concezione del programma e della forma. Dipendendo dalla situazione geografica, dalla forma fisica, dalla composizione del materiale e dall'uso a cui una struttura è finalizzata, i vari modelli esistenti ed emergenti di sviluppo dell'organismo edilizio entreranno in relazione reciproca con i seguenti fattori locali:

– dati climatici (angolo di elevazione del sole, irraggiamento solare stagionale e regionale, temperatura atmosferica, forza e direzione del vento, periodi in cui i venti ricorrono, quantità di precipitazioni, etc.);
– grado di esposizione, aspetto degli spazi aperti e superficie del terreno (angolo di inclinazione, forma, profilo, proporzione, scala, etc.);
– sito, geometria, dimensione e volume degli edifici circostanti, formazioni topografiche, aree con acqua e vegetazione (cambiamento di forma dell'ombra, riflessione, volume, emissione, etc.);
– adattabilità delle masse terrestri esistenti a diventare accumulatori termici;
– flussi di movimenti umani e meccanici;
– tipologie edilizie esistenti ed eredità architettonica.

Materials and forms of construction

Buildings and urban open spaces should be designed in such a way that a minimum of energy is needed to light and service them in terms of harnessing heat for hot water, heating, cooling, ventilation and the generation of electricity from light. To cover all remaining needs, solutions should be chosen that meet the criteria of an overall energy balance and that comply with the latest technical knowledge on the use of environmentally compatible forms of energy.

The use of materials, forms of construction, production technology, transport, assembly and dismantling of building components must, therefore, take account of the energy content and the life cycle of materials.

– Regenerable raw materials that are available in adequate quantities and forms of construction that have a minimal primary energy/"grey" energy content should be given preference.
– The recycling of materials should be guaranteed, with scope for eventual reuse or for ecologically sustainable disposal.
– Load-bearing structures and the skins of buildings must be of great durability so as to ensure an efficient use of materials, labour and energy, and to minimize the cost of disposal. An optimal relationship between production or embedded energy, (also known as enbodied energy), and longevity should be achieved.
– Building elements that serve the passive or active harnessing of solar energy and that can be easily accommodated to constructional, design, modular and dimensional requirements should be subject to further development and given priority in use.
– New systems and products in the field of energy and construction technology should be capable of simple integration into a building and should be easy to replace or renew.

Zur Materialisierung von Gebäuden

Gebäude und umgebende Freiräume sind so zu gestalten, daß für ihre Belichtung, die Gewinnung von Wärme für Heizung und Brauchwasser, für Kühlung, Lüftung und für die Gewinnung von Strom aus Licht möglichst wenig Energie aufgewendet werden muß. Für den verbleibenden Bedarf sind solche Lösungen einzusetzen, die nach den Kriterien einer Gesamtenergiebilanz dem neuesten Stand der Technik zur Nutzung von Umweltenergien entsprechen.

Bei der Verwendung von Materialien, Konstruktionen, Produktionstechnologien, Transport, Montage- und Demontage von Bauteilen müssen daher auch Energieinhalte und Stoffkreisläufe berücksichtigt werden.

– Nachwachsende, ausreichend verfügbare Rohstoffe und Konstruktionen mit möglichst geringen Inhalten an Primärenergie und grauer Energie sind zu bevorzugen.
– Die Einbindung von Materialien in Stoffkreisläufe, eventuelle Wiederverwendungsmöglichkeit oder umweltverträgliche Entsorgung müssen sichergestellt sein.
– Konstruktionen für Tragwerk und Gebäudehülle müssen dauerhaft sein, um den Aufwand hinsichtlich Material, Arbeit, Energie effizient und den Entsorgungsaufwand gering zu halten. Das Verhältnis von eingebetteter Energie und Dauerhaftigkeit ist zu optimieren.
– Bauteile zur direkten und indirekten (passiven und aktiven) Nutzung von Solarenergie, die sich nach konstruktiven und gestalterischen, modularen und maßlichen Anforderungen zur baulichen Integration gut eignen, sind weiterzuentwickeln und bevorzugt einzusetzen.
– Neue Systeme und Produkte im Bereich der Energie- und Gebäudetechnik müssen auf einfache Weise integriert bzw. gegen bestehende ausgetauscht oder erneuert werden können.

Componenti e tecniche della edilizia

Gli edifici e gli spazi urbani aperti dovrebbero essere progettati in modo tale che una quantità minima di energia basti loro per l'illuminazione e serva in termini di calore utile per l'acqua calda e per scopi di riscaldamento, refrigerazione, ventilazione e generazione dell'elettricità dalla luce naturale. Le soluzioni per soddisfare tutte le esigenze rimanenti andrebbero scelte tra quelle che tengono conto dei criteri di un bilancio energetico globale sostenibile e che si conformano con il più innovativo livello di conoscenza tecnica nell'impiego di forme di energia compatibili con l'ambiente.

L'impiego di materiali, forme di costruzione, produzione tecnologica, trasporto, assemblamento e smontaggio delle componenti di un edificio devono pertanto tener conto del loro contenuto energetico e del loro ciclo di vita.

– Dovrebbe essere data la preferenza all'uso di materiali grezzi che siano disponibili in quantità adeguate e a costruzioni che abbiano un'energia primaria minimale/energia grigia contenuta.
– Il riciclaggio dei materiali dovrebbe essere garantito, ai fini dell'eventuale riuso o per realizzazioni ecologicamente sostenibili.
– Le strutture portanti e la pelle degli edifici devono essere di notevole durabilità e garantire un alto grado di efficienza nell'impiego di materiali, lavoro ed energia, ed una minimizzazione dei costi di messa in opera.
– Gli elementi costruttivi che servono per l'impiego attivo e passivo dell'energia solare e che possono essere facilmente adattati alla costruzione, al progetto, alle esigenze modulari e dimensionali, dovrebbero essere soggetti ad un ulteriore sviluppo e dovrebbe esser data loro una priorità nell'utilizzazione.
– Nuovi sistemi energetici e tecnologie costruttive dovrebbero suggerire in un edificio semplici interventi di integrazione, di rimozione e di manutenzione.

Buildings in use

In terms of their energy balance, buildings should be regarded as self-contained systems with an optimal exploitation of environmentally sustainable forms of energy to meet various needs. They should be developed as permanent systems that will be capable of accommodating different uses over a long period.

– Functions should be laid out in plan and section in such a way that account is taken of changes of temperature and thermal zones.
– The planning and execution of buildings and the choice of materials should be based on a flexible concept, so that later changes of use can be accommodated with a minimum expenditure of materials and energy.
– The permeability of the skin of a building towards light, heat and air, and its transparency must be controllable and capable of modification, so that it can react to changing local climatic conditions (solar screening, protection against glare, light deflection, shading, temporary thermal protection, adjustable natural ventilation).
– It should be possible to meet comfort requirements largely through the design of the building by incorporating passive measures with a direct effect. The remaining energy needs in terms of heating, cooling, electricity, ventilation and lighting should be met by active systems powered by ecologically sustainable forms of energy.

The technical and energy resources used in a building should be appropriate to its function. Graphs showing the requirements for different user categories should be reconsidered and, where appropriate, modified. Buildings with special uses, such as museums, libraries, hospitals, etc., should be considered separately, since specific climatic constraints exist for these types.

Gebäude im Gebrauch

Gebäude müssen energetisch als Gesamtsysteme verstanden werden, die für unterschiedliche Ansprüche Umweltenergien bestmöglich nutzen. Sie sind als langlebige Systeme zu entwickeln, die auf Dauer geeignet bleiben, wechselnde Nutzungsarten aufzunehmen.

– Funktionen sollen im Grundriß und Schnitt so geordnet sein, daß Temperaturstufen und thermische Zonierung berücksichtigt sind.
– Planung und Ausführung von Gebäudestruktur und Materialwahl müssen so flexibel konzipiert werden, daß spätere Nutzungsänderungen mit geringst möglichem Material- und Energieeinsatz durchgeführt werden können.
– Die Gebäudehülle muß in ihrer Durchlässigkeit für Licht, Wärme, Luft und Sicht veränderbar und gezielt steuerbar sein, damit sie auf die wechselnden Gegebenheiten des lokalen Klimas reagieren kann (Sonnen- und Blendschutz, Lichtumlenkung, Verschattungen, temporärer Wärmeschutz, variable, natürliche Lüftung).
– Ansprüche an den Komfort sollen weitgehend durch die Gestaltung des Gebäudes mittels direkt wirksamer, passiver Maßnahmen erfüllt werden können. Den noch verbleibenden Bedarf für Heizung, Kühlung, Strom, Belüftung und Beleuchtung sollen umweltenergienutzende, aktive Systeme decken.

Der Aufwand an Technik und Energie muß der jeweiligen Nutzung der Gebäude angemessen sein. Dementsprechende Anforderungsprofile der unterschiedlichen Nutzungskategorien sind zu überdenken und gegebenenfalls anzupassen. So sind auch Gebäude spezieller Art wie Museen, Bibliotheken, Kliniken u. a. gesondert zu betrachten, da hier spezifische gebäudeklimatische Anforderungen bestehen.

Regime d'uso

In funzione del loro bilancio energetico, gli edifici dovrebbero essere considerati come sistemi di autocontrollo capaci di operare uno sfruttamento ottimale di forme di energia sostenibili per l'ambiente, al fine di venire incontro alle differenti esigenze. Si dovrebbe sviluppare una sorta di sistemi permanenti in grado di garantire differenti utilizzazioni a lunga durata.

– Le funzioni dovrebbero essere distribuite in pianta e sezione in maniera tale da tener conto dei gradi di temperatura e delle zone termiche.
– La progettazione e realizzazione degli edifici e la scelta dei materiali dovrebbe essere basata su un concetto flessibile, cosicché i cambiamenti d'uso successivi possano essere realizzati con un dispendio minimo di materiali e di energia.
– La permeabilità della pelle di un edificio a luce, calore e aria e la sua trasparenza, devono essere controllate e suscettibili di modificazione, in modo che esso possa reagire al cambiamento delle condizioni climatiche locali (schermatura dai raggi solari, protezione contro il riverbero, deflessione della luce, ombreggiamento, protezione termica temporanea, ventilazione naturale regolabile).
– Dovrebbe essere possibile venire ampiamente incontro ad esigenze di comfort attraverso una progettazione dell'edificio che incorpori misure passive con un effetto diretto. I restanti bisogni energetici in termini di riscaldamento, refrigerazione, elettricità, ventilazione ed illuminazione, si potrebbero soddisfare con l'uso di sistemi attivi forzati attraverso forme di energia ecologicamente sostenibile.

La tecnica e le risorse energetiche impiegate in un edificio dovrebbero essere appropriate alla funzione che esso svolge. I grafici mostrano i bisogni di differenti categorie di utenza che occorrerebbe considerare e, dove opportuno, modificare. Edifici con destinazioni speciali, come musei, biblioteche, ospedali, etc, dovrebbero venire concepiti separatamente dalle esigenze climatiche specifiche che esistono per queste tipologie.

The city

Renewable forms of energy present an opportunity to make life in cities more attractive. In the realms of energy supply and transport infrastructures, the use of these kinds of energy should be maximized through the actual form of the building. The existing building fabric should be used as far as is practical and possible. The combustion of fossil fuels must be drastically reduced.

The relationship between cities and nature should be developed to achieve a symbiosis between the two. Alterations and other measures carried out in public spaces or existing buildings, or caused by new construction, must take account of the historical and cultural identity of the location and the geographic and climatic conditions of the landscape.

The city must be comprehended in its entirety as a self-contained long-living organism. It must be possible to control the constant changes in its use and appearance, as well as in technology, in order to ensure a minimum of disturbance and a maximum conservation of resources.

Cities are resources in built form and have a high primary energy content. To achieve a closer integration with the overall balance of nature, their various neighbourhoods, buildings and open spaces, their infrastructures, and their functional, transport and communication systems must be subject to a constant process of modification and reconstruction that follows natural cycles of renewal.

The form of the urban and landscape structures that man creates must be governed by the following environmental and bioclimatic factors:

– orientation of streets and building structures to the sun;
– temperature control and use of daylight in the public realm;
– topography (land form, overall exposure, general situation);
– direction and intensity of wind (alignment of streets, sheltered public spaces, systematic ventilation, cold-air corridors);
– vegetation and distribution of planted areas (oxygen supply, dust consolidation, temperature balance, shading, windbreaks);
– hydro-geology (relationship to water and waterway systems).

Die Stadt

Erneuerbare Energien bieten die Chance, das Leben in Städten attraktiver zu gestalten. Für die Infrastruktur der Energieversorgung und des Verkehrs sowie durch die Art der Bebauung ist der Einsatz erneuerbarer Energien zu maximieren. Soweit möglich und sinnvoll, ist bestehende Bausubstanz zu nutzen. Die Verbrennung fossiler Rohstoffe ist drastisch zu reduzieren.

Das Verhältnis von Stadt und Natur ist symbiotisch zu entwickeln. Eingriffe und Veränderungen, die im öffentlichen Raum und an bestehenden Bauten oder durch Neubauten erfolgen, müssen auf die historische und kulturelle Identität des Ortes ebenso bezogen sein, wie auf die geographischen und klimatischen Bedingungen der Landschaft.

Die Stadt muß als langlebiger Gesamtorganismus verstanden werden. Der ständige Wandel in Gebrauch, Technologie und Erscheinungsbild muß möglichst zerstörungsfrei und ressourcenschonend gesteuert werden.

Städte sind gebaute Ressourcen von hohem Primärenergieinhalt. Ihre Quartiere, Bauten und Freiräume, ihre Infrastrukturen, Funktions- und Verkehrsabläufe sind durch laufenden, den natürlichen Erneuerungszyklen folgenden Umbau immer besser in den Gesamthaushalt der Natur einzupassen.

Für die Gestalt der von Menschen geschaffenen Landschafts- und Stadtstrukturen müssen als Umwelt- und als bioklimatische Faktoren bestimmend sein:

– Ausrichtung zur Sonne (Orientierung von Straßen, Gebäudestruktur, Temperaturregelung und Tageslichtnutzung im öffentlichen Raum)
– Topographie (Geländeform, Gesamtexposition, allgemeine Lage)
– Windrichtung und -intensität (Ausrichtung der Straßen, geschützte öffentliche Räume, gezielte Durchlüftung, Kaltluftschneisen)
– Vegetation und Verteilung von Grünflächen (Versorgung mit Sauerstoff, Staubbindung, Temperaturhaushalt, Verschattung, Windbarrieren)
– Hydrogeologie (Bezug zu Wassersystemen)

La città

Le forme d'energia rinnovabile offrono un'importante occasione per rendere la vita nelle città più attraente. Nei campi del rifornimento energetico e delle infrastrutture di trasporto, l'uso di questo tipo di energia dovrebbe essere portato al massimo livello attraverso la opportuna conformazione dell'edificio. Le costruzioni esistenti dovrebbero essere vissute quanto più possibile in maniera pratica. La combustione di carburante di natura fossile deve essere drasticamente ridotta.

La relazione tra città e natura dovrebbe essere sviluppata fino a raggiungere una simbiosi tra i due elementi. Alterazioni e menomazioni che si realizzano in spazi pubblici o in edifici esistenti, a volte causate dall'insediamento di nuove costruzioni, devono tener conto dell'identità storica e culturale del sito e delle condizioni geografiche e climatiche del territorio.

La città deve presentarsi nella sua interezza come un organismo durevole self-contained. Deve essere possibile controllare i costanti cambiamenti del suo uso e del suo aspetto, così come delle tecnologie in essa applicate, in maniera da assicurare un minimo di alterazione e un massimo di conservazione delle risorse.

Le città sono risorse in forma costruita e hanno un alto contenuto di energia primaria. Per il raggiungimento di un'integrazione più vicina al globale equilibrio della natura, il territorio circostante, gli edifici e gli spazi aperti, le infrastrutture, i sistemi di trasporto e di comunicazione, devono tutti essere soggetti ad un costante processo di modificazione e ricostruzione che segua cicli naturali di rinnovo.

Le forme di strutture urbane e paesaggistiche che si vengono a creare devono essere governate dai seguenti fattori ambientali e bioclimatici:

– orientamento del sole, delle strade e delle strutture degli edifici;
– controllo delle temperature e impiego della luce del giorno nell'ambito pubblico;
– topografia (forma della terra, esposizione totale, situazione generale);
– direzione ed intensità del vento (allineamento delle strade, spazi pubblici riparati, ventilazione sistematica, corridoi cold-air);
– vegetazione e distribuzione delle aree piantumate (rifornimento di ossigeno, consolidamento pulviscolare, ombreggiamento, frangi vento);
– idrogeologia (relazione tra acqua e sistemi waterway).

Urban functions such as habitation, production, services, cultural and leisure activities should be co-ordinated with each other where this is functionally possible and socially compatible. In this way the volume of vehicular traffic can be reduced. Production and service facilities can complement each other and be used more intensively and efficiently.

Pedestrians, and vehicles that are not propelled by the combustion of fossil fuels must be given privileged treatment in urban areas. Public transport should enjoy special support. Parking needs should be reduced and the consumption of petrol and other fuel minimized.

An economic use of land, achieved through a reasonable density in new planning schemes coupled with a programme of infill developments, can help to cut expenditure for infrastructure and transport and reduce the exploitation of further areas of land. Measures to restore an ecological balance should also be implemented.

In the public spaces of towns and cities, steps should be taken to improve the urban climate, temperature control, wind protection and the specific heating or cooling of these spaces.

Berlin 3/1996

Städtische Funktionen wie Wohnen, Produktion, Dienstleistungen, Kultur und Freizeit sollen dort, wo dies funktional möglich und sozial verträglich ist, einander zugeordnet werden. So kann der Verkehr von Fahrzeugen reduziert werden. Produktions- und Dienstleistungseinrichtungen können in gegenseitiger Ergänzung intensiver und wirtschaftlicher genutzt werden.

Fahrzeuge, die nicht durch fossile Brennstoffe angetrieben sind, und Fußgänger müssen in den städtischen Quartieren privilegiert behandelt werden. Öffentliche Verkehrsmittel sind zu fördern. Der Stellplatzbedarf ist zu reduzieren, der Treibstoffbedarf zu minimieren.

Eine sinnvolle Dichte bei Neuplanungen, die mit dem Boden haushälterisch umgeht, und Nachverdichtungen können den Aufwand an Infrastruktur und Verkehr sowie den Landverbrauch reduzieren. Ökologische Ausgleichsmaßnahmen sind vorzusehen.

Bei städtischen Räumen sind solche Mittel einzusetzen, die der Verbesserung des Stadtklimas, der Temperatursteuerung, dem Windschutz und der gezielten Erwärmung bzw. Kühlung von Freiräumen dienen.

Funzioni urbane quali, ad esempio, abitazione, produzione, servizi, attività culturali e per il tempo libero, dovrebbero essere tutte mutuamente coordinate, dove questo sia possibile e compatibile dal punto di vista funzionale e sociale. In tal modo può essere ridotto il volume di traffico veicolare. La produzione ed i servizi possono svolgere un ruolo di reciproco completamento e possono essere usati in maniera più intensiva ed efficiente.

Ai pedoni e ai veicoli che non utilizzano propellente a combustibile fossile, deve essere riservato un trattamento privilegiato nelle aree urbane. I trasporti pubblici dovrebbero godere di un supporto speciale, il bisogno di parcheggi dovrebbe essere ridotto e il consumo di petrolio e di altri combustibili minimizzato.

Un attento uso del territorio attraverso il perseguimento di una ragionevole densità nei nuovi schemi di pianificazione, unitamente ad un programma di sviluppo, può aiutare a ridurre le spese per infrastrutture e servizi di trasporto e a limitare lo sfruttamento indiscriminato di ulteriori aree di terreno. Dovrebbero anche essere implementate le misure atte a ristabilire un bilancio ecologico.

Negli spazi pubblici di città grandi e piccole, occorrerebbe compiere importanti passi per migliorare il clima urbano, il controllo della temperatura, la protezione al vento e gli specifici sistemi di riscaldamento e refrigerazione di tali ambienti.

Signatories / Unterzeichner / Firmatari:

Alberto Campo Baeza, Madrid E
Victor López Cotelo, Madrid E
Ralph Erskine, Stockholm S
Nikos Fintikakis, Athens GR
Sir Norman Foster, London GB
Nicholas Grimshaw, London GB
Herman Hertzberger, Amsterdam NL
Thomas Herzog, Munich D
Knud Holscher, Copenhagen DK
Sir Michael Hopkins, London GB

Françoise Jourda, Lyon F
Uwe Kiessler, Munich D
Henning Larsen, Copenhagen DK
Bengt Lundsten, Helsinki FI
David Mackay, Barcelona E
Angelo Mangiarotti, Milan I
Manfredi Nicoletti, Rome I
Frei Otto, Leonberg D
Juhani Pallasmaa, Helsinki FI
Gustav Peichl, Vienna A

Renzo Piano, Genoa I
José M. de Prada Poole, Madrid E
Sir Richard Rogers, London GB
Francesca Sartogo, Rome I
Hermann Schröder, Munich D
Roland Schweitzer, Paris F
Peter C. von Seidlein, Stuttgart D
Thomas Sieverts, Berlin D
Otto Steidle, Munich D
Alexandros N. Tombazis, Athens GR

This document was drawn up by Thomas Herzog in 1994–95 in the context of READ project supported by the European Commission DG XII. The contents were discussed and the wording agreed with leading European architects.

READ = Renewable Energies in Architecture and Design

Der Text wurde im Rahmen eines READ-Projektes, der Europäischen Kommission DG XII, von Thomas Herzog in den Jahren 1994/95 erarbeitet, mit führenden europäischen Architekten diskutiert und im Wortlaut abgestimmt.

= Erneuerbare Energien in Architektur und Design

Il presente testo è stato elaborato da Thomas Herzog, nell'ambito di un progetto READ per la Commissione Europea DG XII nel 1994/95, discusso ed approvato nel contenuto dagli architetti europei che lo portano avanti.

= Energie rinnovabili in architettura e design

Solar Energy in Architecture and Urban Planning

Solarenergie in Architektur und Stadtplanung

Energia solare in architettura e pianificazione urbana

Edited by / Herausgegeben von / A cura di

Thomas Herzog

With contributions by / Mit Beiträgen von / Con contributi di
Norbert Kaiser, Michael Volz

Prestel
Munich · London · New York

This book was published in conjunction with the 4th European Conference on Solar Energy in Architecture and Urban Planning held at the Haus der Kulturen der Welt, Berlin (March 26 to March 29, 1996), and the exhibition held at the Deutsches Architektur-Museum, Frankfurt am Main (December 14, 1996 to February 23, 1997), and further places.

Conference co-ordinator and organizer: WIP, Munich

In collaboration with
European Commission DG XII
Federal Ministry for Regional Planning, Building and Urban Development
Bund Deutscher Architekten BDA
Union Internationale des Architectes UIA
Senate of the City of Berlin
Deutsches Architektur-Museum DAM
Förderverein Deutsches Architektur Zentrum
Eurosolar
READ Group

Co-ordination: Verena Herzog-Loibl with Harriet Brittain

Translations
English: Peter Green
Italian: Alessandra Battisti, Fabrizio Tucci
German: Annette Wiethüchter (33 project descriptions)

Front Cover
Based on a design by MetaDesign, Berlin
Photo: School in Kinkplatz, Vienna, by Helmut Richter (photographer: Mischa Erben)

Frontispiece
Laser simulation model of Linz Congress and Exhibition Hall roof lighting grid (photographer: Peter Bartenbach)

Die Deutsche Bibliothek – CIP-Einheitsaufnahme

Solar energy in architecture and urban planning :
[in conjunction with the 4th European Conference on Solar Energy in Architecture and Urban Planning, held at the Haus der Kulturen der Welt, Berlin (March 26 to March 29, 1996), with the exhibition held at the Deutsches Architektur-Museum, Frankfurt am Main (December 14, 1996 to February 23, 1997), and further places] = Solarenergie in Architektur und Stadtplanung / ed. by Thomas Herzog. With contrib. by Norbert Kaiser ; Michael Volz. [In collab. with European Commission DG XII... Transl., Engl.: Peter Green. Ital.: Alessandra Battisti ; Fabrizio Tucci. German: Annette Wiethüchter]. – Munich ; New York : Prestel, 1996
ISBN 3-7913-1652-4

NE: Herzog, Thomas [Hrsg.]; Kaiser, Norbert; Volz, Michael; European Conference on Solar Energy in Architecture and Urban Planning <4, 1996, Berlin>; Haus der Kulturen der Welt <Berlin>; Deutsches Architektur-Museum <Frankfurt, Main>; Solarenergie in Architektur und Stadtplanung

© 1996, by Prestel Verlag, Munich, London, New York
Second edition 1998
© of project descriptions and illustrations by the authors and architects

Copyright details have been submitted by the architects and manufacturing companies themselves; neither the Editor nor Prestel Verlag shall be held responsible for the accuracy of such details.

All projects marked with ⬡ have been sponsored by the European Commission DG XII as part of Research and Development Programmes.

Photo credits: see page 215

Prestel books are available worldwide. Please contact your nearest bookseller or write to either of the following addresses for information concerning your local distributor:

Prestel Verlag, Mandlstrasse 26, D-80802 Munich, Germany
Phone (89) 38 17 09-0, Fax (89) 38 17 09-35

Prestel Verlag, 16 West 22nd Street, New York,
N.Y. 10010, USA
Phone (212) 627 81 99, Fax (212) 627 98 66

Concept: Verena Herzog-Loibl, Wilfried Wang
Design: Konturwerk, Munich
Offset lithography: Krammer, Reprostudio, Munich
Composition: Max Vornehm GmbH, Munich
Printing and binding: Passavia Druckerei GmbH, Passau

Printed in Germany
ISBN 3-7913-1652-4

Contents

Inhalt
Sommario

Office Buildings · Bürogebäude · Edifici per uffici

Double Façade Systems · Doppelfassaden-Systeme · Sistemi a doppia facciata

Parliament Buildings · Parlamentsgebäude · Edifici parlamentari

Public Administration Buildings · Öffentliche Verwaltungsbauten · Edifici per l'amministrazione pubblica

Cultural Buildings · Kulturbauten · Edifici culturali

Transport Facilities · Verkehrsbauten · Edifici per trasporti

Urban Planning · Siedlungswesen / Städtebau · Pianificazione urbana

Materials, Products, Systems · Materialien, Produkte, Systeme · Materiali, Prodotti, Sistemi

Appendix · Anhang · Appendice

Editor's foreword

Vorwort des Herausgebers
Premessa del curatore

In the mid-1970s, when the so-called energy crisis first made us aware of the finite nature of fossil fuels, architects and urban planners – who are in part responsible for a field that accounts for more than half our energy consumption – were unable to find an immediate answer to this problem. For far too long, energy had been available in unlimited quantities and at a reasonable price; and there had seemed to be no vital need to reduce its consumption. Although there was a great sense of insecurity at the time, the challenge that this new situation presented was at least recognized: the primary function of buildings – the provision of shelter and comfort for man and his belongings – had to be reinterpreted.

The careful husbanding of energy and its more effective use in ecologically sustainable forms (in particular solar energy) came to assume a central role in the work of our profession. This new approach was a pragmatic response to the situation and was not based just on fashionable trends. Now, two decades later, one can point to a number of outstanding structures that reveal an ambitious architectural concept as well as completely new interpretations and intense applications of environmental energy – for heating, cooling, natural ventilation, lighting and the generation of electricity. The buildings in which solar energy has become a factor of the design and has been used in an aesthetically effective form include schools, universities, housing schemes of all kinds and sizes, offices, museums, galleries and many other structures.

In addition, a large number of new products and systems have been developed for the outer skins of buildings, including translucent thermal insulation, improved shading and daylight-deflection systems, new types of glass and new forms of façade construction, the correct application of which can achieve exceptionally good values in the energy household of a building.

"Grey" energy and the life cycles of materials are two other aspects that are being increasingly taken into account. Regenerable, renewable raw materials are coming to assume a much greater importance than in the past in decisions concerning the choice of building materials and the form of construction. The use of recyclable products and minimal quantities of materials for structural membranes is another area where the scope for conserving resources has been recognized.

Als uns Mitte der siebziger Jahre die sogenannte Ölkrise die Endlichkeit der fossilen Energieträger bewußt machte, hatten Architekten und Stadtplaner – mitverantwortlich für den Bereich, in dem mehr als die Hälfte der Energie verbraucht wird – zunächst keine Mittel, darauf zu reagieren. Zu lange war Energie in beliebigem Umfang zu günstigen Preisen verfügbar gewesen, als daß man auf die Minderung des Verbrauchs geachtet hätte. So groß die Unsicherheit zunächst auch war – die Chance wurde erkannt, daß die primäre Aufgabe von Gebäuden neu zu interpretieren war: Menschen und ihren Gütern Schutz und Komfort zu bieten.

Der behutsame Umgang mit Energie ebenso wie der gezielte Einsatz von Umweltenergien – vor allem Solarenergie – wurden in der Sache begründete, von Tagesmoden unabhängige, zentrale Arbeitsthemen des Berufsstandes.

Zwei Jahrzehnte später gibt es prominente Gebäude mit architektonisch ambitioniertem Konzept, welche Umweltenergien ganz neu interpretieren, sie intensiv zur Wärmegewinnung, zur Kühlung, zur natürlichen Lüftung, Belichtung und Stromgewinnung nutzen, bei denen Solarenergie gestaltprägend auch ästhetisch wirksam wird: Schulen und Hochschulen, Wohnhäuser aller Art und Größe, Büro- und Ausstellungsbauten u. v. a. Hinzu kommen neue Produkte und Systeme der Gebäudehülle wie transluzente Dämmung, verbesserte Abschattungs- und Umlenksysteme für das Tageslicht, neue Gläser und Fassadenkonstruktionen, bei deren richtiger Anwendung der Energiehaushalt von Bauten ungewohnt günstige Werte zeigt.

Verstärkt werden demnächst auch graue Energie und Stoffkreisläufe einbezogen. In erheblich umfangreicherem Maße als bisher werden die nachwachsenden, erneuerbaren Rohstoffe bei Material- und Konstruktionsentscheidungen an Bedeutung gewinnen müssen. Auch die konstruktiven Membranen aus recyclebaren Stoffen mit minimalem Materialaufwand werden in ihrem Potential für die Ressourcenschonung erkannt.

Seit kurzem entstehen Konzepte für neue Stadtteile, wo nicht mehr einzelne Solarbauten als Exoten die Ausnahme unter den Häusern sind, sondern wo vielfältige Möglichkeiten der Nutzung solarer Energie und die Strukturen der Bebauungsmuster, der Freiräume und die Infrastruktur miteinbezogen werden. Dadurch geht

Quando a metà degli anni settanta la cosiddetta crisi energetica ci rese consapevoli della natura finita della fonte di energia fossile, architetti e pianificatori – corresponsabili nel settore in cui si consuma più energia – non avevano alcun mezzo per reagirvi. Per troppo tempo l'energia era stata disponibile in quantità illimitate e ad un prezzo ragionevole; cosicché non si era prestata alcuna attenzione alla riduzione del consumo. Al momento questo ingenerò un senso di grande insicurezza – si riconobbe in ciò l'occasione di reinterpretare la funzione primaria dei nuovi edifici, per offrire all'umanità e a ciò che le apparteneva protezione e comfort.

L'amministrazione parsimoniosa dell'energia così come l'impiego specifico di forme ecologicamente sostenibili – in particolare l'energia solare – vennero ad assumere un ruolo centrale nel lavoro della nostra professione – svincolato dalle mode giornaliere.

Attualmente, a due decenni di distanza, vi sono edifici notevoli con un concetto architettonico ambizioso che interpretano in chiave totalmente innovativa l'energia naturale, utilizzandola in modo intenso per raffreddamento, ventilazione naturale, illuminazione e per generare elettricità; edifici in cui l'energia solare, divenendo un fattore che imprime forma, raggiunge efficacia anche dal punto di vista estetico: scuole, università, edifici residenziali di tutte le dimensioni, uffici, musei e così via.

Inoltre, si aggiungono prodotti e sistemi innovativi per l'involucro degli edifici, come l'isolante traslucido, che migliora l'ombreggiatura e la deflessione della luce naturale, nuovi vetri e strutture di facciata, la cui corretta applicazione permette di raggiungere valori eccezionali nel bilancio energetico di un edificio.

Vengono rafforzati da ciò anche l'energia grigia ed il ciclo di vita dei materiali coinvolti nel processo. In notevole e più ampia misura che in passato devono assumere significato le materie prime rinnovabili nel momento della scelta dei materiali e delle forme edilizie. Anche alle membrane costruttive fabbricate con materie riciclabili attraverso una quantità minima di dispendio di materiale va riconosciuto un potenziale nei confronti del rispetto delle risorse.

Da poco si vengono a sviluppare concetti per nuovi quartieri urbani, dove gli edifici che utilizzano energia solare non sono più casi isolati ed esotici

Concepts for new urban districts are now being developed in which structures using solar energy are no longer exotic, isolated examples. Today, the many potential uses of solar energy are seen in conjunction with the structures of urban and building developments, public open spaces and the infrastructure as forming an integral whole. As a result, it has been possible to achieve a considerable reduction in the consumption of energy from fossil fuels for the complex system that the city represents.

Changes are, therefore, taking place on many levels – on an urban scale, in individual developments and in building components – as well as in planning methods and procedures. New political objectives are evolving; the images companies have of themselves and wish to project are undergoing changes, and their readiness to assume responsibility for the environment is being reformulated. It has long been evident that the integration of solar energy into environmental design is an important theme for the future.

The exhibition for which the present catalogue was compiled was organized on the occasion of the 4th European Conference on Solar Energy in Architecture and Urban Planning and will subsequently be shown in other European countries. The exhibition and catalogue provide a survey of achievements to date in the form of finished buildings and projects still in the process of construction. It was possible to execute much of this work to a very high standard as a result of the support for research and development projects granted by the European Commission. From the early 1980s, Dr Wolfgang Palz of the Direction Générale XII – the person responsible for renewable forms of energy – has come to play a very important role. Although he is a physicist, and as such was not immediately familiar with the realm of construction, he recognized that buildings are complex holistic systems and that the structural and aesthetic integration of new solar technology had to be central to their design if the cultural dimension of architecture were to be retained in future constructional concepts and in work on the mass of existing buildings.

The following selection of projects should, therefore, be seen as a general survey of the spectrum of architectural approaches and forms. Within the scope of this catalogue, however, it is not possible to do justice to all aspects of the individual designs. The buildings, projects and products shown here should serve as a source of new ideas and stimulate discussion.

It was important to us to demonstrate the variety of situations, uses and requirements in the different climatic zones of Europe, both in terms of

in diesen Fällen der Verbrauch an fossiler Energie für das komplexe System »Stadt« deutlich zurück.

Veränderungen finden also statt im Bereich der Städte, der Gebäude und der Bauteile – ebenso wie bei den Planungsmethoden und -verfahren. Politische Vorgaben, ein gewandeltes Selbstverständnis und die Verantwortungsbereitschaft von Unternehmen artikulieren sich neu. Längst ist deutlich, daß die Integration von solarer Energie in die Gestaltung der Umwelt zukunftsbestimmend sein wird.

Die Ausstellung und der vorliegende Katalog, die anläßlich der 4. Europäischen Konferenz über Solarenergie in Architektur und Stadtplanung zusammengestellt wurden und die in der Folge an weiteren Orten in verschiedenen europäischen Ländern gezeigt werden sollen, geben Einblick in den Stand des bisher Erreichten, zeigen fertiggestellte Bauten und derzeit laufende Projekte. Vieles davon wurde auf hohem Niveau durch Förderung von Forschung und Entwicklungsarbeit von seiten der Europäischen Kommission möglich. Dabei hat seit Anfang der achtziger Jahre Dr. Wolfgang Palz, in der DG XII verantwortlich für die erneuerbaren Energien, eine zentrale Rolle inne. Obgleich selbst Physiker und als solcher zunächst nicht im Bereich des Bauens fachlich beheimatet, erkannte er sowohl, daß Gebäude als komplexe Gesamtsysteme in den Blick rücken müssen, wie auch, daß die strukturelle und ästhetische Integration neuer Solartechnik zentrale Bedeutung gewinnen muß, wenn die kulturelle Dimension von Architektur bei neuen Baukonzepten und innerhalb des – von der Menge her dominierenden – Altbaubestandes gewahrt werden soll.

Man möge die vorliegende Zusammenstellung als weitgreifenden Überblick verstehen, der vor allem das große Spektrum architektonischer Ansätze und Ausprägungen zeigen will, der aber im vorgegebenen Rahmen keinesfalls den Anspruch erhebt, dem einzelnen Entwurf im Ganzen gerecht zu werden. Die gezeigten Bauten, Projekte und Produkte sollen als Anregung dienen und die Diskussion bereichern.

Wesentlich war uns aber, die Vielfalt der Situationen, der Nutzungen und der in den verschiedenen europäischen Klimazonen ganz unterschiedlichen Ansprüche sowohl an den Komfort als auch an die Steuerung der Einflüsse solarer Einstrahlung sichtbar zu machen.

Entsprechend vielfältig sind die architektonischen Konzepte und baulichen Lösungen, was zeigt, daß qualitätsvolle umweltorientierte Planung mit der Auseinandersetzung und Einbindung von spezifischen lokalen Gegebenheiten und Anforderungen viel mehr zu tun hat als mit schematischen, nor-

tra le case, ma dove le molteplici possibilità di impiego di energia solare e le strutture del tipo edilizio vengono integrate agli spazi aperti ed alle infrastrutture. In questi casi il consumo di energia fossile va sensibilmente riducendosi a favore di un complesso sistema «città».

Alcune trasformazioni hanno luogo anche alla scala cittadina degli edifici e dei componenti – così come nei metodi e nelle procedure di progettazione. Obiettivi politici, una consapevolezza in cambiamento e il senso di responsabilità degli imprenditori sono articolati in maniera nuova.

Da molto tempo è evidente che l'integrazione di energia solare viene ad essere determinante nella progettazione ambientale futura.

La mostra, per la quale il presente catalogo è stato preparato, che verrà in seguito allestita in altre nazioni europee, organizzata in occasione della 4a Conferenza europea sull' Energia Solare in Architettura e Pianificazione Urbana, dà un'idea dello stadio raggiunto finora, mostrando edifici finiti e progetti ancora in corso di costruzione. È stato possibile eseguire gran parte di questo lavoro ad un livello standard molto alto grazie al contributo per la ricerca e lo sviluppo dei progetti stanziato dalla Commissione europea.

Dagli inizi degli anni ottanta il Dr. Wolfgang Palz della Direzione Generale XII – responsabile per le forme rinnovabili di energia – è venuto ad occupare un ruolo molto importante. Sebbene egli sia un fisico, ed in quanto tale non avesse una familiarità immediata con il mondo dell'edilizia, egli riconobbe tanto che gli edifici in qualità di sistemi complessi omnicomprensivi, dovevano essere visti in quest'ottica, quanto che l'integrazione estetica e strutturale di una nuova tecnologia solare avrebbe dovuto assumere un significato centrale, se la dimensione culturale dell'architettura doveva essere assicurata nei nuovi concetti edilizi e all'interno di edifici – in quantità dominante – già esistenti.

La presente selezione di progetti potrebbe essere vista, pertanto, come uno sguardo generale sull'ampio spettro di approcci e forme architettoniche, ma nello spazio di un catalogo non è possibile che venga resa giustizia a tutti gli aspetti dei singoli progetti. Gli edifici ed i prodotti mostrati dovrebbero servire come fonte per nuove idee e per stimolare la discussione.

E' stato sostanziale per noi illustrare la varietà di situazioni, usi e necessità nelle differenti zone climatiche europee, sia in termini di comfort rispetto al controllo dell'irraggiamento solare sia per le sue influenze sul nostro ambiente.

I concetti architettonici e le soluzioni costruttive sono opportunamente varie, ciò dimostra che una progettazione qualitativa orientata ecologicamente

comfort and in respect of the control of solar radiation and its influences on our environment. The architectural concepts and constructional solutions illustrated here are accordingly diverse, which goes to show that qualitative, environmentally-oriented planning has much more to do with the reflection and integration of specific local conditions and needs than with any programmatic, normative precepts, which can quickly lead to uniformity and aesthetic impoverishment.

With the exception of occasional modifications in the interests of consistency, the short descriptions and drawings contained in this catalogue are by the architects of the various projects. It was left to them to decide which characteristics and details of their schemes they wished to describe. The members of the Architectural and Scientific Committee have selected smaller projects by architects who are still relatively unknown, as well as designs for large-scale internationally acclaimed projects by renowned offices. Most of the schemes date from recent years. The inclusion of work by architects who have proved over the last few decades that they belong to the technnical avant-garde and who are evidently addressing their knowledge and creative skills to architectural concepts that focus on the use of solar energy is a positive sign.

There are no detached single-family houses in this documentation. Although, in the previous decade, this building type provided the earliest examples of solar-supported energy supply systems in the realm of housing, from our present viewpoint, this aspect is outweighed by the negative effects on the urban fabric. These include increased land use, low density of development, which results in increased private traffic, and a greater expenditure of constructional and financial resources.

The projects that have a validity for the future are those that take account of the quantities and life cycles of materials and energy, the effects of building on urban space and the environment as a whole, and the conservation of the landscape. For that reason, this documentation also includes a number of older housing developments that were already setting standards some decades ago.

Thomas Herzog

mativen Setzungen, die schnell zu Nivellierung und ästhetischer Verarmung führen können.

Mit gelegentlich geringen Angleichungen wurden Kurztexte und Zeichnungen der verantwortlichen Architekten übernommen. Es blieb ihrer Entscheidung vorbehalten, auf welche Charakteristika ihrer Bauten sie eingingen und welche ergänzenden Angaben sie machten. Die Mitglieder des Architectural and Scientific Committee wählten sowohl kleine Projekte noch unbekannter Autoren aus als auch Entwürfe für weltweit beachtete Großbauten aus den letzten Jahren, die von international bekannten Architekturbüros stammen. Daß sich darunter auch Gebäude von Architekten finden, die in den vergangenen Jahrzehnten bewiesen haben, daß sie auf dem Gebiet des Bauens zur technischen Avantgarde gehören, und die offensichtlich ihr Wissen und ihr kreatives Potential nunmehr auch auf solche architektonische Konzepte richten, deren Schwerpunkt der Einsatz von Solarenergie ist, halten wir für einen großen Gewinn.

Wir zeigen in dieser Dokumentation keine freistehenden Einfamilien-Häuser. Dieser Gebäudetypus gab zwar im vergangenen Jahrzehnt die ersten Beispiele von solargestützten Energieversorgungssystemen für Wohnhäuser, doch muß aus heutiger Sicht die dabei entstehende Problematik in ihrer negativen Auswirkung auf städtische Räume bedacht werden (erhöhter Landverbrauch, geringe Dichte, d. h. erhöhter Individualverkehr, erhöhter bautechnischer und finanzieller Aufwand).

Zukunftsweisend sind solche Arbeiten, welche die Menge und den Zyklus der Stoff- und Energieflüsse und auch die Konsequenzen für den städtischen Raum als Ganzes sowie den Erhalt des Landschaftsraumes berücksichtigen. Es wurden deshalb auch einige ältere Beispiele von Wohnungsbauten in die Dokumentation aufgenommen, die hierzu bereits vor Jahrzehnten Maßstäbe setzten.

ha molto più a che fare con la riflessione e l'integrazione di specifiche condizioni e bisogni locali piuttosto che con ogni precetto programmatico e normativo, che può facilmente condurre all'uniformità ed all'impoverimento estetico.

Fatta eccezione per alcune piccole modifiche, i brevi testi e i disegni sono degli architetti responsabili di ciascun progetto. Si è lasciato decidere loro quali caratteristiche e dettagli dei loro schemi preferissero descrivere. I membri della Commissione Scientifica Architettonica hanno selezionato i progetti più piccoli di architetti ancora sconosciuti, oltre ai progetti su larga scala degli ultimi anni che appartengono a studi di architettura internazionalmente noti.

L'inclusione del lavoro di architetti che hanno provato durante le ultime poche decadi di appartenere all'avanguardia tecnologica e che hanno indirizzato il loro sapere e la loro abilità creativa verso concetti architettonici che si incentrano sull'impiego di energia solare è un segno positivo. Non mostriamo in questa documentazione nessuna casa unifamiliare isolata – sebbene nel decennio precedente questo tipo edilizio abbia costituito i primi esempi di sistemi di riferimento energetico supportati con energia solare in campo residenziale.Da un punto di vista attuale devono essere tenuti in conto e la problematica che da esse deriva e il loro effetto negativo sugli spazi urbani (un più alto uso di terreno, scarsa densità, ossia un maggior traffico privato, ed una maggiore spesa di costruzione e dispendio finanziario). Indicativi per il futuro sono i lavori che tengono conto della quantità dei cicli di vita dei materiali, dell'energia e dell'effetto del costruito sugli spazi urbani e del loro sviluppo come un intero. Perciò nella documentazione sono inclusi anche degli esempi di vecchi edifici residenziali, che già da dieci anni fissano standards.

Considerations on solar architecture

Betrachtungen zur solaren Architektur
Considerazioni sull'architettura solare

Everyone acts reasonably in his or her own way. The reasons that motivate us collectively to realize something, to transform something, are rarely idiosyncratic or subjective. We approach problems logically, we draw on scientifically recognized models as the basis of our preparations. All the same, reason has different temporal dimensions. Thus, for instance, shareholders are interested in a rapid and intensive return on their investment. For them, knowledge of internal processes is not necessarily required. Farmers are also interested in a rapid and intensive return on their labour; many know exactly with which intensity they might cultivate their land, and how long a field needs to lie fallow before it is recultivated. Some, however, pursue their work with an intensity that is ultimately detrimental to the soil. We call this destructive exploitation, and we are immediately reminded of the destruction of large forests. However, a form of destructive exploitation has already existed for a long time in architecture. Societies that follow the current lifestyles – house in the countryside, work in the city or in a techno-park, leisure and consumer activities in the shopping centre, all reached by car – are thereby carrying out a form of destructive exploitation of the future. Most inhabitants of the first world know that such lifestyles in contemporary built structures are not tenable in the long run, that this type of reasoning results only in short-term successes and that it must be replaced by a type of reasoning that is sustained, durable and long lasting. But in the competition of the one type of reason against the other there are currently few people who are prepared to depart from untenable habits. In order to advance the necessary development from a destructive exploitation to a reconstruction in the direction of a balanced relation between our demands and the resources that are available to us, this publication and exhibition should expose ideas and built examples to as many interested people as possible.

The diffusion of exemplary designs in the field of architecture and urban design should demonstrate to anyone the diversity of both qualitative as well as quantitative solutions – even if the balance of either is not always in the same relation – that contribute their part in this phase of reconstruction of societies. What may have looked somewhat unresolved in the seventies and early eighties – houses with applied solar collectors – is the excep-

Jeder handelt auf seine Weise vernünftig; Gründe, die uns gemeinsam bewegen, etwas umzusetzen, etwas zu verändern, sind selten im Alleingang oder subjektiv gefaßt. Wir arbeiten mit logischen Vorsätzen, ziehen wissenschaftlich anerkannte Modelle als Grundlage unserer Vorbereitungen heran. Die Vernunft hat aber verschiedene zeitliche Perspektiven. So sind Aktionäre zum Beispiel an einer baldigen Mehrung der Rendite ihrer Investitionen interessiert. Dabei ist die Kenntnis von betriebsinternen Prozessen nicht unbedingt notwendig. Landwirte sind auch an baldigen Rückflüssen des Ertrages ihrer Arbeit interessiert; viele wissen genau, wie intensiv man einen Acker bestellen darf und wie lange er brach zu liegen hat, bevor man ihn wieder bewirtschaften darf; manche aber betreiben diese Arbeit auch mit einer den Grund und Boden schlußendlich schädigenden Intensität. Wir nennen es Raubbau, und sofort erinnern wir uns auch an das Abholzen großer Wälder. Aber Raubbau gibt es auch schon länger im Bauwesen. Durch die nach wie vor gängigen Vorstellungen von Lebensgewohnheiten – Haus im Grünen, Arbeit in der Stadt oder im Techno-Park, Konsum und Freizeit im Einkaufszentrum, alles erreicht durch den Pendelverkehr mit dem PKW – betreiben derartig ausgerichtete Gesellschaften Raubbau an der Zukunft. Die meisten Menschen in den Industrieländern wissen, daß solche Lebensgewohnheiten in heutigen baulichen Strukturen langfristig nicht haltbar sind, daß diese Art von Vernunft nur kurzfristige Erfolge erzielt und daß sie durch eine Vernunft zu ersetzen ist, die lange Zeit gültige Resultate erreicht. Aber im Wettbewerb der einen Vernunft gegen die andere gibt es derzeit nur wenige, die bereit sind, von unhaltbaren Gewohnheiten Abschied zu nehmen. Um diese notwendige Entwicklung von einem Raubbau zu einem Umbau in Richtung auf eine ausgeglichene Beziehung zwischen unseren Ansprüchen und den uns zur Verfügung stehenden Ressourcen voranzubringen, sollen diese Publikation und die Ausstellung Ideen und gebaute Beispiele so vielen Interessenten wie möglich nahebringen.

Durch die Verbreitung beispielhafter Gestaltungen auf dem Gebiet der Architektur und des Städtebaus kann jedem gezeigt werden, daß es verschiedene Lösungen gibt, die sowohl quantitativ als auch qualitativ, wenn auch nicht immer im gleichen Verhältnis, ihren Beitrag in dieser Umbauphase leisten. Was in den späten siebziger und

Ognuno agisce a suo modo: le ragioni che ci danno motivo di realizzare qualcosa collettivamente, per trasformare qualcosa, sono raramente idiosincrasiche e soggettive. Affrontiamo i problemi con la logica. Attingiamo scientificamente a modelli conosciuti per la base della nostra preparazione. Però la ragione ha differenti dimensioni temporali. Così per esempio, gli azionisti sono interessati ad un immediato ed intenso ritorno del loro investimento. La conoscenza dei processi interni non è necessariamente loro richiesta. I contadini anche sono interessati ad un rapido ed intenso ritorno del loro lavoro; molti sanno esattamente con quale intensità possono coltivare la loro terra, e quanto a lungo un campo debba essere lasciato riposare prima di ricoltivarlo. Alcuni però perseguono il loro lavoro con un'intensità che è ultimamente a detrimento del terreno. Chiamiamo ciò sfruttamento distruttivo, il che ci ricorda immediatamente la distruzione delle grandi foreste. Tuttavia uno sfruttamento distruttivo è già esistito in architettura per lungo tempo.

Le società che adottano gli stili di vita correnti – casa in campagna, lavoro in città o in un tecnoparco, tempo libero ed attività di consumo nel centro commerciale, il tutto raggiungibile con la macchina – stanno portando avanti una forma di sfruttamento distruttiva per il futuro.

La maggior parte degli uomini dei paesi industrializzati sa che tali stili di vita nelle strutture edilizie contemporanee non sono sostenibili a lungo termine, che questo tipo di modo di vivere ha successo solo a breve termine e ciò si deve sostituire con un modo di pensare durevole a lungo termine. Ma nella lotta tra un modo di pensare e l'altro ci sono attualmente poche persone che sono preparate a separarsi da abitudini non più sostenibili. Con lo scopo di procedere in avanti nel necessario sviluppo da uno sfruttamento eccessivo ad una ricostruzione nella direzione di un equilibrato rapporto tra le nostre esigenze e le risorse disponibili, questa pubblicazione e la mostra dovrebbero esporre idee e costituire esempi per interessare quante più persone possibili.

La diffusione di progetti esemplari nel campo dell'architettura e della pianificazione urbana dovrebbe dimostrare ad ognuno le differenze qualitative oltre che quantitative delle soluzioni – persino quando l'equilibrio di entrambe non è sempre nella stessa relazione – che danno il loro particolare contributo in questa fase di ricostruzione della

tion today; buildings and urban quarters have by now integrated various solar energy systems to such an extent that they have become inconspicuous. Precise knowledge coupled with the development of the required design and technical solutions, obviating the need for their explicit display in a design, have reconfirmed the raison d'être of a discipline hitherto in crisis. And in the manner in which the buildings exhibited provide exemplary evidence of the coincidence of use, ambience and resource conservation at the highest level of design, such results once again allow us to speak of significant architecture.

frühen achtziger Jahren generell noch etwas unbeholfen aussah – Wohnhäuser mit aufgestapelten Solarkollektoren – ist nunmehr eher die Ausnahme; Bauten und Quartiere integrieren verschiedenste Solarenergiesysteme mitunter auch so weit, daß man ihnen diese Besonderheit kaum anmerkt. Genaue Kenntnisse, gekoppelt mit der Entwicklung von notwendigen gestalterischen oder technischen Lösungen, ohne daß auf das eine oder auf das andere im Bauwerk dadurch besonders hingewiesen werden müßte, bestätigen die raison d'être einer in der Krise befindlichen Disziplin. Und indem Bauwerke, die hier gezeigt sind, das Zusammentreffen von Nutzung, Ambiente und Ressourcenschonung in vorbildlicher Weise belegen und auch gestalterisch höchstes Niveau zeigen, haben die jeweiligen Ergebnisse auch wieder den Rang von bedeutender Architektur.

società. Ciò che negli ultimi anni settanta ed ancor più recentemente negli anni ottanta appariva come non ben risolto – edifici residenziali con collettori solari applicati – è oggi un'eccezione; gli edifici ed i quartieri urbani hanno da ora integrato vari sistemi di energia solare, talvolta così diffusamente, che si può a malapena notare la loro singolarità. La conoscenza associata alla progettazione delle necessarie forme e soluzioni tecniche, senza che l'una o l'altra debbano essere necessariamente indicate in un progetto, hanno confermato la raison d' ètre di una disciplina finora in crisi. E la maniera in cui gli edifici in mostra provvedono con esemplare evidenza ad una coincidenza d'uso, ambiente e conservazione delle risorse ad un alto livello di progettazione, con tali risultati, ci permette di parlare ancora una volta di architettura significativa.

Wilfried Wang

Prefatory remarks by a member of the scientific committee

Vorbemerkung eines Mitglieds des wissenschaftlichen Komittees
Note preliminari di un membro della commissione scientifica

From my point of view as an engineer, the building projects and concepts documented in this volume represent forward-looking contributions to solar-oriented, energy-saving forms of construction.
A striking aspect of the roughly 150 projects submitted was that relatively few details were given of the energy requirements or the typical energy values.
If we wish to use natural power in buildings – and ultimately that means solar energy – to minimize the consumption of finite forms of energy, we should not allow ourselves to be guided purely by emotions or intuition in our search for solutions. This could lead to a wrong assessment of the effects of various measures. We now have a number of calculating techniques at our disposal that

Die in diesem Band dokumentierten Arbeiten und Gebäudekonzepte stellen aus meiner Sicht als Ingenieur zukunftsweisende Beiträge zum solargerechten und energiesparenden Bauen dar. Beim Prüfen der insgesamt rund 150 eingereichten Arbeiten fiel auf, daß relativ wenig Angaben zum Energiebedarf gemacht wurden oder energetische Kennwerte angeführt waren.
Wollen wir im Bereich des Bauens natürliche Kräfte und damit letztlich solare Energie nutzen, um den Verbrauch an endlicher Energie zu minimieren, so dürfen wir uns bei der Suche nach Lösungen nicht nur von Gefühl und Intuition leiten lassen. Die Auswirkungen verschiedener Maßnahmen könnten dabei möglicherweise falsch eingeschätzt werden. Es stehen uns mittlerweile

Dal mio punto di vista di ingegnere i progetti e i concetti documentati in questo volume rappresentano contributi che guardano avanti a forme edilizie orientate verso il solare e verso il risparmio energetico. Un aspetto impressionante dei quasi 150 progetti proposti è che sono stati relativamente pochi i dati forniti riguardo ai fabbisogni ed ai valori energetici tipo.
Se vogliamo usare fonti naturali nelle costruzioni – e ultimamente ciò significa impiegare energia solare – per minimizzare il consumo delle forme di energia finite, non dovremmo permettere a noi stessi di lasciarci guidare dalle emozioni e dall'intuizione della nostra ricerca di soluzioni. Questo potrebbe portare alla stima errata degli effetti di varie misure. Al momento abbiamo un

allow us to ascertain and quantify the energy needed (for heating, cooling, electricity, etc.) as well as summer temperatures, lighting conditions and the air currents within a building. Technical installations and energy supply concepts should also be taken into account in any design work and in the assessment of solutions.

One area, however, remains beyond the reach of calculations: the use of buildings by people. The way people behave, the way they "handle" a building, whether they understand its technical installations and use them correctly cannot be measured in quantifiable amounts of energy alone. We are called upon to take action to save energy and to reduce the burden on the environment. In many cases, we have no long-term experience on which to draw for new concepts in building and plant that have to be designed in accordance with objectives such as these. We should nevertheless have the courage to venture along new paths and explore unfamiliar things. Many of the projects published in this catalogue reveal new approaches. Only experience will show which are successful.

The danger exists, of course, that spectacular structures will be erected in the name of solar, energy-saving, ecologically sustainable architecture, but which, in fact, do not meet these criteria. Continuing developments will make this apparent, however, and through increased awareness in professional circles and among the public at large we shall certainly succeed in establishing new standards for the future.

Gerhard Hausladen

Rechentechniken zur Verfügung, die es erlauben, den Energiebedarf (für Wärme, Kälte, Strom) und die sommerlichen Temperaturen sowie Lichtverhältnisse und Luftströmungen im Gebäude zu erfassen und zu quantifizieren. Technische Anlagen und Energieversorgungskonzepte müssen ebenfalls in die entwurfliche Arbeit und die Beurteilung von Lösungen einbezogen werden.

Und doch bleibt ein Bereich, der sich unseren Berechnungen entzieht: Die Nutzung eines Gebäudes durch den Menschen. Wie er sich verhält, wie er »mit dem Gebäude umgeht«, ob er technische Anlagen versteht und richtig nutzt, kann durch energetische Kenngrößen allein nicht erfaßt werden.

Wir sind gefordert, etwas zu tun: Energie einzusparen und die Umwelt zu entlasten. Vielfach können wir bei unseren Gebäude- und Anlagekonzepten, die nach solcher Zielsetzung neu entstehen, nicht auf langjährige Erfahrungen zurückgreifen. Wir sollten aber den Mut haben, Neuland zu betreten und ungewöhnliche Dinge aufzugreifen. In vielen der in diesem Katalog veröffentlichten Arbeiten sind neue Ansätze aufgezeigt. Erst die Erfahrung wird uns zeigen, welche Wege erfolgreicher sind.

Natürlich besteht die Gefahr, daß unter dem Anspruch des solaren, des energiesparenden und umweltgerechten Bauens auch spektakuläre Gebäude errichtet werden, die diesen Ansprüchen de facto nicht genügen. Dies wird die künftige Entwicklung jedoch sichtbar machen und der erhöhten Aufmerksamkeit von Fachwelt und Öffentlichkeit wird es sicherlich gelingen, die Maßstäbe für die Zukunft weiterzuentwickeln.

certo numero di tecniche di calcolo a nostra disposizione che ci permettono di verificare e quantificare l'ammontare del fabbisogno energetico (per riscaldamento, refrigerazione, elettricità, etc.) almeno per ciò che riguarda le temperature estive, le condizioni di illuminazione e le correnti d'aria in un edificio. Le installazioni tecniche ed i concetti di rifornimento energetico dovrebbero essere tenuti in conto per ogni lavoro di ideazione ed imposizione delle soluzioni.

Vi è tuttavia un ambito che si sottrae alla sfera dei nostri calcoli: l'uso degli edifici da parte delle persone. Il modo in cui le persone si rapportano ad un edificio e ne fruiscono, se ne conoscono le sue installazioni tecniche e le impiegano correttamente, non può essere compreso solo attraverso quantità energetiche.

Siamo chiamati a fare qualcosa per risparmiare energia e difendere l'ambiente. Nella maggior parte dei casi non possiamo rifarci ad un'esperienza di lunga durata nel progettare edifici ed impianti, coerentemente con i nuovi obiettivi verso cui tendiamo. Dovremmo ciononostante avere il coraggio di avventurarci lungo nuovi percorsi e di esplorare campi a noi pressoché sconosciuti.

In molti dei lavori pubblicati in questo catalogo si rivelano nuovi approcci. Solo l'esperienza ci mostrerà quali strade sono più ricche di successo. Naturalmente esiste il pericolo che strutture spettacolari vengano erette in nome del solare, del risparmio energetico e dell'edilizia ecologicamente sostenibile, ma che de facto non vengono incontro a queste richieste. Gli sviluppi futuri lo renderanno palese, comunque, e attraverso l'accresciuta attenzione nei circoli professionali e tra il pubblico si riusciranno di nuovo a sviluppare gli standards per il futuro.

Principles for Solar Construction – the Path to Solar Standards

Maximen für solares Bauen – auf dem Weg zu solaren Standards
Assiomi per edifici solari – verso nuovi standards

Norbert Kaiser

The purpose of standards

The current debate on solar architecture requires a technical clarification of what are ultimately socio-cultural objectives.

SOLAR STANDARDS may be seen as a contribution to this. They should not be regarded as competing directly with existing standards, nor are they meant to replace them. The purpose of solar standards is to stimulate a new, independent mental approach to design and construction, taking account of bylaws and regulations, complementing and linking them where necessary, and prompting corrections where appropriate.

Initially, this involves a process of integration in our thinking – gaining an overall view of the various energy flows related to the act of building, from the production of energy to service industries; i. e. production energy (also known as embedded or embodied energy), "grey" energy (losses through transport, distribution, etc.), operating energy and induced energy consumed in the course of construction.

These concepts are not based on an apocalyptic vision, nor on one of sacrifice and privation, nor yet on a display of statistical acrobatics aimed at demonstrating possible savings. Before reacting to such demands, one would have to examine a number of pertinent questions: how much, from what source, which, when, by what means, how quickly, when produced, for how long, in what form, and how does one live or work under such conditions? These questions reveal the complexity of the matter. The most important factors governing this whole issue are energy, time and information, which exert a mutual influence on each other. A slow lift, for example, can raise the same load as one with a greater speed, but it will use less energy. Wrongly planned or unnecessary air-conditioning plant will simply replace information with energy. Whereas energy and time are commodities that are irretrievably lost as soon as they are used or designated for a certain purpose, information remains variable, shapable, extendible. As such, it represents the decisive planning tool for conserving resources. In turn, information can be influenced and modified by intelligence, knowledge, creativity and innovation.

Sinn der Standards

Die aktuelle Diskussion über Solararchitektur macht eine technische Verdeutlichung des letztlich sozial und kulturell Gewollten notwendig.

Dazu sollen SOLAR STANDARDS einen Beitrag leisten. Sie stehen dabei nicht in direkter Konkurrenz zu bestehenden Normen oder sollen diese ersetzen. Sie wollen einen neuen, unabhängigen Denkansatz in das Gestalten und Konstruieren bringen, somit Vorschriften einordnen, verknüpfen und soweit notwendig komplementieren oder auch Anstöße zu deren Korrektur geben.

Zunächst geht es um Integration – eine Gesamtbetrachtung aller Energieflüsse im Zusammenhang mit dem Bauen von der Energieproduktion bis hin zur Energiedienstleistung: Herstellungsenergie, graue Energie, Verbrauchsenergie sowie durch die Bebauung induzierte Energie.

Der Denkansatz geht nicht von einer apokalyptischen Vision oder auch nur einem betonten Verzichts- und Einsparungsszenario aus oder versucht statistische Zahlenakrobatik über Einsparungsmöglichkeiten. Dazu wären nämlich erst folgende Überlegungen anzustellen: wieviel? wovon? welche? wann? wobei? wie schnell? wann produziert? wie lange? wie sieht das aus? wie lebt oder arbeitet man damit?

Die Fragen zeigen bereits die Komplexität der Zusammenhänge. Deren wichtigste Faktoren sind Energie, Zeit, Information, welche sich gegenseitig bedingen. Ein Aufzug mit geringer Geschwindigkeit befördert das gleiche Gewicht wie einer mit höherer, jedoch mit weniger Energie. Eine falsch oder unnötig geplante Klimaanlage ersetzt Information durch Energie. Während Energie und Zeit Güter sind, die unwiederbringlich verloren sind, sobald sie ausgegeben oder bestimmt sind, ist die Information noch veränderbar, gestaltbar, erweiterbar, und somit der entscheidende Ansatz des Planers zur Ressourcenschonung. Dabei ist Information beeinflußt und veränderbar durch Intelligenz, Kreativität, Innovation.

In diesem Sinne geht es bei den Standards weniger um das Energiesparen als vielmehr um das richtige Ausgeben der richtigen Energie zum richtigen Zeitpunkt. Es geht nicht um das wohlwollende »Anrechnen« von Solarenergie, sondern um deren

Lo scopo degli standards

L'attuale dibattito sull'architettura solare dà una chiarificazione tecnica di quali siano in definitiva i necessari obiettivi socio-culturali.

I SOLAR STANDARDS devono essere visti come un contributo a ciò. Essi non devono entrare in competizione con gli standards esistenti, né intendono sostituirli. Lo scopo dei solar standards è introdurre un nuovo, indipendente, approccio mentale per la progettazione e la costruzione, tenendo conto di leggi e regolamenti, unendoli e complementandoli dove necessario, o dando anche impulso ad una loro revisione.

In primo luogo ciò comporta integrazione – una considerazione generale di tutte le forme di flussi d'energia in relazione col costruire, dalla produzione di energia fino a quella di prestazione di servizio energetico: energia di produzione, energia «grigia», energia dispersa così come energia indotta attraverso il processo costruttivo.

Questi concetti non si basano su di una visione apocalittica, o su di uno scenario di sacrificio e privazione, né su acrobatici conti statistici di un possibile risparmio. Per giustificare un tale approccio ci si dovrebbe porre per prima cosa un certo numero di domande: quanto? da dove? quale? quando? come? quanto velocemente? quando è stato prodotto? per quanto tempo? in quale forma? come si vive e si lavora in tali condizioni? Queste domande rivelano la complessità della materia. I fattori più importanti che governano l'intera discussione sono energia, tempo e informazione, i quali esercitano tra di loro una reciproca influenza. Un ascensore più lento può portare lo stesso peso di uno molto veloce, ma userà meno energia. Un impianto di condizionamento d'aria mal progettato e non necessario, spenderà solo molta energia anziché trasmettere informazioni. Mentre energia e tempo sono beni che irrimediabilmente si perdono non appena sono usati o designati per un dato scopo, l'informazione resta variabile, plasmabile ed amputabile. In quanto tale essa rappresenta uno strumento decisivo per il mantenimento delle risorse. A turno, l'informazione può essere influenzata o modificata attraverso l'intelligenza, la conoscenza, la creatività e l'innovazione.

In this respect, standards have less to do with saving energy than with the appropriate use of the appropriate form of energy at the appropriate moment. It is not just a matter of benevolently "giving credit" for the complementary use of solar power. What is involved here is a call for its immediate and lasting use as the ultimate source of energy, and the opportunity to achieve a greater individual and social quality of life.

The sun: sensuous and technological aspects

Light, i. e. daylight, which means sunlight, is the immediate source of human well-being. The body is attuned to it via its sensors and actuators. It sees, it feels warmth; and it compensates for too great or too little warmth by reactions of the layers of the skin. It cools itself through perspiration and evaporation or in the play of a light breeze; or it seeks protection in a corner sheltered from the wind. Light has a direct influence on the production of hormones and thus on our moods, on our drive and motivation, and on our desires.
The sun irradiates the body, gives it energy, tans it. The sun shines on the things man sees, transforming them into objects of dynamic beauty imbued with light and shade, colour and space. It gives life to flowers and forests, creates landscapes and is the basis of the growth of our food. The sun heats the earth and the strata of the atmosphere. Through the interplay of temperature differences, it

sofortige und nachhaltige Einforderung als ultimative Energiequelle und die Chance zu mehr individueller und sozialer Lebensqualität.

Sonne: Sinnlichkeit und Technik

Licht, das heißt Tageslicht, das heißt Sonne, ist die unmittelbare Quelle menschlicher Behaglichkeit. Der Körper ist mit Sensoren und Aktoren darauf eingestellt: Er sieht, er fühlt die Wärme, er gleicht ein Zuviel oder Zuwenig an Wärme durch Reaktionen der Hautschichten aus, er kühlt sich durch Verdunstung oder im Spiel einer leichten Brise oder sucht Schutz in einer windstillen Ecke. Licht wiederum hat direkten Einfluß auf die Hormonproduktion und somit auf unsere Laune, Antrieb und Lust.
Die Sonne bestrahlt den Körper, gibt ihm Kraft, bräunt ihn – die Sonne bestrahlt, was der Mensch sieht, und wandelt es in eine dynamische Schönheit von Licht und Schatten, Farben und Räumen. Sie läßt Blumen, Wälder, Landschaften entstehen und unsere Nahrungsmittel wachsen. Die Sonne erwärmt die Erde und Luftschichten, erzeugt durch das Spiel der Temperaturdifferenzen Wind, Regen und Schnee. Die Sonne belichtet und erwärmt Räume, Wasser in Kollektoren, Wind und Wellen. Die Strahlung auf Photozellen läßt sich sogar in Kraft umwandeln.
Unsere sinnlichen Wahrnehmungen durch eigene Körpererfahrung sowie die Wahrnehmung durch Sehen vermittelt eine eigene, vielfältige Ästhetik

In vista di questo, gli standards hanno meno a che fare con il risparmio energetico, e molto più con l'impiego appropriato di forme di energia consone al momento giusto. Questo non è un modo benevolo per «dare credito» all'impiego di energia solare, ma un invito al suo uso immediato e duraturo quale ultimativa fonte di energia, che offre l'opportunità di una più alta qualità della vita sia sociale che individuale.

Il sole: sensualità e tecnica

La luce, ovvero la luce naturale, ovvero il sole, è la fonte immediata del benessere dell'umanità. Il corpo vi si accorda attraverso i suoi sensi e gli apparati del movimento: vede, sente caldo, bilancia il troppo caldo e il troppo freddo attraverso la reazione degli strati cutanei. Si raffredda attraverso la sudorazione e l'evaporazione o nel gioco con una brezza leggera, oppure cerca riparo in un angolo protetto dal vento. La luce ha una diretta influenza sulla produzione degli ormoni e di conseguenza sui nostri umori, sui nostri impulsi, sulle nostre motivazioni e sui nostri desideri.
Il sole irraggia il corpo, gli infonde energia, lo abbronza. Il sole splende sulle cose che l'uomo vede, trasformandole in oggetti di dinamica bellezza imbevuti di luce e di ombra, colore e spazio. Dà vita ai fiori e alle foreste, crea paesaggi ed è alla base della crescita del nostro cibo. Il sole scalda la Terra e gli strati atmosferici. Attraverso l'azione reciproca delle differenze di temperatura,

gives rise to wind, rain and snow. The sun lights and heats rooms, water in collectors, wind and waves. Solar radiation on photo cells can even be converted into electricity and other forms of energy.

Through physical experience and our visual faculty, our sensuous perceptions convey to us an individual, many-sided solar aesthetic that has always been a major source of inspiration for architecture. One aspect of the use of the sun as a form of energy, however, is its discontinuity. The discontinuity of solar radiation was in the past countered to some extent by mobility and by using other forms of energy as a substitute. People migrated in the wake of the summer or sought warmer climes where the land could be cultivated; or they moved from protected to exposed locations and vice versa. Man has adapted his entire pattern of life to the availability of the sun. The most important invention of mankind in the field of solar technology is the burning of biomass created through the process of photosynthesis, i. e. wood. Fire met most of man's basic needs for comfort. It provided him with light when it was dark; it warmed him when he was cold; it could be used to cook food; and it protected him against wild animals. In the course of evolution, man began to exploit fire technically, using it to bake clay and smelt ore.

The first important invention in the realm of building technology to use solar energy was the manufacture of glass. It represented a major innovation, since glass was transparent and facilitated visibility, while providing a protective screen against the elements. The pane of glass was the first step towards an efficient solar collector. The invention was made in the Middle East, long before the Celts coined the word "window" (wind eye), which really suggests an unglazed opening.

The combustion of biomass continued to develop. With higher temperatures, it was possible to smelt more ores and create better tools. Wind and water were the only forms of mechanical energy used. In the 18th century, it became possible for the first time to harness mechanical energy from the combustion process (the steam engine). Up to that time, the fuel used had been almost exclusively wood, which was also an important material in the construction of buildings and ships. As early as the turn of the millennium, the large-scale harvesting of timber without reafforestation had led to permanent ecological damage to whole regions. When wood as a regenerable biological material was no longer available in adequate quantities, man began to exploit the earth's hitherto untouched reserves such as coal. It was on this source of energy, which had been stored for millions of years within the earth and was initially

der Sonne, mit welcher zu arbeiten schon immer wesentliche Inspiration für die Architektur war. Merkmal für die Nutzbarkeit von Solarenergie ist aber die Diskontinuität. Die Diskontinuität der Einstrahlung wurde durch Mobilität sowie den Einsatz von Solarenergie relativiert (man zog dem Sommer oder den Anbaumöglichkeiten hinterher oder wechselte geschützte oder freie Standorte). Der Mensch hat sich in seinem ganzen Lebensrhythmus auf das Sonnenangebot eingestellt. Die wichtigste solartechnische Erfindung der Menschheit war das Verbrennen von durch Photosynthese entstandener Biomasse, Holz. Feuer deckte die wesentlichen Grundbedürfnisse: Es gab Licht, wenn es dunkel war, es wärmte, wenn es kalt war, es schützte vor Angriffen durch Tiere und ermöglichte das Garen von Speisen. In der weiteren Evolution begann man, das Feuer technisch zu nutzen: Brennen von Ton, Schmelzen von Erzen.

Die erste wichtige gebäudetechnische Erfindung zur Nutzung solarer Energie war das Glas. Ein extremer Fortschritt, da man sehen konnte und trotzdem gegen die Einflüsse des Wetters geschützt war. Die Glasscheibe war der erste Schritt zum effizienten Solarkollektor. Erfunden wurde es im Mittleren Osten, lange bevor die Kelten das Fenster – window (wind eye) nannten, was auf eine nicht verglaste Öffnung schließen läßt.

Das Verbrennen von Biomasse entwickelte sich weiter, man konnte mit höheren Temperaturen mehr Erze schmelzen und bessere Werkzeuge herstellen. Als mechanische Energie nutzte man lediglich Wind und Wasserkraft. Im 18. Jahrhundert gelang es, die Verbrennung in mechanische Energie umzuwandeln (Dampfmaschine). Bis etwa zu diesem Zeitpunkt hat man im wesentlichen Holz verbrannt. Dies hatte man auch als Baumaterial für Gebäude und Schiffe benutzt. Soweit nicht wieder aufgeforstet wurde, hatte dieser Verbrauch bereits zur Jahrtausendwende zu bleibenden ökologischen Schäden ganzer Regionen geführt.

Als das Holz als nachwachsende Biomasse nicht mehr reichte, begann man die bislang ungenutzten Reserven der Welt auszubeuten (Kohle). Zunächst als unendlich angesehen, war diese über Jahrmillionen gespeicherte Energie die Voraussetzung für die industrielle Revolution. Die Verbrennungstechnik verfeinerte sich in Motoren, Kraftwerken und man konnte in Gebäuden einen synthetischen Komfort schaffen, welcher unabhängig von der diskontinuierlichen Sonne war.

So wurden Mensch und Gebäude immer mehr von der Natur entfernt, ohne es zu merken, denn der Traum der Architektur, innen/außen zu überwinden und trotzdem ein kontrolliertes Klima bzw. Komfort zu schaffen, hatte sich scheinbar erfüllt. Der zwar

dà origine al vento, alla pioggia e alla neve. Il sole illumina e scalda gli ambienti, l'acqua nei collettori, il vento e le onde. L'irraggiamento solare sulle fotocellule può persino essere convertito in energia.

Attraverso l'esperienza fisica e la nostra capacità visiva, le nostre percezioni sensoriali ci suggeriscono un'estetica solare soggettiva, con molte facce, che è sempre stata una grande fonte di ispirazione per l'architettura.

Un aspetto dell'uso del sole come forma energetica, purtuttavia, è la sua discontinuità. La discontinuità dell'irraggiamento solare era in passato ovviata, in qualche modo, attraverso la mobilità e l'uso ottimizzato dell'energia solare (si migrava sulla scia dell'estate o cercando climi più caldi dove la terra avrebbe potuto essere coltivata; oppure si traslocava da localizzazioni protette a quelle esposte e viceversa). L'uomo ha adattato il suo intero stile di vita alla disponibilità del sole. L'invenzione più importante dell'umanità nel campo della tecnologia solare è la combustione della biomassa venutasi a creare attraverso il processo di fotosintesi, e cioè del legno. Il fuoco va incontro a molte delle necessità basilari dell'uomo. Gli fornisce la luce se è buio, lo riscalda se ha freddo, lo protegge contro gli animali selvaggi, rende possibile la cottura dei cibi. Nel corso dell'evoluzione l'uomo ha cominciato ad esplorare le tecniche del fuoco, usandolo per cuocere l'argilla e per fondere metalli.

La prima importante invenzione nel regno della tecnologia edilizia per l'impiego dell'energia solare è stata la produzione del vetro. Un'innovazione di portata estrema, poiché il vetro era trasparente e facilitava la visibilità, provvedendo allo stesso tempo a creare uno schermo protettivo per gli elementi. Il vetro ha costituito il primo gradino verso un efficiente collettore solare. L'invenzione era stata fatta nel Medio Oriente, molto prima che i Celti coniassero la parola «window» (occhio selvaggio), che realmente suggerisce un'apertura non vetrata.

La combustione di biomasse continuò a svilupparsi. Raggiungendo temperature più alte era possibile fondere più metalli e creare utensili migliori. Il vento e l'acqua erano le uniche forme di energia meccanica usate. Nel diciottesimo secolo, divenne possibile per la prima volta ottenere energia meccanica dal processo di combustione (la macchina a vapore). All'epoca, il combustibile usato era quasi esclusivamente il legno, che rappresentava anche un importante materiale nella costruzione degli edifici e delle navi. Al principio del millennio la produzione di legno su larga scala senza riforestazione ha lasciato un danno ecologicamente permanente su intere regioni della Terra.

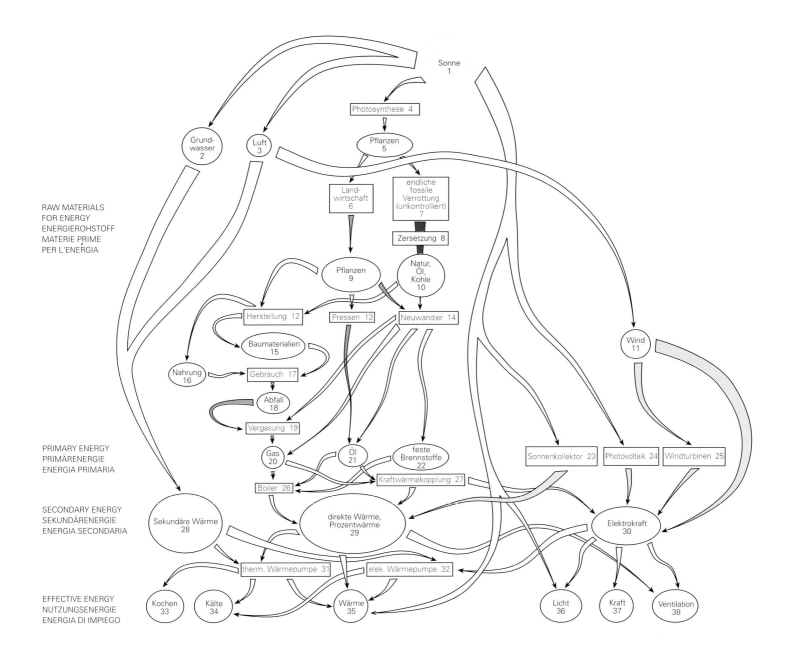

Sonne
1

Photosynthese 4

Grund-wasser 2

Luft 3

Pflanzen 5

Land-wirtschaft 6

endliche fossile Verrottung (unkontrolliert) 7

Zersetzung 8

Pflanzen 9

Natur, Öl, Kohle 10

Herstellung 12

Pressen 13

Neuwandler 14

Wind 11

Baumaterialien 15

Nahrung 16

Gebrauch 17

Abfall 18

Vergasung 19

Gas 20

Öl 21

feste Brennstoffe 22

Sonnenkollektor 23

Photovoltaik 24

Windturbinen 25

Boiler 26

Kraftwärmekopplung 27

Sekundäre Wärme 28

direkte Wärme, Prozentwärme 29

Elektrokraft 30

therm. Wärmepumpe 31

elek. Wärmepumpe 32

Kochen 33

Kälte 34

Wärme 35

Licht 36

Kraft 37

Ventilation 38

RAW MATERIALS FOR ENERGY
ENERGIEROHSTOFF
MATERIE PRIME PER L'ENERGIA

PRIMARY ENERGY
PRIMÄRENERGIE
ENERGIA PRIMARIA

SECONDARY ENERGY
SEKUNDÄRENERGIE
ENERGIA SECONDARIA

EFFECTIVE ENERGY
NUTZUNGSENERGIE
ENERGIA DI IMPIEGO

From the ultimate source of energy to energy supply services

The diagram shows the various transformations solar energy undergoes before being converted into forms of energy supplied to cover human needs for comfort.

☐ direct use (no emission)

☐ simply (physically) converted forms (no emissions)

☐ multiple (biological/physical) converted forms from regenerable raw materials with emissions from combustion (neutral CO_2 balance through short-term absorption cycles)

☐ multiply (biologically/physically) converted forms from finite raw materials with emissions from combustion (relevant in terms of hothouse effect)

Von der ultimativen Energiequelle zur Energie-dienstleistung

Die Graphik zeigt die unterschiedlichen Umwandlungen der Solarenergie bis hin zur Energiedienstleistung, welche den Komfortbedarf des Menschen deckt.

☐ direkte Nutzung (emissionsfrei)

☐ einfach (physikalisch) umgewandelte Nutzung; (emissionsfrei)

☐ mehrfach (biologisch/physikalisch) umgewandelte Nutzung von nachwachsenden Rohstoffen mit Verbrennungsemissionen (CO_2-neutral – durch kurzzeitige Absorptionszyklen)

☐ mehrfach (biologisch/physikalisch) umgewandelte Nutzung von endlichen Rohstoffen mit Verbrennungsemissionen (treibhausrelevant)

Dalla fonte prima d'energia alla prestazione di servizio energetico

Il grafico mostra le diverse trasformazioni dell'energia solare fino al rendimento che soddisfa le necessità di comfort dell'umanità.

☐ Impiego diretto (non inquinante)

☐ Impiego semplice (fisico) trasformato (non inquinante) multiplo (biologico/fisico)

☐ Impiego trasformato di materie prime rinnovabili con inquinamento da combustione (CO_2-neutrale – attraverso cicli di assorbimento a breve termine)

☐ Impiego multiplo (biologico/fisico) trasformato di materie prime finite con inquinamento da combustione (rilevante in termini di effetto-serra)

1 Sun / Sole; 2 Groundwater / Acqua di falda; 3 Air / Aria; 4 Photosynthesis / Fotosintesi; 5 Plants / Piante; 6 Agriculture / Agricoltura; 7 Finite fossil decay (uncontrolled) / Decadimento fossile finito (non controllato); 8 Decomposition / Decomposizione; 9 Plants / Piante; 10 Nature oils, coal / Natura, olio, carbone; 11 Wind / Vento; 12 Production / Produzione; 13 Pressing / Spremitura; 14 New transforming instruments / Nuovi strumenti di trasformazione; 15 Building materials / Materiali da costruzione; 16 Food / Cibi; 17 Brews / Scarti; 18 Waste / Rifiuti; 19 Gasification / Gasificazione; 20 Gas / Gas; 21 Oil / Olio; 22 Solid fuel / Combustibile solido; 23 Solar collector / Collettore solare; 24 Photovoltaics / Fotovoltaico; 25 Wind turbines / Turbine a vento; 26 Boiler / Caldaia; 27 Combined heat and power / Combinazione di forza e calore; 28 Secondary heat / Calore secondario; 29 Direct heat percentage heat / Calore diretto, percentuale di calore; 30 Electrical power / Forza elettrica; 31 Thermal heat pump / Pompa termica di calore; 32 Electrical heat pump / Pompa elettrica di calore; 33 Cooking / Cottura; 34 Cooling / Freddo; 35 Heat / Calore; 36 Light / Luce; 37 Power / Forza; 38 Ventilation / Ventilazione

regarded as infinite, that the Industrial Revolution was built. Combustion techniques in engines and power stations were refined, and it became possible to create a synthetic comfort in buildings that was independent of the discontinuous energy of the sun. As a result, man and architecture became further and further removed from nature without noticing it; for the dream of architecture – overcoming the dichotomy between inside and outside, and nevertheless enjoying a controlled in-door climate and comfort – had, it seemed, been realized. The constant, but synthetic nature of this convenience, however, never achieved the sensuous quality of solar comfort; and the exploitation of these natural resources led to an ecological catastrophe not just in a region of limited area, but on a global scale that represents a threat to mankind. Constructional technology has continued to develop the advantages of glass, for transparency is very much in keeping with the times and with human needs for light and visual contact with nature. Wood as a building material was soon displaced by ostensibly more efficient new materials that appeared to be infinitely reproducible: steel, reinforced concrete, aluminium, plastics, etc. In this case, too, man proceeded on the assumption (and still does on occasion) that by not using wood, and thus not felling trees, he would help to protect the natural environment. On the contrary, however, he began to destroy it more and more, for the manufacture and processing of these materials are particularly energy intensive.

In terms of innovation and in comparison with the development that glass has undergone as a building material in the field of solar technology, the discovery of the photovoltaic principle represented a major leap forward. Up to that time, solar energy had simply been collected and absorbed in the building (or reflected away by shading devices). Now it became possible to convert it into power. Modern architecture is presented with the great opportunity of developing these new technologies and achieving new sensuous qualities with them. The sun offers the highest degree of technical efficiency, both in direct uses (daylight or passive heating) and indirect forms that are free of emission (wind power, photovoltaic installations, thermal collectors). These can be complemented by the use of regenerable building materials and energy-yielding raw materials (biomass) that have a quick regrowth rate.

stetige, aber synthetische Komfort erreichte jedoch nie die Sinnlichkeit des Sonnenkomforts. Die Ausnutzung der Ressourcen (Öl, Kohle, Gas) führte nicht zu einer ökologischen Katastrophe nur einer Region, sondern zu einer Lebensbedrohung der ganzen Menschheit.

Die Gebäudetechnik hat sich zum Vorteil des Glases weiterentwickelt, weil die Transparenz dem Zeitgeist und dem Bedürfnis des Menschen nach Licht und Natur entsprach. Als Baumaterial wurde Holz bald durch angeblich effizientere neue Baustoffe verdrängt, welche auch unendlich herstellbar erschienen: Stahl, Stahlbeton, Aluminium, Kunststoffe. Auch in diesem Fall ging der Mensch (und geht teilweise noch heute) davon aus, daß er durch Nichtverwendung, d. h. Nicht-Schlagen von Holz, die Natur schonen würde, begann aber dadurch, diese mehr und mehr zu zerstören, da diese Materialien in der Herstellung und Verarbeitung besonders energieintensiv sind.

Einen Quantensprung an Innovation, verglichen mit Glas als solarem Baumaterial, wurde durch die Erfindung der Photovoltaik gemacht. Die Sonnenenergie war bislang nur gesammelt und absorbiert worden (oder durch Verschattung reflektiert), nun konnte sie in Kraft umgewandelt werden.

Es ist die Chance heutiger Architektur, die neuen technischen Möglichkeiten zu neuen sinnlichen Qualitäten zu entwickeln. Die Sonne bietet durch direkte (Tageslicht, passive Erwärmung) und indirekte, emissionsfreie Nutzung (Windkraft, Photovoltaik, thermische Kollektoren) die besten technischen Wirkungsgrade. Daneben stehen nachwachsende Baustoffe sowie schnell nachwachsende Energierohstoffe (Biomasse) zur Verfügung.

Quando il legno, come materiale bioecologico rigenerabile, non è risultato più a lungo disponibile in adeguate quantità, l'uomo ha cominciato ad esplorare le fino ad allora incontaminate risorse della Terra, come il carbone. E' su queste fonti di energia, immagazzinate per milioni di anni nel sottosuolo, e viste inizialmente come infinite, che si è costruita la Rivoluzione industriale.

Le tecniche di combustione delle macchine a vapore e delle centrali da combustione furono raffinate, e fu possibile creare negli edifici un comfort artificiale che era indipendente dall'energia discontinua del sole. Come risultato l'uomo e l'architettura vennero sempre più ad allontanarsi dalla natura senza accorgersene; poiché il sogno dell'architettura – affermandosi la dicotomia tra interno ed esterno e tuttavia essendo dotato, lo spazio coperto, di un clima controllato e di un buon comfort – era stato, così sembrava, realizzato.

La costante, ma artificiale natura di questa dotazione, comunque, non ha mai raggiunto la sensuale qualità del comfort solare; e lo sfruttamento di questa naturale risorsa ha condotto ad una catastrofe ecologica non già in una regione di area limitata, ma ad una globale minaccia all'umanità.

La tecnologia costruttiva ha continuato a svilupparsi a vantaggio del vetro, poiché la trasparenza è in totale armonia con i tempi e con le esigenze umane di luce e di contatto con la natura. Il legno come materiale da costruzione era stato subito sostituito con dei materiali apparentemente più efficienti che sembravano essere riproducibili all'infinito: acciaio, calcestruzzo, alluminio, plastica, etc. In questo caso, purtroppo, l'uomo aveva proceduto nell'ipotesi (ed ancora lo fa in qualche occasione), che attraverso il non utilizzo del legno, e quindi non abbattendo gli alberi, avrebbe contribuito a proteggere l'ambiente naturale.

Al contrario però, egli aveva cominciato sempre più a distruggerlo, poiché la produzione e l'elaborazione di questi materiali richiedono un uso particolarmente intensivo di energia.

In termini di innovazione ed in rapporto allo sviluppo a cui il vetro è stato soggetto come materiale da costruzione nel campo della tecnologia solare, la scoperta del fotovoltaico rappresenta un maggiore ed innovativo salto in avanti. Da quel momento, si è potuto raccogliere ed assorbire energia solare nelle costruzioni (oppure rifletterla attraverso un sistema di ombreggiatura). Era quindi divenuto possibile convertirla in energia. Sviluppare queste nuove tecnologie e raggiungere una nuova qualità «sensuale» rappresenta una delle grandi opportunità dell'architettura moderna. Il sole offre i più alti gradi di efficienza tecnica, sia nell'impiego diretto (luce naturale o riscaldamento passivo), che nelle forme indirette, libere da emis-

From the ultimate source of energy to energy services

The efficiency of the direct use of solar radiation is shown in the following example.
Under overcast conditions (standard lighting intensity, in accordance with C. I. E.), a room approximately 20 m^2 in area and 5 m deep requires a high-level window roughly 2 m^2 in size to guarantee adequate daylight. The solar aperture for daylighting is, therefore, approximately 2 m^2.
If one were to illuminate this room with electric light bulbs, under the same cloud conditions – the thermal equivalent of about 100 W/m^2 or less – one would need a photovoltaic installation approximately 40 m^2 in area to generate the necessary electricity. The equivalent solar aperture for an indirect use would, therefore, be about 40 m^2.
If one were to use electricity from a coal-fired power station for the lighting, a radiated surface of approximately one million square metres would be necessary to generate this amount of current, taking into account the various stages of technical conversion, mining, and the formation of coal through decay and photosynthesis.

Von der ultimativen Energiequelle zur Energiedienstleistung

Die Effizienz der unmittelbaren Nutzung der Solareinstrahlung zeigt sich an folgendem Beispiel:
Ein Raum mit ca. 20 m^2 und 5 m Tiefe benötigt bei bedecktem Himmel (Standardleuchtdichte C.I.E.) ein hoch angeordnetes Fenster von ca. 2 m^2, um eine ausreichende Tageslichtbeleuchtung sicherzustellen. Die Solarapertur zur Beleuchtung ist also ca. 2 m^2.
Würde man diesen Raum mit Glühlampen beleuchten, so würde man die gleichen Himmelsbedingungen, welche thermisch in etwa 100 W/m^2 oder sogar weniger entsprächen, bereits ca. 40 m^2 Photovoltaikinstallation benötigen, um den dazu notwendigen Strom zu erzeugen. Die äquivalente Solarapertur einer indirekten Nutzung wären also bereits ca. 40 m^2.
Benutzt man für die Beleuchtung Strom aus einem Kohlekraftwerk, so wäre über den Weg der technischen Umwandlung, Förderung, Kohlebildung durch Verrottung, Photosynthese bei ca. 100 W/m^2 eine Einstrahlungsfläche in der Größenordnung von 1 Mio m^2 notwendig, um diesen Strom zu erzeugen.

sioni (forza del vento, installazioni fotovoltaiche, collettori termici). Oltre a ciò, sono a disposizione materiali da costruzione rigenerabili e materie prime da cui si può ottenere energia (biomassa) con una veloce capacità di ricrescita.

Dalla fonte prima di energia alle prestazioni energetiche

L'efficienza dell'uso diretto delle radiazioni solari è mostrata nel seguente esempio. In condizioni di cielo nuvoloso (illuminazione standard in accordo con il C.I.E.), una stanza di circa 20 mq di superficie e 5 m di profondità richiede un alto livello di finestratura, pari a quasi 2 mq per garantire un adeguato livello di luce naturale.
L'«apertura solare» per la luce naturale è pertanto approssimativamente 2 mq.
Se si dovesse illuminare questo spazio con energia elettrica nelle stesse condizioni di cielo nuvoloso – l'equivalente termico di circa 100 W/mq o anche meno – col fotovoltaico sarebbero necessari 40 mq di superficie di installazione per generare l'elettricità occorrente.
L'apertura solare equivalente per un uso indiretto dovrebbe essere, pertanto, pari a circa 40 mq.
Se si dovesse usare elettricità prodotta da una caldaia a carbone per l'illuminazione, sarebbe necessaria una superficie radiante di approssimativamente un milione di mq per generare 100 W/mq, tenendo in conto i vari gradi di conversione tecnica, estrazione, e formazione del carbone attraverso i processi di decomposizione e di fotosintesi.

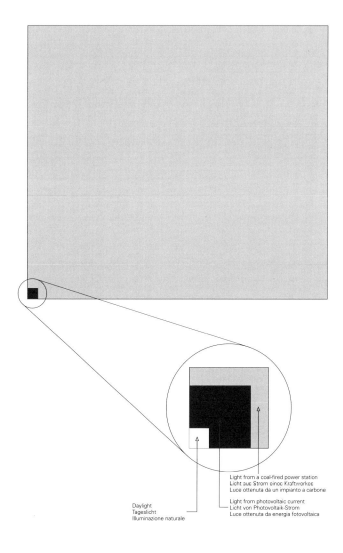

Light from a coal-fired power station
Licht aus Strom eines Kraftwerkes
Luce ottenuta da un impianto a carbone

Light from photovoltaic current
Licht von Photovoltaik-Strom
Luce ottenuta da energia fotovoltaica

Daylight
Tageslicht
Illuminazione naturale

To whom does the sun belong?

The answer is, of course: to everyone, for the sun cannot be taken into personal possession and monopolized. Nevertheless, even if the sun radiates many million times the energy we need on Earth today, it has to be deployed with the utmost care in relation to buildings; for buildings are huge collectors and cast their shadows on other buildings and on the ground, thus taking possession of the sun in their own way.

The exploitation of the sun should be divided into individual (human), technical and social (human and biological) uses.

The most important individual aspect of sunlight in relation to buildings is its visual use, in other words, daylight, lighting and outlook. Direct radiation of the body is desired only occasionally and can, therefore, be restricted to certain zones in which people spend their leisure time (e. g. outdoor areas, balconies, patios, conservatories, verandas, etc.). Solar architecture should provide comfortable conditions for as long as possible in such zones.

In addition to these individual uses of daylight, the heating of a building or the rooms within it by the radiation of the sun may also be described as a

Wem gehört die Sonne?

Antwort: Allen, denn sie kann nicht bewacht werden, d. h. von einem vereinnahmt und monopolisiert werden. Trotzdem – auch wenn die Sonne das vielmillionenfache unseres heutigen Energiebedarfs auf die Erde strahlt – muß man sie in bezug auf Gebäude sehr sorgfältig verteilen, denn Gebäude sind riesige Kollektoren, welche andere Gebäude und die Erde verschatten und somit die Sonne für sich vereinnahmen.

Die Nutzung der Sonne muß aufgeteilt werden in individuelle (menschliche), technische und soziale (menschliche und biologische) Nutzung.

Der wichtigste individuelle Nutzen in bezug auf ein Gebäude ist das Sehen, d. h. Tageslicht, Beleuchtung und Aussicht. Das direkte Bestrahlen des Körpers ist nur zeitweilig erwünscht und kann somit bestimmten Zonen, in welche man sich begibt, vorbehalten bleiben (Außenzonen, Balkon, Terrasse, Wintergarten, Veranda). Solare Architektur muß insbesondere eine möglichst lange komfortable Verweildauer in diesen Zonen einplanen.

Neben der individuellen Tageslichtnutzung wird als passive oder direkte Nutzung die Erwärmung eines Gebäudes bzw. von dessen Räumen durch Solarstrahlung bezeichnet. Diese Erwärmung ist eine

A chi appartiene il sole?

La risposta è, ovviamente, a tutti, poiché il sole non può essere di proprietà individuale o monopolizzato. Ciononostante, anche se sono milioni di anni che il sole irradia l'energia di cui abbiamo bisogno sulla terra oggi, si deve operare una sua accurata ripartizione sugli edifici, poiché essi sono dei collettori enormi che proiettano la loro ombra sugli altri edifici e sul suolo, prendendo così a loro modo possesso del sole.

Lo sfruttamento solare deve essere ripartito negli usi individuali (umani), tecnici e sociali (umani e biologici). Il più importante impiego individuale nel contesto dell'edilizia è l'aspetto visivo, in altre parole: la luce del giorno, l'illuminazione, la vista. L'irraggiamento corporeo diretto è richiesto solo occasionalmente, e può, pertanto, essere ristretto a determinate zone in cui si trascorre il proprio tempo libero (cioè aree esterne, balconi, patii, serre, verande, etc.). L'architettura solare provvede a creare in queste zone condizioni quanto più possibile confortevoli.

In aggiunta a questi usi individuali della luce del giorno, vi è anche il riscaldamento di una costruzione o di ambienti attraverso l'irraggiamento solare, che può essere letto come un uso passivo o

passive or direct use of solar energy. This kind of heating is a mixture of technical and individual uses of solar radiation. At first glance, this form of heating in a comfort zone such as a living room may seem to be at odds with individual comfort needs; for no one would want to live in a collector or a space dominated by solar technology. Technically speaking, the small direct absorption area (primary storage), the temperature limits of rooms, and the convection currents caused by constant supplies of fresh air for the comfort of occupants make the interior of a building an extremely poor collector.

The purely technical use of solar energy should occur in collectors and conversion surfaces (e. g. thermal collectors and photovoltaic installations), from where the energy is transported to storage units or the actual place of use. This is an indirect (or active) use of solar energy, and the technical installation will be positioned on the skin of the building where it is not subject to shade.

Another aspect that has to be considered is the shading of outdoor zones, in other words, the social use of solar energy. Buildings cast shadows on biological collectors too, i. e. areas where plants grow. This results in lower ground temperatures and reduces the amount of time in which one can enjoy and use flowers and plants. Indeed, certain plants may not be able to grow at all under such conditions.

One of the fundamental demands of the Charter is for higher-density development to create more intense neighbourhoods as well as service, supply and cultural catchment areas that will be accessible on foot. In this way, the volume of traffic and the number of infrastructure measures can be reduced. But building to a higher density means that façades will be subject to more shading, depending on the aspect, location, etc. With a relatively regular pattern of development, however, the roofs and top storeys of buildings will remain free of shade, even when the angle of inclination of the sun is small during the winter months. These surfaces will, therefore, be suitable for solar installations.

The direct exploitation of solar energy for heating rooms will be diminished as a result, but this is anyway of minor significance as a technical energy factor on account of the low efficiency of this method. More important in this respect are aspects of visual comfort (outlook) and an occasional glimpse of the sun, even when it is low in the sky in winter. The individual aspect of daylight solar technology is dependent on the intensity of light. Buildings should be designed to receive diffused light, which will be at its most intense when the sun is at its zenith.

Mischform aus technischer und individueller Solarnutzung. Zunächst steht diese Nutzung, soweit sie in einer Komfortzone – also Wohnraum – geschieht, im Gegensatz zu dem individuellen Komfortbedürfnis, denn niemand möchte in einem Kollektor oder einem solaren Technikraum leben. Aufgrund der geringen direkten Absorptionsflächen (Primärspeicher), der Temperaturbegrenzung im Raum sowie der Konvektion durch laufende und zum Wohlbefinden notwendige Frischluftzufuhr, ist das Gebäudeinnere technisch gesehen ein äußerst schlechter Kollektor.

Die rein technische Nutzung der Solarenergie sollte in Kollektor- und Umwandlungsflächen z.B. thermischen Kollektoren, Photovoltaik geschehen, und kann von dort aus zu Speichern oder Verwendungsstellen transportiert werden. Dies ist eine indirekte (auch aktiv genannte) Solaranwendung und wird auf unverschatteten Hüllflächen installiert.

Ein weiterer Aspekt ist die Verschattung der Außenzonen, d. h. die soziale Solarnutzung. Letztlich verschatten Gebäude die Biokollektoren, d. h. die Flächen, auf denen Pflanzen wachsen. Dies hält Kälte länger im Boden und verkürzt die Zeit, zu welcher wir uns an den Pflanzen und Blumen erfreuen bzw. sie nutzen können – manche Pflanzen können erst gar nicht anwachsen.

Eine der fundamentalen Forderungen der Charta ist das verdichtete Bauen zur Schaffung von Nachbarschaften, fußläufigen Einzugsbereichen von Dienstleistungs-, Versorgungs- und Kultureinrichtungen, Reduzierung von Infrastrukturmaßnahmen und Verkehrsaufkommen. Dieses verdichtete Bauen wird Fassadenflächen je nach Ausrichtung, Standort etc. weitgehend verschatten. Bei einigermaßen gleichförmiger Bebauung bleiben Dach und das oberste Geschoß selbst bei sehr flachem Wintersonnenwinkel unverschattet und eignen sich für technische Solarinstallationen.

Die direkte Solarenergienutzung zum Erwärmen der Räume wird eingeschränkt, was wegen der meist geringen Effizienz ohnehin keine signifikante energietechnische Größe ist.

Wichtiger sind Komfortaspekte des Sehens (Aussicht) und das zumindest zeitweilige Sehen der Sonne auch bei flachen Wintersonnenneigungen. Der wichtige individuelle solartechnische Aspekt der Tageslichtbeleuchtung ist von der Leuchtdichte abhängig. Die Gebäude sind ohnehin für diffuses Licht auszulegen, deren größte Leuchtdichte am Zenit ist.

Bei verdichtetem Bauen haben die Außenzonen eine hohe soziale Bedeutung. Eine volle Ausleuchtung dieser Zonen unterstützt den individuellen Komfortaspekt des Sehens. Plätze zum Verweilen, Flanieren oder Spielen sollten jederzeit voll be-

diretto dell'energia solare. Questo tipo di riscaldamento è frutto di una compartecipazione di tecniche e di utilizzazioni individuali d'energia solare. A colpo d'occhio questa forma di riscaldamento in una zona di comfort – come un soggiorno – può apparire in contrasto con le esigenze di comfort individuali; poiché nessuno vorrebbe vivere in un collettore o in uno spazio tecnologico-solare. Da un punto di vista tecnologico, l'estensione limitata delle superfici di assorbimento (aree primarie di accumulo), i limiti di temperatura degli ambienti e la conversione causata dai costanti ricambi di aria fresca rendono l'interno di un edificio un collettore estremamente povero.

Il semplice impiego tecnico dell'energia solare ricorre ai collettori ed alle superfici di conversione (ossia i collettori termici e le installazioni fotovoltaiche), dai quali essa viene trasportata alle unità di accumulo o al posto di utilizzazione immediata. Questo è un uso indiretto (chiamato anche attivo) dell'energia solare, nel quale le installazioni tecniche sono posizionate nella pelle dell'edificio dove non sono soggette ad ombra.

Un altro aspetto che deve essere preso in considerazione è l'ombreggiatura delle zone esterne, in altre parole, l'uso sociale di energia solare. Gli edifici proiettano ombra sui collettori biologici, ad esempio sulle aree dove crescono piante. Ciò produce come risultato l'abbassamento della temperatura a terra e la riduzione del tempo a disposizione per divertirsi e stare in contatto con fiori e piante. In verità ci sono alcune piante che non sono affatto in grado di crescere in tali condizioni.

Una delle esigenze fondamentali della Carta è la richiesta di una più densa forma di sviluppo per creare degli intorni più intensi come aree di servizio, di rifornimento e di drenaggio culturale, aree a cui si potrà accedere a piedi, riducendo il volume del traffico e le dimensioni delle infrastrutture. L'edificato a più alta densità, pertanto, ha come diretta conseguenza che le facciate dovranno essere soggette ad un ombreggiamento maggiore, che dipenderà dalla conformazione, dalla collocazione, etc. Con un modello di sviluppo relativamente regolare, quindi, i tetti e i piani superiori degli edifici dovranno rimanere senza alcuna zona d'ombra, persino quando l'angolo di inclinazione del sole è piccolo nel corso dei mesi invernali. Queste superfici risulteranno così adeguate per ospitare le installazioni solari.

Lo sfruttamento diretto dell'energia solare per riscaldare gli ambienti diminuirà come risultato, ma ciò sarà in ogni caso di minor significato come fattore tecnico-energetico, tenendo conto della bassa efficienza del metodo. Più importante rispetto a questo sono gli aspetti del comfort e della convenienza, come la visione di un bagliore occasionale

In high-density developments, outdoor zones assume a great social significance. Full illumination of these zones strengthens the individual visual sense of well-being. Open spaces where one can stroll, play or spend one's time at leisure should enjoy full sunlight and be naturally heated. This kind of "passive" or direct use of solar energy has a greater degree of sensuous and technical solar efficiency than the equivalent use of sunlight in indoor spaces – if account is taken of the acceptance of outdoor space (through the exclusion of vehicles, for example).

The forms of buildings and their positions in relation to each other automatically lead to a distribution of sunlight and of the individual, technical and social effects it has. In high-density forms of development, the social use will assume central importance.

sonnt und deren Natur erwärmt sein – diese Art der »passiven« oder direkten Solarenergienutzung hat eine höhere sinnliche und solartechnische Effizienz als die Nutzung in einem Raum, wenn man an die Akzeptanz der Außenflächen (Nicht-Nutzen des Autos) denkt.

Die Form der Gebäude sowie ihre Stellung zueinander verteilt die Sonne und somit deren individuelle, technische und soziale Auswirkung.
Bei verdichtetem Bauen steht der soziale Nutzen im Vordergrund.

del sole, persino quando questo è basso nel cielo invernale. Questo aspetto individuale della tecnologia solare d'illuminazione diurna dipende dall'intensità della luce. Gli edifici dovrebbero essere disegnati in modo da ricevere luce diffusa, che sarebbe molto intensa quando il sole è allo zenit. Negli insediamenti ad alta densità, gli spazi esterni assumono un grande valore sociale. La piena illuminazione di queste zone rafforza il senso visivo individuale dello «stare bene». Gli spazi aperti dove si può passeggiare, giocare, o passare un pò di tempo in ozio, dovrebbero godere di piena illuminazione solare ed essere riscaldati naturalmente. Questo tipo di «uso passivo» o diretto di energia solare ha un grado di efficienza solare sensuale e tecnica più alto dell'equivalente impiego della luce diurna negli spazi chiusi – se si tiene in conto l'accoglienza degli spazi esterni (ad esempio attraverso l'esclusione dei veicoli). Le forme degli edifici nella loro posizione in relazione a ciascun altro, automaticamente conducono ad una distribuzione della luce e agli effetti tecnici e sociali che questo comporta. Nelle forme ad alta densità di sviluppo il loro impiego in senso sociale assumerà centrale importanza.

Energy?

No physical entity is treated in such a general, undifferentiated way as energy. Some definition is, therefore, necessary in order to develop strategies in relation to buildings and urban structures:

use   i. e. used for what purpose
form   i. e. state of energy
quality   i. e. actual exploitable energy

Consumption of energy in building

Production energy: (also known as embedded or embodied energy) is the energy invested in building materials through the processes of production, assembly, maintenance, alteration and demolition, and in the course of recycling components or materials.

Operating energy: the energy necessary for maintaining required levels of comfort and operating conditions in buildings.

Induced energy: energy consumption caused indirectly through the process of construction; e. g. commuter traffic or the supply of goods.

Energie?

Mit keiner physikalischen Größe wird so undifferenziert umgegangen wie mit der Energie. Eine Definition folgender Kriterien ist notwendig, um Strategien im Zusammenhang mit Gebäuden und urbanen Strukturen entwickeln zu können:

Nutzung   i. S. wofür ausgeben
Form   i. S. von Energiezustand
Qualität   i. S. tatsächlich nutzbarer Energie

Energieverwendung beim Bauen

Herstellungsenergie: Diejenige Energie, die bei der Herstellung der Baumaterialien, der Errichtung, der Unterhaltung, des Umbaus und des Abbruchs sowie für Recycling gebraucht wird.

Betriebsenergie: Diejenige Energie, welche zur Bereitstellung gewünschter Komfort- und Betriebsbedingungen für Gebäude gebraucht wird.

Induzierte Energie: Die durch die Bebauung indirekt hervorgerufene Energie, zum Beispiel Verkehr durch Pendeln zum Arbeitsplatz oder Bereitstellung von Gütern.

Energia?

Nessuna entità fisica è trattata in maniera così generale ed indifferenziata come l'energia. Si impone pertanto la necessità di una sua definizione per sviluppare strategie in relazione agli edifici ed alle strutture urbane.

Impiego ovvero uso finalizzato ad un certo scopo
Forma   ovvero stato dell'energia
Qualità   ovvero energia effettivamente utilizzabile

Consumo di energia negli edifici

Energia di produzione: energia usata nella produzione dei materiali da costruzione, nella edificazione, manutenzione, modifica e demolizione degli edifici, e nel processo di riciclaggio dei componenti e dei materiali.

Energia di esercizio: energia necessaria per mantenere i livelli richiesti di comfort e le condizioni di funzionamento degli edifici.

Energia indotta: consumo di energia causato indirettamente attraverso i processi di costruzione; per esempio il traffico pendolare, oppure l'insediamento di beni.

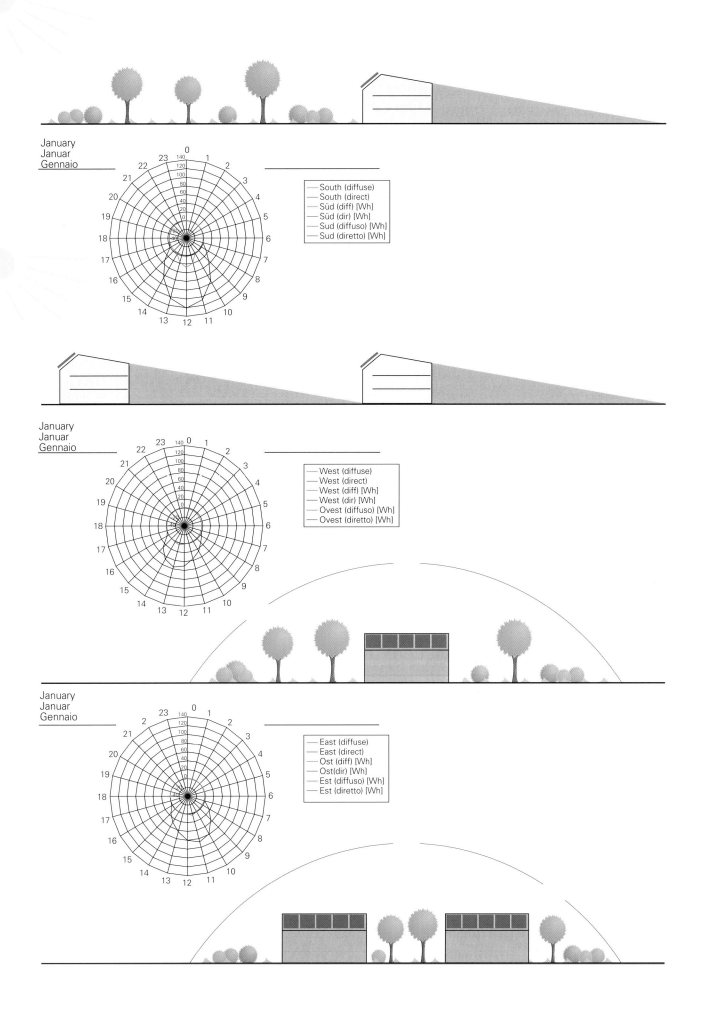

January
Januar
Gennaio

0
140
120
100
80
60
40
20
0

— South (diffuse)
— South (direct)
— Süd (diff) [Wh]
— Süd (dir) [Wh]
— Sud (diffuso) [Wh]
— Sud (diretto) [Wh]

January
Januar
Gennaio

0
140
120
100
80
60
40
20
0

— West (diffuse)
— West (direct)
— West (diff) [Wh]
— West (dir) [Wh]
— Ovest (diffuso) [Wh]
— Ovest (diretto) [Wh]

January
Januar
Gennaio

0
140
120
100
80
60
40
20
0

— East (diffuse)
— East (direct)
— Ost (diff) [Wh]
— Ost(dir) [Wh]
— Est (diffuso) [Wh]
— Est (diretto) [Wh]

For each of these kinds of consumption, the energy passes through various states, from the raw material from which it is obtained to energy services.

Raw materials: non-renewable
combustion: emission as a highly relevant factor
reserves: gas, coal, oil

renewable
combustion: emission of minor relevance
consists of biomass, waste matter

renewable
combustion: no emission
water, wind, sun

The raw materials from which energy is obtained have to be mined, extracted or harvested, in the course of which they are subject to the sequence of processes described below – production, transport, distribution, conversion, etc. For each of these processes, systems are required that, in turn, incur the "expenditure" of production energy, that require an element of natural energy and result in conversion losses. This energy is known as "grey" energy.

The following classification of different forms of energy is taken from David Spreng's book "Graue Energie".

Primary energy
Crude oil, natural gas, coal, uranium, running water, biomass, solar radiation, wind, etc.

Secondary energy
Processed heating oil, petrol, diesel oil, liquid gas, electricity, district heating, etc.
Non-energy products (raw chemicals).

Supply energy
Energy purchased by final consumer.

Usable energy
The energy supplied to consumers for conversion into effective functional energy, e. g. electricity for operating electric motors; hot water for radiators.
Use of energy losses through conversion

Für jeden dieser Verbräuche durchläuft die Energie verschiedene Zustände vom Energierohstoff bis hin zur Energiedienstleistung.

Energierohstoff: erschöpflich
Verbrennung: hoch emissions-relevant
lagernd: Gas, Kohle, Öl

erneuerbar
Verbrennung: gering emissions-relevant
entstehend aus: Biomasse, Abfällen

erneuerbar
Verbrennung: nicht emissions-relevant
Wasserkraft, Wind, Sonne

Dieser Energierohstoff muß gefördert oder geerntet werden und durchläuft die weiter unten definierte Energiekette Herstellung, Transport, Verteilung, Umwandlung etc.
Für jede dieser Stationen sind wiederum Systeme notwendig, die Herstellungsenergie »kosten« und welche Eigenenergie benötigen und Umwandlungsverluste »produzieren«. Diese Energie nennen wir graue Energie.

Die folgende Aufteilung der Energieformen ist David Spreng's Buch »Graue Energie« entnommen.

Primärenergie
genutztes Erdöl, Erdgas, Steinkohle, Uran, Laufwasser, Biomasse, Sonneneinstrahlung, Wind usw.

Sekundärenergie
produziertes Heizöl, Benzin, Dieselöl, Flüssiggas, Elektrizität, Fernwärme usw.
Nichtenergetische Produkte (Chemierohstoffe)

Endenergie
Energie, welche vom Endverbraucher eingekauft wird.

Einsatzenergie
Die dem Verbraucher zur Umwandlung in Nutzenergie bereitgestellte Energie: z. B. Strom an Elektromotor, Warmwasser an Heizkörper.
Energienutzung Umwandlungsverluste

Per ciascuno di questi tipi di consumo, l'energia passa attraverso vari stadi, dalla materia prima da cui è ottenuta, all'energia in regime di servizio.

Materie prime per l'energia:
non-rinnovabili
combustione: inquinamento come fattore rilevante
riserve: gas, carbone, olii

rinnovabili
combustione: inquinamento di minor rilevanza
consiste in: biomasse, rifiuti

rinnovabili
combustione: senza inquinamento
acqua, vento, sole

La materia prima per l'energia deve essere estratta o raccolta e fatta passare attraverso la sotto definita catena energetica di produzione, trasporto, distribuzione, trasformazione, etc. Per ognuna di queste fasi sono di nuovo necessari sistemi, che «costano» energie di produzione e alcuni dei quali hanno bisogno di energia indotta, «producendo» perdite nella trasformazione. Questa è l'energia che chiamiamo «energia grigia».

La seguente divisione di forme di energia è tratta dal libro di David Spreng «Graue Energie» (Energia grigia).

Energia primaria
Petrolio grezzo, gas naturale, carbone, uranio, acqua (in movimento), biomasse, irraggiamento solare, vento, etc.

Energia secondaria
Olio da combustione trattato, petrolio, olio diesel, gas liquido, elettricità, «Fernwärme» (riscaldamento a distanza).
Prodotti non energetici (materie prime chimiche)

Energia fornita
Energia acquistata dal consumatore finale

Energia disponibile
Energia che viene fornita ai consumatori per essere convertita in energia effettiva; ad esempio elettricità per far funzionare un motore elettrico, acqua calda per i radiatori.
Impiego dell'energia liberata per conversione

Energy supply services

(different forms of effective energy)
Various classifications are possible, e. g. according to different kinds of effective energy: heat, power, light, etc.; or different kinds of energy services: mechanical operations, lighting, air-conditioning, etc.

Waste heat

Waste heat is the non-usable – or rather, unused – heat in the entire chain of processes. Whether this heat is really lost or can ultimately be exploited (e. g. through heat-recovery methods) will depend on the particular technical system. The total amount of unused waste heat is an indicator of the rational use of energy and of ecological damage.

Energiedienstleistung

(verschiedene Nutzenergien)
Verschiedene Aufteilungen sind möglich: z. B. Art Nutzenergie: Wärme, Kraft, Licht usw. Art Energiedienstleistung: mech. Antrieb, Beleuchtung, Klimatisierung usw.

Abwärme

Die Abwärme ist die in der gesamten Prozeßkette nicht nutzbare – besser: nicht genutzte – Wärme. Denn ob diese Wärme zu Ab(fall)wärme wird oder weiter genutzt werden kann (z. B. Wärmerückgewinnung), hängt von dem technischen System ab. Die Summe der ungenutzten Abwärme ist ein Indikator für die Rationalität der Energieverwendung und der Umweltbelastung.

Energia di servizio

(diverse forme di energia effettiva)
Sono possibili varie categorie, ossia diversi tipi di energia effettiva: calore, forza, luce, etc.; differenti tipi di energia di servizio: operazioni meccaniche, illuminazione, condizionamento, etc.

Calore di dispersione

Il calore di dispersione è un calore non utilizzabile – o, piuttosto, non impiegato – nell'intera catena del processo. Se poi questo calore risulterà realmente perso, o potrà essere utilizzato al termine del processo (ad esempio attraverso metodi di recupero del calore) questo dipenderà dal particolare sistema tecnico. L'ammontare totale di calore inutilizzato è un efficace indicatore della razionalità con cui l'energia viene impiegata e del livello di danno ecologico.

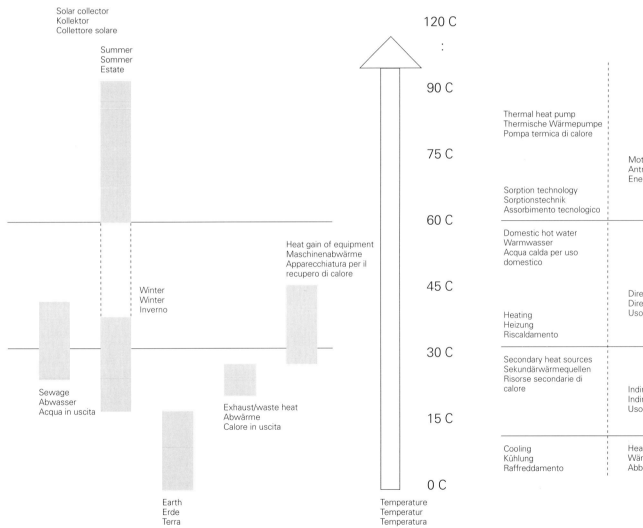

Quality

Entropy
or
energy = exergy + anergia

The amount of material in circulation in our closed planetary system is a fixed quantity. According to the second law of thermodynamics, all processes in a closed system take place in an irreversible sequence proceeding from a higher to a lower state of order. For example, minerals are reduced in size until they reach a state of total fragmentation in which they are no more than worthless rubbish or represent a state of disorder or chaos. This process of fragmentation is called entropy.

Man may still be able to use the residue of raw materials. By applying higher forms of energy, he can, for example, recycle them – i. e. raise them to a higher state – but he cannot create these raw materials anew.

The same applies to energy. This consists of a usable component (exergy) and an element of waste heat (anergia), which is caused in the process of conversion and is not used. As a rule, it is not possible to generate electricity from this waste heat. With the help of energy of a higher order, it can nevertheless be raised to a sufficiently high temperature to make it utilizable within the thermodynamic quality scale (heat pump process). Man can merely retard the process of fragmentation, therefore, by conserving resources and recycling materials in a sensible manner. He cannot halt it completely or reverse it. The physical-biological process of natural evolution alone is capable of doing this – not by reversing the second law of thermodynamics, but with the help of a practically inexhaustible source of energy outside the closed system of our planet, i. e. the sun.

Qualität

Entropie
oder
Energie = Exergie + Anergie

Die Menge der Stoffe in dem geschlossenen Kreislauf unseres Planeten ist konstant. Nach dem zweiten Gesetz der Thermodynamik verlaufen alle Prozesse in einem geschlossenen Kreislauf irreversibel von einem Zustand höherer Ordnung in einen Zustand niederer Ordnung. Beispielsweise Mineralien, die man verkleinert, bis sie in totaler Zersplitterung, Müll oder im Chaos enden. Dieser Prozeß der Zersplitterung wird Entropie genannt.

Der Mensch selbst kann den Müll aus Rohstoffen zwar noch nutzen, er kann ihn unter Hinzunahme von wiederum höherer Energie recyceln, d. h. auf einen höheren Zustand anheben – er selbst kann aber diesen Rohstoff nicht neu herstellen.

Gleiches gilt für die Energie. Diese besteht aus einem nutzbaren Anteil (Exergie) und einem Anteil von Umwandlungsverlusten oder Abwärme, welche nicht genutzt wird (Anergie). Aus Abwärme kann im Regelfall kein Strom mehr erzeugt werden. Die Abwärme kann jedoch unter Zuhilfenahme von Energien höherer Ordnung auf ein so hohes Temperaturniveau gehoben werden, daß diese in der thermodynamischen Qualitätsskala wieder genutzt werden kann (Wärmepumpenprozeß).

Der Mensch kann diese Zersplitterung also nur durch Ressourcenschonung und sinnvolle Wiederaufbereitung verlangsamen. Er kann sie nicht zum Stillstand bringen oder umkehren. Nur die physikalisch-biologische Evolution der Natur ist in der Lage, dies zu tun. Nicht durch Umkehr des zweiten Thermodynamischen Gesetzes, sondern durch eine praktisch unerschöpfliche Energie außerhalb des geschlossenen Systems, der Sonne.

Qualità

Entropia
o
energia = «exergia» + «anergia»

Il totale di materiale in circolazione nel nostro sistema planetario chiuso è una quantità definita. In accordo con la Seconda Legge della Termodinamica, tutti i processi in un sistema chiuso prendono parte ad una sequenza irreversibile da un livello di ordine più alto ad uno più basso. Per esempio, i minerali sono ridotti in pezzi finché essi raggiungono uno stato di frammentazione nel quale non sono altro che cose senza alcun valore, oppure rappresentano uno stato di disordine e di caos. Questo processo di frammentazione è chiamato entropia.

L'uomo può ancora essere in grado di usare questi residui di materie prime. Attraverso l'uso di forme più alte di energia egli può, per esempio, riciclarli – ovvero portarli ad un livello più alto – ma non può da capo ricrearne materia prima.

Lo stesso discorso vale per l'energia. Questa consta di un componente che si utilizza (exergia) e di un elemento di calore di dispersione (anergia) che si viene a creare nel processo di conversione senza essere impiegato. Di regola, non è possibile generare elettricità da questo calore di dispersione. Con l'ausilio di energia di livello più alto, si può tuttavia innalzarlo ad una temperatura sufficientemente alta per renderlo utilizzabile nella scala di qualità termodinamica (processo pompa di calore).

L'uomo può quindi in maniera sensibile meramente ritardare il processo di frammentazione, attraverso la conservazione delle risorse ed il riciclaggio dei materiali. Solo il processo fisico-biologico dell'evoluzione naturale è capace di fare questo – non attraverso il ribaltamento della Seconda Legge della Termodinamica, ma con l'aiuto di una risorsa praticamente inesauribile esterna al nostro sistema planetario chiuso: il sole.

Induced energy

The architect has only an indirect influence on the consumption of energy occasioned by a building; e.g. in the form of communications, traffic and flows of materials, or in the form of production (embedded) energy in relation to the infrastructure. This is more the domain of the urban planner and of politics.

The significance of this issue within the overall scenario of energy consumption can be illustrated by an example from the realm of private traffic. A person who drives more than 10 km a day with a middle-market car consumes as much (primary) energy as he or she would in the home.

Induzierte Energie

Auf die durch ein Gebäude hervorgerufene Energie durch Kommunikation, Verkehr, Stoffflüsse sowie Herstellungsenergie für Infrastruktur hat der Planer des Gebäudes nur indirekt Einfluß – dies ist eher die Domäne der Städtebauer und der Politik.

Die Wichtigkeit im Gesamtszenario des Energieverbrauches zeigt das Beispiel Individualverkehr: Eine Person, die täglich mehr als 10 km mit einem Mittelklassewagen fährt, verbraucht soviel Energie (Primärenergie), wie sie in ihrer Wohnung verbraucht.

Energia indotta

L'architetto ha soltanto un'influenza indiretta sul consumo energetico causato dall'edilizia; ovvero nelle forme di comunicazione, traffico e flusso dei materiali, oppure nelle forme di energia di produzione in relazione con le infrastrutture (ma questo è più il dominio di pianificatori e politici).

Il significato del consumo di energia nello scenario complessivo può essere illustrato attraverso un esempio tratto dal mondo del traffico privato: una persona che guida più di 10 Km al giorno con una macchina media consuma molto di più (energia primaria) che se stesse a casa.

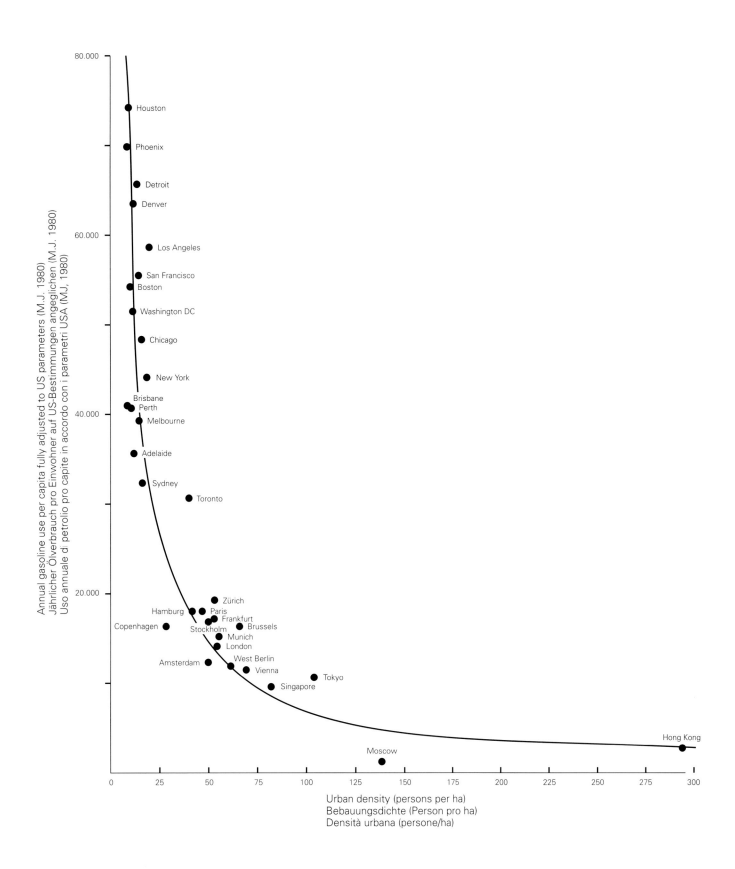

The link between density of development and energy use was made clear by Prof. John Whitelegg in his study "Transport for a Sustainable Future – The Case for Europe".
If one adds the production/embedded energy and the grey energy implicit in the infrastructure to transport-related energy, the need for higher-density development and a social distribution of sunlight in urban planning becomes apparent.

Den Zusammenhang zwischen der Dichte der Bebauung und dem Energieverbrauch machte Prof. John Whitelegg in seiner Studie »Transport for a Sustainable Future – The Case for Europe« deutlich. Addiert man zu der Verkehrsenergie die Herstellungsenergie und die graue Energie für Infrastruktur, so wird hier noch einmal die Notwendigkeit des verdichteten Bauens sowie der sozialen Aufteilung der Sonne im Städtebau klar.

La connessione tra densità di sviluppo ed energia impiegata è stata spiegata dal Prof. John Whitelegg nel suo studio «Trasporti per un futuro sostenibile – Il caso dell'Europa».
Se si aggiunge l'energia di produzione e l'energia grigia implicita nelle infrastrutture per l'energia relativa al trasporto, la necessità di uno sviluppo ad alta densità e di una distribuzione sociale di luce solare nella pianificazione appare evidente.

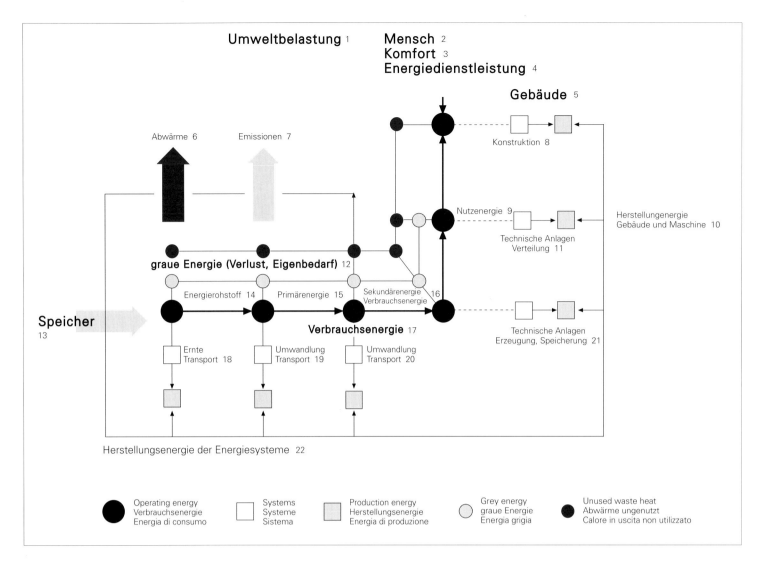

Umweltbelastung 1   Mensch 2
Komfort 3
Energiedienstleistung 4

Gebäude 5

Abwärme 6   Emissionen 7

Konstruktion 8

Nutzenergie 9   Herstellungenergie
Gebäude und Maschine 10

graue Energie (Verlust, Eigenbedarf) 12   Technische Anlagen
Verteilung 11

Energierohstoff 14   Primärenergie 15   Sekundärenergie
Verbrauchsenergie 16

Speicher
13   Verbrauchsenergie 17   Technische Anlagen
Erzeugung, Speicherung 21

Ernte
Transport 18   Umwandlung
Transport 19   Umwandlung
Transport 20

Herstellungsenergie der Energiesysteme 22

● Operating energy Verbrauchsenergie Energia di consumo	□ Systems Systeme Sistema	▨ Production energy Herstellungsenergie Energia di produzione	○ Grey energy graue Energie Energia grigia	◕ Unused waste heat Abwärme ungenutzt Calore in uscita non utilizzato

1 Environmental pollution / Degrado ambientale; 2 Man / Uomo; 3 Comfort / Comfort; 4 Energy supply services / Energia di servizio; 5 Building / Edificio; 6 Waste heat / Calore in uscita; 7 Emission / Inquinamento; 8 Construction / Costruzione; 9 Effective energy / Impiego di energia; 10 Production (embedded) energy: buildings and machinery / Energia di produzione: edifici e macchine; 11 Technical systems: distribu- tion / Impianti tecnici: distribuzione; 12 Grey energy (losses, internal use) / Energia grigia (perdita, fabbisogno proprio); 13 Storage / Accumulatore; 14 Raw materials for energy / Materie prime per l'energia; 15 Primary Energy / Energia primaria; 16 Secondary energy: operating energy / Energia secondaria: Energia di Consumo; 17 Operating energy / Energia di Consumo; 18 Extraction, harvesting, transport / Raccolto, Trasporto; 19 Conversion, transport / Trasforma- zione, trasporto; 20 Conversion, transport / Trasformazione, trasporto; 21 Technical systems: production, storage / Impianti tecnici: produzione, accumulazione; 22 Production energy systems / Energia di produzione del sistema di energia

Energy flows

The diagram above shows the various energy flows for a conventional building development, starting with the raw materials and their processing into primary energy and its conversion into secondary forms of energy such as electricity or district heating, and continuing on to the form of energy used by the end consumer (supplied energy) and distributed to domestic technical installations (usable energy). This comprises the whole system of energy supply services; i. e. the creation of conditions of sensory comfort through light, spatial heating, etc. These conditions of comfort will depend on user requirements and on the characteristics of the building. The building itself and the usable energy, therefore, determine the necessary plant and installation systems. Buildings and systems have to be produced, maintained, removed and recycled – processes that in turn require the consumption of

Energieflüsse

Vorstehende Graphik zeigt die Energieflüsse einer konventionellen Bebauung, beginnend beim Roh- stoff, über dessen Aufbereitung in Primärenergie, die Umwandlung in Sekundärenergie wie Strom oder Fernwärme bis hin zu der Energieform, wel- che der Verbraucher abnimmt (Endenergie) und in seinen haustechnischen Anlagen verteilt (Einsatz- energie), was schließlich zu der Energiedienstlei- stung, d. h. den fühlbaren Komfortbedingungen wie Licht und Raumwärme führt.
Diese Komfortbedingungen sind abhängig von den Erfordernissen bzw. Ansprüchen der Nutzer sowie den Gegebenheiten des Gebäudes. In Konsequenz führt das Gebäude sowie die Einsatzenergie zu notwendigen technischen Anlagensystemen. Sol- che Gebäude und Systeme müssen hergestellt, unterhalten sowie rückgebaut und recycelt wer- den. Dies erfordert Materialien, Stoffe sowie Ener-

Flussi di energia

Il diagramma sopra mostra i vari flussi di energia per lo sviluppo di un edificio convenzionale, par- tendo dalle materie prime e dalla loro trasforma- zione in energia primaria e dalla conversione in forma secondaria di energia come elettricità o «Fernwärme» (riscaldamento a distanza, fino alle forme di energia usate dal consumatore finale (energia di rifornimento) e distribuite alle installa- zioni tecniche domestiche (energia di servizio). Questa comprende l'intero sistema di energia di servizio; ossia la creazione di condizioni di comfort sensibili attraverso la luce, il riscaldamento dell'ambiente, etc.
Queste condizioni di comfort dipenderanno dalle richieste dell'utente e dalle caratteristiche dell'edi- ficio. L'edificio stesso e l'energia fruibile, tuttavia, determinano l'impianto necessario ed i sistemi di installazione. Gli edifici ed i sistemi devono essere

resources in the form of materials and energy. The energy used in this context is production energy (also known as indirect or embedded energy). It is the operating energy used by manufacturers and tradesmen. The generation of this energy is, in turn, an integral part of the overall system of energy production. Grey energy comprises the energy requirements for the generating process as well as the losses incurred through conversion, transport and distribution.

The relevant amounts of production energy within the systems (fixed in quantity and calculated for the full lifespan of an object) together with the grey energy (accompanying the production process and thus variable) should be apportioned to the individual stages of consumption of operating energy.

The horizontal line of the consumer chain represents the supply or infrastructure. The vertical chains represent the service systems and consumption in connection with a building.

If one considers energy flows in relation to a building or to the choice of a certain form of primary energy (including the relevant conversion and distribution systems), a vital question in our race against environmental destruction arises: what energy is expended when?

The corollary of this is: through what planning or political decisions are the consumption of energy and environmental damage irreversibly determined?

gie. Diese Energie ist die Herstellungsenergie (auch indirekte oder eingebettete Energie genannt). Sie ist die Verbrauchsenergie für Hersteller, Handwerker. Herstellungsenergie ist ebenfalls in den Systemen der Energieaufbereitung, in Umwandlung und Transport enthalten. Graue Energie ist der Energieeigenbedarf der Energieerzeugung sowie Verluste durch Umwandlung, Transport und Verteilung.

Den einzelnen Verbrauchsstadien der Betriebsenergie sind die entsprechenden Herstellungsenergien der Systeme (fix und über den Lebenszeitraum) sowie die graue Energie (produktionsbegleitend und somit variabel) zuzuordnen.

Die horizontale Ebene der Verbrauchskette zeigt die Versorgung oder Infrastruktur, die vertikale Verkettung die gebäudebezogenen Installationen und Verbräuche.

Bezieht man die Energieflüsse auf ein Gebäude oder auf die Auswahl einer bestimmten Primärenergie mit den dazugehörigen Umwandlungs- und Verteilungssystemen, so ergibt sich im Wettlauf mit der Umweltzerstörung die Frage, welche Energie wann ausgegeben wird.

Weiterhin: durch welche planerischen oder politischen Festlegungen Energieverbrauch und Umweltschaden irreversibel determiniert werden.

prodotti, mantenuti, rimossi e riciclati – processi che a loro volta richiedono il consumo di risorse in forma di materiali ed energia. L'energia usata in questo contesto è quella di produzione (anche nota come energia indiretta). E' l'energia di servizio usata da produttori e artigiani. La produzione di energia di servizio è, a sua volta, parte integrante del sistema globale della produzione energetica. L'energia grigia comprende le richieste energetiche per processi generativi, oltre alle perdite cui si incorre durante la conversione, distribuzione e trasporto.

L'ammontare particolare di energia di produzione nei sistemi (fissata in quantità e calcolata per l'intera vita dell'oggetto), insieme con l'energia grigia (che accompagna i processi di produzione e per questo variabile), dovrebbero essere collocate agli stadi individuali di consumo di energia di servizio. La linea orizzontale della catena del consumo rappresenta l'approvvigionamento e le infrastrutture. Le catene verticali rappresentano i sistemi di servizio e di consumo in connessione con un edificio.

Se si considerano i flussi di energia in relazione all'edificio o alla scelta di certe forme di energia primaria (inclusi i rilevanti sistemi di conversione e distribuzione), si pone una domanda vitale nella nostra competizione contro la distruzione dell'ambiente: quale energia viene spesa e quando?

Una questione per l'avvenire: attraverso quali pianificazioni o decisioni politiche viene determinato il consumo di energia e il danno all'ambiente in maniera irreversibile?

Time

If one studies the various systems of energy generation or the house as a system, it becomes clear that the production energy contained (embedded) within an object is expended for the lifetime of that object; but it is spent in its entirety today. In other words, it is being expended at a time when we in Europe are producing energy in a way that is extremely damaging for the environment. The overall proportion of emission-free regenerable energy used in Europe today is about 0.1 per cent solar and wind energy and 14.2 per cent waterpower. It will take years or even decades before regenerable energy is substituted for dirty forms of energy to any significant degree. That means we should curtail present-day energy use as much as possible. The production energy (primary energy – approx. 2.0 MWh/m^2) contained in a building is approximately 20 per cent of the operating energy required over its entire lifetime. Considering the spate of building that is likely to take place as a

Zeit

Betrachtet man Systeme der Energieerzeugung oder das System-Haus so wird die Herstellungsenergie zwar für den gesamten Lebenszeitraum, jedoch heute ausgegeben. Heute, d. h. zu einem Zeitpunkt, zu welchem wir Energien in Europa weitgehendst extrem umweltbelastend verfügbar machen. Der Gesamtumfang emissionsfrei regenerativer Energie beträgt derzeit in Europa etwa 0,1 % Sonnen- und Windenergie und 14,2 % Wasserkraft. Bevor diese schmutzige Energie durch regenerative Energie auch zu nennenswerten Anteilen substituiert wird, dauert es leider noch Jahre oder Jahrzehnte.

Dies bedeutet, daß wir insbesondere heutige Ausgaben vermeiden sollten. Die Herstellungsenergie eines Gebäudes (PE – ca. 2,0 MWh/m^2) beträgt ca. 20 % seiner Verbrauchsenergie über den Lebenszeitraum. Bedenkt man den Bauschub, welcher durch die Bevölkerungsexplosion hervorgerufen wird, dann sind diese ca. 20 % Lebenszeitraum-

Tempo

Se si studiano i vari sistemi di generazione dell'energia o il sistema-casa, diviene chiaro che l'energia di produzione è spesa per il complessivo arco di tempo della vita di un oggetto, ma che è spesa oggi, ossia in un'epoca in cui noi rendiamo disponibili in Europa energie estremamente dannose per l'ambiente. La proporzione globale di energia rigenerabile non inquinante usata in Europa è per circa lo 0.1 % energia solare ed energia del vento e per il 14.2 % energia idraulica.

Ci vorranno anni e persino decadi prima che l'energia rinnovabile sostituisca le forme inquinanti di energia ad un livello significativo. Questo significa che noi dobbiamo diminuire l'uso energetico attuale quanto più possibile. L'energia di produzione (energia primaria – approssimativamente 2.0 MWh/mq) contenuta in un edificio è all'incirca il 2 % dell'energia di servizio richiesta durante il suo intero arco di vita. Considerando la spinta a costruire che probabilmente si sta affermando

result of the population explosion, under present-day circumstances, this roughly 20 per cent proportion of the lifespan energy represents a threat to human existence.

The architect in particular, as the person responsible for the planning of a building, has to justify the expenditure of this embedded production energy. A sensible form of construction that conserves resources through its scale and dimensions, together with the appropriate choice of materials – in other words, entropy-conscious building – can in themselves significantly reduce the amount of production energy used.

The amount of operating energy required in terms of the thermal energy consumption of a building is a more or less fixed quantity over a longer period. The only hope in this respect is for better fuels. The consumption of electricity can be quantitatively reduced by the use of short-term technical installations. In view of constant improvements in the technology of power stations and their increasing electrical efficiency (less waste heat), thermal energy acquires a special significance, since it is fixed in amount over a long period.

The consumption of production (embedded) energy in energy generating plant and infrastructure installations is similar to that in buildings. The various forms of this energy represent only one per cent of the energy used during the average lifetime of an installation. Nevertheless, in the context of our present-day environmental conditions, the capacity we are installing centrally – in part redundant in the future – is considerable. Of even greater significance is the fact that long-term central plant means that the present unsatisfactory state of technology is fixed for a long time to come.

Decentralized energy supply services, integrated as far as possible into the building developments themselves and with short-life or exchangeable components, must be given serious consideration when planning service structures.

The decisive factor, therefore, in our struggle to halt the destruction of the environment is the energy expended today in the production process, which is fixed in amount in the long term.

That does not make operating energy any less significant, but its use will occur in part at a later date when alternative forms of energy will have taken the place of energy generated from finite resources.

Achieving a balance of energy along the lifespan axis for a conventional form of construction can be represented as follows.

Energien zu heutigen »Konditionen« eine lebensbedrohende Größenordnung.

Diese Herstellungsenergie hat insbesondere der Architekt als verantwortlicher Planer zu vertreten. Sinnvolle, ressourcenschonende Bauweise in Größe und Dimensionierung, die richtige Materialauswahl, d. h. entropiebewußtes Bauen, kann diese Herstellungsenergie bereits wesentlich reduzieren. Die Verbrauchsenergie ist durch das Gebäude hinsichtlich der Quantität des thermischen Energieverbrauchs langzeitig festgelegt – hier ist nur auf besseren Brennstoff zu hoffen. Der Stromverbrauch kann quantitativ durch Einsatz kurzlebiger technischer Ausrüstung reduziert werden. Der thermischen Energie kommt wegen der Langzeitfestlegung sowie auch der neuen, besser werdenden elektrischen Wirkungsgrade der Kraftwerkstechnik (geringere Abwärme) eine besondere Bedeutung zu. Ähnlich wie beim Gebäude verhält sich der Verbrauch von Herstellungsenergie im Fall von Energieerzeugungs- und Infrastrukturanlagen. Diese Herstellungsenergien machen zwar bei Großkraftwerken nur ein einziges Prozent auf die mittlere Lebensdauer hin gesehen aus, trotzdem ist die Größenordnung, die wir heute – auch schon redundant d.h. auf »Zukunft«– zentral installieren, bei den »Energieumweltkonditionen« schon beachtenswert. Viel entscheidender ist jedoch, daß durch langlebige zentrale Anlagen der heutige (nicht zufriedenstellende) Stand der Technik für sehr lange Zeit festgeschrieben wird.

Dezentrale – möglichst gebäudeintegrierte Energieversorgungsanlagen mit kurzlebigeren bzw. austauschbaren Komponenten sind bei der Abwägung von Versorgungsstrukturen zwingend mit zu überprüfen.

Die heute für die Herstellung ausgegebene und heute langfristig determinierte Energie ist somit die entscheidende im Wettlauf mit der Zerstörung der Umwelt.

Die Verbrauchsenergie wird dadurch nicht unwichtiger. Jedoch wird sie teilweise in spätere Energiesubstitutionszeiten fallen.

Eine Energiebilanzierung auf der Lebenszeitachse stellt sich bei konventioneller Bebauung wie folgt dar:

come conseguenza all'esplosione demografica, nelle condizioni attuali questo circa 20 % di proporzione d'energia nel corso della vita rappresenta una minaccia all'esistenza umana.

L'architetto in particolare, come persona responsabile di un edificio, deve giustificare il consumo di questa energia di produzione. Una forma sensata di costruzione che conservi le risorse attraverso la sua scala e le sue dimensioni, insieme con un'appropriata scelta di materiali – in altre parole un edificio consapevole dell'entropia – può in sé stesso ridurre in maniera significativa l'ammontare di energia di produzione impiegata.

L'ammontare di energia di servizio richiesta in termini di consumo termico energetico di un edificio è più o meno una quantità fissata su un periodo a lungo termine. C'è solo da sperare in migliori combustibili. Il consumo di elettricità può essere quantitativamente ridotto con installazioni tecniche a breve termine.

In vista dei costanti miglioramenti delle centrali di energia e dell'evoluzione della loro efficienza elettrica (meno calore disperso), l'energia termica ha acquistato un significato speciale da quando se ne è fissato un quantitativo totale su un lungo termine.

Il consumo di energia di produzione in un impianto che genera energia e in installazioni per infrastrutture è simile a quello negli edifici. Le varie forme di energia di produzione nei lavori di grossa portata rappresentano soltanto l'uno per cento dell'energia impiegata durante la vita media di un'installazione. Tuttavia, nel contesto delle attuali condizioni ambientali, sono considerevoli i valori che noi stiamo ponendo in posizione centrale – anche in modo ridondante sul futuro. Persino di più grande importanza è il fatto che, con l'impianto centrale a lungo termine, il non soddisfacente stato di tecnologia viene fissato per un lungo tempo a venire.

Gli impianti di approvvigionamento di energia decentralizzati, integrati per quanto possibile negli insediamenti edilizi stessi e con vita breve o componenti sostituibili, si devono tenere in seria considerazione quando si progettano strutture di servizio.

Il fattore decisivo è l'energia spesa attualmente nel processo produttivo, che nel totale è programmato a lungo termine, nella corsa contro la rovina dell'ambiente. L'energia di esercizio non diverrà comunque meno importante. Tuttavia essa diverrà parziale più in avanti, nel periodo di sostituzione energetica.

Effettuando un bilancio energetico, lungo l'asse dell'arco di vita di una forma convenzionale di costruzione, si può realizzare quanto segue:

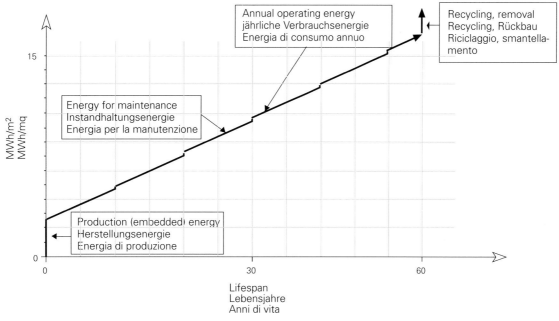

Annual operating energy
jährliche Verbrauchsenergie
Energia di consumo annuo

Energy for maintenance
Instandhaltungsenergie
Energia per la manutenzione

Recycling, removal
Recycling, Rückbau
Riciclaggio, smantella-
mento

Production (embedded) energy
Herstellungsenergie
Energia di produzione

Lifespan
Lebensjahre
Anni di vita

Energy consumption during the lifespan of a building
Energieverbrauch eines Gebäudes über den Lebenszeitraum
Consumo di energia di un edificio durante l'intero arco di vita

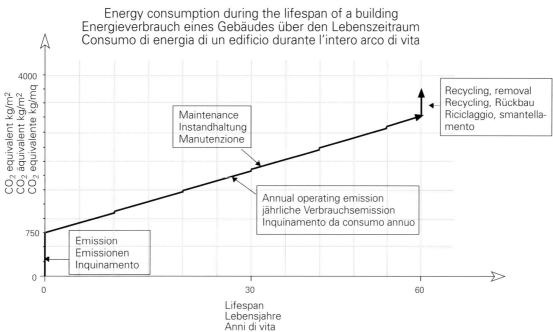

Recycling, removal
Recycling, Rückbau
Riciclaggio, smantella-
mento

Maintenance
Instandhaltung
Manutenzione

Annual operating emission
jährliche Verbrauchsemission
Inquinamento da consumo annuo

Emission
Emissionen
Inquinamento

Lifespan
Lebensjahre
Anni di vita

These graphs show that economies can achieve only a flattening of the curve (cf. the discussion on entropy). To balance out the energy and materials that are taken from nature to create and run a building during its lifetime, solar technology has to be introduced. This comprises the following.

Diese Übersichten machen deutlich, daß man durch Sparen diese Kurve nur abflachen kann (siehe Entropiediskussion). Um das, was von der Natur an Energie und Material für Gebäude während eines Lebenszeitraumes genommen wird, auszugleichen, müssen solartechnische Maßnahmen ergriffen werden. Diese sind:

Questi grafici mostrano che i risparmi possono produrre soltanto un appiattimento della linea (Cfr. la discussione sull'entropia). Per bilanciare l'energia e i materiali tratti dalla natura per creare e gestire un edificio durante il corso della sua vita, si è dovuta introdurre la tecnologia solare. Questa comprende:

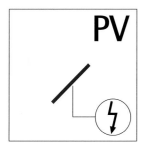

Renewable forms of energy
Erneuerbare Energie
Forme rinnovabili di energia

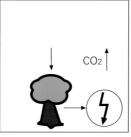

Regenerable forms of energy
Nachwachsende Energie
Forme rigenerabili di energia

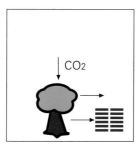

Regrowable materials
Nachwachsende Materialien
Materiali rinnovabili

Renewable forms of energy

E. g. solar energy converted by technical processes and free of emissions (photovoltaic systems, thermal collectors, wind, water power, tidal energy or the direct use of solar energy for natural lighting, heating and ventilation). These forms of energy cause no direct environmental emissions.

Regenerable forms of energy

Biomass in the form of regrowable raw materials that can be converted into energy through combustion, gasification, etc. and that can be neutralized in respect of emissions through replanting. In the latter respect, some raw materials have a comparable growth : yield ratio. For example, 1 m^2 of forest or 1 m^2 of sunflower plantation will yield approximately 1 kWh of energy per annum. The harvest or cultivation cycle of a field of sunflowers is one year; for a forest, it is 50 to 100 years. In other words, given the same cultivated area (or biological collector area), in one case one can compensate for energy use or environmental damage every year, in the other case only after a minimum of 50 years. Arithmetically, of course, after 50 years, the yield is the same, namely 50 kWh. In the one case, the yield is constant, consisting of a small amount annually. In the other case, the yield is zero for 49 years, and then the full amount is harvested in a single process. This raises the whole question of energy liquidity, for a premature withdrawal of these long-term reserves would inevitably result in energy losses – through storage costs, storage waste and the purchase of alternative forms of interim energy, which would be absorbed in use, but which would reduce the period in which CO_2 and energy can be saved up for later.

Regrowable materials

Timber is the classic example of a regrowable building material. It stores energy and CO_2 and requires very little production (embedded) energy. It is, therefore, the ideal material for cutting back on this form of energy. Depending on the particular use and the amount of maintenance required, wood as a building material has a life of between a few years and several centuries. It is also simple to remove and replace. It is, therefore, the ideal investment, a hidden reserve of energy liquidity.

Erneuerbare Energie

Technisch umgewandelte Solarenergie ohne jegliche Emissionen (PV, therm. Kollektoren, Wind, Wasserkraft, Gezeiten oder direkt genutzte Solarenergie für Zwecke wie Tageslicht, Wärme, natürliche Ventilation. Diese Energie bedingt keine direkten Umweltemissionen

Nachwachsende Energie

Biomasse aus nachwachsenden Energierohstoffen, welche durch Verbrennung, Vergasung zu Energie umgewandelt werden und durch gleichzeitige Neuanpflanzung die Emissionen wieder neutralisieren.
Bei letzterer haben einige ähnliche Wachstumsausbeuten, z. B. 1 m^2 Wald oder 1 m^2 Sonnenblumenfeld eine jährliche Energieausbeute von ca. 1 kWh. Der Ernte/Anbauzyklus ist beim Sonnenblumenfeld 1 Jahr, bei Wald 50 bis 100 Jahre, d. h. bei gleicher definierter Anbaufläche (oder biologischer Kollektorfläche) kann man in einem Fall jährlich den Verbrauch bzw. die Umweltschädigung kompensieren, im anderen frühestens alle 50 Jahre. Rechnerisch ergibt dies nach 50 Jahren in beiden Fällen das gleiche Ergebnis: 50 kWh.
In dem einen Fall ist der Ertrag stetig, jedes Jahr nur wenig, in dem anderen Fall ist er 50 Jahre lang gleich Null und dann viel. Hier stellt sich die Frage nach der Energieliquidität, denn ein vorzeitiges Auflösen des Langzeitspeichers wäre mit Energieverlusten verbunden. Denn das Viele oder Mehr an produzierter Energie für die mindestens 50 Jahre (jedoch mit kurzen Kündigungsfristen) »anzulegen«, ist nur mit Verlusten möglich: durch Speicheraufwand, Speicherverluste, Zukauf anderer Energie, welche zwar bei Verbrauch absorbiert wird, jedoch die CO_2- und Energieansparperiode hemmt.

Nachwachsende Materialien

Holz ist das klassische nachwachsende Baumaterial. Es speichert Energie und CO_2, braucht nur sehr geringe Herstellungsenergie. Insoweit ist es das ideale Material zur Einsparung von Herstellungsenergie. Je nach Nutzung und Unterhaltungsaufwand hat das Baumaterial Lebensdauern von einigen Jahren oder Jahrhunderten. Es ist einfach rückzubauen. Es ist die ideale, gut investierte stille Reserve für Energieliquidität.

Forme rinnovabili di energia

Ovvero energia solare non convertita attraverso processi tecnici e non inquinanti (sistemi fotovoltaici, collettori termici, vento, energia idraulica, energia dipendente dalla marea oppure impiego diretto dell'energia solare per illuminazione naturale, riscaldamento e ventilazione). Queste forme di energia non causano alcun inquinamento ambientale diretto.

Forme rigenerabili di energia

La biomassa sotto forma di materie prime rigenerabili che possono essere convertite in energia per combustione, gasificazione, etc., e che possono essere neutralizzate nei confronti delle emissioni attraverso una nuova piantumazione.
Da ultimo, alcune materie prime hanno una crescita comparabile: per esempio un mq di bosco o 1 mq di girasoli produrranno all'incirca un kWh di energia per anno. Il raccolto o un ciclo di coltivazione di un campo di girasoli dura un anno; per un bosco è compreso tra i 50 e i 100 anni, ossia, data una stessa area piantumata (o un'area-collettore biologico), nel primo caso si può compensare l'impiego di energia o il danno ambientale ogni anno, nel secondo caso solo dopo un minimo di 50 anni. Aritmeticamente dopo 50 anni il risultato è lo stesso, vale a dire 50 kWh. Nell'un caso, il profitto è costante, consistendo in un esiguo ammontare annuo. Nell'altro caso, il profitto è zero per 49 anni, poi si ha l'ammontare totale tutto insieme. Qui si pone la questione sulla liquidità di energia, poiché un annullamento anticipato dell'accumulatore a lungo termine è legato alle perdite di energia .
Così «investire» su un solo raccolto, per un periodo minimo di 50 anni (con la possibilità di «ritirare» l'energia con un breve preavviso) risulta inevitabilmente in perdita – per via dei costi e delle perdite di accumulo, e per la rendita di forme alternative di energia, che vengono assorbite nel processo, ma che restringono il periodo in cui CO_2 ed energia possono essere salvate.

Materiali rinnovabili

Il legno è il classico esempio di materiale rinnovabile. Accumula energia e CO_2 e richiede poca energia di produzione. Rispetto a ciò, è il materiale ideale per risparmiare energia di produzione.

Data on wood

In Europe, more timber is planted than is felled. At first sight, this would imply an increase in the potential absorption of carbon dioxide (CO_2). A cubic metre of wood absorbs one tonne of CO_2 in its growth (0.5 t/m³ dry density).

Too little felling of wood (or too little use of timber), however, means that the stock increases in age, and less and less CO_2 is absorbed. After about 50 years, a tree is a good reservoir of carbon, but it no longer absorbs carbon and is, therefore, not a reservoir of oxygen.

On the contrary, trees with no further growth are vulnerable to infestation from insects and fungi and become brittle and break. In conjunction with moisture, wood that has fallen from trees is subject to anaerobic decay and gives off methane. Tall trees shade other plants and take away the light they need to grow. The functions of the biological collector become more and more restricted.

In other words, trees that are no longer biologically efficient have to be felled to make room for new growth and more efficient CO_2 absorption. The energy yield from 1 m³ of timber is roughly 2,500 kWh. About 75 per cent of every cubic metre of wood can be cut into squared timbers, boards, battens, etc. This represents about 0.75 t of CO_2 stored in the building material and a pri-

Exkurs Holz

In Europa wird mehr Holz aufgeforstet als geschlagen. Dies führt vordergründig zu einer Erhöhung unseres Potentials an CO_2-Absorption
1 m³ = 1 t CO_2 (0,5 t/m³ Darrdichte)
Das zu geringe Schlagen (bzw. Verwenden von Holz) hat zur Folge, daß der Bestand immer älter wird und immer weniger CO_2 absorbiert wird. Nach ca. 50 Jahren ist ein Baum zwar ein guter Kohlenstoffspeicher jedoch kein Kohlenstofffänger und somit auch kein Sauerstoffspeicher.
Im Gegenteil, Bäume ohne weiteres Wachstum sind Pilz- und Insektenbefall ausgesetzt, brechen. Fallholz in Verbindung mit Feuchte setzt durch anaerobe Fäulnis Methan frei, die Baumkrone nimmt anderen Pflanzen das Licht zum Wachsen weg – der biologische Kollektor wird in seiner Wirkung immer mehr eingeschränkt.
Dies bedeutet, daß biologisch nicht mehr effizienter Baumbestand geschlagen werden müßte, um neuem Wachstum und effizienter CO_2-Absorption Platz zu machen.
Die Energieausbeute aus 1 m³ Holz beträgt etwa 2500 kWh. Aus 1 m³ Holz können ca. 75 % Kanthölzer, Bretter, Latten geschnitten werden. Dies ergibt eine Speicherung in Baumaterial von 0,75 to CO_2 und eine Primärenergie von ca. 1875 kWh (bezogen auf 1 m³ Festholz).

Dipendendo dal particolare uso e dalla quantità totale di manutenzione richiesta, il legno come materiale da costruzione ha una vita che varia da pochi anni a molti secoli. È anche semplice da rimuovere e sostituire. È, quindi, l'investimento ideale, una riserva nascosta di liquidità energetica.

Excursus sul legno

In Europa è stato piantato più legno di quanto se ne sia abbattuto. Ciò dovrebbe implicare un incremento nel potenziale assorbimento del Biossido di Carbonio (CO_2) – 1 mc di legno assorbe 1 t di CO_2 durante la sua crescita (0.5 t/mc «Darrdichte», densità a secco).
L'abbattimento di troppo poco legno (oppure l'uso di troppo poco legname) significa, però, che il suo quantitativo invecchia sempre più e assorbe sempre meno CO_2. Dopo circa 50 anni, un albero costituisce una buona riserva di Carbonio, ma esso non assorbirà Carbonio più a lungo, per cui non sarà anche una buona riserva di Ossigeno. Piuttosto, gli alberi che non hanno un'ulteriore crescita sono vulnerabili ad infestazioni di insetti e funghi e divengono fragili e facili a rottura. Sotto l'azione dell'umidità, il legno caduto dagli alberi è soggetto ad un decadimento anaerobico e sprigiona Metano. Gli alberi alti fanno ombra sulle altre piante e sottraggono loro la luce di cui esse hanno bisogno per crescere.
Ciò significa che la funzione di collettore biologico si fa sempre più ristretta, ossia gli alberi che non sono più a lungo efficienti biologicamente devono essere abbattuti per far posto ai nuovi che crescono e ad un più efficiente assorbimento di CO_2.
Il guadagno energetico di 1 mc di legno è circa 2500 kWh. Circa il 75 % di ogni mc di legno può essere tagliato in legni squadrati, tavole, traverse, etc.
Questo rappresenta all'incirca 0.75 t di CO_2 accumulate nei materiali da costruzione ed un'energia primaria contenuta pari all'incirca a 1.875 kWh (per mc di legno non tagliato).
Un 25 % di legno è di scarto, ma questo può essere usato per generare funzioni energetiche, producendo un profitto di 625 kWh di energia insieme a 0.25 t di emissione di CO_2.
All'incirca 660 kWh di energia primaria sono necessari per abbattere, trasportare, segare, piallare, etc., 1 mc di edificio in legno. Approssimativamente 200 kWh di questa sono richiesti per il processo meccanico, il resto è usato termicamente per l'essiccazione. La maggior parte del processo di essiccazione può essere ottenuta impiegando tecnologia solare.

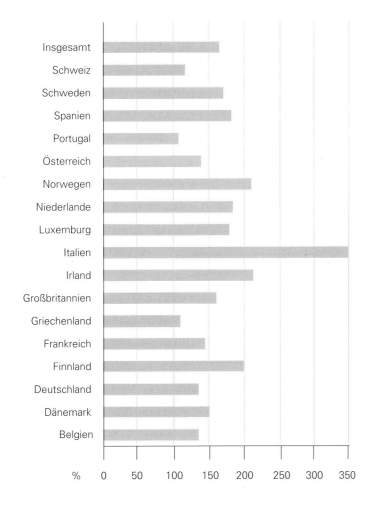

mary energy content of approximately 1,875 kWh (per cubic metre of uncut timber).

Twenty-five per cent of the timber is waste, but this can be used for energy generating purposes, producing a 625-kWh energy yield together with 0.25 t of CO_2 emission.

Approximately 660 kWh of primary energy are needed to fell, transport, saw, plane, etc. one cubic metre of building timber. Roughly 200 kWh of this are required for mechanical processing; the rest is used thermally for drying. The bulk of the drying process, however, can be carried out employing solar technology.

The energy yield from the waste from a cubic metre of building timber amounts to about 830 kWh. A surplus of energy is, therefore, guaranteed. This will usually lie between 200 and 600 kWh/m³ timber.

The aim of solar standards

En route to our goal, there are many options open in the form of potential savings, the rational use of energy, or aspects such as the complementary use of solar energy or its substitution for other forms of energy. A number of guidelines, recommendations and standards already exist in this respect, although they are certainly capable of improvement. The decisive factor is the ultimate goal, which must be defined clearly and independently of the many possible routes leading to it. The period in which this goal may be attained is dependent on many factors: politics, subsidies, market conditions, costs, etc., but above all on the energy we ourselves can invest in this process in

25 % ist Abfall, welcher zu energetischen Zwecken genutzt werden kann: Dies ergibt 625 kWh Energieausbeute, verbunden mit 0,25 to CO_2-Emission. Für das Schlagen, Transportieren, Sägen, Hobeln werden ca. 660 kWh PE, bezogen auf 1 m³ Bauholz, benötigt. Davon sind ca. 200 kWh antriebsbedingt, der Rest dient zum Trocknen. Den größten Teil des Trocknungsprozesses kann man jedoch solartechnisch bewerkstelligen.

Bezogen auf 1 m³ Bauholz beträgt die Energieausbeute des Abfalls ca. 830 kWh, so daß sich in jedem Fall ein Energieüberschuß ergibt, der zwischen 200 und 600 kWh/m³ Bauholz liegt.

Ziel der Solar Standards

Auf dem Weg zu diesem Ziel gibt es vielfältige Wege des Sparens, der rationellen Energieverwendung, des komplementären oder substituierenden Einsetzens von Solarenergie. Dafür gibt es Empfehlungen, Normen, die sich sicher verbessern lassen. Entscheidend ist das Ziel, welches eindeutig und unabhängig von den zahlreichen Wegen zu definieren ist. Der Zeitraum, dieses Ziel zu erreichen, ist von vielen Faktoren abhängig: Politik, Subventionen, Markt, Kosten etc. – vor allem aber von der Energie, welche wir selbst einbringen können: Kreativität, Innovation. Es ist die Komponente Information in dem Energie-Zeit-Informations-Dreieck – und damit sollen sie sofort anfangen. Das Ziel sollte so definiert sein:

Ein Gebäude hat der Natur das, was es ihr genommen hat, über den Lebenszeitraum zurückzugeben.

In der Analogie zur Betriebswirtschaftslehre kön-

Il profitto energetico ricavabile dallo scarto di 1 mc di legno da costruzione ammonta a 830 kWh. E' quindi garantito un surplus di energia, che normalmente si aggirerà tra i 200 ed i 600 kWh/mc di legno.

Lo scopo dei solar standards

Sulla strada verso questo obiettivo, ci sono molte opzioni aperte nella forma di risparmio di potenziale, uso razionale di energia, o aspetti come l'impiego complementare di energia solare, o la sua sostituzione con altre forme di energia. Un certo numero di linee guida, prescrizioni e standards già esiste al riguardo, anche se questi sono certamente suscettibili di miglioramento. Il fattore decisivo è l'obiettivo estremo, che deve essere definito in maniera chiara ed indipendente dalle molte possibili strade che a questo possono condurre. Il periodo in cui tale obiettivo sarà raggiunto dipende da molti fattori: politica, sovvenzioni, condizioni di mercato, costi, etc., ma soprattutto dall'energia che noi stessi possiamo investire in questo processo sotto forma di creatività e di pensiero innovativo. Ciò rappresenta la componente di informazione nel triangolo formato da energia-tempo-informazione e da questo deve subito avere inizio. Lo scopo deve essere definito come segue:

Nel corso della sua vita, un edificio dovrebbe risarcire la natura di ciò che le ha sottratto.

Per cogliere un'analogia nel campo degli affari, possiamo considerare ciò che prendiamo dalla natura come un prestito per assicurarci il nostro benessere. Affinché l'ordine ecologico non collassi, dobbiamo saldare questo debito in un periodo

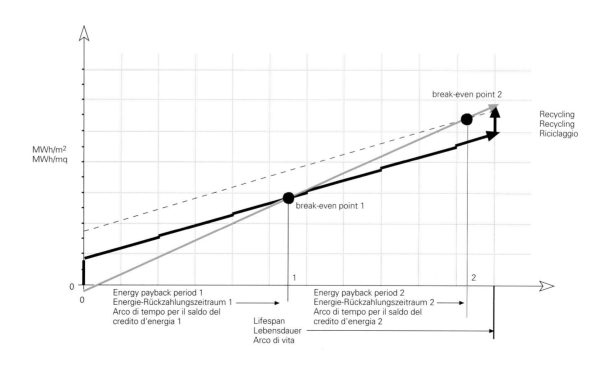

the form of creativity and innovative thinking. This represents the informational component in the triangle formed by energy, time and information, and we should address our attention to this point at once.

The goal may be defined as follows.

In the course of its life, a building should restore to nature what it has taken from it.

To take an analogy from the field of business management, we may regard what we take from nature as a loan to secure our sense of well-being. If the ecological order is not to collapse, we must repay this loan over a period that should not exceed the lifespan of the building.

The loan sum itself should be kept to a minimum through the rational use of energy in the realms of production and operation. This will facilitate an economical repayment by means of regenerative forms of energy with a minimum of emissions.

In business management, the point on the graph where costs (consumption) are covered, and profit (regenerative production) begins is known as the break-even point. The length of time up to this point is the (energy) pay-back period.

The following graph illustrates this.

The debt in terms of production and operating energy can be discharged through the use of regenerative forms of energy. The ecological break-even point 1 will be reached in the energy pay-back period 1. The energy required for removal and recycling will not be covered by this, however, so that initial profits will have to be set aside to cover later expenditure.

The break-even point between overall expenditure and yield is shown in the graph: i. e. the ecological break-even point 2 and the related energy pay-back period 2.

nen wir das, was wir von der Natur nehmen, als Kredit für unser Wohlbefinden ansehen. Soll das ökologische Ordnungssystem nicht zusammenbrechen, so muß dieser Kredit mit einer Maximallaufzeit des Lebenszeitraumes eines Gebäudes zurückgezahlt sein.

Die Kreditsumme selbst hält man durch rationelle Energieverwendung bei Herstellung und Verbrauch so gering als möglich, um die Tilgung mit regenerativer (möglichst emissionsfreier) Energie wirtschaftlich zu gestalten.

Die Betriebswirtschaftslehre nennt den Schnittpunkt zwischen Kosten (Verbrauch) und Ertrag (regenerative Erzeugung) break-even-point und den Zeitraum bis dahin (Energy) pay-back-period. Nachstehende Graphik zeigt das System:

Die Herstellungs- und Verbrauchsenergie wird durch den Einsatz regenerativer Energie getilgt und hat in einem Zeitraum Energy-pay-back-period 1 den ökologischen Break-even-point 1 erreicht. Dieser deckt jedoch nicht die Rückbau- und Recycling-Energie ab, so daß sich zunächst Gewinne für die spätere Ausgabe bilden müssen.

Auf der entsprechenden Hilfslinie ergibt sich dann der Schnittpunkt für die Gesamtausgaben mit den Erträgen, der ökologische Break-even-point 2 und die Energy-pay-back-period 2.

Das Beispiel zeigt ein herkömmliches Gebäude, dafür notwendige regenerative Energiesysteme ließen sich gebäudeintegriert gar nicht installieren – geschweige denn derzeit nachhaltig wirtschaftlich realisieren.

Die nachstehende Graphik zeigt die Strategie auf dem Weg zum Ziel. Zunächst muß die Herstellungsenergie durch massiven Einsatz erneuerbarer Materialien gesenkt werden und Abfallteile dieser Materialien entlastend zu einem regenerativen

di tempo che non ecceda il corso della vita dell'edificio.

Lo stesso debito sarà contenuto al minimo attraverso l'uso razionale di energia nel mondo della produzione e delle attività dell'uomo, cosicché sarà possibile dar forma ad un ammortamento economico per mezzo di forme rigenerative di energia (possibilmente prive di inquinamento).

L'economia aziendale chiama il punto di intersezione tra i costi (consumo) e il profitto (produzione rigenerativa) «break-even-point» e l'arco di tempo fino a quel punto (energia) «pay-back-period».

Il seguente grafico illustra questo sistema:

Il debito in termini di energia di produzione di servizio può essere saldato attraverso l'impiego di forma rigenerative di energia. L'ecologico break-even-point 1 si raggiungerà nell'energy-pay-back-period 1. L'energia richiesta per la demolizione ed il riciclaggio non sarà, però, coperta attraverso questo, in maniera tale che i profitti iniziali potranno essere messi da parte per coprire le spese successive.

Il break-even-point tra spesa totale e profitto è mostrato nel grafico, dove si può vedere l'ecologico break-even-point 2 ed il relativo pay-back-period 2.

L'esempio mostra un edificio convenzionale dove i necessari sistemi rigenerativi di energia non si lasciano affatto installare in maniera integrata con l'edificio – e tanto meno attualmente permettono di realizzare un'operazione sostenibile dal punto di vista economico.

Il seguente diagramma mostra la strategia seguita per ottenere questi risultati. Prima di tutto, l'energia di produzione contenuta è stata ridotta con un impiego massivo di materiali rinnovabili.

Lo scarto di questi materiali potrebbe essere usato

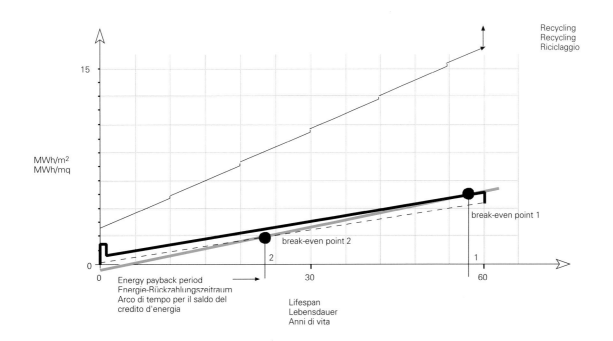

This example is based on a conventional building in which it would not be possible to integrate the necessary regenerative energy systems, let alone ensure their long-term economical operation. The following diagram shows the strategy to be pursued to achieve these goals. First of all, the production/embedded energy content has to be reduced by an extensive use of renewable materials. Waste from these materials should be employed to relieve the energy load with renewable forms of energy. In the event of the building being dismantled or demolished and components recycled, the renewable energy contained in the materials will make a positive contribution to the energy balance. In the graph, the relevant break-even line between expenditure and yield is now below the consumption line. If this can be lowered – through the intelligent exploitation of primary energy, for example – a solar "repayment installation" can be realized, which could be integrated into the building with scope for economical operation.

STANDARDS FÜR SOLARES BAUEN (Standards for solar building), edited by Norbert Kaiser in the context of the European research project READ 1.

Energiebeitrag eingesetzt werden. Die in den Baumaterialien gespeicherte regenerative Energie wirkt sich beim Rückbau/Recycling statt belastend entlastend auf die Energiebilanz aus. Die entsprechende Hilfslinie als Schnittlinie Ausgabe/Ertrag liegt nun innerhalb der Verbrauchslinie. Wird diese durch entsprechende Maßnahmen, insbesondere intelligente Primärenergieausnutzung gesenkt, so ergibt sich eine solare »Rückzahlungsinstallation«, welche im Normalfall ins Gebäude integriert werden und auch eine Chance auf wirtschaftliche Realisierung haben kann.

STANDARDS FÜR SOLARES BAUEN
Bearbeitung: Norbert Kaiser im Rahmen des europäischen Forschungsprojektes READ 1.

per ammortare il debito energetico con forme di energia rinnovabile. Nell'eventualità che l'edificio venga smantellato o demolito ed i componenti riciclati, l'energia rinnovabile contenuta nei materiali verrà a creare un contributo positivo per il bilancio energetico. La linea ausiliaria equivalente alla linea di separazione spesa/profitto è ora entro la linea del consumo. Se questa si potrà abbassare con adeguati provvedimenti – soprattutto attraverso l'impiego intelligente di energia primaria – si realizzerà un'«installazione-rimborso» solare, che potrà essere normalmente integrata nell'edificio rappresentando così anche una chance dal punto di vista economico.

STANDARDS FÜR SOLARES BAUEN (Standards per edifici solari) a cura di Norbert Kaiser nell'ambito del progetto di ricerca europeo READ 1.

SOLAR STANDARDS – a first step
Case Study: Solar City Project in Pichling, Linz

The study is based on the energy data compiled by the city of Linz:
room heat: 65 kWh/m^2 floor area/annum – for two-storey developments
60 kWh/m^2/a – for three-storey developments
hot water: 30 kWh/m^2/a, the solar-thermal content of which = 10 kWh/m^2/a.
In accordance with the principles of the SOLAR STANDARDS now being drawn up, the consumption of electrical energy, the energy supply and energy production were all taken into account in this project, and the annual primary energy consumption was restricted to
< 100 kWh/m^2/a.

Secondary targets were agreed for the individual uses of energy (general rules); but within the given parameters, the planner was free to decide on the main points of emphasis and the active solar tech-

SOLAR STANDARDS – ein erster Schritt
Fallstudie am Projekt: Solar City Linz Pichling

Ausgangsbasis waren die Energie-Kenn-Ziffern der Stadt Linz:
Raumwärme: 65 kWh/m^2/a bei zwei Geschossen
60 kWh/m^2/a bei drei Geschossen
Warmwasser: 30 kWh/m^2/a, davon solarthermisch: 10 kWh/m^2/a

Den Grundsätzen der in Bearbeitung befindlichen SOLAR STANDARDS entsprechend, wurden der elektrische Energieverbrauch, die Energiebereitstellung und Energieproduktion mit in die Überlegungen einbezogen und der jährliche Primärenergieverbrauch begrenzt auf:
< 100 kWh/m^2/a.

Dabei wurden Unterziele für die Einzelverbräuche (allgemeine Regeln), ansonsten jedoch die freie Wahl des Planers bei den Schwerpunkten sowie für die Grundversorgung komplettierende aktive

SOLAR STANDARDS – un primo passo
Caso di studio:
il progetto per Solar City Linz Pichling

Le basi di partenza sono state gli indici energetici della città di Linz:
calore per ambiente: 65 kWh/mq/anno su due piani
60 kWh/mq/anno su tre piani
acqua calda: 30 kWh/mq/anno di cui
termica solare: 10 kWh/mq/anno
In questi ambiti, ai principi dei SOLAR STANDARDS che si trovano in elaborazione vengono riferiti nelle nostre considerazioni il consumo di energia elettrica, la disponibilità del servizio energetico e la produzione di energia, e il consumo di energia primaria confinato a:
< 100 kWh/mq/anno

Contemporaneamente gli obiettivi nei confronti dei singoli consumi (regole generali), come del resto il libero discernimento del progettista tanto sui punti più importanti quanto sui criteri dell'ap-

nology to be installed to complement the basic supply. The criteria governing levels of comfort and the operational systems, together with the values to be applied in documenting the findings, were determined in advance.

The planning was to reflect the following criteria. In addition to complying with functional constraints, the skin of the building and the ratio of the skin to the volume (A/V ratio) were to be optimized in terms of the lighting engineering. Vision, lighting and heating requirements must, therefore, be treated as separate entities.

Creating visual links

This is a wholly architectural consideration, not a matter of solar technology. Minimum dimensions for openings should not be fixed in advance. The architect should, however, determine a minimum area to be kept free of shading.

Daylighting

Windows and indoor spaces should be laid out in such a way that, under overcast conditions (as defined by C.I.E. 16, E-3,2) with an external intensity of illumination of approx. 10,000 lux, a level of 200 lux can be achieved in the depth of rooms. This will largely determine the sizes of windows, the depths of rooms and the A/V ratio. In this respect, one is concerned with comfort requirements and a criterion for energy saving, both of which exert a great influence on the architecture.

Constructional physics of the outer skin and storage masses

The minimum solar aperture is determined by requirements for visual contact and daylighting. Where the aperture is to be enlarged to increase passive solar energy gains for heating the building, the relevant solar elements (sunlit rooms, solar walls, conservatories or verandas) should be precisely planned, and the relationship between the solar aperture and the degree of shading to which it is subject on the one hand and the effective primary and secondary energy storage volumes and ventilation on the other hand should be determined.

Excessively large storage masses should be avoided in order to economize on resources and to minimize the consumption of production energy. Insolation areas for the efficient exploitation of solar energy (in winter) should be dimensioned with the utmost care. The same applies conversely to shading and ventilation for heat dissipation and cooling in summer. (Space does not allow a more detailed description of the relationships between ventilation, storage mass and solar aperture. In general, however, one can say that a sunlit room is

Solartechnik vereinbart. Vorgeschrieben wurden Komfort- und Betriebskriterien sowie Werte für das anzuwendende Nachweisverfahren.

Die Planung sollte folgende Kriterien beinhalten: Gebäudehülle sowie A/V-Verhältnis sind neben den funktionalen Notwendigkeiten lichttechnisch zu optimieren: Dazu müssen die Funktionen: Sehen, Beleuchten sowie Erwärmen getrennt betrachtet werden.

Sichtkontakt

Dieser richtet sich ausschließlich nach architektonischen Anforderungen und ist nicht Bestandteil der Solartechnik. Es sollten auch keine Mindestgrößen für Öffnungen vorgeschrieben sein. Der Architekt sollte jedoch ein Minimum an abschattungsfreien Flächen vorgeben.

Tageslichtbeleuchtung

Die Fenster und Räume sollten so angeordnet sein, daß bei bedecktem Himmel nach C.I.E. 16 (E-3.2) und Außenbedingungen von ca. 10 000 lux in der Raumtiefe noch 200 lux erzielt werden können. Dies bestimmt im wesentlichen die Größe der Fenster, die Raumtiefe sowie das A/V-Verhältnis. Hier handelt es sich um eine Behaglichkeitsanforderung sowie um ein Kriterium der Energieeinsparung, die großen Einfluß auf die Architektur haben.

Bauphysikalische Ausstattung der Hüllflächen und Speichermassen

Die Einrichtungen für Sichtkontakt und Tageslichtbeleuchtung ergeben die Mindestsolarapertur. Soweit diese aus Gründen der Verbesserung passiver Solargewinne zur Erwärmung des Gebäudes erhöht werden soll, ist die jeweilig adäquate Solarinstallation (Sonnenzimmer, Sonnenwand oder Wintergarten bzw. Veranda) genau durchzuplanen und das Verhältnis der Solarapertur und deren Abschattung zum wirksamen Primärbzw. Sekundärspeicher und der Ventilation zu bestimmen.

Dabei sind im Sinne von Ressourcenschonung und zur Minimierung von Herstellungsenergie überdimensionierte Speichermassen zu vermeiden – es sollte sorgsam mit der Größe der Einstrahlungsflächen für eine effiziente Solarausnutzung umgegangen werden (Winter) bzw. Abschattung und Ventilation für den Entwärmungsfall (Sommer) der Vorrang gegeben werden. (Auf eine detailliertere Darstellung der Verhältnisse: Ventilation/Speicher/Solarapertur wird hier aus Platzgründen verzichtet. Generell kann angemerkt werden, daß ein Sonnenzimmer sich technisch nicht zu hohem passivem Solargewinn eignet. Ein Wohnraum darf nicht zu einem Kollektor gemacht werden.)

provvigionamento di base, sono divenuti conciliabili con la tecnica solare attiva usata in modo complementare.

I criteri di comfort e d'esercizio sono stati necessariamente prescritti così come verificati i valori usati a questo scopo.

La progettazione dovrebbe tenere in considerazione i seguenti criteri:

l'involucro dell'edificio e il rapporto A/V sono, accanto alle necessità funzionali, da ottimizzare sul piano della tecnica di illuminazione. Per questo le funzioni vedere, illuminare, riscaldare sono da separare.

Contatto visuale

Questo si accorda esclusivamente con le esigenze architettoniche e non è un elemento proprio della tecnica solare. Inoltre non si dovrebbe prescrivere alcun dimensionamento minimo. L'architetto dovrebbe tuttavia pretendere un minimo di superfici libere da ombreggiamento.

Illuminazione naturale

Le finestre e gli ambienti dovrebbero essere disposti in modo tale che con un cielo coperto sui 16 «C.I.E.» (E-3.2), in condizioni esterne di circa 10 000 lux, si possano ancora ottenere 200 lux nella profondità degli spazi interni. Questo determina in sostanza la dimensione della finestra, la profondità dell'ambiente e il rapporto A/V. Si tratta di un'esigenza di comodità e di un criterio di risparmio energetico, il che esercita un notevole influsso sull'architettura.

Dotazioni fisico-costruttive delle superfici d'involucro e delle masse d'accumulo

Dalle installazioni per il contatto visuale e per l'illuminazione naturale scaturisce la minima apertura solare. In ragione della volontà di incrementare alla base il miglioramento del guadagno solare passivo per il riscaldamento degli edifici, la relativa adeguata installazione solare (stanza solare, parete solare o Wintergarten, in altre parole, veranda) è da progettare attentamente, così come è da determinare il rapporto dell'apertura solare e del suo ombreggiamento per ottenere un efficace accumulo primario o secondario e la ventilazione. Oltre a ciò è da evitare un sovradimensionamento delle masse d'accumulo per un senso di riguardo delle risorse e dell'impiego dell'energia di produzione – questo dovrebbe essere praticato attentamente per un efficiente sfruttamento solare (d'inverno), e si dovrebbe dare la precedenza a ombreggiamento e ventilazione per favorire il calo di riscaldamento (d'estate). (In questa sede, per mancanza di spazio, si rinuncia ad una più dettagliata descrizione dei rapporti di ventilazione/accu-

technically not suitable for large-scale passive energy gains. A living room should not be turned into a collector.)

Heat distribution systems for conditioning internal spaces

The temperature level for the transmittance of heat should be kept as low as possible. The flow temperature should be under 35°C. The advantages of any deviations from this rule should be proved in advance. The installed load of a building in respect of heating energy should be limited to the annual energy requirements divided by 1,200 (hours of full operation). Appropriate storage measures should be implemented to ensure that the hot-water requirements do not increase this load.
The energy required for air-conditioning the rooms includes the following:

- energy consumption for heating rooms, including heating fresh air supply by combustion, and the equivalent production energy contained in pure storage masses; i.e. solid storage elements over and above the basic construction (50-year life-span);
- energy consumption for movement of air;
- energy consumption for air-conditioning systems. This energy consumption had to be 5 per cent below the specific energy levels originally laid down for Linz. Furthermore, only the values for multi-storey structures are valid. The purpose of drawing up an energy code cannot be to "reward" lower-density types of building development – which already contain a greater degree of (embedded) production energy and result in an increased consumption of transport energy – with an even higher allowance for operational energy. On the contrary, this extra consumption of energy must be saved elsewhere.

Hot water

The specific annual energy requirement should be limited to a calculated figure of 25 kWh/m²/a – in the first instance through water economies – without taking into account any contributions in the form of solar energy. With an energy supply from combined heat and power, it will not be necessary to install a thermal solar system. In its place, the following measures can be implemented:

- further proved economies in the use of water to achieve a figure of 20 kWh/m² per annum through the installation of special fittings and equipment;
- economies in room temperature amounting to 10 kWh/m² per annum, plus an 8W/m² reduction in the installed thermal load;
- installation of an appropriate photovoltaic system.

Wärmeverteilungssystem zur Raumkonditionierung

Das Temperaturniveau zur Wärmeübertragung soll so niedrig wie möglich gehalten werden. Die Vorlauftemperatur sollte unter 35°C liegen. Im Falle von Abweichungen hiervon sollten die Vorteile nachgewiesen werden. Der Anschlußwert des Gebäudes für Heizenergie sollte auf den Jahresenergieverbrauch geteilt durch 1200 (Vollbetriebsstunden) begrenzt werden. Durch geeignete Speichermaßnahmen ist sicherzustellen, daß der Warmwasserbedarf diesen Anschlußwert nicht erhöht.
Die Energiemengen für die Raumkonditionierung setzen sich somit zusammen aus:

- Wärmeverbrauch der Räume inkl. Lüftungswärme durch Verbrennung und äquivalente Herstellungsenergie von reinen Speichermassen, d. h. über normale Konstruktion hinaus angeordnete Massivspeicher (50 Jahre Lebensdauer)
- Energieverbrauch für Luftbewegung
- Energieverbrauch für Konditionierungssysteme

Dieser Verbrauch mußte die von Linz ursprünglich vorgegebenen, spezifischen Energie-Kenn-Zahlen um 5% unterschreiten, wobei ausschließlich die Werte der mehrgeschossigen Bauweise gelten. Es kann nicht Sinn einer Energie-Kenn-Zahl sein, daß weniger verdichtet stehende Bauten, welche bereits mehr Herstellungsenergie verbrauchen und mehr Aufwand an Verkehrsenergie verursachen, auch noch mit höherer Betriebsenergie »belohnt« werden. Vielmehr müssen sie dieses Mehr an Energie an anderer Stelle sparen.

Warmwasser

Der spezifische Jahresenergieverbrauch sollte zunächst durch Wassersparmaßnahmen ohne Einrechnung eines solaren Deckungsbeitrages auf rechnerisch 25 kWh/m²/a begrenzt sein. Bei einer Energiebereitstellung aus Kraft-Wärme-Kopplung muß kein thermisches Solarsystem installiert werden. Als Ersatz sollten wahlweise folgende Maßnahmen gelten:

- weitere nachgewiesene Wassereinsparung durch Armaturen auf 20 kWh/m²/Jahr
- Einsparung von Raumwärme von 10 kWh/m²/Jahr sowie Senkung des thermischen Anschlußwertes des Gebäudes um 8 W/m²
- Installation eines entsprechenden Photovoltaikanteils

Eine Kombination der genannten Möglichkeiten ist erlaubt. Der Anschluß von Geschirrspülmaschine und Waschmaschinen an die Warmwasseranschlüsse muß sicherlich obligatorisch sein.

mulo/apertura solare. In generale si può notare che una stanza «solare» non si adatta tecnicamente a più alti guadagni di energia solare passiva. Uno spazio abitabile non può essere reso un collettore.)

Sistema di distribuzione del calore per il condizionamento degli edifici

Il livello di temperatura per la trasmissione di calore deve essere mantenuto il più basso possibile. Temperatura di preriscaldamento < 35° C. In caso di differente funzionamento, devono esserne verificati i vantaggi . Il valore-limite di utenza dell'edificio per energia di riscaldamento dovrebbe essere, nell'ambito del consumo energetico annuo ripartito su 1200 ore di pieno esercizio. Tramite l'adozione di appropriate masse d'accumulo, ci si deve assicurare che il fabbisogno di acqua calda non incrementi questo valore-limite di utenza.
Le quantità energetiche per il condizionamento degli ambienti quindi si compongono come segue:

- fabbisogno di calore degli ambienti incl. calore d'aerazione per combustione ed equivalente energia di produzione da masse d'accumulo reali, cioè, in addizione ad una normale costruzione, dall'installazione di masse di accumulo esterne (periodo di vita 50 anni).
- consumo di energia per la circolazione dell'aria
- consumo di energia per il sistema di condizionamento

Questo consumo dovrebbe essere di circa il 5% al di sotto delle prescritte «Energie-Kenn-Zahlen» (Norme sui valori energetici): cosa che vale solo per i valori degli edifici multipiani. Non può avere alcun senso, nell'ottica dell'Energie-Kenn-Zahlen», che edifici di minore densità, che impiegano più energia di produzione e causano più energia di traffico, vengano anche «ricompensati» con una più alta energia di esercizio. Essi dovrebbero, al contrario, risparmiare in altro luogo questo di più di energia consumata.

Acqua calda

Lo specifico consumo di energia annuo dovrebbe per il momento essere confinato ad un aritmetico 25 kWh/mq/anno, attraverso provvedimenti per il risparmio dell'acqua senza includere il contributo di una copertura solare.
Mettendo a disposizione un impianto di cogenerazione, non deve essere installato nessun sistema solare termico. In cambio dovrebbero essere valide a scelta le seguenti misure:

- ulteriore verifica del risparmio di acque ottenuto attraverso la rubinetteria di 20 kWh/mq/anno
- risparmio di calore interno di 10 kWh/mq/anno ed abbassamento del valore-limite di utenza dell'edificio intorno a 8 W/mq.

A combination of the above measures is acceptable. The connection of dishwashers and washing machines to the hot-water supply system will certainly be obligatory.

Use of heat pumps
The use of heat pumps should be permitted only if a minimum coefficient of performance (COP) of 5 is achieved. This must take into account the drive mechanisms of all ancillary services (but not the heating pump). This COP requires the exploitation of good secondary heat sources, such as waste air or water.

Overall consumption of thermal energy
Depending to the system of evaluation, the total energy consumption resulting from these uses should not exceed:
- 70 kWh/m^2/a in the case of dwellings > 60 m^2 floor area
- 75 kWh/m^2/a in the case of dwellings < 60 m^2 floor area.

These figures include ancillary forms of energy such as operational current.

Electrical energy needs of occupants
The electrical energy needed for mechanical services over which the building developer has some influence is included in the thermal energy contingent. It is virtually impossible, however, to control the use of the occupants' own equipment. The electrical loading per dwelling unit should, therefore, be reduced by a process of load management (e.g. locking devices to prevent the simultaneous use of heavy-load equipment such as cookers, washing machines, dryers and dishwashers).
The consumption of energy can thus be calculated at approx. 35 kWh/m2/a, but it will vary according to the size of dwelling and/or the number of occupants.

Primary energy needs
The relation between effective energy and applied primary energy should be > 75 per cent.
This presupposes the combined use of heat and power for the supply of energy. In the case of the system area in Pichling, the purchase or input of additional power can be ignored in any calculations, and it should be assumed that the form of operation allows no waste heat to be destroyed at any time.
This also means that, for insufficient heat in winter and insufficient electricity in summer, optimized or regenerative solutions have to be found in terms of the primary energy consumption, solutions that should guarantee an overall primary energy consumption of less than 100 kWh/m^2/a.

Anwendung von Wärmepumpen
Diese Anwendung sollte nur dann zugelassen werden, wenn eine Mindestleistungszahl von 5 erreicht wird. Dies muß alle Antriebe der peripheren Anlagen (nicht Heizungspumpe) mit beinhalten. Diese Leistungszahl erfordert den Anschluß guter Sekundärwärmequellen wie z. B. Abluft oder Abwasser.

Gesamtverbrauch thermischer Energie
Die Summe dieser Verbräuche nach dem Bewertungsystem darf allerdings
- bei Wohnungen > 60 m^2 WNF   70 kWh/m^2/a
- bei Wohnungen < 60 m^2 WNF   75 kWh/m^2/a

nicht überschreiten. Dies schließt Hilfsenergien wie Antriebsstrom mit ein.

Elektrischer Energiebedarf der Nutzer
Der vom Bauträger beeinflußbare elektrische Energiebedarf für die Haustechnik ist in dem Teil der thermischen Energie eingerechnet. Die Auswahl der Geräte des Nutzers ist kaum zu beeinflussen. Der elektrische Anschlußwert pro Wohneinheit ist durch ein Lastmanagement (Verriegelung der Spitzenverbraucher Kochen, Waschmaschine, Trockner, Geschirrspülmaschine) zu reduzieren.
Der Stromverbrauch kann so mit ca. 35 kWh/m^2/a kalkuliert werden und variiert nach Wohnungsgröße bzw. Personenbelegung.

Primärenergiebedarf
Das Verhältnis der Nutzenergie zur eingesetzten Primärenergie soll > 75 % sein.
Dies setzt eine Kraft-Wärme-Kopplung zur Energieerzeugung vorraus, was jedoch für die Systemgrenze Pichling ohne Stromzukauf oder Stromeinspeisung zu betrachten und in der Betriebsweise rechnerisch so anzunehmen ist, daß zu keinem Zeitpunkt Abwärme vernichtet wird.
Weiter bedeutet dies, daß für fehlende Wärme im Winter und fehlenden Strom im Sommer primärenergetisch optimierte bzw. regenerative Lösungen gefunden werden müssen, die insgesamt den Gesamtprimärenergieverbrauch unter 100 kWh/m^2/a sicherstellen.

- installazione di una opportuna aliquota di foto-voltaico.

È concessa una combinazione delle menzionate possibilità. Il collegamento delle lavastoviglie e delle lavatrici agli attacchi per l'acqua calda deve essere obbligatorio.

Applicazione della pompa di calore
Si dovrebbe permettere questo impiego solo al raggiungimento del valore di potenza minimo di 5. Questo deve comprendere tutti i comandi degli impianti periferici (esclusa la pompa di riscaldamento). Questo valore di potenza esige il collegamento di buone fonti di calore secondarie come ad esempio aria in uscita o acqua di scarico.

Impiego totale di energia termica
La somma di questi fabbisogni a seconda del sistema di valutazione non può tuttavia oltrepassare i seguenti valori:
- per gli appartamenti > 60 mq Superficie netta abitabile   70 kWh/mq/anno
- per gli appartamenti < 60 mq Superficie netta abitabile   75 kWh/mq/anno

il che include l'energia di supporto quale la corrente di azionamento.

Fabbisogno di energia elettrica per l'utente
Il fabbisogno di energia elettrica, influenzabile dalle società finanziarie del settore edile, è incluso nel calcolo d'ambito dell'energia termica. Gli strumenti dell'utente sono appena influenzabili. Il valore limite di utenza elettrica per un'abitazione è da ridurre attraverso una gestione del carico energetico (limitazione dei picchi di consumo di cucine, lavatrici, essiccatori, lavastoviglie).
Il consumo di corrente può così essere calcolato intorno a circa 35 kWh/mq/anno e variare a seconda della grandezza dell'appartamento, ovvero del numero di persone.

Fabbisogno di energia primaria
Il rapporto dell'energia utile sull'energia primaria impiegata deve essere > 75 %.
Ciò impone un impianto di cogenerazione per la produzione di energia. Ciò è tuttavia da considerare per il limite del sistema di Pichling senza l'acquisto o la fornitura d'energia, e così il consumo e i valori sono da calcolare in maniera tale che in nessun momento venga abbattuto il calore in uscita.
Ciò significa che per il calore e la corrente mancanti rispettivamente di inverno e d'estate, ottimizzati in termini di energia primaria, si devono trovare soluzioni rigenerative, che complessivamente assicurino il consumo totale di energia primaria al di sotto di 100 kWh/mq/anno.

Housing

Wohnungsbau
Edifici per abitazione

Halen Housing Complex, Bern	CH	Atelier 5, Bern
Housing Development, Passau	D	Hermann Schröder, Sampo Widmann, Munich
Beck Apartment Building, Lenzburg	CH	Metron Architekturbüro AG, Brugg
Housing Complex, Götzis	A	Karl Baumschlager, Dietmar Eberle, Norbert Schweitzer, Werner Wertaschnigg, Bregenz
Osuna Housing, Seville	E	Pilar Alberich Sotomayor, Angel Diaz Dominguez, Jaime Lopez de Asiaín, Seville
Housing Development, Brünnerstrasse-Empergergasse, Vienna	A	Arge - Martin Treberspurg, Georg Reinberg, Erich Raith, Vienna
Stadlau Housing Complex, Vienna	A	Arge - Martin Treberspurg, Georg Reinberg, Erich Raith, Vienna
Apartment Building, Altötting	D	Demmel + Mühlbauer, Munich
Settlement of Low Cost Housing, Florence	I	Paolo Puccetti, Florence
Urban Restoration, Kalenderpanden, Amsterdam	NL	Loof & Van Stigt/Energiebedrijf, Amsterdam
Hostel for Youth Educational Institute, Windberg	D	Thomas Herzog, Munich
Multiple-Dwelling Block, Perlach, Munich	D	Doris & Ralph Thut, Munich
Low-Energy House, Stuttgart	D	Kilian + Hagmann, Stuttgart
Houses with Zero Energy Heating, Trin	CH	Andrea-Gustav Rüedi-Marugg, Chur
Terrace House Prototype, London	GB	Bill Dunster, London
House in the Hillside, Aldrans	A	Horst Herbert Parson, Innsbruck

Halen Housing Complex, Bern

Siedlung Halen, Bern
Complesso residenziale Halen, Berna

Architects: Atelier 5, Bern
Planning and execution: 1955–1961

Siedlung Halen is situated in a clearing in a wood close to the city of Bern. Under rigorous discipline it was designed as high-density dwelling units.

The houses (two types, 4 and 5 m wide, both three stories high) were constructed as simply and as economically as possible. Great care was taken to protect private space, interior as well as exterior, from prying eyes and to acoustically insulate each unit fully.

Cars are parked in a large garage. Paths on the whole estate are preserved for pedestrians. The central road alone may be used for limited service access.

The key aspect of this project is the communal facilities. With the purchase of a house each owner acquires ownership of a 79th part of all the public areas and installations. The glazed front of the houses faces south. They have only minimal exterior walls.

Die Siedlung Halen wurde auf einer Waldlichtung in der Nähe von Bern errichtet. Die Wohneinheiten wurden mit äußerster Disziplin und Systematik in großer Dichte auf dem Grundstück zusammengefügt.

Die einzelnen Häuser (2 Typen, 4 und 5 m breit, beide dreigeschossig) wurden so einfach und ökonomisch wie möglich konstruiert. Alles wurde unternommen, um die privaten Innen- und Außenräume vor Einblicken zu schützen und jedes Haus vom anderen akustisch einwandfrei zu isolieren. Die Autos werden in einer großen Einstellhalle untergebracht, die Wege in der ganzen Siedlung sind verkehrsfrei. Einzig in der zentralen Straße gibt es einen beschränkten Zubringerdienst.

Um Raum und Verantwortung für die Gemeinschaft zu schaffen, erwirbt jeder Anwohner ein 79stel der gesamten öffentlichen Anlagen und Einrichtungen im Miteigentum. Die verglaste Front der Häuser ist nach Süden orientiert. Sie haben einen nur geringen Außenwandanteil.

La pianificazione della «Siedlung Halen», situata in una radura boschiva nei pressi della città di Berna, è stata animata da una volontà di sistematizzare i caratteri dell'insediamento con rigorosa disciplina, da cui l'idea guida di concentrare quanto più possibile sul terreno l'insieme delle unità d'abitazione.

La costruzione dei due tipi di case (larghe 4 e 5 m), disposte su tre piani, è stata elaborata nell'ottica della massima economia e semplicità. Grande attenzione è stata posta nel preservare l'intimità degli spazi interni dagli sguardi indiscreti e assicurare un perfetto isolamento acustico a ciascuna abitazione.

La presenza di un ampio garage per le macchine ha permesso la totale pedonalizzazione delle stradine dell'insediamento. Solo l'asse principale permette un servizio di rifornimento, peraltro limitato allo stretto necessario.

La collettività è il tema centrale del progetto: ciascun abitante ha acquistato in comproprietà, oltre alla sua casa, un 79simo della totalità del sito con i servizi e le attrezzature. Il fronte vetrato delle case è orientato verso sud. Esse hanno una parete esterna di tamponamento dimensionata al minimo.

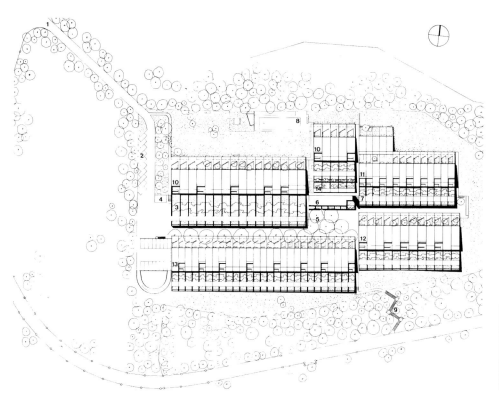

a-a

b-b

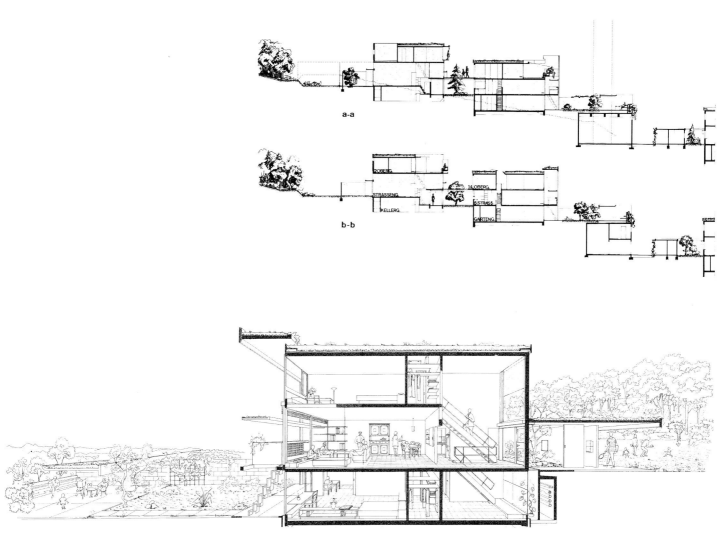

49

Housing Development, Passau (Germany)

Wohnanlage, Passau-Neustift
Complesso residenziale, Passau

Architects: Hermann Schröder, Sampo Widmann, Munich
Planning and execution: 1985–1989

Collaborators: I. Burgstaller, W. Fischer, T. Fusban, S. Lautner, D. Mruck
Clerk of works: Hartmut Geffke
Structural Engineer: Karl Wagner
Landscaping: Donata und Christoph Valentien
Energy Consultant: Roberto Gonzalo
Colour concept: Gabriele Schröder

This housing scheme in Passau represents one of eight groups developed by the Bavarian building authorities, using ideas borrowed from public-funded housing in Scandinavia and Holland. In those countries, it is quite common to build rented public housing in the form of terraced houses or similar dwelling types, usually in small groups. This helps to achieve a better socio-spatial structure, a higher habitable quality and lower construction costs.

To minimize the energy requirements for heating in the Passau scheme, a high degree of compactness in the layout of the houses was aimed at, which reduced the external surface area. This also helped to reduce building costs, with a reduction in the areas of expensive façade construction. Wind lobbies were placed in front of the houses in the form of unheated steel and glass structures. Connected to glass shafts leading to the upper floors, these lobbies also function as warm-air collectors. The correct operation of these constructional features (i.e. controlled opening and closing of doors, ventilation flaps and the windows to the shafts), enables additional thermal gain to be made. Increased thermal insulation (which cost contraints precluded here) and further development of the wind-lobby/warm-air collector system could help to achieve an even more favourable energy balance in this type of housing.

Die Wohnanlage in Passau ist eine von acht Hausgruppen, die von der bayerischen Baubehörde in Anlehnung an den sozialen Wohnungsbau in Skandinavien und Holland errichtet wurde. In diesen Ländern ist es üblich, die Mietwohnungen des sozialen Wohnungsbaus als Reihenhäuser oder reihenhausähnliche Haustypen in meist kleinen Gruppen zu errichten, wobei eine bessere sozialräumliche Gliederung, ein höherer Wohnwert und geringere Baukosten erzielt werden.

In Passau wurde zur Minimierung des Heizenergiebedarfs ein möglichst hoher Kompaktheitsgrad der Häuser durch Reduzierung der Außenflächen angestrebt. Dies deckte sich mit dem gleichzeitigen Bemühen, die Baukosten zu senken, da so die teuren Fassadenflächen verringert wurden. Die ohnehin nötigen Windfänge wurden als ungeheizte Stahl-Glas-Konstruktionen vor die Häuser gestellt und als Warmluftkollektoren genutzt, in dem sie mit den in die oberen Geschosse geführten gläsernen Schächten verbunden wurden. Bei richtiger Bedienung (rechtzeitiges Öffnen und Schließen von Türen, Luftklappen und den Fenstern zu den Schächten) ist ein zusätzlicher Wärmegewinn möglich. Durch eine weitere Erhöhung der Wärmedämmung (die hier aus Kostengründen auszuschließen war) und eine Weiterentwicklung des »Windfang-Warmluftkollektors« könnte eine noch günstigere Energiebilanz dieser Haustypen erreicht werden.

Questo complesso residenziale a Passau, rappresenta uno degli otto gruppi di edifici residenziali realizzati dalle autorità bavaresi, facendo uso dei concetti di fondo alla base dell'esperienza pubblica scandinava ed olandese. In queste nazioni, è abbastanza comune che si costruiscano residenze pubbliche da affittare in forma di case a schiera o insediamenti di questo tipo, normalmente in piccoli gruppi, per ottenere una struttura socio-spaziale migliore, una più alta qualità abitativa e dei costi di costruzione più bassi.

Per minimizzare le richieste energetiche nello schema di riscaldamento di Passau, si è mirato ad ottenere un alto grado di compattezza nel concepire il layout delle case per ridurre la superficie esterna. Tutto ciò ha inoltre prodotto un notevole contenimento dei costi dell'edificio, ed una particolare riduzione dell'onere relativo alla costruzione della facciata. I necessari paravento trovano posto sul fronte delle case nella forma di acciaio non temperato e strutture di vetro. Connessi con sfiatatoi vetrati che conducono ai piani più alti, questi paravento funzionano anche come collettori per l'aria calda. La corretta gestione di questi impianti (ad es. il controllo dell'apertura e chiusura delle porte, i «flaps» di ventilazione e le finestre degli sfiatatoi) fa si che si possa guadagnare calore addizionale. Attraverso l'uso di isolanti termici (i cui costi proibitivi ne hanno reso impossibile l'applicazione in questo caso) e un ulteriore sviluppo del sistema paravento/collettori di aria calda, si potrebbe arrivare ad ottenere un equilibrio energetico più vantaggioso in questo tipo di residenze.

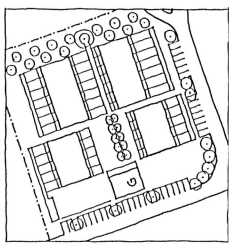

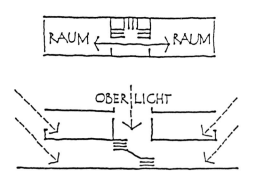

The depth makes a central roof light necessary and the stairs are so arranged that they become part of the living space.

Große Haustiefe erfordert Aufhellung der Mitte und räumlich wirksame Anordnung der Treppe, »Wohntreppe«.

La profondità dell'abitazione richiede un'illuminazione centrale dal tetto e le scale sono accomodate in maniera tale da divenire parte dello spazio di soggiorno.

Beck Apartment Building, Lenzburg (Switzerland)

Mehrfamilienhaus Beck, Lenzburg
Complesso residenziale, Lenzburg

Architects: Metron Architekturbüro AG, Brugg
Planning and execution: 1993–1994

Collaborators: Gian Battista Castellani, Lucia Vettori
Clerk of works: Thomas Sacchi
Structural Engineer: Kurt Kaufmann, HSK
Acoustics: Bruno Gandet
Colour concept: Matthis Beck
Energy Consultant: Beat Züsli

The three-storey building is situated in the park of a villa, adjacent to the old part of town.

The task was to build un-subsidized, high-quality apartments for rent. Ecological and, in particular, energy aspects were to receive special attention.

For architectural and urban planning reasons the building was designed to be long and narrow. The clear orientation towards the south favours the pre-established energy goals. Rooms which can be let with either one of two adjoining units, allow a variation of apartment sizes. Continuous balconies along the entire south side of the building give outdoor space to the rooms.

The south façade is completely glazed whilst the rear is almost totally enclosed in large prefabricated elements. This creates an interesting interior atmosphere. In addition there is a solar powered hot water supply. The three apartments beside the road have a controlled ventilation system with a heat recovery installation.

Das dreigeschossige Haus steht im Garten einer Villa, in unmittelbarer Nähe der Altstadt.

Die Aufgabe bestand darin, nichtsubventionierten Mietwohnungsbau von hoher Wohnqualität mit starker Gewichtung von ökologisch-energetischen Aspekten zu realisieren.

Aus architektonisch-städtebaulichen Gründen wurde ein schmaler, langer Gebäudekörper gewählt, der mit seiner eindeutigen Südorientierung auch den energetischen Anforderungen Rechnung trägt. Der Grundriß läßt eine Variation der Wohnungsgrößen mit sogenannen Schaltzimmern zu. Die durchgehende Balkonschicht an der Südseite dient den Wohnungen als Außenraum.

Die vollständige Verglasung der Südfassade und die stark geschlossene Rückfassade (vorfabrizierte Großtafelelemente) unterstützen die Grundkonzeption und führen zu einer interessanten innenräumlichen Situation.

Zusätzlich wurde eine solare Warmwasserversorung und in den drei an der Durchgangsstraße gelegenen Wohnungen eine kontrollierte Lüftung mit Wärmerückgewinnung installiert.

L'edificio a tre piani è situato nel parco di una villa adiacente alla parte antica della città.

Il compito era quello di realizzare appartamenti di alta qualità da affittare senza sussidi, nei quali l'aspetto ecologico, e soprattutto quello energetico, avrebbero dovuto godere di un particolare riguardo.

Per ragioni di progettazione architettonica ed urbana la costruzione è stata concepita in forma stretta e allungata, tale da sfruttare al meglio l'orientamento verso Sud per favorire il raggiungimento dei risultati energetici desiderati. Alle stanze possono essere attribuite una o due unità ad esse opportunamente collegate, il che comporta una significativa variazione del taglio degli appartamenti. Ad arricchire l'atmosfera degli ambienti interni contribuiscono vari fattori. I balconi che corrono continui lungo il lato meridionale dell'edificio generano una sorta di appendice esterna per le stanze. Inoltre il prospetto a Sud è completamente vetrato mentre in quello opposto si fa uso di elementi prefabbricati quasi totalmente chiusi.

Inoltre viene utilizzato un approvvigionamento solare d'acqua calda ed i tre appartamenti dietro la strada hanno un sistema di controllo di ventilazione con installato un sistema di recupero del calore.

Hot water
14 m² sun collectors to preheat water using solar energy
Building envelope
Highly insulated construction with minimal points of heat loss
Controlled ventilation
Apartments in noisy locations have mechanical ventilation with heat recovery.
Passive solar energy use
Large glass surface of the south façade, optimized window surface at the north, east and west façade. Massive inner walls and concrete ceiling function as thermal mass.

Warmwasser
14 m² Sonnenkollektoren zur solaren Vorwärmung des Warmwassers
Gebäudehülle
Hochwärmedämmende Konstruktion mit minimalen Wärmebrücken
Kontrollierte Wohnungslüftung
Mechanische Wohnungslüftung mit Wärmerückgewinnung in den lärmexponierten Wohnungen
Passive Sonnenenergienutzung
Großflächige Verglasung der Südfassade, optimierte Fensterflächen an Nord-, Ost- und Westfassade. Massive Innenwände und Betondecken als Speichermasse.

Acqua calda
14 mq di collettore solare per il riscaldamento solare dell'acqua calda
Involucro dell'edificio
Costruzione altamente isolata con minimizzazione dei ponti termici
Ventilazione controllata
Gli appartamenti esposti al rumore hanno una ventilazione meccanica con scambio di calore
Uso passivo di energia solare
Ampie superfici vetrate sulla facciata meridionale, ottimizzano la superficie delle facciate Nord, Est ed Ovest. Muri interni massivi e soffitti in calcestruzzo funzionano come massa d'accumulo termico.

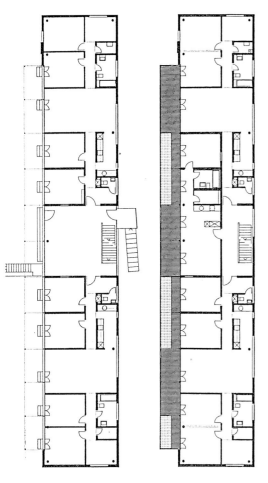

Housing Complex, Götzis (Austria)

Wohnhäuser, Götzis
Complesso residenziale, Götzis

Architects: Karl Baumschlager, Dietmar Eberle, Norbert Schweitzer, Werner Wertaschnigg, Bregenz
Planning and execution: 1994

With its three curved blocks, the development represents an architectural termination to the sloping flank of the Sonderberg. The scheme comprises two-, three- and three-and-a-half-room flats with a nursery school in block 1. Some of the ground floor dwellings also have gardens.

In each of the spaces between the blocks are a sand pit and benches. In the central area, a paved open space with a fountain is planned. The individual private gardens are screened off by hedges from the lower-lying entrances to the blocks and from the access route.

The clearly articulated, compact form of the buildings and their alignment make them ideally suited to the passive exploitation of solar energy. The compact blocks are of solid construction with polystyrene-insulated façades.

Heat is supplied from a central gas-fired condensing heating system. Heat emission is via radiators and in part via a sub-floor installation. Hot water is supplied from decentralized electric heaters.

Die Wohnanlage bildet mit drei bogenförmig angeordneten Baukörpern einen architektonischen Abschluß zum Abhang des Sonderbergs. Es entstehen dabei Zwei-, Drei- und Drei-einhalb-Zimmer-Wohnungen, im Erdgeschoß teilweise mit Garten. In Haus 1 ist ein Kindergarten untergebracht.

Jeweils in den Hauszwischenräumen sind Sandkästen mit Sitzbänken vorgesehen. Im zentralen Bereich wurde ein Festplatz mit einem Brunnen geplant. Die einzelnen Privatgärten werden gegen die tieferliegenden Hauszugänge sowie den Erschließungsweg durch Hecken abgegrenzt.

Der klare, kompakte Baukörper ist durch seine Südorientierung für die passive Nutzung von Sonnenenergie geeignet. Die durch ein durchgehendes Vordach geschützten Balkone verhindern im Sommer eine zu starke Überwärmung der südlichen Wohnräume.

Die kompakten Gebäude sind in Massivbauweise mit Polystyrol-Dämmfassade ausgeführt.

Die Wärme wird durch die Gas-Kondensationsheizung zentral bereitgestellt. Die Wärmeabgabe erfolgt über Radiatoren und teilweise beheizte Fußböden. Das Brauchwasser wird elektrisch dezentral erwärmt.

Con i suoi tre blocchi curvati, il complesso rappresenta una sorta di testata architettonica del fianco collinare del Sonderberg.

Lo schema è comprensivo di appartamenti di due, tre e tre camere e mezzo, con un asilo nel primo blocco, alcuni dei quali al piano terreno hanno anche i giardini.

In ciascuno degli spazi compresi tra i blocchi ci sono vasche di sabbia e panchine, mentre nell'area centrale è stato progettato uno spazio aperto pavimentato con fontana. I giardini privati individuali sono schermati attraverso delle siepi dalle entrate più basse ai blocchi e dalle stradine di accesso. La chiara e compatta articolazione dell'edificio è, attraverso il suo orientamento a Sud, la conformazione ideale per lo sfruttamento passivo di energia solare.

I blocchi compatti sono di solida costruzione con facciate isolate tramite polistirolo. Il calore è garantito da un sistema di riscaldamento centralizzato con caldaia a gas. La rete di riscaldamento funziona attraverso i radiatori e in parte con installazioni a pavimento, mentre l'acqua calda è fornita da caldaie elettriche autonome.

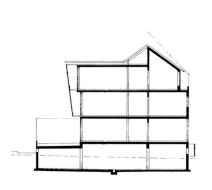
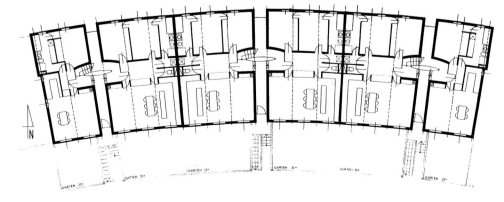

Osuna Housing, Seville

Wohnanlage, Sevilla
Complesso residenziale, Siviglia

Architects: Pilar Alberich Sotomayor, Angel Diaz Dominguez, Jaime Lopez de Asiaín, Seville
Planning and execution: 1983–1991

Consultant: Valeriano Ruiz
Monitoring: J. E. R., Junta de Andalucia

The site is to the south-east edge of the urban area of Osuna. It creates a new neighbourhood, extending the existing town.

The design was developed from a two-storey single house prototype, which was constructed and its climatic performance monitored for 18 months, before the design was finalized.

The Andalucian climate is one of hot summers, requiring cooling, and of mild winters. Some winter heat is required. Heating: Solar collection is by way of direct gain to each habitable room, all of which face south in most of the dwellings. Heat distribution is by natural convection. The dwellings have high thermal inertia, with concrete floors and heavy partitions in order to provide adequate daily thermal storage.

Cooling: External gains are controlled by deciduous trees and creepers which will cover the pergola to the south of each house. The roof overhang is designed to screen high-altitude summer sun. Stack ventilation, predominantly in evening and at night, across the plan and section, admits air from the north façade and expels it at roof level.

Energy Savings: Monitored results in the prototype showed a passive system contribution of about 70 % of winter heating.

Am südöstlichen Rand des Bezirks Osuna entsteht ein neuer Stadtteil. Der Entwurf der Gesamtanlage erfolgte unter Verwendung eines zweistöckigen freistehenden Haus-Prototyps, der gebaut und dessen klimatische Leistung 18 Monate lang gemessen und ausgewertet wurde, bevor der endgültige Entwurf entstand.

Das andalusische Klima hat heiße Sommer, die Kühlung erforderlich machen, und milde Winter, in denen man wenig Heizung braucht.

Heizung: Jeder Wohnraum – größtenteils nach Süden ausgerichtet – wird direkt über Solarkollektoren mit Heizwärme versorgt, die durch natürliche Konvektion verteilt wird. Die Wohnungen sind mit ihren Betondecken und dicken Trennwänden thermisch inert, so daß tagsüber für adäquate Wärmespeicherung gesorgt ist.

Kühlung: Außenwärme wird von Laubbäumen und Kletterpflanzenbewuchs der nach Süden gelegenen Pergolen abgekühlt. Der Dachvorsprung bietet Schatten vor der Hochsommersonne. Horizontale und vertikale Luftschacht-Ventilation läßt von der Nordseite her, vorwiegend abends und nachts, Frischluft ein, die über das Dach wieder abgeleitet wird.

Energieeinsparungen: Die Messungen am Prototyp ergaben einen Beitrag des passiven Systems von etwa 70 % der Winter-Heizleistung.

Il sito si colloca sul margine Sud-orientale dell'area urbana di Osuna. Si viene così a creare un nuovo sobborgo, che si collega direttamente con la città esistente determinandone un'estensione.

Il progetto si è fondato sullo sviluppo di un prototipo di casa isolata a due piani, che era già stata costruita e le cui prestazioni climatiche erano state controllate per diciotto mesi, prima che fosse redatta la versione finale del complesso.

Il clima andaluso è caratterizzato da calde estati che richiedono refrigerazione e inverni temperati, durante i quali di rado è usato il riscaldamento.

Riscaldamento: tutte le stanze abitabili, che in gran parte degli alloggi affacciano verso Sud, vengono direttamente riscaldate dal calore che, raccolto per mezzo di collettori solari, viene distribuito per convezione naturale. Gli appartamenti hanno un'alta inerzia termica, con pavimenti in calcestruzzo armato e partizioni pesanti allo scopo d'immagazzinare un'adeguata quantità giornaliera d'energia.

Refrigerazione: gli aumenti di temperatura esterni sono controllati attraverso alberi decidui e piante rampicanti che copriranno la pergola a Sud di ciascuna casa. Il tetto in aggetto è stato progettato per schermare il sole quando, d'estate, raggiunge la massima altezza. Camini di ventilazione, specialmente durante le ore serali e notturne, prendono aria dalla facciata Nord e la espellono a livello del tetto.

Risparmio energetico: i risultati controllati attraverso monitor nel prototipo hanno dimostrato che il sistema passivo offre un contributo per il riscaldamento invernale di circa il 70 %.

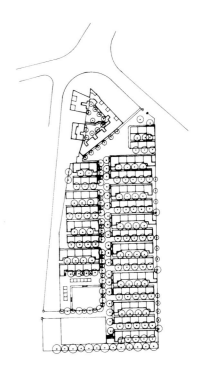

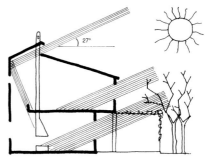

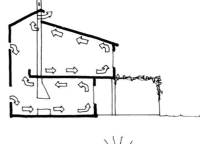

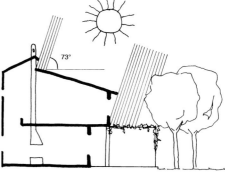

Housing Development Brünnerstrasse-Empergergasse, Vienna

Wohnhausanlage Brünnerstraße-Empergergasse, Wien
Insediamento residenziale Brünnerstraße-Empergergasse, Vienna

Architects: Arge – Martin Treberspurg, Georg Reinberg, Erich Raith, Vienna
Planning and execution: 1993–1996

Project Leader: F. Mühling
Realization: Konrad Beyer & Co.,
Baugesellschaft m.b.H.
Structural Engineer: Stella & Stengel

The project forms part of the urban extension area along Brünnerstrasse. The street is subject to heavy traffic. The development is laid out in the form of a long, five-storey dwelling strip, with ten south-facing rows of terraced houses leading from it on the quieter eastern side. At the front of the terraces are conservatories. On the south the roof and upper storeys project in a series of steps to provide adequate shading in summer.

This layout favoured the creation of a protected open space with an agreeable micro-climate at the heart of the estate. The space, to which all dwellings are oriented, opens on to the adjoining landscaped areas.

The passive use of solar energy, a high degree of thermal insulation and an adequate storage mass help to reduce the consumption of energy. The installation of ventilation plant (air supply and extract), with facilities for heat recovery and the pre-heating of fresh air, ensures comfortable living conditions, and reduces energy consumption even further.

Das Projekt ist Teil des Stadterweiterungsgebietes an der Brünnerstraße. Der Lage an der stark befahrenen Straße entspricht ein langer, fünfgeschossiger Riegel mit Wohnungen. Im Osten des Riegels befinden sich, in geschützter Lage, zehn südorientierte Reihenhauszeilen, denen Wintergärten vorgelagert sind. An ihrer Südfassade springen Dach und Obergeschosse stufenförmig vor, um im Sommer eine ausreichende Beschattung sicherzustellen.

Durch diese Anordnung der Gebäude war es möglich, im Innern der Siedlung einen geschützten, kleinklimatisch günstigen und zu den angrenzenden Grünräumen ausgerichteten Freibereich zu schaffen, zu dem sich alle Wohnungen hinorientieren. Durch passive Nutzung der Sonnenenergie, hohe Wärmedämmung und entsprechende Speichermasse wird ein niedriger Energieverbrauch erreicht. Der Einsatz einer Be- und Entlüftungsanlage mit Wärmerückgewinnung und Vorwärmung der Frischluft schafft hohe Lebensqualität und vermindert den Energieverbrauch zusätzlich.

Il progetto si viene a conformare come parte dell'estensione urbana lungo la Brünnerstrasse. La via è soggetta a un traffico pesante, perciò l'edificio è stato concepito come una lunga striscia di appartamenti di cinque piani, che da lì conduce al più pacifico lato ad Est e alle case a schiera che si affacciano a Sud. Le serre sono collocate sul prospetto principale delle case a schiera. A Sud il tetto e i piani più alti si proiettano in una serie di gradoni per procurare un'adeguata ombreggiatura estiva.

Questo schema progettuale favorisce la creazione di uno spazio aperto, protetto, nel cuore del complesso, con un gradevole microclima, spazio verso il quale tutti gli appartamenti sono orientati e che si congiunge naturalmente con il paesaggio. L'uso passivo di energia solare, con un alto grado di isolamento termico, e un'adeguata massa per l'accumulo, aiutano a ridurre il consumo di energia. L'installazione di un impianto di ventilazione con mezzi per accumulare il calore e preriscaldare l'aria fredda, assicurano delle condizioni di vita confortevoli e riducono ulteriormente il consumo di energia.

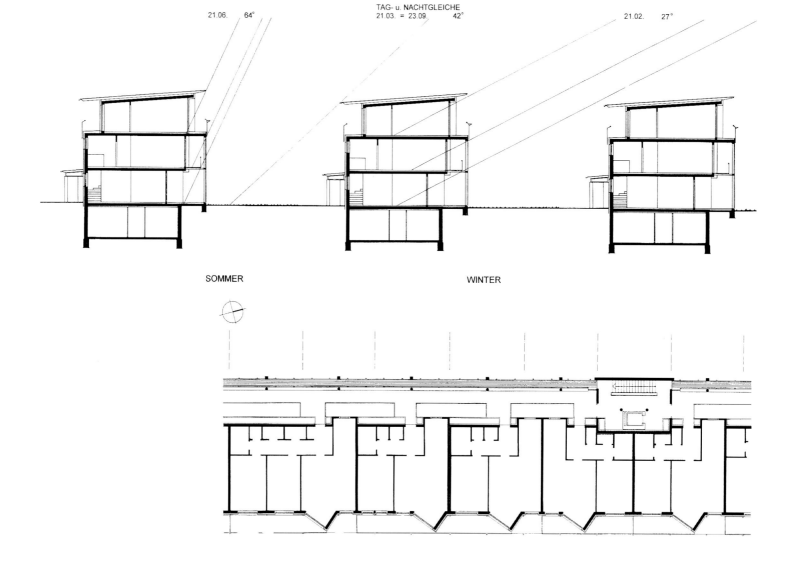

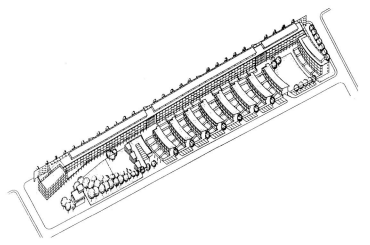

Stadlau Housing Complex, Vienna

Siedlung Stadlau, Wien
Complesso residenziale Stadlau, Vienna

Architects: Arge – Martin Treberspurg, Georg Reinberg, Erich Raith, Vienna
Planning and execution: 1988–1991

Clerk of works: Werkstatt Wien
Realization: Fa. HOWE
Structural Engineer: Helmut Lutz
Colour concept: with Michael Weese

The project is located on the edge of the city of Vienna. The "character" of the area, dominated by self-build houses, is part of the new design.

All dwellings are orientated to the south. Together with a community-centre they form a small unit beside a restored pond.

The houses are strictly zoned: a northern zone includes all ancillary rooms and the stairs; a central zone, which excludes all bioclimatic negative influences, is orientated to the south (and includes all living and sleeping rooms). The southern zone which contains integrated sun-spaces (glass houses), serves as a transition area to the open air and provides shadow during summer.

The buildings are highly insulated and use the sun in a passive way, including south-oriented windows (direct) and automatically controlled sun spaces (indirect).

The houses were built within the publically subsidized housing programm of Vienna and are rented to the occupants.

Das Projekt liegt am Stadtrand von Wien in einer Umgebung von größtenteils selbstgebauten Häusern. Dieser Charakter wurde im städtebaulichen Konzept übernommen.

Die Wohnbauten sind alle nach Süden orientiert und bilden mit dem Gemeinschaftshaus einen kleinen Platz um einen schon zuvor vorhandenen und sanierten Teich.

Die Gebäude selbst sind strikt zoniert: eine Nordzone mit allen Erschließungen und Versorgungseinrichtungen, eine Mittelzone, die baubiologisch störungsfrei und südorientiert ist, den Wohnraum und die Schlafräume enthält, sowie eine südliche Sonnensammel- und Beschattungszone.

Die Gebäude sind hoch wärmegedämmt, die passive Nutzung der Sonnenenergie erfolgt direkt über die Südfenster sowie indirekt über eine automatisierte Steuerung aus dem Wintergarten.

Die Häuser wurden im Rahmen des geförderten Mietwohnungsbaues realisiert.

Il progetto si colloca nella periferia di Vienna, in un'area caratterizzata da case auto-costruite, un concetto a tal punto dominante da divenire parte integrante della nuova ideazione urbanistica e architettonica.

Tutti gli appartamenti sono orientati a Sud e concorrono a formare insieme ad un centro comunitario, una piccola piazza, dietro ad uno stagno già esistente ed ormai risanato.

Le case sono rigidamente zonizzate: una zona a Nord include tutti i servizi e le scale; una zona centrale, che esclude tutte le influenze bioclimatiche negative, è orientata a Sud ed include tutti gli ambienti di soggiorno e le camere da letto. La zona a Sud provvede all'immagazzinaggio dell'energia solare e in estate all'ombreggiatura.

Gli edifici sono altamente isolati e fanno uso passivo di energia solare tramite l'orientamento meridionale delle finestre (sistema diretto) e l'illuminazione solare degli spazi controllata automaticamente (sistema indiretto).

Le abitazioni sono state realizzate con i finanziamenti pubblici stanziati per il programma residenziale di Vienna e vengono affittate a coloro che ne hanno effettivamente bisogno.

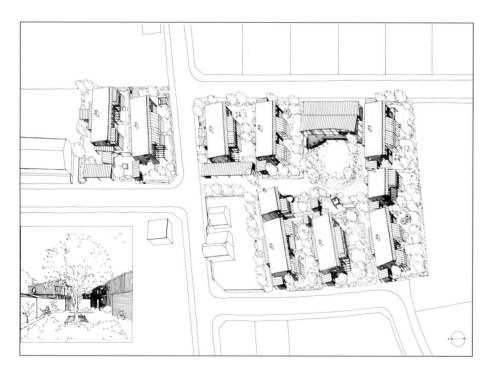

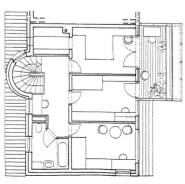

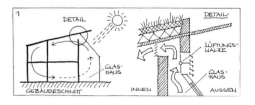

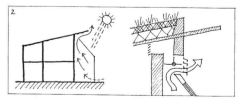

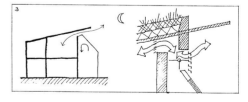

1   Energy gain
    Energiegewinn
    Guadagno energetico

2   Protection against extreme overheating, ventilation
    Schutz gegen extreme Überhitzung durch Lüftung
    Protezione contro l'estremo surriscaldamento,
    attraverso la ventilazione

3   Ventilation of the bedroom
    Lüftung des Schlafzimmers
    Ventilazione della zona notte

4   The conservatory is separated from the house.
    Das Glashaus wird vom Haus getrennt.
    La serra è separata dalla casa.

Apartment Building, Altötting (Germany)

Wohngebäude, Altötting
Edifici per appartamenti, Altötting

Architects: Demmel + Mühlbauer with Lengdobler, Munich
Planning and execution: 1991–1994

Collaborator: German Deller
Structural Engineer: Seeberger und Friedel
Services Engineer: Siegfried Piegsa
Energy Consultant: Roberto Gonzalo

Flexibility, a minimization of costs, and ecological sensitivity were major factors determining the design of these two rows of terraced houses. The development provides accommodation for families, single-parent households and handicapped people. The different widths of the houses reflect the different financial resources. Each house has a separate car port. These structures help to create a new urban spatial dimension. In addition to providing parking space, they also contain a large storeroom and a multi-purpose space at first floor level. All the buildings have a laminated-timber skeleton frame with structurally integrated, prefabricated, timber façade panels.

The dividing walls between houses consist of two 17.5 cm skins of sandlime bricks.

Solar energy is used both passively and actively. The use of condensate boilers enables gas consumption to be reduced to a minimum. The high level of thermal insulation means that a compact boiler is adequate for each row of houses. The calculated energy requirements of approximately 50 kWh/m²/annum have been substantiated by the figures for the initial heating period.

Flexibilität, Kostenminimierung und ökologische Rücksichtnahme waren die Eckdaten beim Entwurf dieser beiden Reihenhauszeilen. Die Bebauung bietet Wohnraum für Familien, Alleinerziehende und Behinderte. Die unterschiedliche Breite der Häuser reflektiert die finanziellen Möglichkeiten der Bewohner. Jedes Haus hat seinen eigenen Carport. Diese Gebäudeteile tragen dazu bei, eine neue stadträumliche Dimension zu schaffen. Sie bieten nicht nur Platz fürs Auto, sondern enthalten einen großen Lagerraum sowie einen Mehrzweckraum im Obergeschoß. Alle Häuser sind Fachwerkbauten aus laminierten Holzträgern mit integrierten vorgefertigten Fachwerkfeldern, ebenfalls aus Holz. Die Trennwände zwischen den einzelnen Häusern bestehen jeweils aus zwei 17,5 cm dicken Kalksandsteinmauern. Solarenergie wird sowohl passiv als auch aktiv genutzt. Die Verwendung von Kondensatheizkesseln führt zu minimalem Gasverbrauch, und aufgrund der massiven Wärmedämmung reicht pro Häuserzeile eine einzige Kompaktanlage aus. Der kalkulierte Energieaufwand von jährlich etwa 50 kWh/m² ist von den Zahlen der ersten Heizperiode bestätigt worden.

Flessibilità, minimizzazione dei costi e sensibilità ecologica sono i maggiori fattori che hanno influenzato il disegno di queste due linee di case a schiera. L'insediamento fornisce alloggi per famiglie, per singole coppie e per persone handicappate e i diffenti tagli abitativi riflettono le diverse disponibilità finanziarie.

Le strutture residenziali nelle quali ciascuna casa ha un suo proprio posto macchina, e che, in addizione all'area di parcheggio fornita, contengono anche un grande magazzino e un ambiente multifunzionale a livello del primo piano, vogliono contribuire a creare una nuova dimensione dello spazio urbano.

Tutte le costruzioni hanno un telaio con scheletro in legno lamellare e pannelli di facciata in legno prefabbricati e strutturalmente integrati. La parete divisoria tra le case a schiera è costituita da due strati di 17,5 cm di muratura in mattoni di calce e sabbia.

L'energia solare viene impiegata sia in maniera attiva che passiva. L'uso di caldaie a liquido condensato permette di contenere al minimo il consumo del gas. L'alto livello di isolamento termico fa sì che la caldaia compatta risulti adeguatamente calibrata per ciascun blocco di abitazioni. Il fabbisogno di energia calcolata approssimativamente intorno a 50 kWh/mq l'anno è confermato dalle cifre emerse dall'iniziale periodo di riscaldamento.

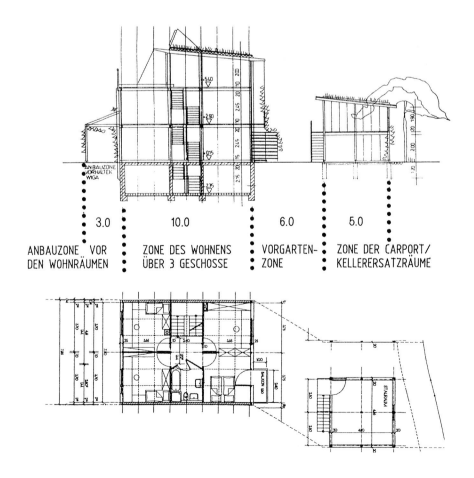

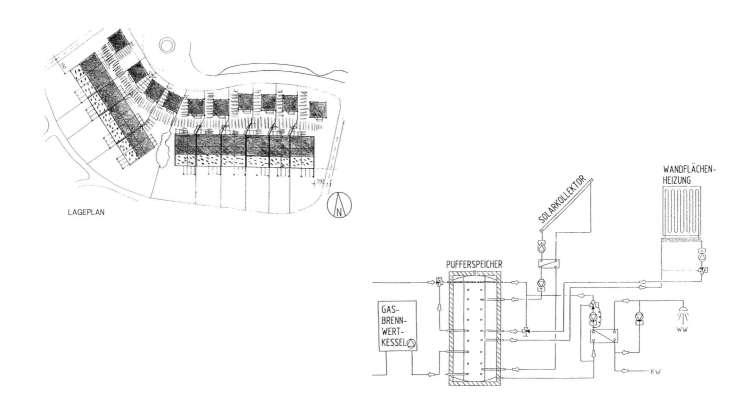

LAGEPLAN

PUFFERSPEICHER

SOLARKOLLEKTOR

WANDFLÄCHEN-HEIZUNG

GAS-BRENN-WERT-KESSEL

WW

KW

Settlement of Low Cost Housing, Florence

Wohnanlage zu niedrigen Baukosten, Florence
Complesso residenziale a basso costo, Firenze

Architect: Paolo Puccetti, Florence
Planning and execution: 1980–1983

Collaborator: Gianclaudio Papasogli
Engineers: Daniele Parigi, Maurizio Tanzi

This settlement was conceived by applying the fundamental concepts of bioclimatic design and of maximum use of solar energy, as requested by the inhabitants.
A favourable site was selected and careful analysis of local climate and environmental factors was carried out.
Cost effective energy conservation measures, such as wind protection schemes and summer self-shading solutions were integrated.
The design of building forms, apertures, indoor space distribution and choice of appropriate material for a high comfort level followed bioclimatic principles.
Use was made of architecturally integrated, reliable, passive and active solar technologies, compatible with common construction technologies and low maintenance costs.
The contribution of solar energy achieved over 50 % of space heating demand and over 80 % of domestic hot water demand.

Diese Anlage wurde auf Wunsch der Bewohner unter Berücksichtigung der Grundlagen des bioklimatischen Bauens sowie der maximalen Ausnutzung von Sonnenenergie geplant:
Hierfür wurde ein günstiges Grundstück ausgewählt, dann erfolgten gründliche Untersuchungen des örtlichen Klimas und anderer Umweltfaktoren. Kostengünstige Energiekonservierung (z. B. durch Windschutzsysteme) und selbstauslösende Beschattungssyteme im Sommer wurden in den Entwurf einbezogen. Die Gestaltung von Bauformen, Öffnungen, Innenraumaufteilung und die Wahl der Baustoffe erfolgte nach bioklimatischen Gesichtspunkten. Ziel war dabei ein Höchstmaß an Komfort. Verläßliche passive und aktive Solartechnik wurde architektonisch integriert. Sie ist vereinbar mit normalen Bauprozessen und niedrigen Instandhaltungskosten. Die Solarenergie deckt über 50 % des Heizenergie- und mehr als 80 % des Bedarfs für Warmwasser.

L'insediamento è stato concepito applicando i concetti fondamentali della progettazione bioclimatica per la massima utilizzazione dell'energia solare, come espressamente richiesto dagli abitanti:
– scelta del luogo più favorevole e analisi accurata del clima locale e dei fattori ambientali;
– integrazione edilizia di soluzioni a costi contenuti per la conservazione dell'energia, e di schemi progettuali per la protezione dai venti freddi e per l'ombreggiamento estivo;
– progettazione bioclimatica delle forme, delle aperture, della distribuzione degli spazi interni e scelta appropriata dei materiali ai fini di un alto livello di comfort interno;
– integrazione architettonica esteticamente valida di tecnologie solari attive e passive, compatibili con le tecnologie usuali a basso costo di realizzazione;
– contributo solare ottenuto superiore al 50 % del fabbisogno di energia per riscaldamento e superiore all' 80 % per quello di acqua calda ad uso domestico.

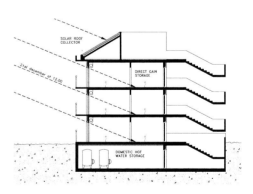

Urban Restoration, Kalenderpanden, Amsterdam

Stadtsanierungsprojekt Kalenderpanden, Amsterdam
Intervento di recupero dei Kalenderpanden, Amsterdam

Architects: Loof & Van Stigt/Energiebedrijf Amsterdam
Planning and execution: 1994–1996

Energy installations: DWA Installatieen energieadvies
Daylight Consultant: LITE
Building physics: Climatic Design Consult

The twelve warehouses, built in 1840, bear the names of the months, from which they take their collective name: Kalenderpanden ("Calender Buildings"). Each of the twelve warehouse bays measures 6 m x 41 m. On the upper two floors, three bays open out into a single space (18 m wide). The construction consists of heavyweight brick walls, heavy wooden beams and original cast-iron columns on the upper two floors. The Kalenderpanden have been in use as warehouses until recently.

The exterior appearance of the building will be maintained. The interior is divided into four parts, named after the four seasons. In each "season", an inner courtyard, or atrium, is created to allow penetration of daylight. The architectural design and energy scheme reflect the four seasons. Domestic apartments are situated at the front facing south. Commercial apartments are situated at the rear of the block, forming a noise buffer between a high voltage switching station and the apartments.

The main energy measures proposed are four different concepts for the inner courtyards, optimal orientation of both domestic and commercial apartments, a high level of insulation, high efficiency equipment, collective application of solar hot water systems, a canal-coupled heat-pump and approximately 800 m² of PV-panels.

Die im Jahr 1840 erbauten zwölf Lagerhäuser tragen die Namen der zwölf Monate und heißen daher »Kalenderhäuser«. Jedes mißt in der Grundfläche 6 x 41 m. In den zwei Obergeschossen wurden jeweils drei zu 18 m breiten Räumen zusammengefaßt. Die Konstruktion besteht aus starken Ziegelmauern, schweren Holzbalkenträgern und Gußeisenstützen in den oberen zwei Geschossen. Bis vor kurzem wurden die Kalenderpanden noch als Lagerhäuser genutzt.

Das äußere Erscheinungsbild der Häuser bleibt unverändert. Das Innere wird viergeteilt und nach den vier Jahreszeiten benannt. In jeder »Saison« entsteht ein Innenhof, ein Atrium, durch das Tageslicht ins Gebäudeinnere dringt. Sowohl der architektonische Entwurf als auch das Energiekonzept spiegeln die Jahreszeiten wider. Wohnungen sind in den Vorderhäusern mit Blick nach Süden untergebracht. Geschäftsetagen befinden sich im hinteren Teil des Blocks und bilden einen Lärmpuffer zwischen dem Hochspannungs-Umspannwerk und den Wohnungen.

Die vorgeschlagenen Hauptenergiemaßnahmen erfolgen nach vier verschiedenen Konzepten für die Innenhöfe und basieren auf optimaler Orientierung von Wohnungen und Büros, guter Isolierung, hochwertiger Gebäudetechnik, Verwendung einer gemeinsamen solarbeheizten Warmwasseranlage, einer mit der Gracht verbundenen Wärmepumpe und etwa 800 m² PV-Fläche.

I dodici magazzini, costruiti nel 1840, portano il nome dei mesi, ragion per cui hanno come nome collettivo Kalenderpanden («Edifici Calendario»). Ciascuno di essi misura 6 m x 41 m. Sui due piani più alti, tre campate si fondono in un unico spazio di 18 m di ampiezza.

La costruzione consiste di pesanti muri di mattoni, massicce travi di legno e colonne originali in ghisa che corrono lungo i due piani di altezza. I Kalenderpanden sono stati usati come magazzini fino a poco tempo fa.

E' stato mantenuto l'aspetto esterno, mentre quello interno è stato diviso in quattro parti, chiamate come le quattro stagioni. In ciascuna di esse è stata creata una corte interna, o atrio, per la penetrazione della luce solare. Le caratteristiche delle quattro stagioni vengono rispettate tanto nella progettazione architettonica quanto nello schema di funzionamento energetico. Gli alloggi sono collocati nella parte anteriore dell'edificio esposta a sud. Gli uffici sono situati nel retro del blocco e costituiscono una barriera al rumore tra una stazione di commutazione ad alto voltaggio e gli alloggi.

I principali provvedimenti energetici seguono quattro diversi concetti per le corti interne e si basano sull' ottimale orientamento sia degli spazi residenziali che di quelli commerciali, sull' elevato grado d'isolamento termico, sull' alta efficienza delle apparecchiature impiegate, e sull' applicazione ad uso collettivo di sistemi solari, per ottenere acqua calda, una pompa di calore a canale accoppiato e approssimativamente 800 mq di pannelli fotovoltaici.

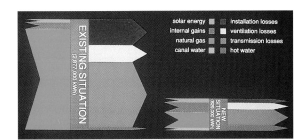

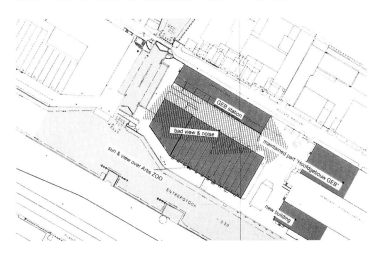

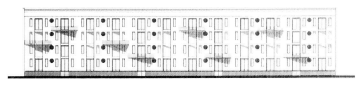

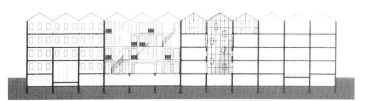

Hostel for Youth Educational Institute, Windberg (Germany)

Wohnheim der Jugendbildungsstätte, Windberg
Centro di accoglienza per la formazione giovanile, Windberg

Architects: Thomas Herzog with Peter Bonfig, Munich
Planning and execution: 1987–1991

Site Architect: Walter Götz
Interior Design: Verena Herzog-Loibl
Landscape Architect: Anneliese Latz

Windberg is a small community on the southern slopes of the Bavarian Forest. The monastery complex at the heart of the village comprises a number of buildings for the religious order and an educational centre for young people.

To conserve energy, account was taken of the time in use and temperature requirements of certain spaces. Those that are used for several hours at a time, therefore, were separated from those used for only a short period. They were also built with different materials.

The southern tract of the building contains the rooms in use for longer periods. Its external wall was clad on the outside with a layer of Translucent Thermal Insulation. The maximum temperature on the outer face is reached in the early afternoon. During the summer months, a broad roof projection and external blinds protect the rooms against overheating. The northern part of the building houses sanitary facilities, storage and circulation areas. These spaces are used only briefly at certain times of day; e.g. the shower rooms. Hot water is supplied by tubular collectors in the south-facing roof slope, and there is a swift-functioning warm-air heating system. To minimize heat losses due to ventilation, a heat-recovery plant was installed in the roof space.

Windberg ist ein kleiner Ort auf einem südlichen Ausläufer des Bayerischen Waldes. Neben dem Orden beherbergt das Kloster dort eine Jugendbildungsstätte.

Für die Gestaltung des Grundrisses war die Dauer der Benutzung der einzelnen Raumarten und das dann erforderliche Temperaturniveau von besonderer Bedeutung. Deshalb sind die Räume, die über Stunden hin genutzt werden, von solchen, die nur kurzzeitig genutzt werden, getrennt und aus anderen Materialien konstruiert.

Im südlichen Gebäudeteil liegen die durchgehend genutzten Räume. Hier ist die schwere und thermisch träge reagierende Außenwand mit TWD abgedeckt. Auf ihrer Oberfläche erreicht die Temperatur ihr Maximum in den frühen Nachmittagsstunden. Gegen Aufheizung im Sommerhalbjahr schützen ein großer Dachüberstand und außenliegende Jalousetten.

Im nördlichen Gebäudeteil befindet sich der Sanitär-, Abstell- und Erschließungsbereich. Diese Räume werden nur kurz und zu bestimmten Tageszeiten genutzt, wie z. B. zum Duschen. Das Warmwasser wird über Röhrenkollektoren auf dem südlichen Dach gewonnen. Die schnell wirkende Heizung erfolgt durch Warmluft. Um den Lüftungsverlust zu minimieren, wurden Wärmerückgewinnungsanlagen im Dachraum installiert.

Windberg è una piccola comunità sul versante meridionale della foresta bavarese. Il monastero nel cuore del villaggio comprende un certo numero di edifici religiosi ed un centro per la formazione dei giovani.

Al fine di conservare energia si è tenuto conto dei livelli di temperatura richiesti per certi ambienti. Quelli che sono usati per molte ore al giorno sono separati da quelli che lo sono solo per un breve periodo di tempo. Questi ultimi sono stati costruiti anche con materiali differenti.

Il lato a Sud dell'edificio contiene degli spazi vissuti per lunghi periodi. Il suo muro perimetrale è stato rivestito all'esterno con uno strato di isolante termico traslucente. La temperatura massima sulla faccia più esterna si raggiunge nel primo pomeriggio. In estate un sistema di oscuramento esterno protegge il muro dal surriscaldamento. La parte a Nord dell'edificio ospita servizi sanitari, magazzini e zone connettive. Questi spazi sono usati solo per breve tempo in determinati momenti del giorno, come gli ambienti doccia. L'acqua calda viene rifornita dai collettori tubolari sul fianco del tetto che affacciano a Sud e c'è inoltre un sistema di riscaldamento a funzionamento veloce d'aria calda. Per minimizzare le perdite di calore dovute alla ventilazione, un impianto di recupero del calore è stato installato nello spazio del tetto.

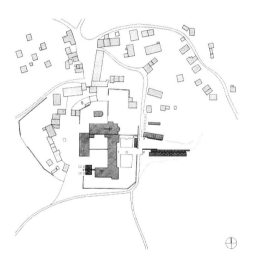

1   Translucent insulation and sun protection
Transluzente Wärmedämmung + Sonnenschutz
Isolamento termico traslucente + protezione dall'irraggiamento solare

5   Heat pipe collectors
Röhrenkollektoren
Collettore tubolare

8   Mechanical ventilation system with heat recovery
Mechanische Lüftungsanlagen mit Wärmerückgewinnung
Ventilazione meccanica con scambio di calore

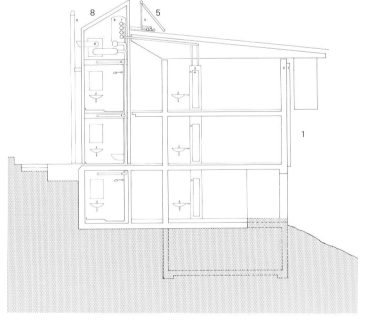

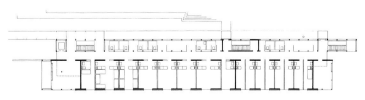

Multiple-Dwelling Block, Perlach, Munich

Mehrfamilienhaus, München-Perlach
Residenze plurifamiliari, Monaco-Perlach

Architects: Doris & Ralph Thut, Munich
Planning and execution: 1974, 1977–1978

The block is designed for six families and was erected as a self-help building scheme. A flexible, low-cost construction system was used as a vehicle for communicative planning and living processes. The occupants leave their individual traces in this space. In addition to its energy-related function, the large communal conservatory integrated into the scheme plays a spatial-communicational role.

Solar energy is used both passively and actively. The control of the indoor climate of the building is mainly natural, by means of a free convection system, both in summer and winter. This results in a considerable reduction of the energy required to meet the usual standards of comfort in housing.

Das Wohnhaus ist für sechs Familien ausgelegt und wurde in Selbstbauweise errichtet. Ein flexibles vorgefertigtes low-cost-Bausystem wird als Medium eines kommunikativen Planungs- und Lebensprozesses eingesetzt. Die Bewohner hinterlassen darin ihre individuellen Spuren. Das große gemeinschaftliche Glashaus ist – neben seiner energetischen Funktion – räumlich-kommunikativ definiert und in das Konzept integriert.

Kombination von passiver und aktiver Nutzung der Sonnenenergie. Die weitgehend natürliche Klimatisierung des Gebäudes durch freie Konvektion, sowohl für den Sommer- als auch Winterbetrieb, reduziert den Energiebedarf entscheidend, der zur Schaffung der in Wohngebäuden üblichen Behaglichkeitskriterien benötigt wird.

Il blocco di appartamenti è stato progettato per sei famiglie ed edificato secondo la logica dell'autocostruzione. Un sistema edilizio flessibile ed economico è stato usato come veicolo per una progettazione comunicativa e per processi da vivere. Gli abitanti lasciano effettivamente le loro tracce in questo spazio. In aggiunta alla sua funzione relazionata all'energia, è stata integrata allo schema una grande serra comunale che gioca il ruolo di comunicazione spaziale.

L'energia solare è impiegata sia in maniera attiva che passiva. Il controllo del clima interno dell'edificio è principalmente naturale, attraverso l'uso di un sistema di convezione libera, sia in estate che in inverno. Questo ha come risultato una considerevole riduzione dell'energia richiesta per ottenere gli standards normali di comfort nelle residenze.

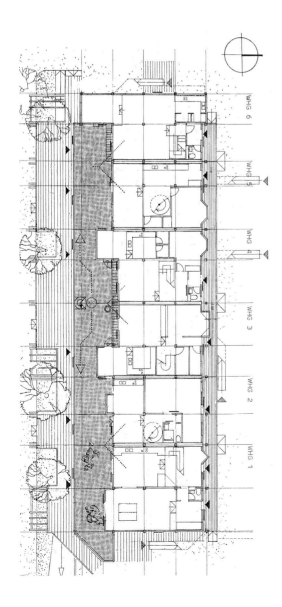

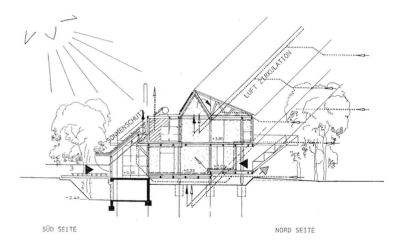

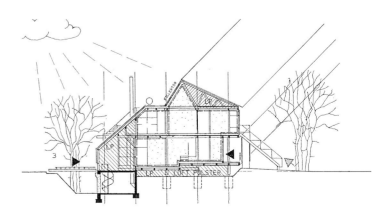

Low-Energy House, Stuttgart

Niedrigenergiehaus, Stuttgart
Casa a basso consumo energetico, Stoccarda

Architects: Kilian + Hagmann, Stuttgart
Planning and execution: 1993 –1994

The positioning of the site on a south-west facing slope, and the goal of a "low energy-house", were the determining factors for this project.
The evaluation of plan and elevation, the heat, solar and static data were optimized by a computer simulation.
It showed that the orientation of the building maximized energy gains on the south-west side, and minimized energy losses on the north-east, by using small openings and high heat insulation.
Therefore the ancillary rooms were concentrated in a service block to the north-east, whilst the living rooms were opened to the south-west.
Along with the window surfaces, a Translucent Thermal Insulation-System functions as solar absorber. Automatic shading systems and air ventilation conditioning flaps prevent overheating in summer. The appearance of the building changes according to the season, time of day and weather. The average u-value of the building is under 0,3 W/m²K.

Die Lage des Grundstücks, ein nach Südwesten offener Hang, war zusammen mit dem Ziel »Niedrigenergiehaus« bestimmende Grundlage.
Die Betrachtung von Grundriß und Aufriß, von Statik, Heiz- und Solartechnik wurde durch eine Computersimulation optimiert. Es zeigte sich, daß die Orientierung des Gebäudes maximale Energiegewinne auf der Südwestseite ermöglichte, bei geringen Energieverlusten durch kleine Öffnungen und hohe Wärmedämmung im Nordosten. Somit wurden die Funktionsräume in einem Serviceblock im Nordosten zusammengefaßt, die Wohnräume nach Südwesten geöffnet.
Zusätzlich zu den Fensterflächen wirkt das TWD-System als Solarabsorber. Durch automatisch gesteuerte Verschattungsanlagen und Lüftungsklappen wird eine Überhitzung im Sommer vermieden. Entsprechend den Jahres- und Tageszeiten ändert sich das Erscheinungsbild des Hauses. Auch die Witterung bildet sich am Gebäude ab. Der durchschnittliche k-Wert der Gebäudehülle liegt unter 0,3 W/m²K.

Due sono stati i fattori determinanti di questo progetto: la posizione del sito collocato su un pendio esposto a Sud-Ovest; e il raggiungimento dell'obiettivo di realizzare una casa a basso consumo di energia.
Pertanto le stanze di servizio sono state condensate in un blocco a Nord-Est, mentre gli ambienti di soggiorno si aprono a Sud-Ovest. Per ciò che riguarda la valutazione del riscaldamento e del soleggiamento, sono stati ottimizzati i dati statici a disposizione in pianta ed elevato attraverso una simulazione effettuata al computer, grazie alla quale si è evinto che l'orientamento dell'edificio che garantiva il massimo guadagno di energia per il riscaldamento e soleggiamento era quello Sud-occidentale, mentre in quello Nord-orientale sarebbe stato possibile minimizzarne le perdite facendo uso di aperture di piccole dimensioni.
Insieme alla superficie delle finestre è stato impiegato il sistema d'Isolamento Termico Traslucido, che svolge la funzione di assorbire il calore solare. Inoltre l'impiego di un sistema di ombreggiatura automatico e dei flaps (ventilazione ad aria condizionata) preserva efficacemente dal surriscaldamento estivo. I prospetti dell'edificio vengono così a mutare insieme al mutare delle stagioni, dei diversi momenti del giorno e del tempo atmosferico. Il valore-k medio dell'edificio è risultato essere di 0.3 W/mqK.

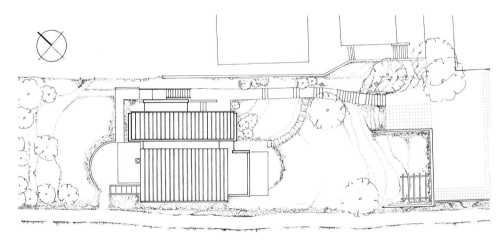

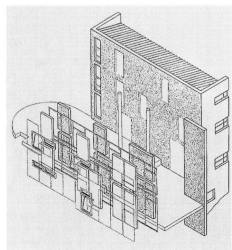

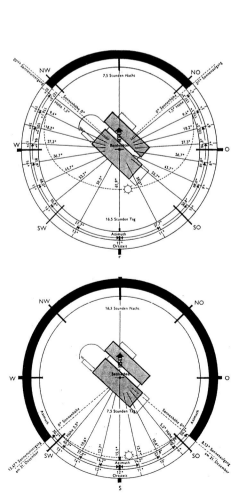

71

Houses with Zero Energy Heating, Trin (Switzerland)

Nullheizenergie-Häuser, Trin
Casa a basso consumo energetico, Trin

Architect: Andrea-Gustav Rüedi-Marugg, Chur
Planning and execution: 1991–1994

Collaborator: Maurus Frei
Structural Engineer: Jürg Konzett

Despite the many different functional and environmental constraints to which this development was subject and the requirments made of it in terms of solar energy and ecology, it is the strict reductionist architectural concept that dominates the design.

The houses are heated entirely by the penetration of the sun. As a result, no heating installation was necessary. The planning of energy requirements is based on the solar radiation available in the month of December. The site provides ideal conditions for this. Free of mist and situated on a south-facing slope that cannot be developed, it is sheltered to the north by a wood. The main features of the energy design are as follows.

A continuous outer skin is permeable to diffusion, with high thermal insulation values. There is a 50 m² area of special south-facing glazing with thermally separated frames. The inner surfaces are optimized for the absorption of 18 kW solar radiation (overwarming of indoor air: max, 3 K). On the warm side of the thermal insulation, 200 t of material are available (floors, ceilings and walls) with 70 kWh/K storage capacity as a bad-weather reserve. A minimum air exchange in the depths of winter is sufficient (ventilation via windows), thanks to the bioligically compatible materials chosen for the construction.

During the period from mid-November to mid-February, a great degree of awareness and discipline is required in controlling room temperatures. In other words, no solar shading or curtains are permissible. Floor areas may be covered to a maximum of 30–40 % by furniture and carpets.

No artificial lighting is necessary during daylight hours. Hot water is supplied by vacuum tubular collectors between the window strips in the south façade.

Trotz einer Vielzahl funktionaler, solarenergetischer, ökologischer und baubiologischer Rahmenbedingungen stand die konsequent reduktionistische Architektur im Vordergrund. Die Häuser werden zu 100 % durch das eindringende Sonnenlicht beheizt, somit sind keinerlei haustechnische Installationen notwendig. Die Energieplanung ist auf die im Dezember zur Verfügung stehende Sonnenstrahlung ausgelegt. Die nebelfreie, unverbaubare Südhanglage mit Wald auf der Nordseite bietet ideale Voraussetzungen. Hauptmerkmale:

Lückenlos hochwärmegedämmte, diffusionsoffene Gebäudehülle.

50 m² Spezial-Südverglasung mit thermisch getrennten Rahmen.

Die inneren Oberflächen sind für die Aufnahme von 18 kW Sonneneinstrahlung optimiert (Innenluftüberwärmung max. 3 K).

Warmseitig der Wärmedämmung stehen 200 t Material (Böden, Decken und Wände) mit 70 kWh/K Speicher-Kapazität als Schlechtwettersicherheit zur Verfügung.

Die gewählten baubiologischen Materialien lassen im tiefsten Winter einen besonders kleinen Luftwechsel zu (Fensterlüftung).

Die Zeit von Mitte November bis Mitte Februar verlangt einen bewußten und disziplinierten Umgang mit der Raumtemperatur: Das bedeutet weder Sonnenschutz noch Vorhänge, die Bodenfläche darf nur zu 30–40 % mit Möbeln und Teppichen bedeckt sein.

Tagsüber ist keine künstliche Beleuchtung notwendig. Das Warmwasser wird von Vakuum-Röhren-Kollektoren zwischen den Fensterbändern der Südfassade aufgeheizt.

Nonostante i reali vincoli funzionali ed ambientali a cui questo insediamento è stato soggetto le richieste fatte in termini di energia solare e biologia costruttiva sono state il preciso concetto architettonico dominante del progetto. Le case sono interamente riscaldate attraverso l'irraggiamento solare, per cui non c'è stato bisogno di installare alcun impianto termico. La pianificazione energetica si è basata sull'irraggiamento solare del mese di dicembre. Il sito prescelto fornisce le condizioni ideali. Libero da foschia e situato su un territorio in pendenza non edificabile che guarda a Sud, è protetto a Nord da un bosco. I maggiori componenti del progetto sono stati i seguenti:

una pelle esterna continua permeabile alla diffusione del calore, con alti valori di isolamento termico. Una speciale area a Sud di 50 mq vetrata con telai termicamente separati. Le superfici interne sono ottimizzate per assorbire 18 kW di radiazioni solari (surriscaldamento di aria interna: massimo 3 K). Sul lato caldo dell'isolamento termico, vi sono 200 t di materiale (fra pavimenti, soffitti e pareti) con 70 kWh/K di capacità di accumulo a costituire una riserva per il cattivo tempo. Un minimo cambio d'aria nel cuore dell'inverno è sufficiente (attraverso le finestre), grazie alla compatibilità biologica dei materiali scelti per la costruzione. Da metà novembre a metà febbraio, è richiesto un alto grado di consapevolezza e disciplina nel controllo delle temperature degli ambienti. In altre parole, non sono ammesse ombreggiature o tende e le superfici pavimentate possono essere coperte per un massimo del 30–40 % da mobili o tappeti.

Non è necessaria un'illuminazione artificiale durante le ore diurne, ed inoltre l'acqua è riscaldata da un collettore vacuo-tubolare posto tra le finestre a nastro della facciata meridionale.

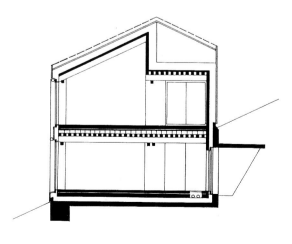

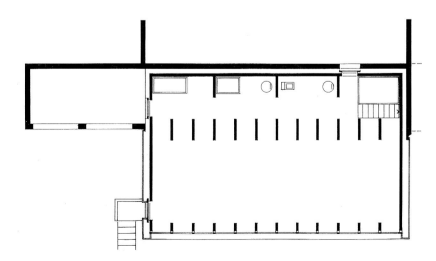

Terrace House Prototype, London

Reihenhaus-Prototyp, London
Prototipo di casa a schiera, Londra

Architect: Bill Dunster, London
Planning and execution: 1993–1995

Structural Engineer: Mark Lovell
Environmental Engineer: John White

Within the sustainable housing terrace, each household has its own intelligent sunspace which can be used for food production, solar energy collection and as seasonably occupiable extra living space. The glasshouse is self-irrigating, self-draining, self-shading and self-venting, using low cost horticultural components. As the home increasingly becomes the place of work and accommodation for two generations, leisure can be combined with horticultural cultivation. The traditional vegetable allotment is merged with the leisure generated conservatory, combining two ingredients already essential to a typical suburban lifestyle, to create a sustainable urban form.

The individual house prototype was largely self-built on a low budget, with low embodied energy content. It received 95 % of finance through the local building society. Active solar systems are being added as they become affordable. The energy saving due to the passive solar strategy is around 23 kWh/m²/annum. The total consumption of 67 kWh/m²/annum at present will reduce as active components are added. Thermal performance exceeds UK building regulations by 20 %.

Jeder Haushalt hat seinen eigenen »intelligenten« Sonnenplatz, der zum Gemüseanbau, zur Speicherung von Solarenergie und, je nach Jahreszeit, als zusätzlicher Wohnraum genutzt werden kann. Das Glashaus ist ausgestattet mit selbstauslösenden Bewässerungs- und Drainagevorrichtungen, Beschattungs- und Belüftungssystemen. Hierfür wurden preisgünstige Einzelteile aus dem Gewächshausbau verwendet. Da die eigene Behausung zunehmend auch Arbeitsplatz ist, sowie Wohnung für zwei Generationen, können Freizeitaktivitäten und Gemüse- und Obstanbau miteinander verbunden werden. Das Gemüsebeet »verwächst« mit dem Wintergarten; so werden zwei Elemente kombiniert, die bereits zuvor für den typischen Vorort-Lebensstil wesentlich waren, und eine dauerhafte städtische Form geschaffen.

Der Prototyp entstand zum großen Teil im Eigenbau zu niedrigen Baukosten, mit im Baukörper begründetem Niedrigenergiehaushalt. Zu 95 % wurde es von der Wohnungsbaugesellschaft des Bezirks finanziert. Aktive Solarenergiesysteme werden eingebaut, sobald sie erschwinglich sind. Die Energieeinsparung durch passive Solarenergienutzung beläuft sich auf etwa 23 kWh/m² im Jahr. Der Gesamtverbrauch von jährlich 67 kWh/m² verringert sich, wenn eine aktive Solarenergiegewinnung hinzukommt. Der Wärmebedarf liegt um 20 % unter dem von den britischen Bauvorschriften geforderten Wert.

Con la casa a schiera sostenibile, ciascun abitante ha il suo proprio spazio soleggiato intelligente, che può essere usato per la produzione di alimenti, per la raccolta di energia e stagionalmente come spazio ulteriore di soggiorno. La serra è auto-irrigante, auto-drenante, auto-ombreggiante e auto-ventilante, e si serve di componenti utilizzate solitamente nell'agricoltura a basso costo. In questo modo la casa diviene sempre più il posto di lavoro e d'alloggio per due generazioni, dove si possono unire tempo libero e coltivazione agricola. Il tradizionale concetto di orto si fonde con quello di serra generato per il tempo libero, combinando due elementi ancora essenziali al tipo di vita suburbano, al fine di creare una forma urbana sostenibile.

Il prototipo di casa monofamiliare a basso consumo energetico è stato in larga parte autocostruito con un budget basso, e finanziato al 95 % da una società di costruzione locale. Sistemi di energia solare attiva saranno aggiunti non appena possibile.

Il risparmio energetico annuo, dovuto allo sfruttamento di energia solare passiva, è all'incirca di 23 kWh/mq. L'attuale consumo totale annuo di 67 kWh/mq verrà ridotto non appena saranno aggiunti i componenti attivi. La prestazione termica supera del 20 % quella regolamentata per un edificio UK.

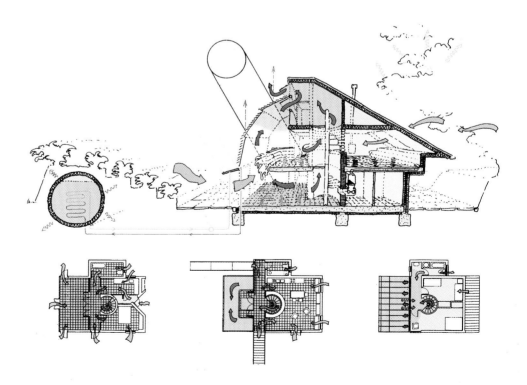

Summer day
Zero energy cooling

Sommertag
Null-Energie-Kühlung

Giornata estiva
Raffreddamento senza
consumo energetico

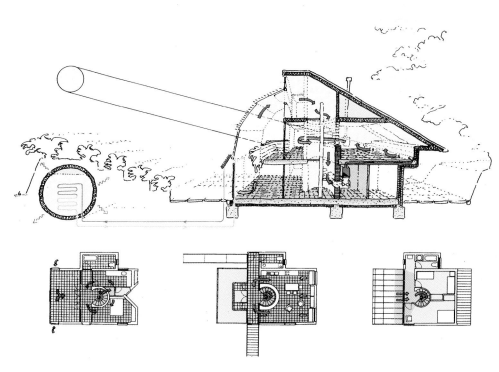

Winter day
Wintertag
Giornata invernale

House in the Hillside, Aldrans (Austria)

Haus im Hang, Aldrans
Casa nella collina, Aldrans

Architect: Horst Herbert Parson, Innsbruck
Planning and execution: 1984–1986

Built for an artist, the house is divided into three different zones set out in accordance with simple geometric principles. In the entrance zone is a single-storey exhibition space, with a tall conservatory structure behind it. This serves as a central source of light, and as a heat storage area and thermal buffer. Beyond it, to the rear, are the various living spaces spread over three underground levels. The effect of these spaces is determined largely by the quality of the daylight entering them and by the visual links both within the house and to the outside world. A further aspect of the spatial quality is the awareness that one is within a highly civilized "cave" that satisfies the desire for withdrawal and shelter.

The house – which was conceived from the outset as a terrace-house prototype to be continued alongside – takes up only a small area of the site and represents an alternative to the usual developments on sloping sites. The exploitation of a constant earth temperature of 8 °C below a depth of 1.50 metres results in a stabilising of the outdoor temperature in winter and has a cooling effect on the house in summer. The thermal insulation to the walls below ground consists of 8 cm water-resistant, impervious insulating slabs.

Dieses Haus für eine Künstlerin ist in drei unterschiedliche Zonen aufgeteilt, die nach einfachsten geometrischen Prinzipien geordnet sind: Im Eingangsbereich befindet sich ein eingeschossiger Ausstellungsraum, dahinter ein hohes Glashaus als zentrale Lichtquelle, Wärmespeicher und Wärmepuffer, und noch weiter hinten in drei unterirdischen Ebenen die diversen Wohnräume. Die Wirkung der Räume beruht vor allem auf der Qualität des eindringenden Tageslichts und den Blickbeziehungen nach außen und innen – aber auch auf dem Bewußtsein, eine »kultivierte Höhle« vorzufinden, die die Sehnsucht nach Zurückgezogenheit und Schutz befriedigt.

Das Haus im Hang – von Anfang an zur seitlichen Fortführung als Reihenhaustyp gedacht – beansprucht wenig Grundfläche und stellt eine Alternative zu üblichen Hangbebauungen dar. Die Nutzung der konstanten Erdtemperatur von 8 °C ab 1,50 m Tiefe bewirkt im Winter eine Herabsetzung der Außentemperatur und im Sommer eine Abkühlung des Hauses. Die Wärmedämmung der Wände zum Erdreich erfolgt durch 8 cm dicke, wassersichere und geschlossenporige Dämmplatten.

Costruita per un artista, la casa è suddivisa in tre differenti zone scaturite in accordo con dei semplici principi geometrici. All'entrata c'è uno spazio-esposizione ad un solo piano, con un'alta struttura-serra subito dietro. Questo spazio serve come fonte centrale di luce, e come area per l'accumulo del calore e cuscinetto termico. Al di dietro, sul retro, ci sono vari spazi residenziali che si articolano su tre livelli. L'effetto di questi spazi è determinato principalmente dalla qualità della luce che li attraversa, e dalle connessioni visive sia della casa sia del mondo esterno. Un ulteriore aspetto della qualità spaziale è la consapevolezza di trovarsi all'interno di una «caverna» altamente civilizzata che soddisfi il desiderio di trovare rifugio e riparo.

La casa occupa soltanto una piccola area del sito e rappresenta un'alternativa agli insediamenti usuali nei luoghi collinari.

L'ottenimento di una temperatura costante di 8° C ad una profondità di 1.5 m permette di avere una temperatura esterna stabile in inverno ed un effetto refrigerante in estate. L'isolamento termico dei muri sotto terra consiste in 8 cm di lastra isolante impermeabile.

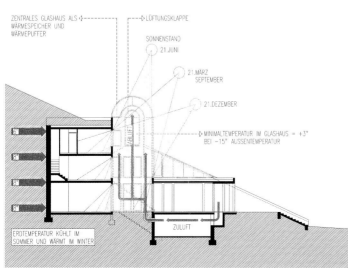

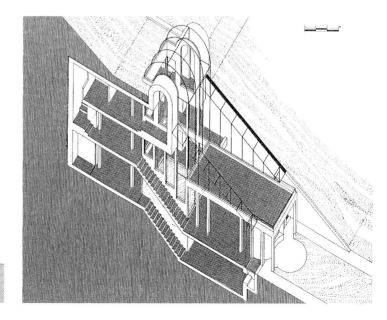

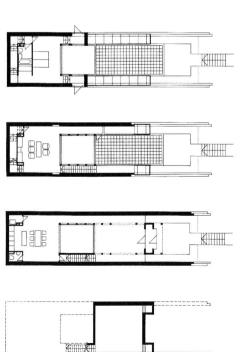

Education & Research Buildings

Bildungsbauten
Edifici per la formazione e la ricerca

Triple Sports Hall for the School in Kinkplatz, Vienna

Dreifachturnhalle der Ganztagshauptschule Kinkplatz, Wien
Palestra scolastica nella Kinkplatz, Vienna

Architect: Helmut Richter, Vienna
Planning and execution: 1992–1994

Structural Engineer: Vasko-Heinrich
Building physics and energy calculations: Erich Panzhauser
Glass façade: Brüder Eckelt & Co.

The complex was designed to accommodate 500 pupils and comprises two different types of school: a general secondary school and a secondary school for information technology. The ensemble consists of three long tracts extending in a northerly direction each with double classroom wings, and a circulation zone with a glazed south face. From this zone, direct access is provided to the main large-scale spaces, such as the triple sports hall, entrance hall and recreation space.

The triple sports hall is sunk to a depth of seven metres into the slope. On its open façade it is fully glazed. The glazing system was specially designed for the extensive application foreseen in this scheme and consists of two layers of thermally isolated double glazing. The outer layer is made of green-tinted, sun-filtering, single-glazed safety glass, whilst the inner layer is of laminated safety glass, which is covered with a 30 % white-dot grid. The point fixings are attached to the inner panels to prevent the formation of cold bridges at the points of connection. A sophisticated ventilation system supported by blinds helps to avoid overheating in summer. The massive enclosing walls which are partly in the earth have a very favouarble effect.

Das Gebäude wurde für 500 Schüler ausgelegt und beherbergt eine Hauptschule mit Mittel- und Ganztagsschule und eine Informatik-Hauptschule.

Der Baukörper besteht aus drei fingerartig gegen Norden ausgreifenden zweischultrigen Klassentrakten und einer gegen Süden verglasten Erschließungszone, an die die Großräume (Dreifachturnhalle, Eingangs- und Pausenhalle) angelagert sind.

Die Dreifachturnhalle ist sieben Meter tief in den Hang gegraben, aber sonst vollständig verglast. Das Verglasungssystem wurde speziell für diesen großflächigen Einsatz entwickelt und besteht aus einer zweischaligen thermisch getrennten Isolierverglasung. Als Außenscheibe dient grünlich getöntes Sonnenschutz-Einscheiben-Sicherheitsglas, als Innenscheibe Verbundsicherheitsglas, zu 30 % mit weißem Punktraster bedruckt (g-Wert 21%, k-Wert 1,8 W/m^{2}K).

Die Punktbefestigung wurde an der Innenscheibe angebracht. Durch diese technische Innovation wird verhindert, daß Kältebrücken im Haltepunkt entstehen.

Zur Vermeidung einer Überhitzung in den Sommermonaten kommt ein von Markisen unterstütztes, differenziertes Belüftungssystem zum Einsatz. Sehr günstig wirkt sich hier die an das Erdreich grenzende massive Umfassungswand aus.

Il complesso è stato progettato per 500 scolari ed ospita due differenti tipi di scuole: una secondaria inferiore sia a metà tempo che a tempo pieno ed una secondaria di informatica. Il corpo dell'edificio consta di tre elementi simili a delle dita, contenenti le classi disposte su entrambi i lati, che si estendono verso nord, e a sud di una zona di apertura vetrata, con cui si accede ai grandi ambienti (la palestra, l'atrio e lo spazio di ricreazione).

La palestra è incassata per sette metri nel terreno in pendenza, ma per il resto è totalmente svetrata.

Il sistema vetrato è stato progettato con questo schema per prevederne in particolare l'impiego estensivo e consiste in un duplice strato di isolamento termico inserito tra il doppio vetro. I punti di fissaggio sono alloggiati nella parte interna del pannello per prevenire con questa innovazione tecnica la formazione di ponti termici nei punti di attacco. Un sofisticato sistema di ventilazione supportata da quello di oscuramento serve ad evitare il surriscaldamento estivo. Il muro di cinta massivo che confina con il terreno influisce in questo caso in maniera estremamente vantaggiosa.

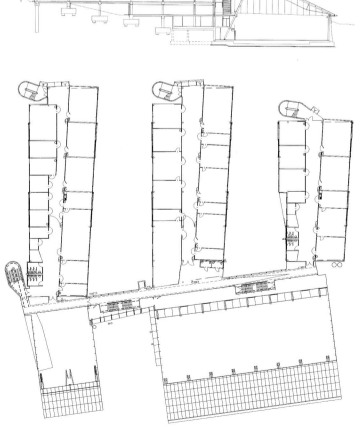

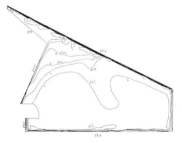

Temperature contour plot
Temperatur Raumzonenschema
Schema delle temperature rilevate

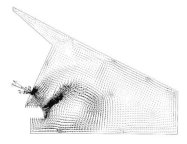

Velocity vector plot
Geschwindigkeit Konvektionsschema
Schema della velocità di convezione

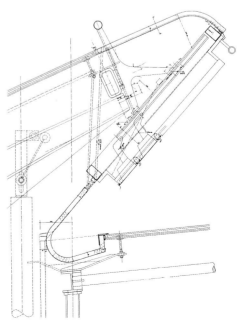

Lycée Polyvalent, Fréjus (France)

Lycée Polyvalent, Fréjus
Liceo Polivalente, Fréjus

Architects: Sir Norman Foster and Partners, London
Planning and execution: 1991–1993

The site for the 900 student Lycée straddles a hill with fine views out towards the sea and hills. The building is linear in form, two storeys high and maximizes views to the south. The internal arrangement establishes a "street" with all classrooms opening off it, thus becoming the social focus for the Lycée.

The method of ventilating the building in the hot climate relies on techniques used in traditional Arabic architecture. The use of a concrete structure provides thermal mass in order to absorb temperature variations. The choice of building form enhances natural ventilation using stack effect, thus avoiding the need to mechanically ventilate the building. The lofty internal street creates a solar chimney to induce the flow of air. Traditional features such as brise-soleil are also used to shade the south elevation.

Das Gelände des Gymnasiums für 900 Schüler liegt auf einer Anhöhe mit schöner Aussicht auf das Meer und die hügelige Landschaft ringsum. Das Gebäude hat eine linear angelegte Form, ist zweistöckig und auf den Panoramablick nach Süden ausgerichtet. Die innere Gliederung erfolgt entlang einer »Straße«, von der alle Klassenzimmer erschlossen werden und die so zum Mittelpunkt des Schullebens wird. Das Belüftungs- und Luftkühlungssystem für diesen Bau verwendet Techniken der traditionellen arabischen Architektur. Das Tragwerk aus Stahlbeton bildet die Speichermasse zur Regulierung von Temperaturschwankungen. Die Wahl der Gebäudeform fördert dank einer Kaminsogwirkung die natürliche Belüftung, so daß auf mechanische Belüftungssysteme verzichtet werden kann: Der hohe Innenraum der »Straße« wirkt wie ein Sonnenkamin, der die Luftzirkulation fördert. Auch traditionelle Elemente wie der »brise-soleil« werden zur Beschattung der Südfassade eingesetzt.

Il sito del Liceo per 900 studenti si colloca a cavallo di un'altura con un'incantevole vista verso il mare e il paesaggio collinare circostante. L'edificio è di forma lineare, ha un'altezza di due piani ed enfatizza in particolare la visione del panorama verso Sud. La sistemazione interna viene a costituire una «strada» dove si affacciano tutte le classi, strada che pertanto diviene il fulcro della vita sociale del Liceo. Il sistema di ventilazione dell'edificio produce un clima caldo coerentemente con le tecniche in uso nella architettura araba tradizionale. L'impiego di una struttura in calcestruzzo armato mette a disposizione una massa termica in grado di assorbire le variazioni di temperatura. Conformare un edificio in maniera da valorizzare la ventilazione naturale sfruttando l'effetto camino, fa in modo che l'edificio eviti il bisogno di essere ventilato meccanicamente: così la strada interna elevata crea un camino solare atto a introdurre il flusso dell'aria. Tecniche convenzionali quali i «brise-soleil» sono invece utilizzate per ombreggiare il lato a sud.

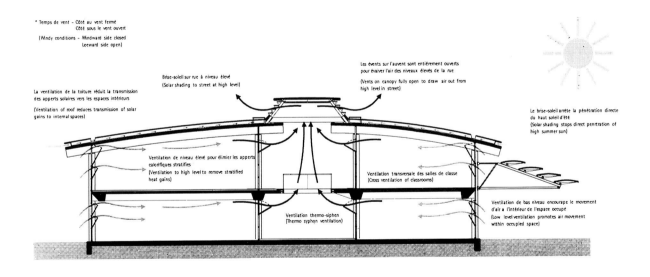

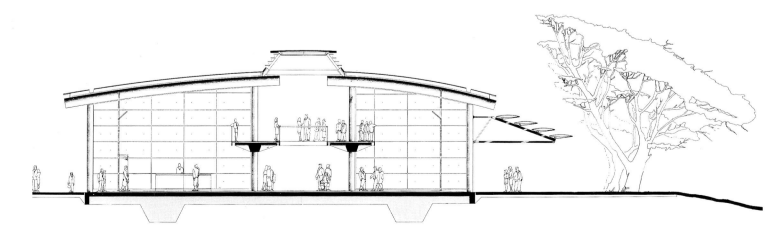

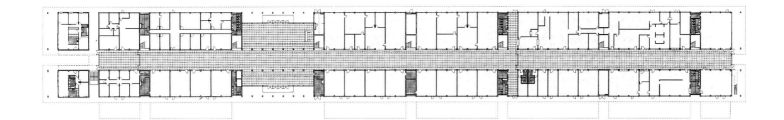

Sports Centre, Odenwald School (Germany)

Sporthalle Odenwaldschule
Palestra scolastica, Odenwald

Architects: plus +, Peter Hübner, Neckartenzlingen
Planning and execution: 1992–1995

Energy Engineer: Transsolar Energietechnik
Project Architect: Martin Grün
Structural Engineer: Sobek + Rieger

The aim was to produce a well integrated building with minimized investment and running costs.

The different approaches of the architects and engineers involved at the design stage revealed the logical possibilities of each part of the building. The glass superstructure which runs across the hall to take a movable curtain, also works as a skylight and, due to the stack effect, enhances the natural ventilation of the hall. The stiffening rib of the floor plate, called for by static demands, is also used as an air duct to the hall and ground heat exchanger, as well as an installation duct.

With the interdisciplinary work of the design team it was possible to reduce the technical installations by increasing the climatic performance of the building itself.

Das Gebäude sollte sich bei niedrigen Investitions- und Unterhaltskosten in die Umgebung und die bestehende Bebauung integrieren. Der unterschiedliche Ansatz von Architekten und Klimaingenieuren ermöglichte die konsequente Mehrfachnutzung von Gebäudeelementen. Der verglaste Dachaufbau über die gesamte Hallenbreite verbessert die Tageslichtversorgung und wirkt durch den Kamineffekt als zusätzlicher Antrieb der natürlichen Belüftung. Eine aus statischen Gründen notwendige Versteifung der Bodenplatte wurde als Kanal ausgeführt, der gleichzeitig als Zuluftkanal und Erdwärmetauscher dient. Außerdem wird er als Installationskanal genutzt.

Durch die interdisziplinäre Zusammenarbeit war es möglich, die technischen Installationen zu reduzieren und die raumklimatische Funktionalität wieder mehr dem Gebäude zu übertragen.

Obiettivo principale dell'operazione era quello di produrre un edificio ben integrato con costi d'investimento e di gestione minimizzati.

I differenti approcci sviluppati durante lo stadio progettuale degli architetti e degli ingegneri hanno rivelato le razionali potenzialità di ciascuna parte della costruzione. La sovrastruttura vetrata che corre lungo la sala ad ospitare una parete mobile, lavora anche come lucernario ed intensifica la naturale ventilazione della sala stessa dovuta all'effetto camino. Un irrigidimento del solaio a piastra, necessario per motivi statici, è stato realizzato come un canale che allo stesso tempo è usato come condotto di aerazione, come scambiatore di calore con il terreno ed anche come condotto d'installazione impiantistica. Con il lavoro interdisciplinare di progettazione in team è stato possibile ridurre la presenza d'installazioni meramente tecnologiche attraverso l'incremento di funzionalità dell'edificio stesso.

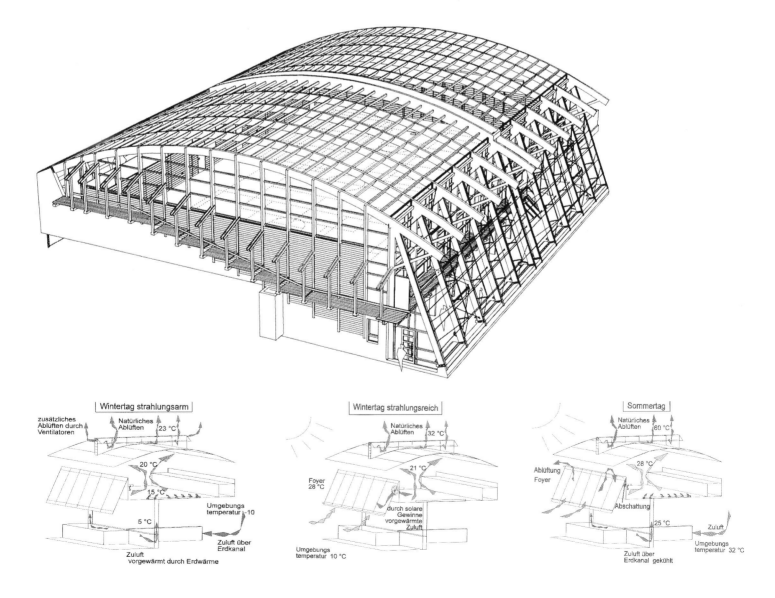

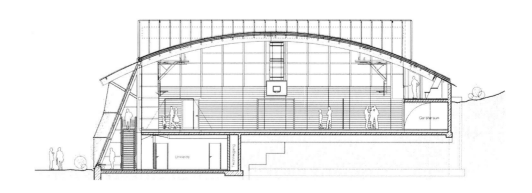

Vice-Chancellor's Office, Académie des Antilles et de la Guyane, "La Boîte à Vent"

Rektoratsgebäude, Martinique
Rettorato dell'Accademia delle Antille, Martinica

Architects: Christian Hauvette, Paris, Jérôme Nouel, Martinique
Planning and execution: 1989 –1994

The "Rectorat de l'Académie des Antilles et de la Guyane" is an 8,000 m² building housing the administrative offices of the National Education Service.

The building is located on the island of Martinique, in the French West Indies. The climate in this region is tropical, constant heat and high humidity. The main speciality of this building, which could be qualified as experimental, is that it was designed to dispense with the need for electric air-conditioning, even though the latter has become standard practice in Martinique. Natural atmospheric climatic-control represents a real advantage over artificial cooling. In addition to reduced energy consumption in kilowatt/hours the building has achieved the elimination of the "thermal-shock" effect which is experienced when one passes from an air-conditioned interior to the exterior. The architecture was specifically conceived in such a way as to adapt to the working mode in a tropical climate. The tradewinds are harnessed so that they gently traverse the building, bringing with them a refreshing cool breeze. There is a fine line between too much wind which blows paper off the desks and not enough wind which causes drops of sweat to fall onto this same paper.

Das Rektoratsgebäude der Antillen-Akademie hat eine Geschoßfläche von 8000 m² und beherbergt die Büros des Bildungsministeriums von Guyana. Es wurde auf der Insel Martinique erbaut, die zu den französischen Antillen gehört. Das Klima ist tropisch: ständig hohe Temperaturen und hohe Luftfeuchtigkeit. Das Spezielle an diesem Gebäude, das als experimentell eingestuft werden kann, ist die Abwesenheit von elektrischen Klimaanlagen, die sonst auf Martinique zum Standard geworden sind. Eine natürliche Klimaregulierung durch Ausnutzung atmosphärischer Strömungen hat ihnen gegenüber viele Vorteile. Außer einem reduzierten Energieverbrauch in kWh, hat das Gebäude dadurch auch die »Thermalschockwirkung« vermieden, die man erfährt, wenn man vom gekühlten Hausinnern nach draußen tritt. Der architektonische Entwurf hat die spezielle Arbeitsweise in einem tropischen Klima berücksichtigt. Ziel war es, die Passatwinde zu »zähmen« und sie als sanfte Brise durch den Bau zu lenken, die das Raumklima erfrischt. Es galt, den feinen Grat zu treffen zwischen zu starkem Wind – der das Papier vom Tisch weht – und einem zu schwachen Lufthauch – der Schweißtropfen auf das nämliche Papier tropfen läßt.

Il Rettorato dell'Accademia delle Antille ha un'estensione di 8000 mq ed ospita gli uffici amministrativi del Ministero della Pubblica Istruzione della Guyana. L'edificio è situato nell'Isola di Martinica, appartenente alle Antille francesi. Il clima in questa regione è tropicale con temperatura elevata e un alto grado di umidità.

Lo spunto più originale di questo edificio, che potrebbe essere definito sperimentale, consiste nel fatto che è stato progettato per ovviare al bisogno di un impianto di condizionamento d'aria ad elettricità, nonostante l'uso di quest'ultimo sia divenuto una pratica abituale in Martinica. Un controllo climatico atmosferico naturale rappresenta un vantaggio reale rispetto ad una refrigerazione artificiale, ed inoltre viene a ridurre il consumo di energia in Kilowatt/ora. Esso introduce nell'edificio un altro vantaggio: l'eliminazione del thermal-shock, ovvero dello sgradevole effetto che si percepisce passando da un interno con aria condizionata all'esterno.

L'architettura è stata specificamente concepita in maniera tale da adattarsi al sistema lavorativo di un luogo a clima tropicale: gli Alisei sono stati convogliati in modo da attraversare dolcemente l'edificio, procurando una leggera brezza refrigerante. Ed è, questa brezza, quella linea sottile di vento a cavallo fra il troppo vento che scompiglia i fogli dai tavoli e il vento non sufficiente a far cadere le gocce di sudore sulla stessa carta.

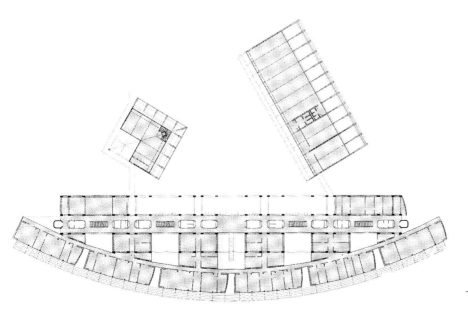

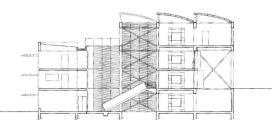

International School, Lyon

Internationale Schule von Lyon
Scuola internazionale, Lione

Architects: Jourda & Perraudin, Lyon
Planning and execution: 1989–1992

Structural Engineer: Agibat Mti
Services Engineer: Cabinet Nicolas
Quantity Surveyor: E2 CA
Monitoring: Contrôle et Prévention

Facing the confluent of the Rhône and the Saône, the classroom building unfolds along the banks of the river, beside the entrance to the Gerland park on the Rhône.

This temperate area is entirely open in summer by means of a system of motorized glass plates. The eastern and southern façades of the classroom building are entirely faced in glass, which is protected by suspended pare-soleil whose angles vary with the position of the sun during class hours. To the east the building circumscribes the "Centre of Life" that focusses all the spaces common to the three schools (primary school, intermediate school, and upper school), a village covered by a suspended and planted canopy. The communal buildings are organized under this roof. Connected to the three school halls, and grouped along an interior street are the library, games room, canteens, annexes to the gymnasiums, conference areas and laboratories. Between these buildings, protected by the roof, the "exterior" yet sheltered public spaces of the Centre of Life are to be found: interior street, terraces, gymnasiums.

Gegenüber dem Zusammenfluß von Rhône und Saône entfaltet sich am Ufer das Gebäude mit den Klassenzimmern. Der guttemperierte Raum ist im Sommer mittels eines motorisch betriebenen Glaslamellensystems ganz zu öffnen. Die Ost- und Südfassaden sind vollständig verglast und werden von Sonnensegeln verschattet, deren Neigung sich während des Unterrichts nach dem Einfallwinkel der Sonnenstrahlen ausrichtet.

Im Osten legt sich das Gebäude um das »Lebenszentrum«, das alle Gemeinschaftsräume der drei Schulen (Grundschule, Mittel- und Oberstufe des Gymnasiums) umfaßt und das von einem bepflanzten Dach als große Klimahülle überspannt wird. Unter dieser mit den drei Hallen der Schule verbundenen Überdachung sind die Gemeinschaftsräume um eine innere Straße gruppiert: Bibliothek, Spielsaal, Restaurants, Nebengebäude der Sporthallen, Versammlungsräume und Laboratorien. Zwischen diesen Bauten befinden sich die öffentlichen »äußeren« Räume: innere Straße, Terrassen, Sporthallen.

Affacciato sulla confluenza del Rodano e della Soana, l'edificio delle aule di lezione si sviluppa sugli argini del primo, quasi ad accompagnare l'ingresso del parco di Gerland lungo il fiume. Lo spazio degli ambienti interni gode di un microclima temperato e d'estate è completamente aperto grazie al sistema di lamelle di vetro motorizzate. Le facciate Est e Sud dell'edificio delle classi, totalmente vetrate, sono protette da elementi parasole sospesi, la cui inclinazione varia in funzione dell'angolo dei raggi del sole durante il corso giornaliero delle ore.

A Est il complesso si sviluppa intorno al «Centro di Vita» che focalizza tutti gli spazi comuni alle tre scuole (elementare, media e superiore), a formare una sorta di villaggio coperto da un grande telo impiantato e sospeso. Sotto la copertura, collegata con i tre atri delle scuole, sono organizzati gli edifici di servizio collocati lungo una strada interna: biblioteca, sala giochi, ristoranti, locali annessi alle palestre sportive, spazi di riunione e laboratori. Nell'edificio, protetti dalla copertura, trovano posto gli spazi pubblici «esterni» ma protetti dal «Centro di Vita»: strada interna, terrazzamenti, palestre sportive.

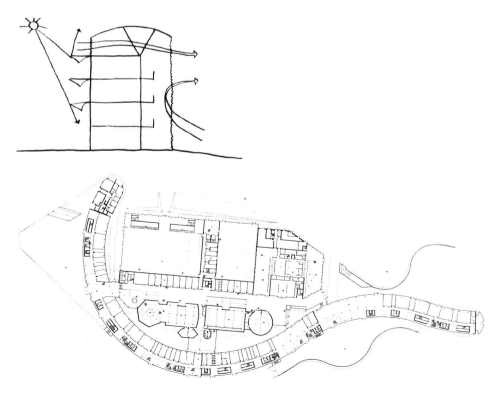

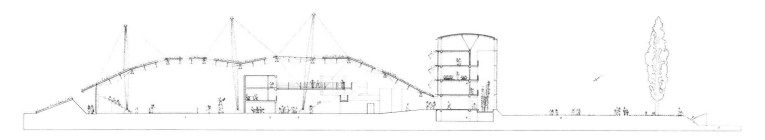

University of Trondheim (Norway)

Universität Trondheim
Università di Trondheim

Collaborators: Knud Larsen, Troels Troelsen,
Niels Roloff, Per Knudsen, Flemming Larsen
Engineer: R.G-P.-Gruppen
Landscaper: AS Landskabsarkitekterne

Architect: Henning Larsen, Copenhagen
Competition: 1972; **planning and execution:** 1975–1978, 1990–1993

A university is a very complex, constantly changing organism, which can be adapted to new requirements and forms of organization. The design of the building was based on analysis of the needs of the university and philosophical consideration of its integration within the town. The idea of integration motivated a structural form for the building which would allow the possibility of a variety of spatial combinations.

The complex covers a net of about 100 x 100 m within which the buildings are placed like blocks in a town. Streets between them are glazed over and function as climate controlled contact zones between the different faculties and departments of the university.

The complex has a three-dimensional structure which allows openness and flexibility, enabling the separate functions to grow and change. It is laid out horizontally in a form which is subordinated to the dramatic natural surroundings. Detailed analysis was made of daylighting to the internal streets, use of materials, traffic and access.

Eine Universität ist ein ein sehr komplexer, sich ständig wandelnder Organismus, der neuen Anforderungen und Organisationsformen angepaßt werden muß. Der Entwurf des Gebäudes basierte auf der Funktionsanalyse des Universitätsbetriebs und auf philosophischen Überlegungen zur Integration des Bauwerks in das Stadtgefüge. Der Integrationsgedanke führte zu einer Gliederungsform, die eine Vielfalt von räumlichen Kombinationen ermöglicht.

Der Entwurf des Gesamtkomplexes basiert auf einem Grundraster aus ca. 100 x 100 m großen Feldern, in dem die Gebäudeteile wie Stadtblöcke angeordnet sind. Die Straßen sind glasgedeckt – klimatisierte Kontaktbereiche zwischen den verschiedenen Fakultäten und Universitätsabteilungen. Das Tragwerk des Baukomplexes ist dreidimensional und erlaubt daher Offenheit und Flexibilität, so daß einzelne Funktionsbereiche wachsen und verändert werden können. Die Räume sind in der Horizontale angelegt und in ihrer Form der dramatisch wirkenden Umgebung angepaßt.

In detaillierten Studien wurden Tageslichtlenkung in den »Straßen«, Verwendung von Materialien, Verkehr und Erschließung untersucht.

Un'università è un organismo complesso in costante cambiamento, che si può adattare a nuove esigenze di forma e di organizzazione. Il progetto dell'edificio si è basato sull'analisi delle esigenze dell'università e su considerazioni filosofiche della sua integrazione con la città. L'idea di integrazione ha motivato una forma strutturale della costruzione che avrebbe permesso una varietà di combinazioni spaziali.

Il complesso copre una superficie netta di circa un ettaro su cui gli edifici si collocano come dei blocchi in una città. Le strade fra di essi sono vetrate e funzionano come zone di contatto a clima controllato tra le differenti facoltà e dipartimenti dell'università.

La struttura tridimensionale del complesso permette apertura e flessibilità ed è in grado di separare le funzioni di crescita e di cambiamento. La sua conformazione orizzontale è stata pensata in maniera da essere subordinata alla drammatica natura del circondario. Si è operato uno studio dettagliato dell'illuminazione naturale delle strade interne, dell'uso dei materiali e delle vie di accesso.

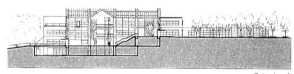

Snitt A – A

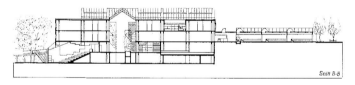

Snitt B-B

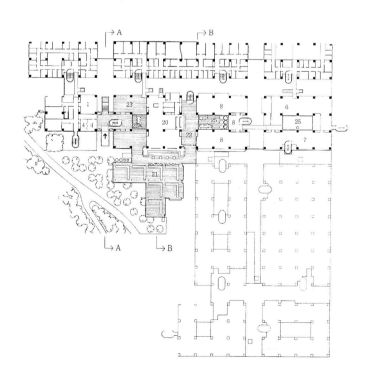

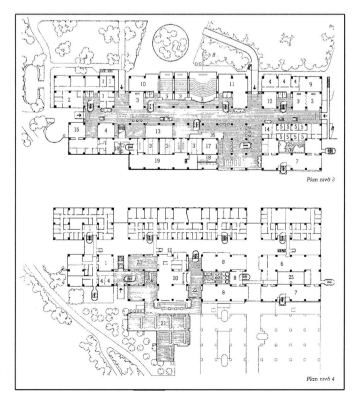

Plan nivå 3

Plan nivå 4

Professional Training Centre, Herne-Sodingen (Germany)

Fortbildungsakademie, Herne-Sodingen
Centro di formazione, Herne-Sodingen

Architects: Jourda & Perraudin, Lyon, with HHS, Kassel
Competition: 1991–1992; **planning and execution:** 1994–1997

Structural and Services Engineer: Ove Arup
& Partners
Quantity Surveyor: BDM Partner

The project is part of the IBA Emscher Park, in the centre of the borough of Herne-Sodingen, created on the site of an old pithead around which the town has grown since the beginning of the century.

The project proposes to extract a piece of the park, to protect it by a glass box measuring 13,000 m² and to create within this a temperate all year round micro-climate, controlled by extensive natural ventilation, sprays, sun-screens etc.

This gigantic glasshouse, constructed according to the logic of industrial manufacturing, is supported by large wooden and metal extendable trees on a regular grid.

Within this new ecological environment, two long wooden buildings house the training and accomodation facilities. They will be protected from the wind and, given the simple materials and construction techniques used, will subsequently be able to be easily modified and adapted.

Das Projekt entstand im Rahmen der IBA Emscher Park. Die Akademie wird in einem im Zentrum der Gemeinde Herne-Sodingen gelegenen Park errichtet werden, angelegt auf einem alten Zechengelände, um das herum sich die Stadt seit dem Beginn des Jahrhunderts entwickelt hat.

Das Projekt schlägt vor, einen Teil des Parks mit einer gläsernen Hülle von 13 000 m² Grundfläche zu schützen und darin ein kontrolliertes, mildes Mikroklima zu schaffen, mittels einer ausgedehnten natürlichen Ventilation, Becken mit Wasserzerstäubern, Schattensegeln usw.

Dieses gigantische Glashaus ist in der Logik industrieller Fertigung konstruiert. Getragen von großen metallenen und hölzernen Baumstützen, ist die Hülle regelmäßig gerastert und erweiterbar.

Im Innern stehen zwei lange Holzgebäude mit den Ausbildungs- und Wohnräumen. Sie werden gegen Wind geschützt sein und so durch die Einfachheit ihrer Konstruktion und ihrer Materialien spätere Modifizierung oder Anpassung leicht ermöglichen.

L'edificio, inserito nell'ambito dell'IBA Emscher Park al centro del comune di Herne-Sodingen, è situato all'imbocco di un pozzo minerario intorno al quale dall'inizio del secolo si è sviluppata la città.

Il progetto propone di isolare una parte del parco, proteggerla con un involucro di vetro di 13 000 mq e di crearvi, al riparo dalle intemperie, un microclima temperato tutto l'anno e controllato grazie all'ausilio di un'abbondante ventilazione naturale, di vasche con nebulizzatori, di vele per l'ombreggiatura, ecc.

La gigantesca serra, costruita coerentemente con la logica della fabbricazione industriale, è supportata da grandi strutture ad albero miste di legno e metallo su di una griglia regolare ed estensibile.

All'interno di questo nuovo ambiente ecologico, due lunghi edifici in legno ospitano locali per la formazione e l'accomodamento che saranno protetti dal vento e che, per la semplicità della loro logica costruttiva e dei materiali in essi impiegati, risulteranno oltremodo modificabili e facilmente adattabili.

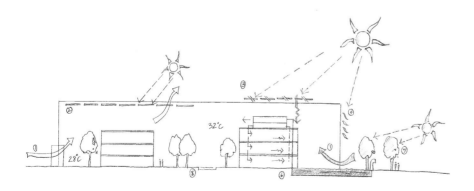

Typical summer day

1   Doors open for views and natural ventilation
2   Buoyant hot air rises and escapes through open rooflights drawing fresh air in at low level.
3   Solar water heater
4   Photovoltaic cells (solar shades)
5   Trees shade glass envelope from low angle sun
6   Cool fresh air drawn in from shade areas outside glass envelope.
7   Vegetation and water features shade and cool the glass envelope by evaporation.

Typischer Sommertag

1   Offene Türen für Ausblicke und natürliche Belüftung
2   Aufsteigende warme Luft entweicht durch offene Dachoberlichter, so daß von unten Frischluft nachströmt.
3   Solarenergie zur Warmwasseraufbereitung
4   Photovoltaikzellen (Beschattungselemente)
5   Bäume schützen die Glashülle vor Sonnenlicht mit flachem Einfallwinkel.
6   Kühle Frischluft wird über schattige Außenbereiche ins Innere gesogen.
7   Pflanzenbewuchs und Wasserbecken beschatten und kühlen die Glashülle durch Evaporation.

Tipica giornata estiva

1   Porte aperte per la vista e per la ventilazione naturale
2   L'aria calda ascendente fuoriesce attraverso lucernari aperti sul tetto, così da procurare al di sotto una corrente di aria fredda
3   Energia solare per il trattamento solare dell'acqua calda
4   Cellule fotovoltaiche (elementi di ombreggiatura)
5   Ombra degli alberi con bassa angolazione del sole
6   Aree ombreggiate all'esterno
7   Le piante e l'acqua ombreggiano e raffreddano l'involucro vetrato attraverso l'evaporazione

Ventilation elements in roof glazing, used as tracked shading components with photovoltaic power generation for direct radiation

A Vertical section
   Tracked PV-shading component with holograms
   Ventilation
   PV-module as roof glazing
B View from below
C Section A-A through tracked PV-shading element
   Glass
   Holograms
   Resin
   Solar cell
   Glass

Lüftungselemente in der Dachverglasung: in Bahnen ange-ordnete Beschattungsmodule mit Photovoltaik-Stromerzeu-gung bei direkter Sonneneinstrahlung

A Vertikalschnitt
   In Bahnen angeordnete PV-Beschattungselemente mit integrierten Hologrammen
   Ventilation
   PV-Modul als Dachverglasung
B Ansicht von unten
C A-A Querschnitt durch PV-Beschattungselement
   Glas
   Hologramme
   Harz
   Solarzelle
   Glas

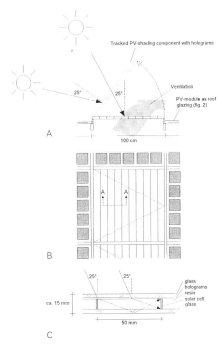

Tracked PV-shading component with holograms

Ventilation

PV-module as roof glazing (fig. 2)

25° 25°

100 cm

A

B

25° 25°

glass
holograms
resin
solar cell
glass

ca. 15 mm

50 mm

C

Gli elementi di ventilazione sulla copertura vetrata, usati come componenti ombreggianti, insieme alla strumenta-zione per generare energia fotovoltaica, per irraggiamento diretto.

A Sezione verticale
   Componente tracciato con ombreggiatura-PV con ologrammi integrati
   Ventilazione
   Modulo-PV per la copertura
B Vista da sotto
C Sezione A-A sugli elementi-PV ombreggianti
   Vetro
   Ologrammi
   Resina
   Celle solari
   Vetro

New Development for the University of Ulm (Germany)

Neubauten für die Universität, Ulm
Nuovi edifici dell'Università di Ulm

Architects: Steidle + Partner, Munich
Planning and execution: 1988–1994

Structural Engineer: Sailer + Stepan

The underlying idea of the design was to create an urban neighbourhood with streets and squares in the landscape of the Eselsberg in Ulm.

A 400-metre-long timber deck structure that accommodates the teaching areas and has intensive public use, performs the role of a main street. The oblique south face of this tract consists of glazed openings boldly coloured timber panels and an outer layer of timber trellis-work for creepers. This creates a transition between the structure and the natural environment and enables the indoor climate to be controlled naturally. This "main artery" also provides access, via gallery-like corridors, to the two-storey institute buildings on the north side. Using simple structural forms, building techniques and materials, it was possible to achieve naturally lit and ventilated spaces within the given cost limits, with renewable wood as the principle architectonic aspect of the construction materials.

Grundgedanke des Entwurfs war die Schaffung eines Stadtviertels mit seinen Straßen und Plätzen in der Landschaft des Ulmer Eselsbergs.

Die Funktion der Hauptstraße übernimmt ein 400 m langer Holzbrückenbau, der die publikumsintensiven Lehrbereiche beherbergt. Dessen schräggestellte Südfassade aus verglasten Feldern, intensiv farbig behandelten Holzpaneelen und einer vorgelagerten zweiten Schicht von Holzspalieren für Rankgewächse besteht. So wird ein Übergang vom Gebäude zur Natur geschaffen und die natürliche Klimatisierung des Hauses bewirkt. Diese »Hauptschlagader« erschließt zudem, über galerieartige Flure, die nordseitig angelagerten zweigeschossigen Institute. Mit einfachen Strukturen, Bautechniken und Materialien wurden natürlich belichtete und belüftete Räume im Rahmen der Kostenlimitierung geschaffen und der nachwachsende Rohstoff Holz als architektonisch bestimmendes Baumaterial eingesetzt.

L'idea che sottende il progetto è stata quella di creare un intorno urbano con strade e piazze nel paesaggio dell'Eselsberg a Ulm.

Una struttura di legno a ponte lunga 400m che accoglie le aule di insegnamento e quelle ad uso più spiccatamente pubblico, svolge un ruolo di strada principale.
La facciata a Sud obliqua di questo tratto consiste in pannelli di legno audacemente colorati ed un altro strato di legno a graticcio. Questo viene a creare una transizione tra la struttura e l'ambiente naturale e fa in modo che la climatizzazione interna venga controllata naturalmente.
Questa arteria principale provvede anche all'accesso attraverso una galleria con corridoi agli edifici su due piani nel lato Nord. Usando semplici forme strutturali, tecniche e materiali costruttivi, è stato possibile ottenere spazi illuminati e ventilati naturalmente, a costi limitati, con l'impiego del legno, materia prima rinnovabile, in qualità di materiale da costruzione determinante per l'architettura.

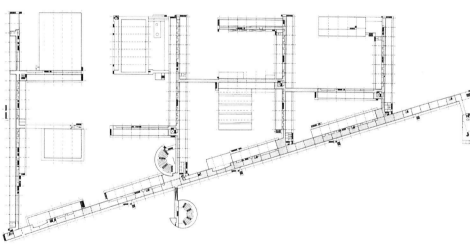

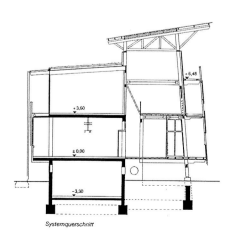

Systemquerschnitt

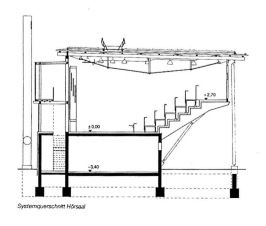

Systemquerschnitt Hörsaal

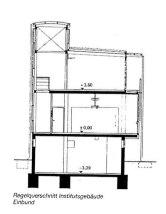

*Regelquerschnitt Institutsgebäude
Einbund*

Queen's Building, De Montfort University, Leicester (Great Britain)

Universitätsgebäude, Leicester
Edificio universitario, Leicester

Architects: Short * Ford and Associates, London
Planning and execution: 1989–1993

The 10,000 m² Queen's Building accommodates a complete University School of Engineering and Manufacture, with some 2000 staff and students. The teaching and research relates to the practical business of Manufacturing Technology, and much of it is heat producing at a prodigious scale. However this building is almost wholly naturally lit and naturally cross-, and stack-ventilated; the first results are very encouraging. The hypothesis is that the optimal form for this building distributes its considerable volumes into narrow section elements, with free elevations on two or even three sides. Thus it is possible for such a building, whilst it is attempting to strike a rhythm with its immediate sensible environment, to exploit its inherently more flexible form to repair a hole in the surviving urban fabric.

Das Queen's Building mit einer Gesamtgeschoßfläche von 10 000 m² beherbergt die gesamte Universitätsfakultät für Maschinen- und Anlagenbau mit etwa 2000 Studenten und Lehrkräften. Lehre und Forschung beschäftigen sich mit der Industrieproduktion, zum großen Teil von Wärmeerzeugung in enormer Größenordnung. Das Gebäude wird fast vollständig natürlich belichtet. Querlüftung und Kamineffekt sorgen für eine natürliche Belüftung. Erste Ergebnisse sind sehr ermutigend. Die Hypothese war, daß die optimale Form des Gebäudes seine beträchtliche Masse in schmale Abschnitte auflöst, mit aufgelösten Fassaden auf zwei oder sogar drei Seiten. So ist es für ein derartiges Gebäude möglich, mit seiner unmittelbaren Umgebung in einem gemeinsamen Rhythmus zu korrespondieren und zugleich seine eigentlich viel flexiblere Form einzusetzen, um im noch verbliebenen Stadtgefüge eine Lücke zu füllen.

Nell'area di 10 000 mq del Queen's Building, inaugurata nell'Ottobre 1993, trovano posto un'intera facoltà d'ingegneria e tecnologie industriali, con almeno 2000 persone tra staff e studenti.
L'insegnamento e la ricerca sono strettamente correlati con le attività pratiche e inerenti le diverse tecnologie di lavorazione ed è ingente la quantità di calore prodotta a questo fine. Ciò nonostante la costruzione è quasi interamente illuminata naturalmente, e ventilata con camini d'aerazione, il che sta iniziando a produrre risultati molto incoraggianti.
L'ipotesi è che la conformazione ottimale da attribuire ad un edificio di questo tipo comporti il dissolvimento dei suoi considerevoli volumi in elementi a sezione stretta, con prospetti liberi su due e persino tre lati. Da ciò è possibile evincere che un tale edificio, mentre tenta di mantenere vivo il rapporto con l'immediato ambiente sensibile, può conformarsi coerentemente con quest'obiettivo in modo più flessibile, per riparare ad un buco nella metodologia d'intervento nei confronti delle aree industriali urbane che ancora sopravvivono.

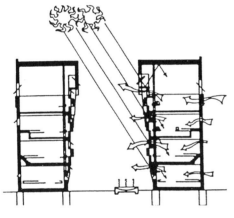

The principles of the natural ventilation strategy. With so much mass and so little solar gain the building should work well.

Natürliches Belüftungskonzept. Mit so viel Baumasse und so wenig Sonnenwärmegewinn sollte das Gebäude angenehm klimatisiert sein.

Principi della ventilazione naturale. Con una tale massa e con un guadagno di energia solare così basso, l'edificio dovrebbe essere climatizzato gradevolmente.

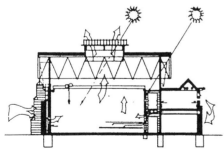

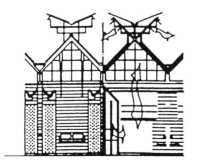

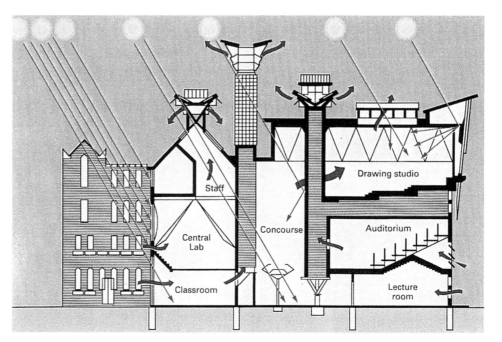

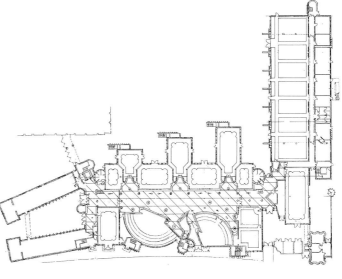

Science and Technology Park, Gelsenkirchen (Germany)

Wissenschaftspark Gelsenkirchen
Parco della Scienza, Gelsenkirchen

Architects: Kiessler + Partner, Munich
Planning and execution: 1989–1995

Design: Uwe Kiessler, Hermann Schultz,
Vera Ilic, Stefanie Reithwiesner
Clerk of works: Norbert Muhlak, Michael Föglein

The technology centre for research and development into ecological energy technologies is the largest of the projects in the Emscher Park architectural exhibition (IBA) at Gelsenkirchen-Ückendorf. The complex consists of a 300 m long glazed arcade beside an irregularly formed artificial lake, with nine pavillons leading from it, creating a comb-like form. The entire lower third of the long glass façade can be electronically opened to create something akin to a public "pavement".
In Summer the boundary between inside and outside is blurred. Park, arcade and by extension the Institute merge into a single space.

Das Technologiezentrum für zukunftsorientierte Forschung und Entwicklung ist das größte Projekt der Internationalen Bauausstellung IBA Emscher Park. Die an einem unregelmäßig geformten, künstlichen See gelegene, 300 m lange, öffentliche Arkade bildet das Rückgrat der ganzen Anlage, von der aus das dreigeschossige Galeriegebäude und die neun Pavillons kammartig erschlossen werden. Die große Glasfassade kann im unteren Drittel mittels elektrisch betriebener Hubelemente in ganzer Länge geöffnet werden. Die Grenze zwischen innen und außen wird somit im Sommer praktisch aufgehoben; Park, Arkade und anschließendes Institut verschmelzen zu einer Raumeinheit.

Il centro tecnologico per la ricerca e lo sviluppo nel campo delle tecnologie innovative è il più esteso dei progetti presentati all'Esposizione architettonica (IBA) effettuata nell'Emscher Park a Gelsenkirchen-Ückendorf. Il complesso consiste di una galleria vetrata lunga 300 m che si affaccia su un lago artificiale di forma irregolare, con nove padiglioni aggregati a pettine. L'intera parte bassa dell'ampia facciata vetrata, per tutta la sua lunghezza e per circa un terzo della totale superficie, può essere aperta elettronicamente a formare una sorta di percorso pubblico. Nei mesi estivi il confine fra interno ed esterno è praticamente rimosso e il parco, la galleria e l'intera estensione dell'istituto si fondono in un unico spazio.

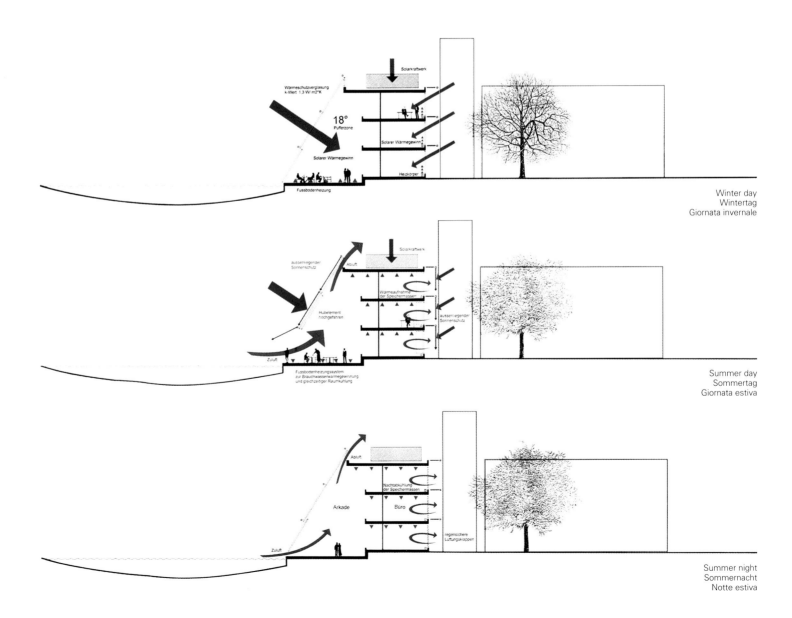

Winter day
Wintertag
Giornata invernale

Summer day
Sommertag
Giornata estiva

Summer night
Sommernacht
Notte estiva

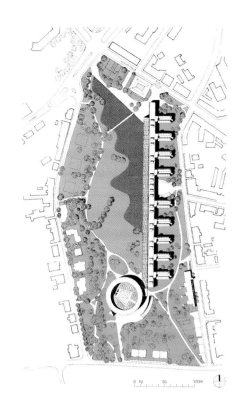

Office Buildings

Bürogebäude
Edifici per uffici

Office Building, Athens	GR	Alexandros N. Tombazis and Associates, Athens
The Ionica Building, Cambridge	GB	RH Partnership, Cambridge
PowerGen Headquarters, Coventry	GB	Bennetts Associates, London
Commerzbank Headquarters, Frankfurt a.M.	D	Sir Norman Foster and Partners, London
debis Headquarters, Potsdamer Platz, Berlin	D	Renzo Piano Building Workshop, Genoa/Paris
Offices and Housing, Potsdamer Platz, Berlin	D	Richard Rogers Partnership, London
Ludwig Erhard Haus, Stock Exchange, Berlin	D	Nicholas Grimshaw and Partners, London
Bianchi Palace, Bioclimatic Restoration, Perugia	I	Francesca Sartogo, Massimo Bastiani, Valerio Calderaro, Rome
Centre for Renewable Energy Sources (C.R.E.S.), Athens	GR	Nikos Fintikakis, Athens
Lloyd's Register of Shipping Headquarters, Hampshire	GB	Richard Rogers Partnership, London
UNESCO Workshop, Vesima	I	Renzo Piano Building Workshop, Genoa/Paris

Double Façade Systems

Doppelfassaden-Systeme
Sistemi a doppia facciata

Double Façade for an Office and Housing Development, Munich	D	Steidle + Partner, Munich
Double Façade for Düsseldorf City Gate	D	Petzinka, Pink und Partner, Düsseldorf
Double Façade for RWE Headquarters, Essen	D	Ingenhoven, Overdiek und Partner, Düsseldorf

Office Building, Athens

Bürogebäude, Athen
Uffici, Atene

Architects: Alexandros N. Tombazis and Associates, Athens
Planning and execution: 1991–1995

This 4,000 m² office building is situated in central Athens on a major road. Office accommodation is on six floors, with a bank at ground and first basement level. The building is oriented south. The main element of the design is the double steel structure of the façade which dominates the aesthetic of the building and controls the penetration of sun-light.

From a bioclimatic point of view the main point was to keep the use of energy as low as possible, especially in cooling the building. This was achieved by insulation of the opaque elements, effective shading of the south façade whilst allowing sufficient daylight in working hours, and use of a natural ventilation system for cooling.

Dieses 4000 m² große Bürogebäude befindet sich im Zentrum von Athen an einer der großen Hauptstraßen. Es beherbergt Büroräume auf sechs Etagen und eine Bank im Erd- und ersten Untergeschoß. Die Fassade ist nach Süden gerichtet. Das Hauptelement des Entwurfs bildet die doppelte Stahlkonstruktion der Fassade, die das Eindringen des Sonnenlichts kontrolliert und die Ästhetik des Gebäudes prägt.

Aus bioklimatischer Sicht lag das Hauptaugenmerk darauf, den Energieverbrauch, besonders beim Kühlen des Gebäudes, soweit wie möglich zu senken: durch Isolieren der opaken Elemente, richtige Beschattung der Südfassade sowie die Sicherstellung ausreichenden natürlichen Lichts während der Arbeitszeit und durch natürliches Lüften als Kühlmethode.

L'edificio per uffici si inserisce con i suoi 4000 mq, in una delle strade principali del centro di Atene, con una banca presente al piano terra e al primo piano basamentale, e gli uffici distribuiti su sei piani. L'orientamento della costruzione è a Sud, e l'elemento di spicco è costituito dalla struttura binata d'acciaio sulla facciata, che oltre ad essere la dominante estetica della costruzione, svolge la funzione di controllo della penetrazione di luce solare nell'edificio.

Dal punto di vista bioclimatico l'obiettivo centrale era quello di mantenere il più basso possibile il consumo energetico, soprattutto per quel che riguardava la refrigerazione dell'edificio. Il risultato desiderato è stato ottenuto attraverso l'attento isolamento termico degli elementi opachi, l'impiego di ventilazione naturale come sistema di refrigerazione, e l'effettiva ombreggiatura della facciata meridionale, che allo stesso tempo permette una sufficiente illuminazione naturale nelle ore di lavoro.

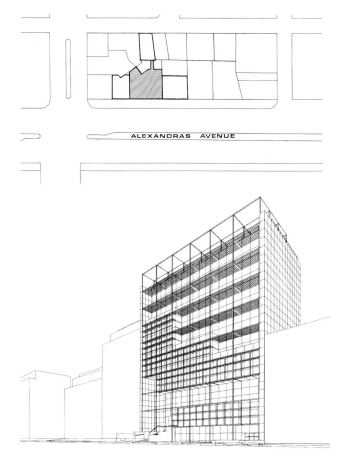

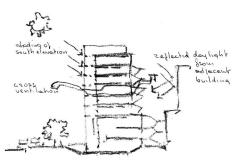

shading of
south elevation

reflected daylight
from
adjacent
building

cross
ventilation

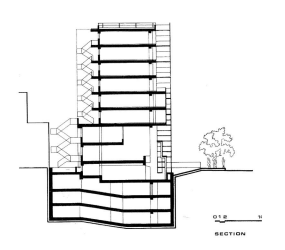

0 1 2   10

SECTION

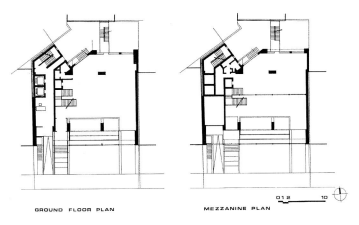

GROUND FLOOR PLAN   MEZZANINE PLAN

0 1 2   10

The Ionica Building, Cambridge

Hauptsitz von Ionica, Cambridge
Sede centrale della Ionica, Cambridge

Architects: RH Partnership, Cambridge
Planning and execution: 1992–1994

Environmental Engineer: Battle McCarthy
Building Services Engineer: Rybka Battle Ltd.
Daylight and Acoustic Consultant: Cambridge Architectural Research
Wind Tunnel Testing: University of Bristol
Structural Engineer: Hannah, Reed Associates
Quantity Surveyor: Davis Langdon & Everest

The new headquarters for the telecommunications company Ionica at Cambridge demonstrates the principle of environmental control by structure, creating a low-energy, mixed-mode office building. It achieves occupant comfort by combining natural ventilation with a mechanical peak-lopping system.

The building operation depends on the use of wind and solar-driven ventilation, thermal mass with night-time cooling, ventilation machinery for peak-lopping in mid-summer and mid-winter, and a sophisticated computer control system. It was designed using extensive environmental testing including a wind tunnel, artificial sky, and computer simulation.

The Ionica building won the 1995 RICS award for Energy Efficient Building of the Year.

Das neue Hauptverwaltungsgebäude für die Telekommunikationsfirma Ionica in Cambridge demonstriert die Steuerung von Umweltfaktoren durch die Konstruktion, so daß ein Niedrigenergie-Bürohaus mit einer Mischung aus unterschiedlichen Energiemedien entsteht. Es erzielt Nutzerkomfort, indem es natürliche Be- und Entlüftung mit einem mechanisch gesteuerten Ausgleichsystem für Extremsituationen kombiniert. Das Betreiben des Gebäudes basiert auf der Nutzung einer von Windkraft und Solarenergie angetriebenen Be- und Entlüftung, der thermischen Masse des Baukörpers mit nächtlicher Abkühlung, der Ventilationsanlage, die bei extremen Temperaturen im Winter und im Hochsommer die Innentemperatur ausgleicht und einem ausgeklügelten Computersteuerungssystem. Bei diesem Entwurf wurden eingehende Tests durchgeführt, bei denen Windkanal, künstlicher Himmel und Computersimulationen zum Einsatz kamen.

Das Ionica-Gebäude erhielt den 1995er RICS Award for Energy Efficient Building of the Year.

Il nuovo quartier generale per la compagnia di telecomunicazioni Ionica a Cambridge, è la dimostrazione che il principio del controllo ambientale applicato per strutturare impianti a basso consumo energetico, ha sconvolto la tipologia dell'edificio per uffici. Il comfort di coloro che vi lavorano è ottenuto attraverso la combinazione di una ventilazione naturale con un sistema meccanico «peak-lopping» (bloccaggio dei picchi estremi di temperatura).

Il funzionamento dell'edificio si basa sullo sfruttamento del vento e della ventilazione «solar-driven» (regolata dall'energia solare), e sulla presenza di masse termiche con raffreddamento notturno, di macchine di ventilazione per il peak-lopping nei periodi centrali dell'estate e dell'inverno e di un sofisticato sistema di controllo computerizzato. Durante la fase progettuale si è fatto un largo impiego di esperimenti ambientali, incluso un tunnel del vento, un cielo artificiale e un sistema di simulazione al computer.

L'edificio per uffici della Ionica ha vinto il premio RICS nel 1995 quale Energy Efficient Building dell'anno.

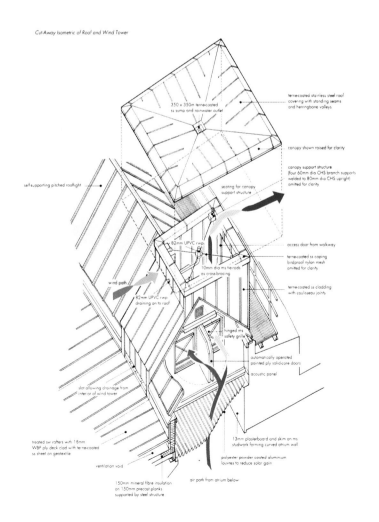

Cut-Away Isometric of Roof and Wind Tower

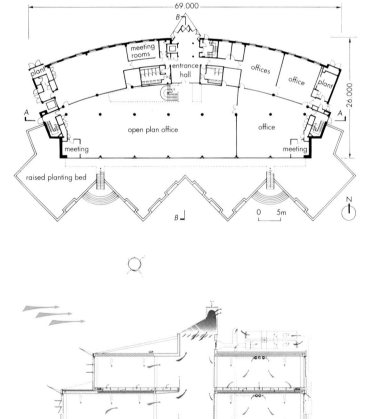

PowerGen Headquarters, Coventry (Great Britain)

Hauptsitz von PowerGen, Coventry
Sede centrale della PowerGen, Coventry

Architects: Bennetts Associates, London
Planning and execution: 1991–1994

Structural Engineer: Curtins Consulting Engineers
Services Engineer: Ernest Griffiths & Son
Acoustic Consultant: Arup Acoustics
Lighting Consultant: Equation Lighting Design
Landscape Architect: Mark Westcott Design

The PowerGen Headquarters building of 13,600 m² is one of a new generation of low energy, naturally ventilated office buildings using structure to temper the internal environment. The building is simply arranged on three floors with four floorplates per floor on either side of a long atrium. The focus of the design is on the workplace and the individual.

The exposed coffered concrete frame of the main structure is used to modify the building's internal climate through its mass. Three combined stair towers and business centres in the atrium help to encourage social contact and improve internal communications.

The building level was raised and the ground level lowered to provide an undercroft, reducing the impact of parking and providing more area for the landscape.

Bei der PowerGen Hauptverwaltung mit 13 600 m² Geschoß-fläche handelt es sich um ein Beispiel einer neuen Generation von Bürogebäuden mit niedrigem Energiebedarf und natürlicher Be- und Entlüftung, bei denen das Tragwerk zur Temperaturregelung im Innern eingesetzt wird. Ausgangspunkte des Entwurfs sind der Arbeitsplatz und der einzelne Nutzer. Der kassettierte Sichtbetonrahmen des Haupttragwerks beeinflußt durch seine Masse das Innenklima. Drei zusammenhängende Treppenhäuser und Geschäftszentren im Atrium fördern soziale Kontakte und erleichtern die interne Kommunikation. Durch Anheben des Gebäudes und Absenken des Bodens ergab sich eine Art unterirdisches Gewölbe, so daß die Parkplätze nicht aufs Gelände übergreifen und mehr umgebender Freiraum erhalten blieb.

La sede centrale della PowerGen, di 13 600 mq, è uno degli edifici per uffici a basso consumo energetico della nuova generazione, ventilati naturalmente con l'uso di strutture atte a temperare le condizioni ambientali interne. Il progetto focalizza la sua attenzione sulla qualità del posto di lavoro e sul comfort dell'individuo. La costruzione si sviluppa in maniera semplice su tre piani con quattro piattaforme per piano che hanno su ciascun lato un grande atrio. Il telaio di calcestruzzo a vista della struttura portante ha una massa termica tale da poter esercitare una significativa influenza sulla climatizzazione interna dell'edificio. Tre torri di scale collegate fra loro e il business center nell'atrio assolvono al ruolo di incoraggiare il contatto sociale e di migliorare le relazioni interne. Il livello della costruzione è stato rialzato, mentre è stato abbassato quello del terreno per ridurre l'impatto visivo e fisico del parcheggio e fornire più area al paesaggio circostante.

1

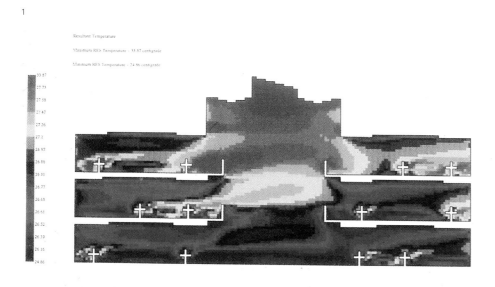

2

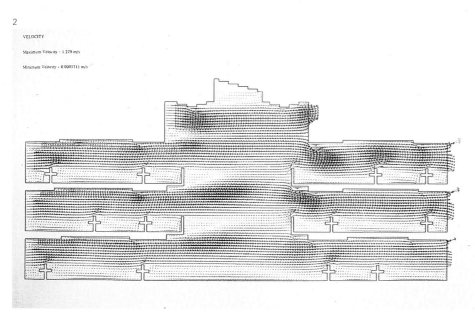

3

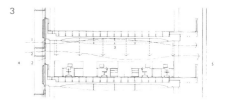

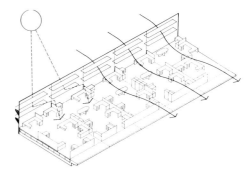

1 Computer model illustrating the radiant cooling effect of exposed concrete structure, without which the offices would be several degrees warmer.
2 Computer model showing the movement and velocity of air across the building.
3 The requirements of the client dictated an office width of 12 m. This allows a high degree of good natural daylight to penetrate and enables a natural ventilation system.

1 Computerdarstellung der Abstrahlung von Kühle durch die Sichtbetonwände. Ohne dies wären die Temperaturen in den Büros um einige Grad wärmer.
2 Computerdarstellung der Luftströme und Luftstromgeschwindigkeiten innerhalb des Gebäudes.
3 Der Bauherr wünschte eine Büroraumbreite von 12 m. Dadurch sind eine hohe Tageslichtausnutzung und natürliche Belüftung der Räume möglich.

1 Modello al computer che mostra l'effetto radiante refrigerante della struttura cementizia esposta, senza il quale gli uffici sarebbero più caldi di molti gradi.
2 Modello al computer che mostra il movimento e la velocità dell'aria attraverso l'edificio.
3 La richiesta del committente imponeva una profondità di ufficio di 12 m. Ciò permette che un alto grado di luce naturale penetri all'interno e rende possibile un sistema di ventilazione naturale

Commerzbank Headquarters, Frankfurt am Main

Hauptsitz der Commerzbank, Frankfurt a. M.
Sede centrale della Commerzbank, Francoforte

Architects: Sir Norman Foster and Partners, London
Planning and execution: 1992–

The new sixty-storey headquarters for Commerzbank in Frankfurt is the world's first ecological high-rise tower. The design transforms the fundamental nature of a large office building by developing new ideas for the ecology and working patterns of an office environment, including natural ventilation with opening windows. Generous winter gardens spiral up the tower to become the visual and social focus for four-storey clusters of offices. These gardens are linked to a central atrium, running the full height of the building, which acts as a natural ventilation chimney for the inward looking offices.

The plan of the tower is triangular in form, each side being gently curved to maximize space efficiency. Lifts, staircases and services are placed in the three corners. The lifting pattern is designed to reinforce the village-like clusters of offices and gardens. Pairs of vertical masts, enclosing the corner cores, support eight-storey vierendeel beams, which in turn support clear span office floors. Thus, not only are there no columns within the offices, but the vierendeels also enable the gardens to be totally free of structure.

Der sechzigstöckige Neubau für den Hauptsitz der Commerzbank in Frankfurt gilt als das erste »ökologische« Hochhaus der Welt. Der Grundcharakter eines Bürobaus wurde verändert, indem neue Ideen zu Ökologie und Arbeitsabläufen im Bereich des Büros entwickelt wurden, u. a. die einfache Lüftung durch Fenster, die man öffnen kann. Großzügige Wintergärten »klettern« in einer Spirale durch den Turm nach oben, als visueller und sozialer Treffpunkt für jeweils einen vierstöckigen Büroblock innerhalb des Hochhauses. Diese Wintergärten sind mit einem zentralen Atrium verbunden, das bis zum oberen Gebäudeabschluß reicht und als natürlicher Lüftungsschacht für die nach innen gerichteten Büros dient.

Der Grundriß des Turms ist dreieckig, jede Seite ist leicht gekrümmt, wodurch die Flächennutzung optimiert wird. Aufzüge, Treppen und Versorgungsleitungen sind in den drei Ecken untergebracht, und zwar so, daß die Erschließung die »dörfliche« Anordnung von Büros und Gärten betont. Vertikale Doppelmaststützen einschließlich der Kerne in den Ecken tragen acht geschoßhohe Vierendeel-Träger, die ihrerseits freie Spannweiten über den großen Büroflächen ermöglichen. Somit sind nicht nur die Büroräume stützenfrei, sondern die Vierendeels erlauben auch eine freitragende Konstruktion im Bereich der Gärten.

La nuova sede a sessanta piani per gli uffici della Commerzbank a Francoforte rappresenta la prima torre high-rise ecologica del mondo. Il progetto opera una vera e propria trasformazione della concezione canonica di un grande edificio per uffici attraverso l'applicazione di idee innovative sensibili al problema ecologico, che hanno conosciuto sviluppo anche nello studio di nuovi modelli di lavoro, per i quali è previsto che un ufficio si articoli includendo una ventilazione naturale con finestre apribili. Generosi winter-garten si sviluppano a spirale su per la torre per divenire il fulcro visuale e sociale del gruppo di uffici al quarto piano. Questi giardini, percorrendo l'intera altezza dell'edificio, sono collegati all'atrio centrale, che a sua volta si comporta come se fosse un camino di ventilazione degli uffici che si affacciano all'interno.

La pianta della torre è di forma triangolare con ciascun lato leggermente curvato per rendere massima l'efficienza spaziale e con i tre angoli occupati da ascensori, scale e servizi. Il sistema di sollevamento è in effetti progettato in maniera tale da rafforzare l'idea della forma di villaggio dei gruppi di uffici e di giardini. Un paio di pilastri verticali, compresi nella parte centrale degli angoli, sopportano per otto piani le travi Vierendeels, che allo stesso tempo sorreggono interamente la campata dei piani ufficio. Pertanto, non solo non ci sono pilastri negli uffici, ma grazie all'impiego delle Vierendeels, anche i giardini godono di una struttura completamente libera.

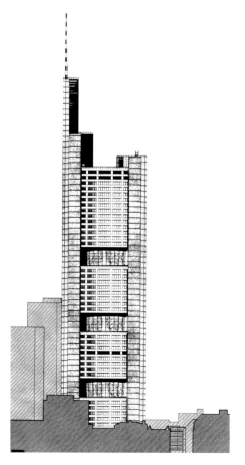

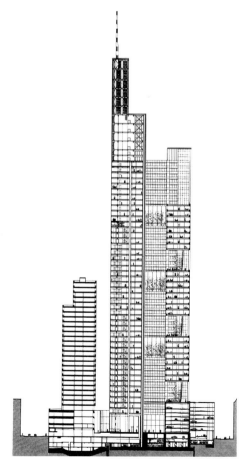

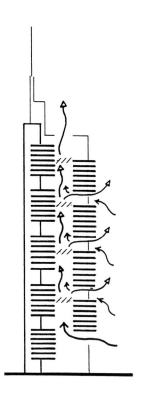

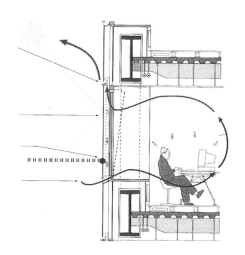

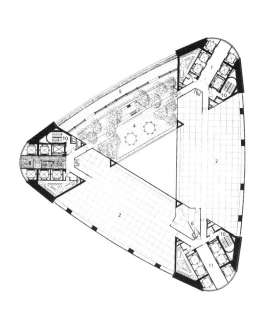

debis Headquarters, Potsdamer Platz, Berlin

debis-Hauptverwaltung, Potsdamer Platz, Berlin
Sede centrale della debis nella Potsdamer Platz, Berlino

Architects: Renzo Piano Building Workshop, Genoa/Paris
Planning and execution: 1992 –

Bernard Plattner (Associate Architect),
Christoph Kohlbecker, Drees & Sommer

Seventeen new buildings with a variety of uses, to be realized by the end of 1998, are the outcome of an international competition won by RPBW. The debis headquarters is merely one structure within the Daimler Benz project in Potsdamer Platz, Berlin. This urban space in the middle of the reunited city still bears the marks of two adjacent peripheral urban situations.

The debis development is intended as an example of entrepreneurial responsibility for the environment and the future. This 21-storey high-rise building will be ventilated largely by natural means through a transparent double-layer façade. It is based on development of functional systems and detailed investigations.

Auf der Grundlage eines internationalen Realisierungswettbewerbes (1. Preis RPBW) werden bis Ende 1998 insgesamt 17 neue Gebäude mit unterschiedlichen Nutzungen entstehen. Die debis-Hauptverwaltung ist ein Gebäude innerhalb des Daimler Benz, Potsdamer-Platz-Projektes in Berlin. Noch heute zeichnet sich der Potsdamer Platz inmitten der Gesamtstadt durch zwei angrenzende Stadtränder aus.

Die debis-Hauptverwaltung wird als Beispiel für unternehmerische Umwelt- und Zukunftsverantwortung stehen. Durch eine transparente Doppelfassade wird das einundzwanziggeschossige Hochhaus weitgehend natürlich be- und entlüftet, deren Entwicklung auf detaillierten Untersuchungen zur Funktionsweise basiert.

I nuovi diciassette edifici con differenti utilizzazioni che saranno realizzati a partire dalla fine del 1998 sono il risultato di un concorso internazionale vinto dal RPBW. La sede centrale della Daimler-Benz non è che una delle strutture del progetto di insediamento nella Potsdamer Platz a Berlino. Questo spazio urbano nel mezzo della città riunita porta ancora i segni delle due adiacenti situazioni periferiche.

Il complesso della debis è inteso come un esempio di responsabilità imprenditoriale per l'ambiente ed il futuro. L'edificio consta di ventuno piani e sarà condizionato principalmente con sistemi di ventilazione naturali ed un sistema trasparente a doppia facciata. Esso è basato sullo sviluppo dei sistemi di funzionamento e su una ricerca dettagliata.

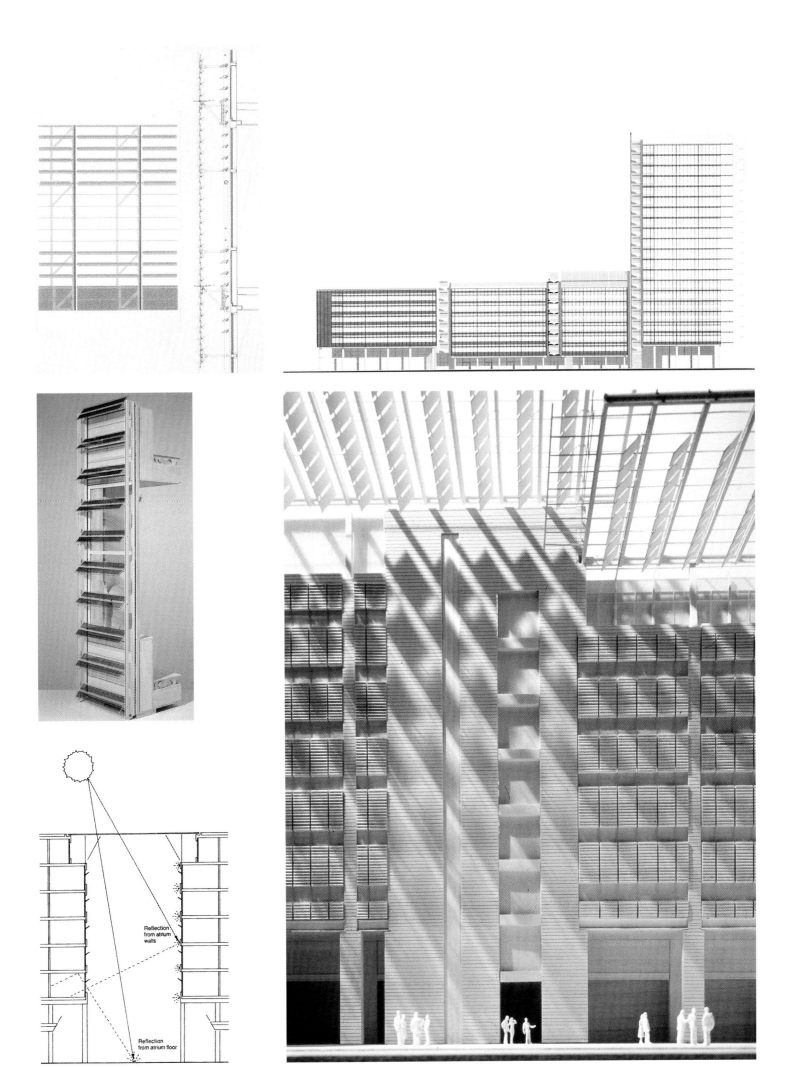

Reflection from atrium walls

Reflection from atrium floor

111

Offices and Housing, Potsdamer Platz, Berlin

Büro- und Wohngebäude am Potsdamer Platz, Berlin
Uffici e residenze nella Potsdamer Platz, Berlino

Architects: Richard Rogers Partnership, London
Planning and execution: 1992 –

Structural Engineers: Weiske & Partner GmbH/Ove Arup & Partners
Services Engineers: RP & K Sozietät/Schmidt Reuter
Quantity Surveyor: Davis Langdon & Everest
Landscape Architect: David Jarvis Associates

In 1993 debis-Immobilienmanagement appointed Richard Rogers Partnership to design the buildings B4, B6, B8 as part of the Potsdamer Platz project in Berlin.

The buildings have mixed use with retail, offices and housing. The gross floor area is approximately 18,000 m² per building.

A passive environmental approach was adopted which responded to climatic conditions and urban context. This involved opening up courtyards according to solar orientation, using building mass for night-time free cooling, passive use of solar energy and natural ventilation, as well as new buiding materials and intelligent controls.

With these principles the energy consumption can be optimized. The buildings are naturally ventilated and daylight levels are good.

1993 beauftragte debis-Immobilienmanagement Richard Rogers Partnership mit der Planung der Gebäude B4, B6, B8 im Rahmen des Potsdamer-Platz-Projekts in Berlin.

Die Gebäude haben eine Mischnutzung mit Einzelhandel, Büros und Wohnungen. Die BGF beträgt ca. 18 000 m² pro Gebäude.

Es wurde ein passiver, umweltbezogener Ansatz gewählt, indem die Planung den klimatischen Bedingungen und dem städtebaulichen Kontext angepaßt wurde. Dies betraf das Öffnen der Innenhöfe und die Orientierung zur Sonne hin, die Schaffung von thermischer Masse mit nächtlicher Auskühlung, die passive Nutzung von Solarenergie, eine natürliche Be- und Entlüftung wie auch neuartige Werkstoffe und intelligente Steuerungssysteme.

Durch Anwendung dieser Grundsätze kann der Verbrauch an Betriebsenergie optimiert werden. Die Gebäude sind natürlich belüftet, und der Einfall von ausreichendem Tageslicht wurde sichergestellt.

Nel 1993 la debis-Immobilienmanagement ha commissionato alla Richard Rogers Partnership il progetto degli edifici B4, B6, B8 nell'ambito dei progetti della Potsdamer Platz a Berlino.

Gli edifici hanno un uso misto per commercio al dettaglio, uffici e appartamenti.

E' stato adottato un approccio ambientale passivo che rispondesse alle condizioni climatiche ed al contesto urbano. La costruzione si è sviluppata aprendosi su corti interne in accordo con l'orientamento solare, usufruendo della massa edilizia per il raffreddamento notturno, e impiegando l'energia solare e la ventilazione naturale passivamente, oltre che nuovi materiali e sistemi di distribuzione intelligenti.

Attraverso questi principii il consumo di energia può essere ottimizzato. Gli edifici sono ventilati in maniera naturale e raggiungono un buon livello di illuminazione naturale.

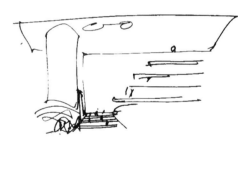

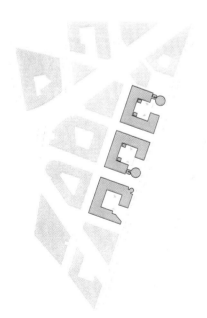

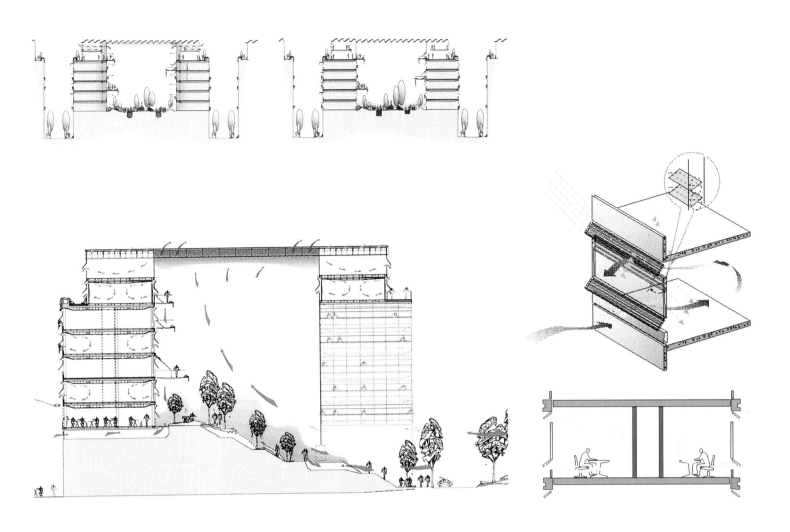

Ludwig Erhard Haus, Stock Exchange, Berlin

Ludwig Erhard Haus, Börsen- und Kommunikationszentrum, Berlin
Borsa Valori Ludwig Erhard Haus, Berlino

Architects: Nicholas Grimshaw and Partners, London
Competition: 1991; **execution:** 1994 –

The design objective for the Berlin Stock Exchange was to enclose a high quality environment. Natural air movement and daylight are maximized, and occupants can benefit from individual control. Two atria have been inserted between the office spaces and the exterior which act as thermal buffer zones to mitigate the effects of the harsh Berlin climate and reduce heating loads. The stack effect will be exploited to promote passive ventilation within the atria and the adjacent offices. Although comparisons are difficult, estimates for energy consumption for the Stock Exchange building are as low as 121 kWh/m^2 where a conventional air conditioned building's consumption would be expected to be in the order of 150 kWh/m^2.

Ein Ziel des Entwurfs für das Berliner Börsenzentrum war es, ein qualitativ hochwertiges Innenraummilieu zu schaffen. Frischluftzufuhr und -zirkulation sowie Tageslichtlenkung (die von den Nutzern selbst gesteuert werden können) wurden daher optimiert. Zwei Innenhöfe zwischen Büroflächen und Außenhaut fungieren als Wärmepuffer, die das rauhe Berliner Winterklima fernhalten und den Heizenergieverbrauch reduzieren sollen. Die Kaminsogwirkung produziert eine passive Belüftung der Atrien und der angrenzenden Büros. Obwohl Vergleiche schwierig sind, wird der niedrige Energiebedarf der Börse auf 121 kWh/m^2 geschätzt, wogegen konventionell klimatisierte Gebäude etwa 150 kWh/m^2 verbrauchen würden.

L'obiettivo del progetto per la Borsa Valori di Berlino è stato quello di ottenere all'interno un'alta qualità ambientale. I movimenti dell'aria e l'illuminazione naturale, che possono essere regolati dagli utenti stessi, sono stati ottimizzati. Due zone d'atrio sono state inserite quali zone di cuscinetto-termico tra l'esterno e gli spazi con destinazione ad ufficio, per mitigare gli effetti del rigido clima berlinese. L'effetto camino produrrà una ventilazione passiva tra i due atri e gli uffici adiacenti. Sebbene le comparazioni siano difficili, il basso fabbisogno energetico della Borsa Valori è stimato intorno a 121 kWh/mq, contro i circa 150 kWh/mq che verrebbero impiegati in un edificio climatizzato in maniera convenzionale.

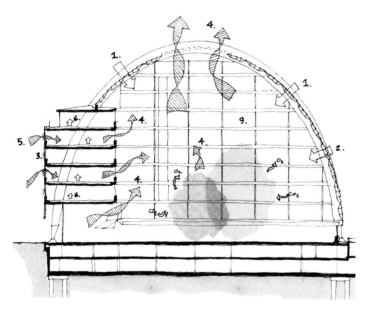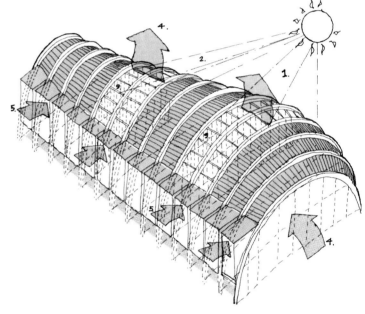

1 Atria encourage the penetration of natural light into the building.

2 High use of natural lighting reduces requirements for artificial lighting and hence mitigates associated cooling load demands.

3 Glass louvers provide external shading, preventing overheating in perimeter offices.

4 "Stack effect" exploited promoting passive ventilation within atria and adjacent offices.

5 Opening windows in perimeter offices supports natural ventilation.

6 Induction displacement ventilation units in conference rooms and Stock Exchange, installed beneath perimeter sills, provide ventilation and cooling in extreme summer conditions.

9 Atria behave as passive thermal buffer zones between office space and exterior in order to reduce heating loads.

1 Atrien fördern das Eindringen von Tageslicht in das Gebäude.

2 Hohe Tageslichtausnutzung reduziert den Einsatz von Kunstlicht und den damit verbundenen Klimatisierungsaufwand.

3 Glaslamellen sorgen für Beschattung und verhindern ein Überheizen der Anliegerbüros.

4 »Kaminsogwirkung« wird ausgenutzt zur passiven Lüftung der Atrien und der anliegenden Büros.

5 Öffnen der Bürofenster zur natürlichen Ventilation.

6 Induktions-Konvektions-Ventilatoreinheiten in Konferenzräumen und in der Börsenhalle unter den Fensterbänken sorgen für Belüftung und Klimatisierung bei hochsommerlichen Temperaturen.

9 Die Atrien fungieren als passive Wärmepuffer zwischen den Büros und dem Außenraum und reduzieren so die Heizlast.

1 L'atrio favorisce la penetrazione della luce naturale nell'edificio.

2 Alti gradi di luce naturale riducono il bisogno di luce artificiale e inoltre, associati alla refrigerazione, riducono i costi.

3 Lamelle vetrate provvedono all'ombreggiatura, prevenendo il surriscaldamento sul perimetro degli uffici.

4 «L'effetto camino» viene utilizzato per la ventilazione passiva dell'atrio e degli uffici adiacenti.

5 Le finestre che si aprono sul perimetro degli uffici favoriscono una ventilazione naturale.

6 Unità per l'induzione-convezione e ventilazione dell'aria nella sala conferenze e nella Borsa, poste al di sotto dei davanzali delle finestre, provvedono alla ventilazione e alla refrigerazione in condizioni estreme di temperatura estiva.

9 Gli atri fungono da zone di cuscinetto termico intermedie tra spazi-ufficio ed esterno, per ridurre l'onere del riscaldamento.

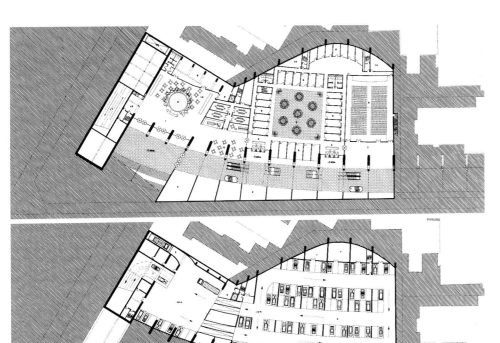

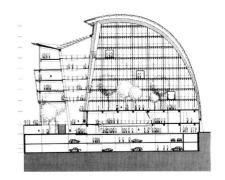

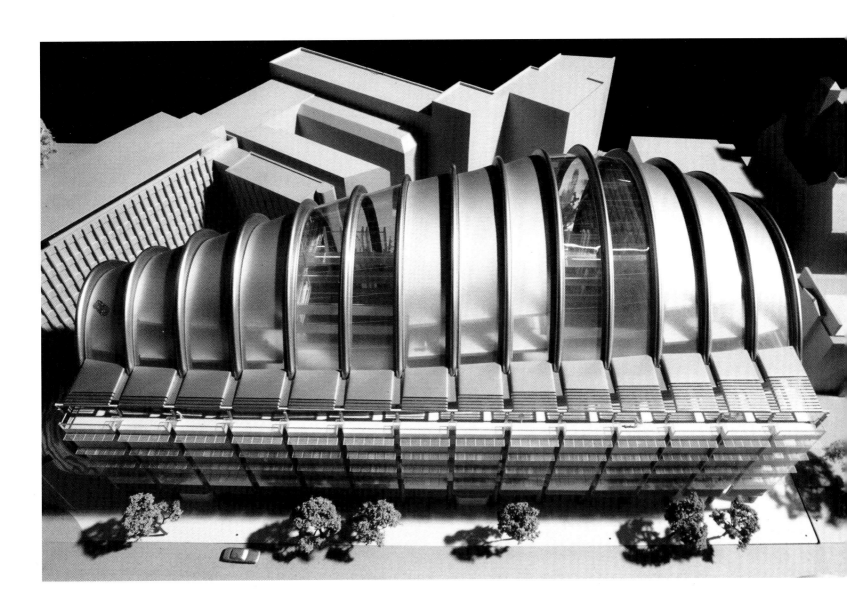

Bianchi Palace, Bioclimatic Restoration, Perugia (Italy)

Palazzo Bianchi, Bioklimatische Restaurierung, Perugia
Restauro bioclimatico di un palazzo monumentale, Perugia

Architects: Francesca Sartogo, Massimo Bastiani, Valerio Calderaro, Rome
Planning and execution: 1992 –1995

Bianchi Palace is a typical "casa corte" organized around a central atrium. The 18th century restoration of the building and its employment as municipal offices have altered its original characteristics. The project proposes to restore its original typological and bioclimatic structure. The atrium will be restructured in terms of its dimension, articulation and function, optimizing the thermal potentialities and the stack effect. A traditional "Impluvium" roof with photovoltaic panels and with a transparent "holographic optical" roof covering, capable of filtering and directing solar radiation into the "atrium," will be fitted, with the purpose of warming and creating better daylighting and energy use.

Der Palazzo Bianchi ist ein typisches Atriumhaus (casa a corte) mit dem Innenhof in der Mitte. Ein Umbau im 18. Jahrhundert und seine Funktion als Sitz städtischer Behörden haben den ursprünglichen Charakter des Gebäudes verändert. Das Projekt schlägt die Wiederherstellung der originalen typologischen und bioklimatischen Konstruktion vor: durch Wiederaufbau des Atriums in den alten Dimensionen, in der ursprünglichen Gliederung und Funktion; durch Optimierung seiner thermischen Möglichkeiten und des Kaminsogeffekts; durch ein traditionelles Dach mit einem Impluvium aus Photovoltaik-Feldern und transparenten holographisch-optischen Platten, die das Sonnenlicht filtern und in den Hof lenken, so daß er erwärmt wird und bessere Tageslichtbedingungen bietet.

Palazzo Bianchi è una tipica «casa a corte» organizzata intorno ad un atrio centrale. La ristrutturazione settecentesca e la funzione ad uffici comunali alterano le sue preesistenti caratteristiche. Il progetto propone il ripristino della struttura originale tipologica e bioclimatica attraverso: la ricostruzione dell'«atrio» nella sua dimensione, articolazione e ruolo; l'ottimizzazione delle potenzialità termiche e dell'effetto camino; l'integrazione sulla costruzione di un tetto tradizionale ad «Impluvium» di pannelli fotovoltaici e di una copertura trasparente a «lastra olografica ottica» capace di filtrare e canalizzare le radiazioni solari nell'«atrio» al fine di riscaldare e produrre migliore illuminazione naturale ed energia.

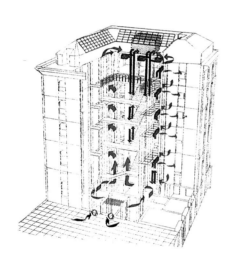

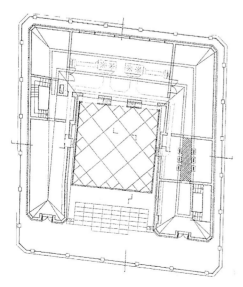

Centre for Renewable Energy Sources (C.R.E.S.), Athens

Zentrum für erneuerbare Energiequellen (C.R.E.S.), Athen
Centro per le Risorse di Energia Alternativa (C.R.E.S.), Atene

Architect: Nikos Fintikakis, Athens
Planning and execution: 1990–1997

Project Manager: Synthesis and Research Ltd;
G. Albanis, N. Fintikakis, M. Tzavelis
Civil Engineer: Structural Design SA
L. Logothetis, G. Parigoris
Mechanical Engineer: Talos Engineering SA;
N. Kouleimanis, A. Sgouropoulos

The "New Centre for Renewable Energy Sources", sponsored by C.R.E.S., is to be built in the historic surroundings of Poseidon's temple at Cape Sounion, close to the city of Athens. The intention of the Architectural design is to protect the environment, reflect it – a silver curve on the ground is a horizontal mirror of the dawn and sunset – and nullify any building volume (a non Building), which might violate the surrounding harmony. The Center is equipped with passive and hybrid solar systems, which both supplement the building energy requirements and provide adequate means for performing laboratory measurements and supporting pilot soft energy projects.

Der Neubau des C.R.E.S. wird in der Nähe von Athen in der geschichtsträchtigen Gegend um den Poseidon-Tempel am Kap Sunion entstehen. Bei diesem Bau wollte man die Umwelt schonen und sie zugleich reflektieren – ein gekrümmtes silbernes Gebilde am Boden, ein horizontaler Spiegel der Morgendämmerung und des Abendrots. Der Entwurf wollte sozusagen jegliches gebaute Werk annullieren, das die Harmonie der Umgebung stören könnte (ein »Nicht-Gebäude« schaffen). Das Zentrum verfügt über passive und hybride Solarenergieanlagen, die sowohl den Energiebedarf des Gebäudes decken helfen, als auch Strom für Labormessungen und Pilotprojekte sanfter Energietechnologie liefern.

Il «Nuovo Centro per le Risorse di Energia Alternativa», promosso dal C.R.E.S., è stato costruito nei dintorni dello storico Tempio di Poseidon a Capo Sounion, non lontano dalla città di Atene. L'intento della progettazione architettonica è stato quello di proteggere e addirittura riflettere l'ambiente (una curva argentea sul terreno, uno specchio orizzontale dell'alba e del tramonto), annullando la volumetria dell'edificio (un non-edificio), che avrebbe potuto violare l'armonia dell'intorno. Il centro è attrezzato sia con sistemi solari passivi sia con sistemi ibridi, che supportano insieme le esigenze energetiche dell'edificio, e mette a disposizione mezzi adeguati per il monitoraggio delle prove di laboratorio e per la sperimentazione di progetti pilota di soft-energy.

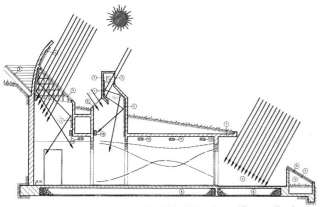

Summer – Natural lighting / Sommer – Natürliche Beleuchtung / Estate – Illuminazione naturale

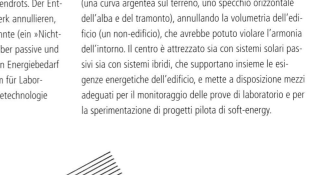

Winter – Natural lighting / Winter – Natürliche Beleuchtung / Inverno – Illuminazione naturale

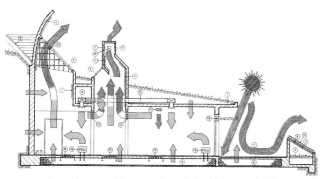

Summer – Thermal behaviour / Sommer – Thermisches Verhalten / Estate – Comportamento termico

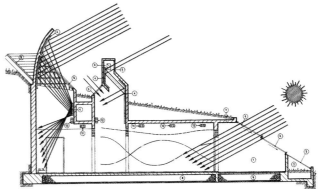

Winter – Thermal behaviour / Winter – Thermisches Verhalten / Inverno – Comportamento termico

1 Greenhouse for heating / Gewächshaus als Heizkammer / Serra per riscaldamento
2 Greenhouse for experiments / Gewächshaus für Experimente / Serra per esperimenti
3 Solar chimney / Solarkamin / Camino solare
4 Mirror (reflector) / Spiegel (Reflektor) / Specchio (riflettore)
5 Fixed glass surfaces / Fest montierte Glasscheiben / Superficie vetrata fissa
6 Sliding glass surfaces / Schiebe-Glasscheiben / Superficie vetrata scorrevole
7 Shading / Beschattung / Ombreggiatura
8 Gravel (thermal storage) / Kiesschicht (Wärmespeicher) / Ghiaia (accumulatore termico)
9 Solar water collector / Solarbeheizter Wasserspeicher / Collettore solare per l'acqua
10 Lights on at 100% capacity / Beleuchtungskörper mit 100% Lichtleistung / Luce al 100 % di capacità
11 Lights on at 50% capacity / Beleuchtungskörper mit 50% Lichtleistung / Luce al 50 % di capacità
12 Movable insulation panel / Verstellbare Isolierplatten / Pannelli isolanti removibili
13 Opening with damper / Öffnung mit Luftklappen / Aperture con valvola di tiraggio
14 Fresh air duct / Frischluftschacht / Condotto d'aria fresca
15 Floor heating / Fußbodenheizung / Pavimento riscaldato
16 Fan coil unit / Ventilatorgewinde / Unità fan coil
--- Natural lighting / Tageslichtbeleuchtung / Illuminazione naturale
---- Artificial lighting / Kunstlichtbeleuchtung / Illuminazione artificiale
-- Total lighting level / Kombinierte Gesamtbeleuchtung / Livello totale di illuminazione

Lloyd's Register of Shipping Headquarters, Hampshire (Great Britain)

Lloyd's Register of Shipping, Hauptverwaltung, Hampshire
Sede centrale della Lloyd's Register of Shipping, Hampshire

Architects: Richard Rogers Partnership, London
Planning and execution: 1992–1994

Structural Engineer: Anthony Hunt/YRME
Services Engineer: Ove Arup & Partners
Quantity Surveyor: AYH Partnership
Landscape Architect: Janet Jack

The offices are distributed in a series of six linked pavilions which circumscribe a country park. Because of the sensitive nature of the site the single-storey buildings are set into the contours of the gently sloping terrain, so as to reduce their visual impact. The stability of the ground temperature, together with a degree of earth sheltering, allow for a natural ventilation system.

Fresh air is taken in via the under floor plenum and circulates through the office space by natural displacement. This is aided by the positive pressure of the floor void and the negative pressure exerted by skylights and ventilation chimneys. The curved shape of the roof is designed to accelerate air movements creating aerodynamic suction which enhance stack effect.

Die Büros sind in sechs miteinander verbundenen Pavillons untergebracht, die im Halbkreis einen Landschaftspark einrahmen. Wegen des sensiblen Standorts im ländlichen Raum wurden die einstöckigen Bauten in die Konturen des sanft abfallenden Geländes eingefügt, um sie nicht zu sehr ins Auge springen zu lassen. Dadurch, daß die Häuser halb im Hang eingegraben sind und der Boden eine konstante Temperatur hat, wurde es möglich, ein natürliches Be- und Entlüftungssystem vorzusehen.

Frischluft wird den Büros über unter den Fußböden befindliche Luftkammern zugeführt. Sie zirkuliert durch natürliche Konvektion, zusätzlich gefördert durch den Überdruck des Hohlraumbodens und den Sog, der von Oberlichtern und Ventilationsschächten erzeugt wird. Die gewölbte Dachform soll Luftbewegungen beschleunigen und die Sogwirkung verstärken.

Gli uffici sono distribuiti in sei padiglioni collegati in serie che circoscrivono un parco regionale. A causa della delicata natura del sito, gli edifici a un solo piano sono posti sul margine del terreno leggermente in declivio, così da ridurre il loro impatto visuale. Un sistema naturale di ventilazione è reso possibile dalla stabilità della temperatura del terreno e dal fatto che gli edifici sono in parte interrati.

L'aria fresca è incanalata al piano interrato e circola attraverso lo spazio ufficio con un movimento naturale, favorito dalla pressione positiva del piano vuoto e da quella negativa esercitata dai lucernari e dai camini di ventilazione. Il profilo curvo del tetto è progettato per accelerare il movimento dell'aria e per valorizzare l'effetto camino.

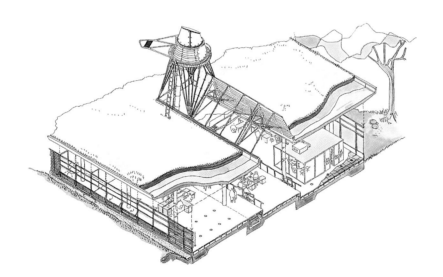

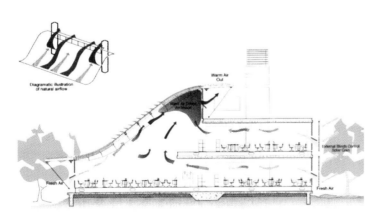

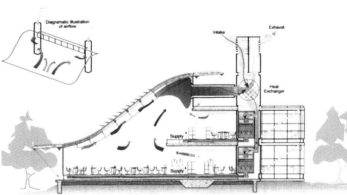

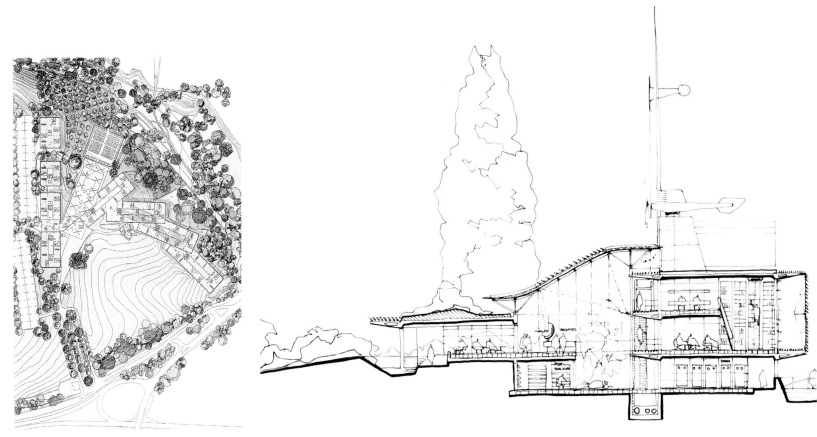

119

UNESCO Workshop, Vesima (Italy)

UNESCO Entwicklungszentrum, Vesima
Centro UNESCO per lo sviluppo, Vesima

Architects: Renzo Piano Building Workshop, Genoa/Paris
Planning and execution: 1989–1991

The UNESCO workshop sits on a steep hill near Genoa, over-looking the sea. It is like a penumbra barrier, lightweight wood and glass architecture that holds at bay the very thing that gives it life – the all-embracing sunlight that floods the scene. The workshop is defined architecturally by sunlight, but also uses sophisticated technology to mitigate its harmful effects. The roof is made of glass and is fitted with sensor-operated blinds that respond to variations in light intensity, with a calculated delay that makes the light creep slowly but perceptibly around the workshop. The curtains shielding the windows that fill in the sides of the buildings and the lower terrace facing the sea operate in the same way: the tiny movements they make as they slowly respond to the shifting sun indicate the pressure the outside exerts on the inside.

Das UNESCO Entwicklungszentrum liegt an einem Abhang zum Meer, in der Nähe von Genua. Das Labor ist wie eine Schattenbarriere, ein leichter Bau aus Holz und Glas der genau das in Schach hält, was ihm Lebendigkeit verleiht – das alles überströmende Sonnenlicht. Der Laborbau definiert sich architektonisch vom Sonnenlicht her, setzt aber auch raffinierte Technik ein, um dessen schädlichen Einfluß zu mildern. Das Dach besteht aus Glas und ist mit sensor-gesteuerten Jalousien ausgestattet, die auf unterschiedliche Lichtintensität reagieren und mittels kalkulierter Verzöge-rung das Licht langsam, in seinem Verlauf um das Gebäude herum spürbar machen. Die Lamellenvorhänge vor den Sei-tenfenstern und vor den Fenstern zur Seeterrasse funktio-nieren genauso: ihre langsame, kaum merkliche Bewegung, in Reaktion auf den wechselnden Sonnenlichteinfall, ist ein Indikator für den Druck, den die Außenbedingungen auf das Innere ausüben.
Die Bauform selbst erzeugt im Innern Luftströmungen, und die natürliche Be- und Entlüftung wird durch eine Kon-vektion von unten nach oben gefördert.

Il laboratorio per lo sviluppo UNESCO è situato in una zona collinare sul mare nei pressi di Genova. Il laboratorio è simile ad una barriera per la penombra, un'architettura leg-gera di legno e vetro in armonia con la baia, che ne viene ravvivata. La luce naturale abbraccia tutto ciò che riempie la scena. Il laboratorio architettonicamente definito dalla luce, fa anche uso di sofisticate tecnologie per mitigare i suoi effetti dannosi. Il tetto è realizzato in vetro ed è fornito di un sistema di oscuramento funzionante a sensore, che risponde alle variazioni di intensità della luce, con un ritardo calcolato che fa sì che essa penetri gradualmente ma in maniera per-cettibile nel laboratorio. Le tende che proteggono le finestre, che occupano le parti laterali dell'edificio e la terrazza più bassa che affaccia verso il mare, funzionano alla stessa maniera: il più piccolo movimento che esse compiono per rispondere lentamente al cambiamento del sole sta ad indi-care la pressione che l'esterno esercita sull'interno.

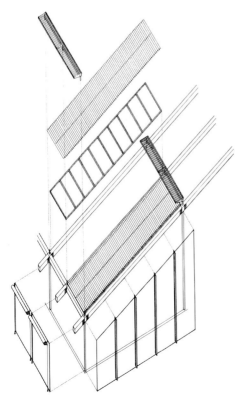

Double Façade for an Office and Housing Development, Munich

Doppelfassade an einem Büro- und Wohngebäude, München
Doppia facciata per un complesso di uffici e abitazioni, Monaco

Architects: Steidle + Partner, Munich
Planning and execution: 1994–1997

The façades of the housing and offices are structurally identical, designed as plain surfaces punctuated by simple openings with timber casements.

Here, where the curtain wall construction provides acoustic insulation, the inner wooden casements can be opened for natural ventilation. During periods when the volume of traffic is smaller, or in cases of emergency, individual windows in the outer skin can be opened, too. At the client's wish, the office spaces were also provided with air-conditioning and a soffit temperature control system.

The space between the external rendering and the steel and glass façade extends over four storeys. In winter, the glass flaps at the top can be closed by an electric motor activated by temperature sensors. The air-temperature gain in this cavity – caused by thermal emission from the building and solar radiation – results in a reduction of energy losses. The principle is similar to that of a box casement. In the event of fire, the top flaps, activated by a smoke-detector system, are automatically opened to prevent the transfer of fire from one floor to another as a result of the overheating of the cavity.

Die Fassaden von Wohn- und Bürogebäude sind strukturell gleich als Lochfassade mit Holzfenstern ausgeführt.

Das Bürogebäude liegt mit seiner Nordfassade an einer innerstädtischen Hauptverkehrsstraße. Die Straßenansichten des Bürogebäudes erhalten eine vorgehängte Stahl-Glas-Fassade.

Hier besteht trotz des starken Verkehrslärms die Möglichkeit einer natürlichen Belüftung: Beim Öffnen der inneren Holzfenster dient die vorgehängte Stahl-Glas-Fassade als Schallschutz. In Zeiten mit weniger Verkehr (oder zu Rettungszwecken) lassen sich individuell auch die Fensterflügel der Außenhaut öffnen. Auf Wunsch des Bauherrn wurden diese Büroräume zusätzlich mit einer Lüftungsanlage und Deckenkühlpaneelen ausgerüstet.

Der über vier Geschosse durchgehende Luftraum zwischen Putz- und Stahl-Glas-Fassade kann im Winter an oberster Stelle durch gläserne Klappen – elektromotorisch betätigt und von Temperaturfühlern gesteuert – verschlossen werden. Die Erwärmung des Luftzwischenraums durch Wärmeabstrahlung des Gebäudes und durch Sonneneinstrahlung, führt zur Reduzierung von Energieverlusten, ähnlich der Wirkungsweise eines Kastenfensters. Im Brandfall werden die oberen Klappen, über Rauchmelder ausgelöst, wieder geöffnet, um einen Brandüberschlag von Geschoß zu Geschoß durch Überhitzung des Luftzwischenraums zu verhindern.

Le facciate della costruzione sia per le residenze che per gli uffici sono uguali, progettate come facciate bucate con delle finestre di legno. La facciata dell'edificio ad uffici è collocata a Nord e dà su di una via trafficata del centro; essa è realizzata in acciaio e vetro ed è appesa dal lato della strada.

Qui vi è la possibilità di un'areazione naturale nonostante i forti rumori del traffico. Durante l'apertura delle finestre di legno la facciata in acciaio e vetro viene utilizzata come schermo acustico. Quando il volume di traffico diminuisce (oppure in caso di emergenza) si possono aprire anche le finestre individuali della pelle esterna.

Per volontà del cliente gli ambienti-ufficio sono stati anche provvisti di aria condizionata e di un sistema di controllo della temperatura a soffitto. Lo spazio tra l'intonaco esterno e la facciata in acciaio e vetro si estende per quattro piani, ed in inverno i flaps vetrati sulla sommità possono essere chiusi attraverso un motore elettrico attivato con sensori di temperatura. Il riscaldamento dell'aria ottenuto in questa cavità ventilata - causato dall'emissione termica dell'edificio e dall'irraggiamento solare - porta ad una riduzione delle perdite di energia. Il principio è simile a quello dei comparti-menti stagni. Durante un incendio, i flaps superiori, attivati da un sistema di rilevamento del fumo, si aprono automaticamente per prevenire la propagazione del fuoco da un piano ad un altro attraverso il surriscaldamento della cavità ventilata.

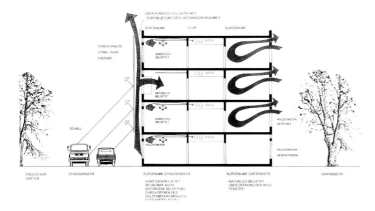

OBERER ABSCHLUSS GEÖFFNET
DURCHLÜFTUNG DES LUFTZWISCHENRAUMES

BÜRORAUME   FLUR   BÜRORAUME

VORGEHÄNGTE
STAHL-GLAS-
FASSADE

KÜNSTLICH
BELÜFTET

NATÜRLICH
BELÜFTET

KÜNSTLICH
BELÜFTET

SCHALL

HOLZFENSTER
GEÖFFNET

HOLZFENSTER
GESCHLOSSEN

ENGLISCHER
GARTEN   STRASSENSEITE   BÜRORAUME STRASSENSEITE   BÜRORAUME GARTENSEITE   GARTENSEITE

KÜNSTLICH BELÜFTET
BEI BEDARF AUCH
NATÜRLICHE BELÜFTUNG
DURCH ÖFFNEN DES
HOLZFENSTERS MÖGLICH

NATÜRLICH BELÜFTET
ÜBER ÖFFNUNG DER HOLZ
FENSTER

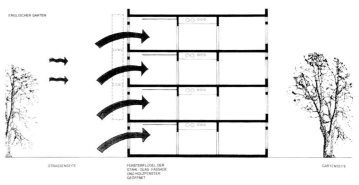

ENGLISCHER GARTEN

STRASSENSEITE   FENSTERFLÜGEL DER
STAHL-GLAS-FASSADE
UND HOLZFENSTER
GEÖFFNET   GARTENSEITE

3   SOMMER-NACHTAUSKÜHLUNG

 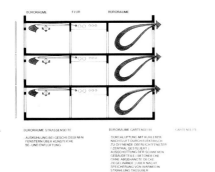

BÜRORAUME   FLUR   BÜRORAUME

STRASSENSEITE   BÜRORAUME STRASSENSEITE   BÜRORAUME GARTENSEITE   GARTENSEITE

AUSKÜHLUNG BEI GESCHLOSSENEN
FENSTERN ÜBER KÜNSTLICHE
BE- UND ENTLÜFTUNG

DURCHLÜFTUNG MIT KÜHLER
NACHTLUFT DURCH ELEKTRISCH
ZU ÖFFNENDE OBERLICHTFENSTER
ZENTRAL GESTEUERT
AUSSCHÜTTUNG DER SCHWEREN
GEBÄUDETEILE I BETONDECKE
OHNE ABGEHÄNGTE DECKE
ZIEGELWÄNDE I ÜBER NACHT
SPEICHERUNG VON WÄRME EIN
STRAHLUNG TAGSÜBER

4   WINTER-KLIMAPUFFER

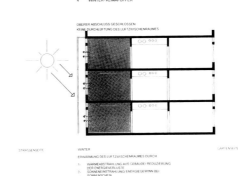

OBERER ABSCHLUSS GESCHLOSSEN
KEINE DURCHLÜFTUNG DES LUFTZWISCHENRAUMES

STRASSENSEITE   WINTER   GARTENSEITE

ERWÄRMUNG DES LUFTZWISCHENRAUMES DURCH

WÄRMEABSTRAHLUNG AUS GEBÄUDE I REDUZIERUNG
DER ENERGIEVERLUSTE
SONNENEINSTRAHLUNG I ENERGIEGEWINN BEI
SONNENSCHEIN

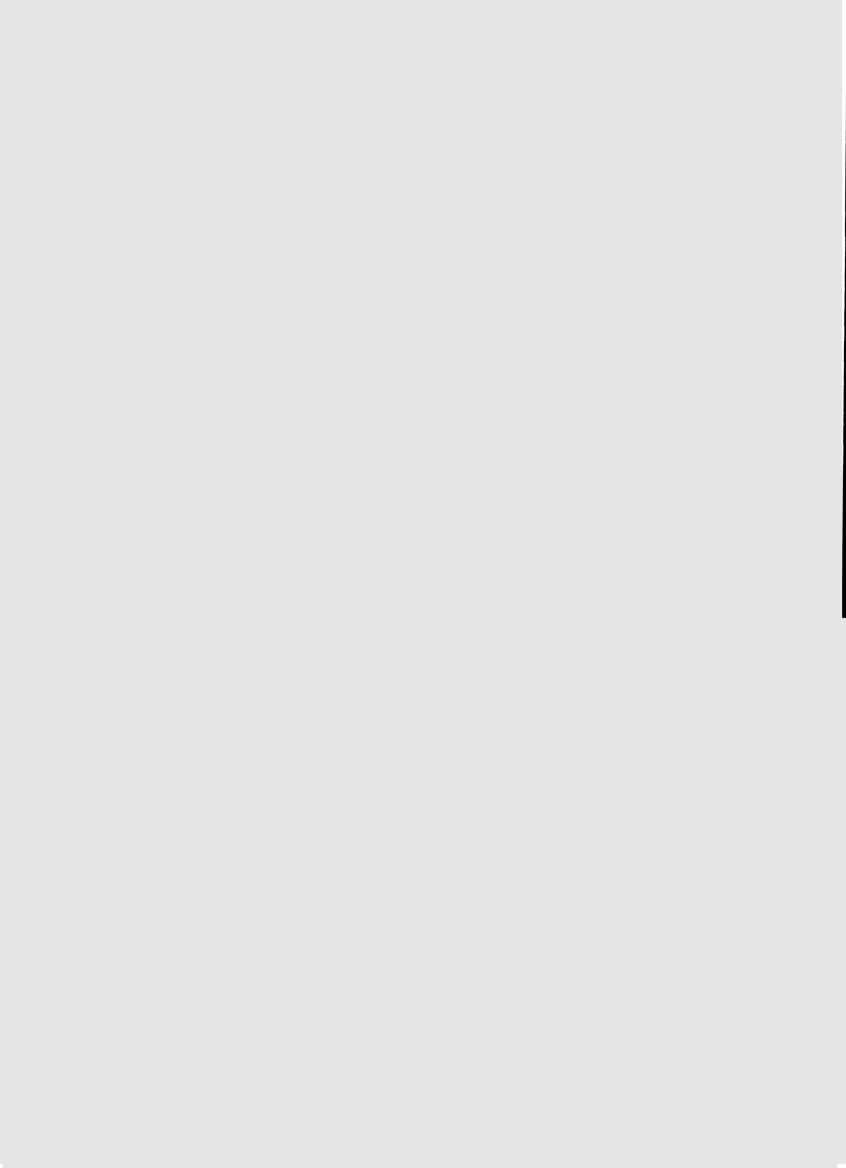

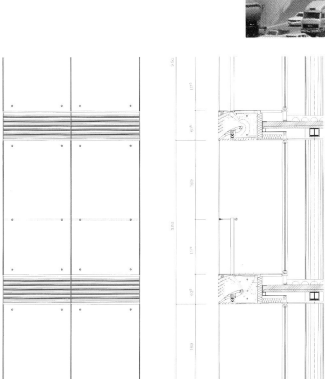

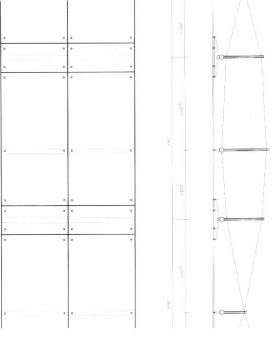

,
vorak,
ahinbas,
M. Slawik,

z m , questo alto blocco si eleva su
olo piano che permette una veduta
sul lago attraverso la sua facciata vetrata

ato di pelle esterna è una facciata ventilata,
nte svetrata, e ha un alto grado di traslucidità gra-
impiego dell' «Opti-white», un vetro super traspa-
te.

La pelle esterna consiste di un singolo strato di vetro di sicurezza rinforzato. Questo è separato dal vetro termico interno
a doppio spessore con dei «flaps» scorrevoli attraverso uno
spazio di 50 cm, che ospita anche la schermatura solare.
Aprendo gli elementi nella facciata ci si assicura che, fatta
eccezione per le condizioni atmosferiche con temperature
estreme oppure venti da bufera, gli ambienti possono essere
ventilati naturalmente.

E' stato possibile minimizzare la presenza di installazioni
tecniche attraverso l'impiego della capacità di accumulo
termico della struttura stessa e la forma naturale di ventilazione. Ottime condizioni climatiche per gli uffici sono
garantite dall'installazione addizionale di un impianto di
ventilazione con un piccolo scambio d'aria e sistemi di
refrigerazione a soffitto.

L'intero sistema di installazioni tecniche è alloggiato negli
elementi di soffitto. Al contempo le unità di soffitto forate
incrementano il potenziale di accumulo termico dell'edificio
e l'effettivo raffreddamento dei soffitti stessi.

stär-
werden

vierung der
ürliche Lüftung
chen Einbau einer
hsel und einer Kühl-
ng der Büroräume sicher-

en Deckenelementen der Büro-
, gleichzeitig wird durch die perfo-
Speicherfähigkeit des Gebäudes und
er Kühldecke genutzt.

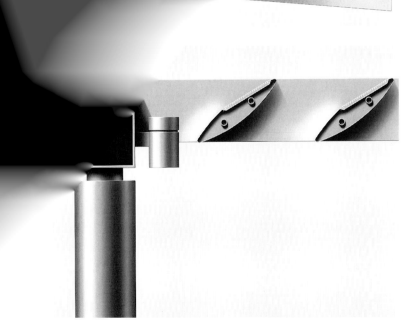

1   Multi-functional ceiling element to be
    integrated into performed concrete
    ceilings for example

    Multifunktionales Deckenelement zum
    Einbau z.B. in geformte Betonrohdecken

    Elemento di soffitto multifunzionale per
    installazioni, per esempio integrato in
    soffitti conformati in cemento

2   Photovoltaic slats

    Photovoltaik-Lamelle

    Lamelle fotovoltaiche

3   Façade detail showing sun protection,
    glass construction, optional blinds, air
    intake and extraction.

    Fassadendetail mit Sonnenschutz,
    Glasaufbau, Blendschutz (optional),
    Belüftung, Entlüftung

    Dettaglio di facciata con protezione dal
    sole, struttura vetrata, protezione anti-
    abbagliamento (optional), aerazione,
    estrazione dell'aria

3

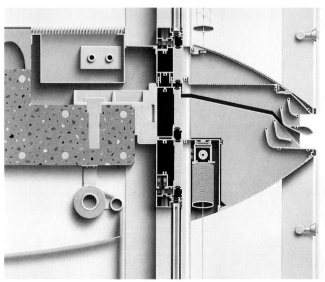

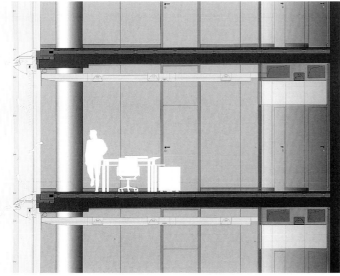

Parliament Buildings

Parlamentsgebäude
Edifici parlamentari

New Parliamentary Building, Westminster, London	GB	Michael Hopkins & Partners, London
New German Parliament, Reichstag, Berlin	D	Sir Norman Foster and Partners, London

Public Administration Buildings

Öffentliche Verwaltungsbauten
Edifici per l'amministrazione pubblica

German Foundation for the Environment, Osnabrück	D	Erich Schneider-Wessling, Cologne
Inland Revenue Centre, Nottingham	GB	Michael Hopkins & Partners, London
The Solar Wall, Toledo	E	Norbert Kaiser, Duisburg
Public Library, Pompeu Fabra, Mataró, Barcelona	E	Miquel Brullet i Tenas, Barcelona

New Parliamentary Building, Westminster, London

Neues Parlamentsgebäude, Westminster, London
Nuovo Parlamento, Westminster, Londra

Architects: Michael Hopkins & Partners, London
Planning and execution: 1992 –

Engineer: Ove Arup & Partners
Lighting Consultant: Bartenbach LichtLabor

The New Parliamentary Building is in a city centre location with the problems of noisy, polluted surrounding streets and security considerations. Because of this the design is based on a mechanically ventilated system. Air ducts are integrated into the external walls, increasing in width en route to the roof-based air plant and chimneys. These perform air exhaustion and intake. Energy is recovered through a thermal wheel at the interface between the two air paths. Air is introduced into rooms through a ventilated floor void, using a displacement principle. The upper surface of the vaulted precast concrete floor units provides thermal storage and the lower surface a ceiling finish that reflects natural light, in conjunction with light shelves above the windows. The solar contribution to heating is through gains recovered from the ventilated window blinds within a triple-glazed cavity, linked into the ventilation system. Cooling is carried out by ground water, so eliminating the need for CFC refrigerants. The energy target for this building is 90 kWh/m^2 per annum.

Das neue Parlamentsgebäude entsteht auf einem innerstädtischen Grundstück mit allen Problemen des Straßenlärms und der Luftverschmutzung in der unmittelbaren Umgebung sowie der Sicherheitserfordernisse. Aufgrund dieser Gegebenheiten setzt der Entwurf ein mechanisches Ventilationssystem ein. In den Außenmauern befinden sich Luftschächte, die sich nach oben zur Lüftungsanlage und den Kaminen auf dem Dach erweitern. Diese führen dem Gebäude Frischluft zu und saugen verbrauchte Luft ab. Energierückgewinnung erfolgt über ein Wärmerad an der Schnittstelle zwischen den zwei Luftwegen. Die Räume werden über Luftkammern in den Fußböden belüftet, und zwar nach dem Konvektionsprinzip. Die obere Schicht der vorgefertigten, gewölbten Betondeckenelemente sorgt für Wärmespeicherung, ihr Oberflächenfinish spiegelt Tageslicht, das von Lichtschaufeln an die Decken geworfen wird. Der Solarenergieanteil für die Beheizung des Gebäudes besteht aus Wärmegewinnen mittels der ventilierten Fensterjalousien in einem dreifach verglasten Hohlraum, der Teil des Belüftungssystem ist. Kühlung erfolgt über das Grundwasser, was den Verzicht auf FCKW-haltige Kühlaggregate ermöglicht. Der angestrebte Energiebedarf für das Gebäude ist 90 kWh/m^2 jährlich.

L'edificio del Nuovo Parlamento è collocato al centro della city, con grossi problemi di rumore, d'inquinamento, essendo interamente circondato da strade, e con l'esigenza di rispetto delle norme di sicurezza. Per queste ragioni il progetto si è basato su un sistema di ventilazione meccanica. I condotti d'aria sono perfettamente integrati con le pareti esterne, e si vanno ad incrementare in ampiezza durante il percorso verso la copertura, dalla quale fuoriescono camini di aerazione. Questi immettono nell'edificio aria pulita e ne espellono aria viziata. Viene recuperata energia attraverso una conversione di calore all'interfaccia tra i due percorsi dell'aria. Questa è introdotta negli ambienti attraverso un piano vuoto ventilato, che fa uso di un sistema di distribuzione principale. La superficie superiore, in unità di cemento prefabbricato voltato, provvede all'accumulo termico, mentre la superficie inferiore, un soffitto di finitura che riflette l'illuminazione naturale, opera come diffusore della luce sopra le finestre. Il contributo dell'energia solare al riscaldamento è aumentato grazie al quantitativo recuperato dai sistemi di oscuramento delle finestre ventilate che presentano una cavità con triplo vetro, in unione al sistema di ventilazione. La refrigerazione è ottenuta attraverso l'uso di acque freatiche, così da eliminare il bisogno dei refrigeranti CFC. Lo scopo è quello di ridurre il fabbisogno energetico annuo che per questo edificio è pari a 90 kWh/mq.

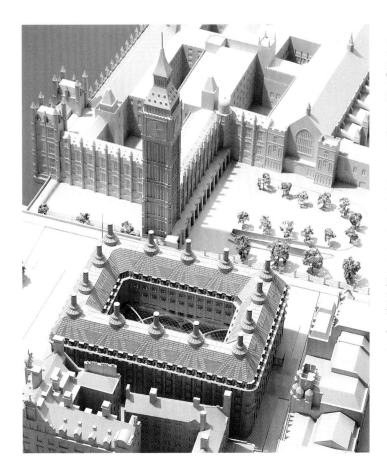

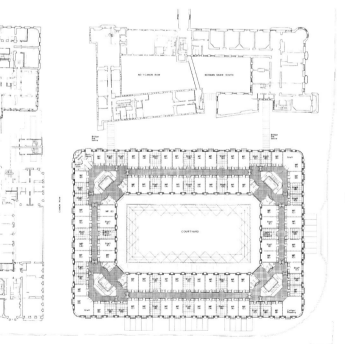

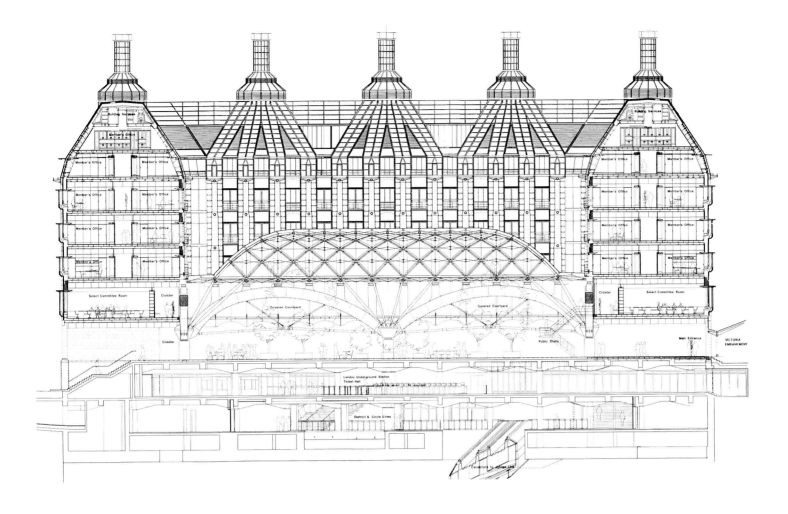

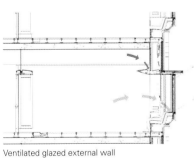

Ventilated glazed external wall

Belüftete Außenverglasung

Parete esterna vetrata ventilata

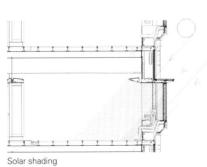

Solar shading

Sonnenschutz

Schermatura solare

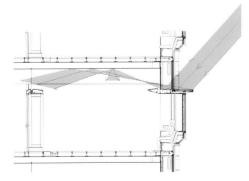

External wall daylighting performance

Tageslichtlenkung, Einfall über die Außenverglasung

Illuminazione naturale, incidenza sopra la parete esterna vetrata

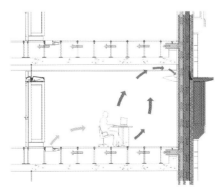

Ventilated floor voids

Lüftungskammern im Fußboden

Camere di ventilazione a pavimento

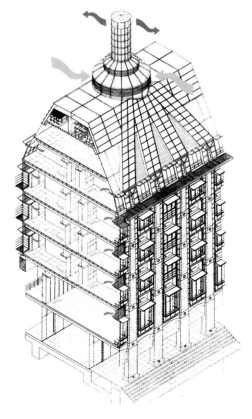

Offices serviced by rooftop ventilation plant

Büros werden von der Lüftungsanlage auf dem Dach mit Frischluft versorgt

La ventilazione degli uffici è controllata da un impianto posto sulla sommità del tetto

New German Parliament, Reichstag, Berlin

Reichstag, Berlin
Nuovo Parlamento Tedesco, Reichstag, Berlino

Architects: Sir Norman Foster and Partners, London
Planning and execution: 1993 –

The proposals are rooted in four major issues: the workings of Parliament, the history of the Reichstag, ecology/energy, and the economics of realizing the project.

The principal level will be recreated allowing the grand ceremonial entrance, now blocked up, to be re-opened as a democtratic main entrance for everyone.

It is essential that the processes of democracy be revealed and made accessible. The roof is designed to become a major public space, a symbol announcing the new unified Germany. The roof structure will deflect controlled daylight into the Plenary Chamber below and also scoop out air as part of the system for natural ventilation. The structure will also contain an array of photovoltaic cells as a part of the energy system and provide support for an elevated viewing deck with access by helical ramps. As well as having the best views, the public are symbolically above the politicians who are answerable to them.

Extensive use is made of natural ventilation and light, combined with sophisticated systems of cogeneration and heat recovery, demonstrating the potential for environmental systems which are pollution-free.

Die theoretische Basis des Projekts bilden vier Punkte: Arbeitsweise des Bundestags, Geschichte des Reichstagsgebäudes, Ökologie/Energie und die zur Realisierung des Projekts erforderlichen Mittel. Das Hauptgeschoß wird wiederhergestellt, so daß das große, zeremonielle Eingangsportal, das jetzt verschlossen ist, wieder geöffnet werden kann als ein auf demokratische Weise interpretierter Haupteingang für jedermann.

Es ist ganz wichtig, daß die Arbeit des demokratischen Staates offenliegt und zugänglich ist. Der Entwurf sieht vor, daß das Dach zum großen öffentlichen Platz wird, Symbol für das neue vereinigte Deutschland. Vom Dach wird mittels Deflektoren Tageslicht in den Plenarsaal gelenkt; als Teil des natürlichen Belüftungssystems wird über das Dach auch Abluft abgesogen. In die Dachkonstruktion werden außerdem Photovoltaik-Zellen integriert, die ihren Beitrag zur Stromversorgung des Baus leisten. Das Dach trägt eine erhöhte Aussichtsplattform, die man über spiralförmige Rampen erreicht. Besucher haben so nicht nur den besten Rundblick, sie stehen als Vertreter der Öffentlichkeit auch symbolisch über den Politikern, die ihnen Rechenschaft schuldig sind.

Weitgehend werden natürliche Ventilation und Tageslichtlenkung eingesetzt, verbunden mit hochentwickelten Anlagen zur Kraftwärmekopplung sowie Wärmerückgewinnung. Hierdurch wird demonstriert, was umweltfreundliche Systeme vermögen.

Le proposte progettuali si sono fondate sui quattro maggiori argomenti di discussione: i lavori del Parlamento, la storia del Reichstag, ecologia/energia e l'economia di realizzazione del progetto.

Il livello principale dell'edificio verrà ricreato seguendo la grande entrata cerimoniale, ora bloccata, per poi essere riaperta in qualità di ingresso democratico destinato a qualsiasi persona. E' infatti essenziale che il processo di democrazia sia manifesto e reso accessibile. La copertura è stata progettata in modo da divenire uno spazio pubblico di grande importanza, un simbolo che annunci la nuova Germania. La sua struttura defletterà, regolandola, la luce del giorno nella sottostante Camera Plenaria, ed ancora ricambierà l'aria in qualità di parte di un sistema di ventilazione naturale. Essa conterrà anche un apparato di celle fotovoltaiche, parte del sistema energetico, e provvederà a sostenere un ponte panoramico elevato a cui si accederà attraverso rampe elicoidali. Cosicché, godendo della vista migliore, le persone del pubblico siano simbolicamente presenti al di sopra dei politici che li rappresentano.

Viene fatto un grande impiego della ventilazione e dell'illuminazione naturale, combinate con sofisticati sistemi di cogenerazione e ricovero del calore, che dimostrano quanto ampio sia il potenziale dei sistemi ecologici noninquinamenti.

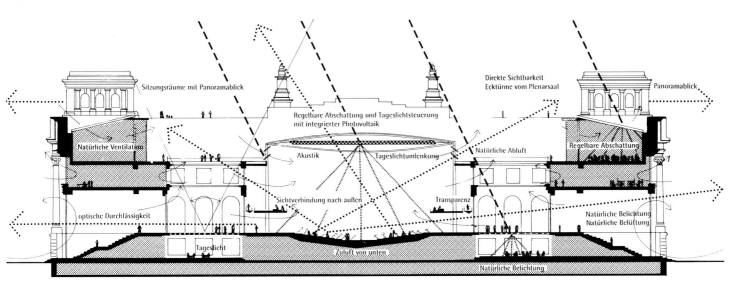

Sitzungsräume mit Panoramablick
Direkte Sichtbarkeit Ecktürme vom Plenarsaal
Panoramablick
Regelbare Abschattung und Tageslichtsteuerung mit integrierter Photovoltaik
Natürliche Ventilation
Akustik
Tageslichtumlenkung
Natürliche Abluft
Regelbare Abschattung
Sichtverbindung nach außen
Transparenz
Natürliche Belichtung
Natürliche Belüftung
optische Durchlässigkeit
Tageslicht
Zuluft von unten
Natürliche Belichtung

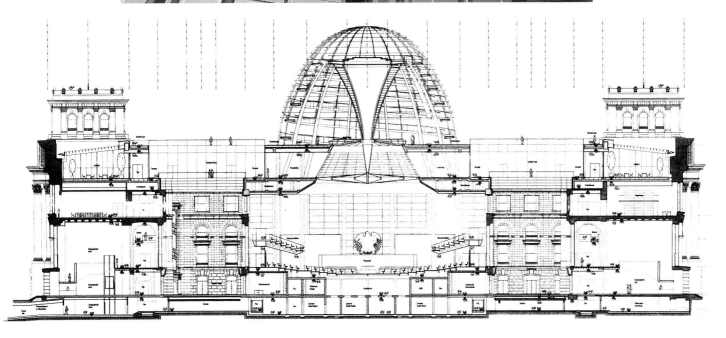

German Foundation for the Environment, Osnabrück

Deutsche Bundesstiftung Umwelt, Osnabrück
Seda della Fondazione Tedesca per l'Ambiente, Osnabrück

Architect: Erich Schneider-Wessling, Cologne
Planning and execution: 1991–1995

The distinctive form of the building is a response to the natural environment – a park-like site in an area of two- and three-storey villa developments. The glass structure echoes the outlines of the trees and encloses a magnificent 160-year-old group of beeches at the centre, transforming the external space into a secluded courtyard.

The façade is a fully-glazed timber and aluminium construction. Drawn over it is a light trellis-work for climbing plants, which guarantee a natural form of solar shading. In conjunction with glazed elements, a double-layer façade can be created with conservatory areas that function as buffer zones.

The radial layout results in a sequence of dynamically tapering and expanding internal spaces that are ideally suited for a mixture of uses. "Sun traps" above the centres of the circular sections allow light to penetrate deep into the building and illuminate it naturally. During the daytime, artificial lighting is not necessary.

Situated along the north of the development are the entrance hall, staircases and ancillary spaces. Short internal routes, which help to reduce the circulation areas to a minimum, create a quality of compactness and permit a high degree of flexibility.

Die besondere Form des Gebäudes ergibt sich unter Berücksichtigung der natürlichen Situation – eine Parklandschaft im Villenviertel mit zwei- bis dreigeschossiger Bebauung. Das gläserne Gebäude folgt den Baumkonturen, umschließt die imposante 160 Jahre alte Buchengruppe als Mittelpunkt und verwandelt so den Außenraum zum Innenhof.

Die Fassade, eine vollverglaste Holz-Alu-Konstruktion, wird von einem leichten Rankgerüst begleitet, das durch die Bepflanzung den natürlichen Sonnenschutz garantiert und, ergänzt um Glaselemente, die Pufferfunktion von Wintergärten übernehmen kann.

Durch die radiale Anordnung entwickeln sich im Innern die Räume zu dynamisch enger und weiter werdenden Folgen, die ideal für Kombizonen geeignet sind. »Sonnenfänger« über den Mittelpunkten der Ringe leiten das Licht tief ins Gebäude hinein und belichten es auf natürliche Weise. Auf Kunstlicht kann während des Tages verzichtet werden. An den Nordseiten liegen die Eingangshalle, die Treppenhäuser, und Nebenräume. Kurze Wege im Inneren verringern Verkehrsflächen, erzeugen Kompaktheit und lassen große Flexibilität zu.

La forma distintiva dell'edificio scaturisce dall'ambiente naturale - un luogo simile ad un parco in un'area con dei complessi di ville a due e tre piani. La struttura vetrata riecheggia il profilo degli alberi ed include al centro un vecchio gruppo di magnifici faggi di 160 anni, trasformando così lo spazio esterno in una corte isolata.

Il prospetto è una struttura in legno e alluminio totalmente vetrata. E' stato disegnato su questa un luminoso graticcio per le piante rampicanti, che garantiscono una forma naturale di schermatura solare. In aggiunta agli elementi vetrati, può venirsi a creare una doppia facciata con aree adibite a serra che funzionano come zone di cuscinetto.

Lo schema progettuale radiale è il risultato di una sequenza dinamica di spazi che si restringono e si dilatano, situati idealmente a formare una commistione di usi. «Trappole solari» al di sopra dei centri dei settori circolari permettono che la luce penetri profondamente nell'edificio e lo illumini naturalmente. Pertanto durante le ore diurne non occorre la luce artificiale. Situate lungo il lato Nord del complesso ci sono le hall di entrata, le scale principali ed i servizi. Brevi percorsi interni aiutano a ridurre al minimo le aree di circolazione, creando in questo modo una «condensazione» di qualità ed offrendo allo stesso tempo un alto grado di flessibilità.

Ground floor / Erdgeschoß / Piano terreno

1 Foyer / Foyer / Foyer
2 Cafeteria / Caféteria / Caffetteria
3 Kitchen / Küche / Cucina
4 Terrace / Terrasse / Terrazza
5 Meeting room / Besprechung / Sala riunioni
6 Conference room / Konferenzraum / Sala conferenze
7 Library / Bibliothek / Biblioteca
8 Connection to old villa / Verbindungsgang zur alten Villa / Collegamento alla vecchia villa
9 WC / WC / WC
10 Disabled WC / Behinderten-WC / WC handicappati
11 Store-room / Lagerräume / Magazzino
12 Refuse area / Müllraum / Deposito rifiuti
13 Service access / Eingang Anlieferung / Accesso di servizio
14 Workshop / Werkstatt / Officina
15 Office / Büro / Ufficio
16 Caretaker / Hausmeister / Portineria

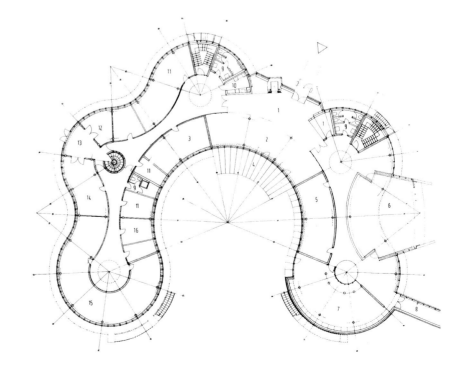

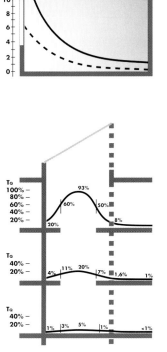

Inland Revenue Centre, Nottingham (Great Britain)

Inland Revenue Centre (Finanzamt für Staatsabgaben), Nottingham
Inland Revenue Centre (Sede dell'Ufficio Imposte), Nottingham

Architects: Michael Hopkins & Partners, London
Planning and execution: 1992–1995

Engineer: Ove Arup & Partners
Lighting Consultant: Bartenbach LichtLabor

The Inland Revenue Complex is a new office campus of courtyard and L-shaped buildings. Its many energy-saving features are based on the minimum application of mechanical air-conditioning systems. The design makes provision for increased use of daylight and effective solar screening by light shelves and independently-operated blinds. The building is mainly naturally ventilated through the perimeter walls. Stair towers act as stack-effect flues to assist in ventilation. The floors are exposed internally and provide thermal storage and a light-reflecting surface. The whole complex is heated by an existing district heating system fed from a refuse incineration plant. The overall energy target is 110 kWh/m^2 per annum.

Der Inland-Revenue-Komplex ist ein neues Verwaltungszentrum mit Hofhäusern und L-förmigen Bauten. Die Basis für seine zahlreichen energiesparenden Maßnahmen war die Verwendung von möglichst wenig mechanischen Klimaanlagen. Der Entwurf sieht eine vermehrte Tageslichtnutzung vor sowie effiziente Sonnenschutzelemente (Lichtschutz-Simse und unabhängig voneinander verstellbare Jalousien). Das Gebäude wird weitgehend über die Außenmauern natürlich belüftet. Treppenhäuser wirken als Luftschächte zur Förderung der Ventilation. Im Innern sind die Fußböden nicht verkleidet und sorgen so für Wärmespeicherung und dienen als lichtreflektierende Oberflächen. Der gesamte Gebäudekomplex wird über das örtliche Fernwärmenetz beheizt, das seine Heizleistung aus einer Müllverbrennungsanlage bezieht. Der angestrebte Gesamtenergieverbrauch beträgt 110 kWh/m^2.

Il complesso Inland Revenue è un nuovo grande centro per il terziario con edifici conformati a corte o a L. Le sue caratteristiche di risparmio energetico si basano sull'applicazione minima di sistemi meccanici per il condizionamento dell'aria. Il progetto adotta misure per incrementare l'uso della luce naturale così come di schermature solari attraverso cornicioni e persiane che si possono manovrare indipendentemente. La costruzione è in gran parte ventilata naturalmente attraverso i muri perimetrali. Le torri-scala agiscono come canne di ventilazione per produrre l'effetto-camino. All'interno i pavimenti non sono rivestiti, fornendo così una massa termica per immagazzinare calore ed una superficie riflettente. L'intero complesso è riscaldato attraverso un sistema zonale esistente alimentato da un impianto d'incenerimento di rifiuti. L'obiettivo finale è quello di avere un consumo annuo di energia pari a 110 kWh/mq.

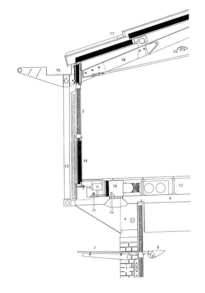

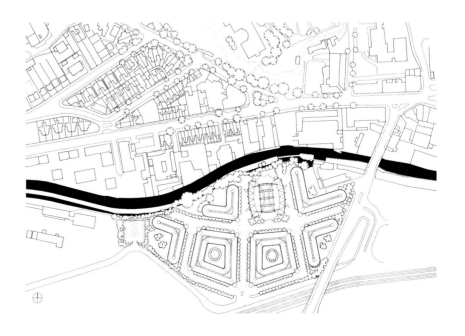

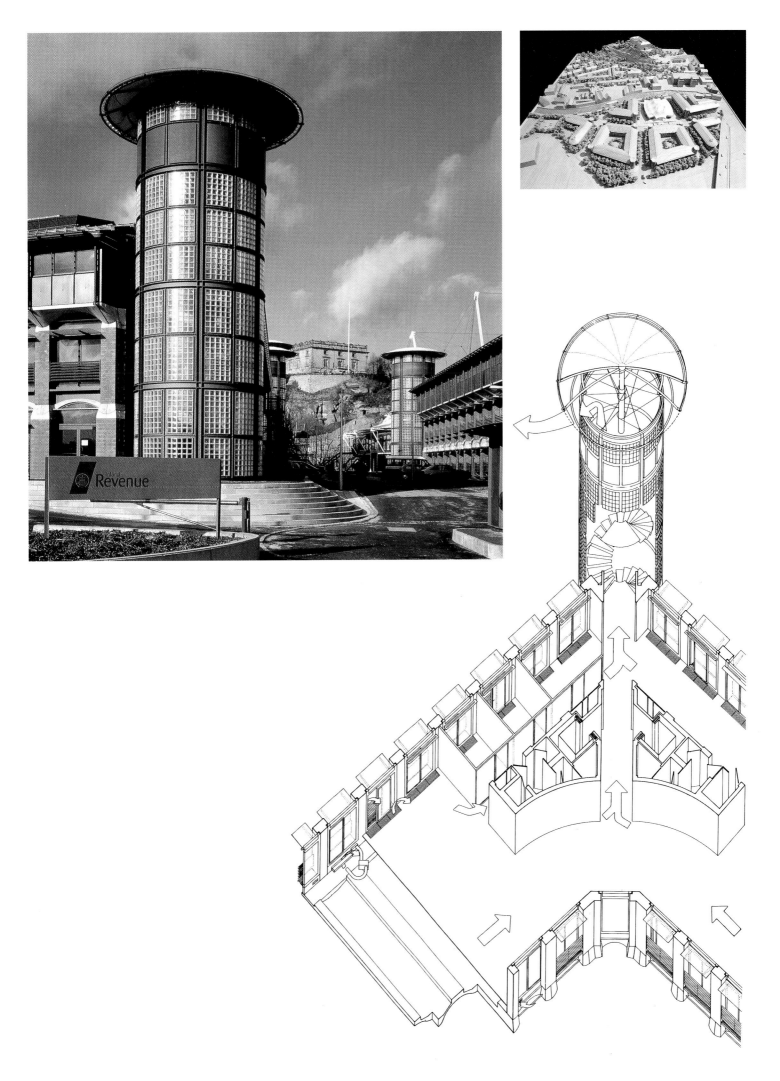

The Solar Wall, Toledo (Spain)

Die Solarwand, Toledo
La Parete Solare, Toledo

Design: Norbert Kaiser, Kaiser Bautechnik Ingenieurgesellschaft mbH, Duisburg
Planning and execution: 1993–1995

Collaborators: Jürgen Brehmer, Jan Wienold

Near Toledo in Spain a 1 MW peak PV Plant was erected by a consortium of leading European power utilities with the intention of balancing the summer water shortage and consequent electricity shortfall of the Castrejon hydro power plant.

Electricity and water are very precious in this area. Water used to produce electricity is in competition with agricultural needs. Therefore the seminar building had to demonstrate technical solar means for heating, cooling, ventilation, daylighting and water purification.

An existing massive concrete sculpture – the former aggregate assembly tower of a concrete plant – was selected to be the basic structure for the demonstration building. Besides the aesthetic challenge the massive structure provided an excellent thermal store. The shape, which formed a funnel towards the sun, was an ideal prerequisit for a collector. The Solar Wall integrates all systems for collection, production and conversion of electricity for water and space heating, as well as the sorption machine for dehumidification and adiabatic cooling, solar thermal water purification and photovoltaics. Cavities formed behind the collector systems contain a graduated thermal installation for the recirculation of solar heated air, thermally supported exhaust, as well as air supply which motivates ventilation. All technical functions (except storage) are integrated in this wall.

The design evolution using the sun and the Rio Tajo water as sole resources, revealed the sculpture from the sun's view as an Indalo – an old spanish neolitic totem, demonstrating mankind and nature with the most spectacular combination of light and water: a rainbow.

In der Nähe von Toledo entstand im Auftrag eines Konsortiums führender europäischer Stromerzeuger ein Solarkraftwerk mit einer Spitzenleistung von 1 MW peak. Ziel war der Ausgleich der sommerlichen Wasserknappheit und der daraus folgenden reduzierten Stromleistung des Castrejon-Wasserkraftwerks.

Strom und Wasser sind in dieser Gegend sehr kostbar. Der Wasserbedarf des Kraftwerks konkurrierte mit dem der Landwirtschaft. Daher sollte ein Seminargebäude die Möglichkeiten der Solarnutzung zur Erwärmung, Kühlung, Ventilation, Beleuchtung sowie Wasseraufbereitung demonstrieren.

Eine bestehende massive Betonskulptur – der Montageturm für Betonfertigteile des ehemaligen Betonwerks – wurde für das Modellbauwerk verwendet. Sie stellte nicht nur eine ästhetische Herausforderung dar, sondern bot auch eine ausgezeichnete Wärmespeichermasse. Die Form, wie ein Trichter zur Sonne ausgerichtet, bot ideale Voraussetzungen für die Installation eines Sonnenkollektors.

Die Solarwand integriert alle Kollektor-, Aufbereitungs- und Umwandlungssysteme für Warmwasser, zur Raumheizung sowie als Antrieb für ein Sorptionsgerät zum Kühlen, zur solarthermischen Wasseraufbereitung und Photovoltaik. Die sich konstruktiv ergebenden Kammern hinter den unterschiedlichen Kollektorsystemen sind graduiert wärmetechnisch ausgestattet für solare Umlufterwärmung, thermisch gestützte Entlüftung sowie Zuluft zu verwenden. Alle Gebäudefunktionen mit Ausnahme der Speicher sind in dieser Wand integriert. Sonneneinstrahlung und das Wasser des Rio Tajo sind die einzigen Energiequellen und zeigen den Bau vom Stand der Sonne aus als »Indalo« – ein neolithisches spanisches Totem, das Mensch und Natur in der faszinierendsten Kombination von Wasser und Licht darstellt: im Regenbogen

Nei pressi di Toledo un impianto fotovoltaico con un picco di 1 MW è stato costruito da un consorzio di enti europei erogatori di energia che rivolgono particolare attenzione a bilanciare la carenza di acqua estiva e di conseguenza l'inadeguata elettricità prodotta dall'impianto idroelettrico Castejon.

Elettricità ed acqua sono molto preziose in quest'area. L'acqua usata per produrre elettricità è in competizione con le esigenze agricole. Perciò l'edificio sperimentale dovrebbe dimostrare la possibilità di impiego di energia solare per riscaldamento, refrigerazione, ventilazione così come la depurazione delle acque.

Una scultura massiva di cemento già esistente – la torre di una precedente produzione a catena di montaggio di un impianto in calcestruzzo – fu selezionata per essere la struttura di base per l'edificio dimostrativo. Accanto alla sfida estetica, la struttura massiva provvedeva ad un eccellente accumulo termico.

La conformazione ad imbuto rivolto verso il sole costituiva un prerequisito ideale per un collettore.

La parete solare integra tutti i sistemi di collettori, di trattamento e trasformazione di acqua calda per il riscaldamento degli ambienti oltre ad un sistema per azionare un apparato di assorbimento per il raffreddamento, per il trattamento termico solare delle acque e per il fotovoltaico. Le cavità dietro i differenti sistemi di collettori sono termicamente graduate ed equipaggiate per un ricircolo di aria riscaldata attraverso il sole, basato sull'aerazione termica oltre che su aria supplementare da utilizzare. Tutte le funzioni costruttive ad eccezione dell'accumulo sono integrate nella parete. L'irraggiamento solare e l'acqua del Rio Tajo quali uniche fonti di energia, rivelano la struttura dal punto di vista solare come un Indalo – un antico Totem spagnolo neolitico, che stava a dimostrare umanità e spirito di natura con la più spettacolare combinazione di acqua e luce: l'arcobaleno.

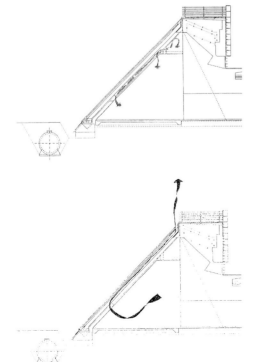

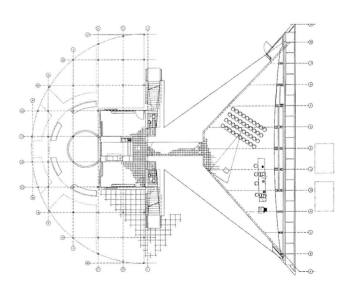

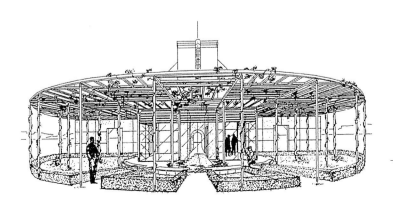

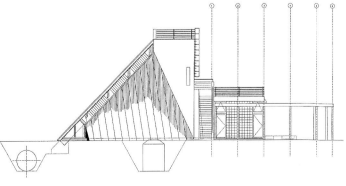

Public Library, Pompeu Fabra, Mataró, Barcelona

Öffentliche Bibliothek Pompeu Fabra, Mataró, Barcelona
Biblioteca pubblica Pompeu Fabra, Mataró, Barcellona

Architects: Miquel Brullet i Tenas, Barcelona
Planning and execution: 1993–1995

Leader Company: TFM SA, Oscar Aceves,
Main Partners: Genec (Cen de Cadarache),
Michael Chantant; ZSW, Ursula Eicker;
Universitat de Barcelona, Jordi Andreu

The name of the Library, Pompeu Fabra, derives from the philologist who normalized the Catalan language. It is a 1600 m² building standing in a public square, the Plaça d'Occitània, Mataró.

The building is rectangular in form and oriented so that the main façade faces south. The accommodation, including reading rooms, conference facilities and service rooms is on two levels with a basement.

The goal of the project was to create the optimum equilibrium between the integrated solar energy system, energy savings, achieving a comfortable internal climate lighting level, and the aesthetic and economic requirements.

The main energy source is the photovoltaic system which has been installed on the south façade and the roof by means of four tilted parapets.

Die Bibliothek wurde nach dem Philologen Fabra benannt, der die katalanische Sprache vereinheitlichte. Das Gebäude mit einer Grundfläche von 1600 m² steht auf der Plaça d'Occitania in Mataró. Es ist ein Parallelepiped, dessen Hauptfassade nach Süden orientiert ist. Das Bauwerk ist unterkellert, und auf zwei Geschossen befinden sich alle Räume, einschließlich Lesesäle, Konferenzzimmer und Technikräume. Ziel des Entwurfs war die Schaffung eines bestmöglichen Gleichgewichts zwischen integrierter Solarstromversorgung, Energie-Einsparungen, angenehm temperiertem Innenklima, guter Innenbeleuchtung sowie ästhetischen und wirtschaftlichen Ansprüchen. Haupt-Energiequelle ist das Photovoltaik-System auf vier geneigten »Brüstungen«, die an der Südfassade und auf dem Dach installiert wurden

Il nome Pompeu Fabra deriva alla biblioteca dal filologo che ha codificato il linguaggio catalano. L'edificio di 1600 mq di superficie si erge su uno spazio pubblico, la Placa d'Occitania, a Mataró, conformato rettangolarmente e orientato in modo da avere il prospetto principale esposto a Sud. In esso trovano posto sale di lettura, spazi per conferenze e stanze di servizio all'interno di due piani con un basamento.

Lo scopo del progetto era quello di ottenere un equilibrio ottimale tra un sistema integrato ad energia solare e l'obiettivo del risparmio energetico, soddisfacendo allo stesso tempo le richieste di un clima interno piacevole, di una buona illuminazione, ed esigenze di natura estetica ed economica. La maggiore fonte di energia è rappresentata dal sistema fotovoltaico installato sulla facciata meridionale e sul tetto attraverso l'impiego di quattro parapetti inclinati.

The PV façade and skylights will produce approximately 75 Mw/h per year, more energy than is needed for the estimated consumption of the library. Thermal needs of the building will be reduced by about 30 % thanks to use of the warm air produced by the PV.

Die Photovoltaik-Installation an Fassade und Oberlichtern produziert ca. 75 MW/h pro Jahr, mehr Strom, als für den geschätzten Verbrauch im Bibliotheksgebäude. Der Bedarf des Gebäudes an Heizenergie wird unter Verwendung der durch die PV erwärmten Luft um 30 % reduziert.

L'installazione in facciata ed i lucernari originano circa 75 MW/h all'anno, ed inoltre la corrente elettrica che è utilizzata per il fabbisogno stimato per la biblioteca. La richiesta di energia termica dell'edificio viene ridotta di circa il 30 % grazie all'uso di aria calda prodotta attraverso il PV.

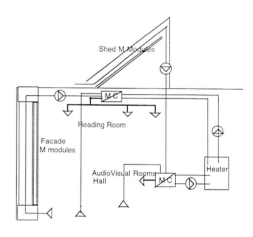

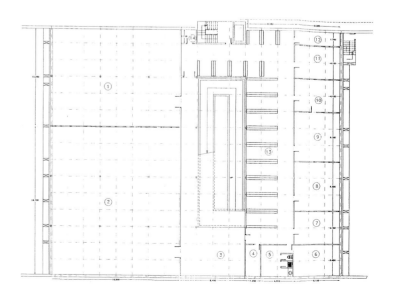

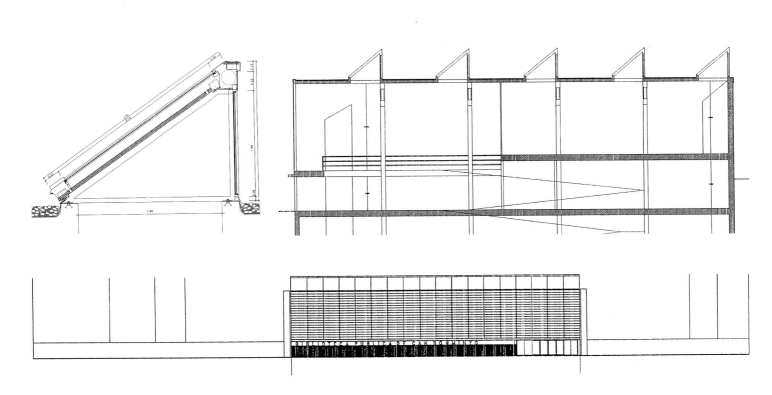

Cultural Buildings

Kulturbauten
Edifici culturali

Congress and Exhibition Hall, Linz	A	Herzog + Partner, Thomas Herzog, Hanns Jörg Schrade, Munich
Cultural Centre, Remchingen	D	Helmut Striffler, Mannheim
Cardiff Bay Opera House, Wales	GB	Manfredi Nicoletti, Rome
Museum of Natural History, Florence	I	Design team at the University of Florence
Exhibition Pavilion, Stuttgart	D	Jockers + Partner, Stuttgart
New Acropolis Museum, Athens	GR	Manfredi Nicoletti, Lucio Passarelli, Rome
Shelter for Archaeological Site, Santorini	GR	Nikos Fintikakis, Athens
Restoration of Historic Baths, Rhodes	GR	A. Paraskevopoulou, N. Zarifis, A. Angelopoulos, Rhodes
Youth Forum (JUFO), Möglingen	D	plus+, Peter Hübner, Neckartenzlingen
Buddhist Retreat Centre, Holy Island, Scotland	GB	Andrew Wright and Consultants, London
Jean-Marie Tjibaou Cultural Centre, Nouméa	F	Renzo Piano Building Workshop, Genoa/Paris

Congress and Exhibition Hall, Linz (Austria)

Ausstellungs- und Kongreßgebäude, Linz
Centro per esposizioni e congressi, Linz

Architects: Herzog + Partner, Thomas Herzog with Hanns Jörg Schrade, Munich
Planning and execution: 1986–1994

Project Supervisor: Heinz Stögmüller, Architect
Collaborators: R. Schneider, A. Schankula, K. Beslmüller
Structural Engineer: Sailer + Stepan with Kirsch-Muchitsch
Mechanical Engineer: M. Bloos with Greif
Consultants: V. Herzog-Loibl (Interior), A. Latz (Landscape), LichtLabor Bartenbach (daylighting), ISE of FHG (solartechnical measurements)

To ensure a maximum degree of internal flexibility, all congress and exhibition spaces are laid out under the single roof of a large hall structure 204 x 80 m in extent. The structure represents a reinterpretation of the "crystal palace" theme.

One of the primary considerations was to provide an outdoor quality of daylight for the interior of the building.
A new system was developed, consisting of extremely thin louvre grids between the panes of the double glazing. The louvres reflect solar radiation and allow only diffused light to enter the building, thus preventing overheating in summer as well as glare caused by direct sunlight. These additional daylight and temperature control systems influence the outer skin of the building in its technical functioning, its construction and aesthetic effect.

Fresh air is supplied via inlets in the floor of the hall and window strips which occur at the point where the plane of the roof changes. Along the crown of the roof are continuous openings with louvres to regulate the extraction of air in summer. The form of the large "spoiler" or capping piece over this opening reinforces the suction effect along the entire length of the building.

Zum Zweck maximaler innerer Flexibilität sind alle Kongreß- und Ausstellungsräume unter dem Dach einer großen Halle von 204 x 80 m angeordnet. Dabei wird das Thema »Glaspalast« neu interpretiert.
Im Vordergrund stand das Bemühen, Tageslichtqualitäten, wie sie unter freiem Himmel vorherrschen, durch eine vollflächige Verglasung im Gebäudeinnern verfügbar zu machen.
Ein neuartiges System aus hauchdünnen Lamellenrastern zwischen den Gläsern der Isolierscheiben reflektiert die direkte solare Srahlung von Süden, läßt nur Streulicht von Norden passieren und verhindert so die Überhitzung im Sommer sowie die Blendung. Durch diese zusätzliche Lenkfunktion von Tageslicht und Temperatur verändert sich die Gebäudehülle sowohl in ihrer technischen Funktionalität und ihrem Aufbau als auch in ihrer ästhetischen Wirkung.
Die Zuluft tritt über Quelluftauslässe im Boden der Halle und über seitliche Fensterbänder am Höhenversatz des Daches ein. Am Firstpunkt befinden sich durchlaufende, mit Lamellen regulierbare Öffnungen für die Fortluft im Sommer. Ein großer Flügel darüber begünstigt durch seine Querschnittsform die Sogwirkung zum Zweck der Entlüftung auf die ganze Länge des Gebäudes.

Al fine di assicurare il massimo grado di flessibilità interna, tutti gli spazi di congresso e di esposizione si dispiegano al di sotto della singola copertura di una grande struttura a hall che si estende per 204 x 80 m. La struttura rappresenta una reinterpretazione del tema del «Crystall Palace».
Una tra le considerazioni primarie era garantire una qualità della luce naturale per gli spazi interni dell'edificio. E' stato pertanto sviluppato un nuovo sistema sottilissimo di retini di lamelle tra gli strati isolanti dei vetri, che riflettono l'irraggiamento solare diretto proveniente da Sud, lasciando passare solo la luce diffusa da Nord, prevenendo così il surriscaldamento estivo oltre che l'abbagliamento. Questa luce diurna addizionale e i sistemi di controllo della temperatura influenzano la pelle esterna dell'edificio nella sua funzione tecnica, nella sua costruzione e nell'effetto estetico.
L'aria fresca è rifornita tramite piccole prese d'aria nel pavimento della hall e le finestre a nastro collocate nel punto in cui cambia il piano del tetto. Sul punto di colmo della copertura ci sono aperture continue con lamelle regolabili per l'estrazione dell'aria durante l'estate.
Un alettone sulla sommità agevola attraverso la sua forma trasversale l'effetto risucchio per l'intera lunghezza dell'edificio.

Cross-section with daylight factor curve (DF)
Querschnitt mit Kurven des Tageslicht-Quotienten (DF)
Sezione trasversale con la curva del fattore luce naturale (DF)

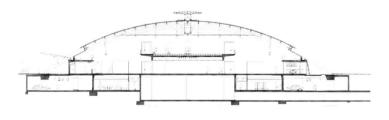

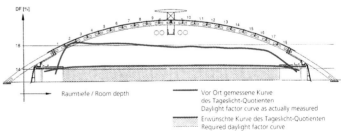

Vor Ort gemessene Kurve des Tageslicht-Quotienten
Daylight factor curve as actually measured
Erwünschte Kurve des Tageslicht-Quotienten
Required daylight factor curve

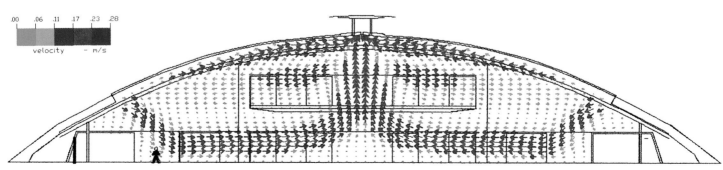

Air speed vectors in cross-section through exhibition hall

Vektordarstellung der Durchströmungsrichtung und -geschwindigkeit im Hallenquerschnitt

Vettori velocità dell'aria nella sezione trasversale attraverso la sala esposizioni

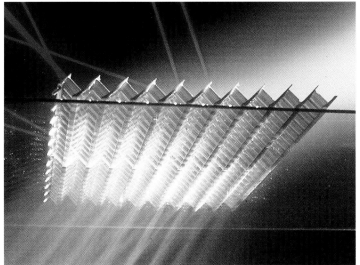

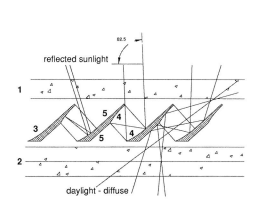

reflected sunlight

82.5

1

3

5 4

5 4

2

daylight - diffuse

Cultural Centre, Remchingen (Germany)

Kulturhalle Remchingen
Centro culturale, Remchingen

Architect: Helmut Striffler, Mannheim
Planning and execution: 1987–1990

Lighting Consultant: Bartenbach LichtLabor

The conception of the building was the result of a competition. The aim was to create a space for cultural events which would be artificially lit in the evenings and naturally lit during the day. Because of its location near a noisy main street and the demand to open the entrance hall towards the landscape there was no choice but to get daylight from the roof. In order to create the impression of a uniform level of cheerful light in the hall, the daylight-guiding and daylight-distribution were carefully planned and executed together with Christian Bartenbach.

As a result the hall has very good adaptability. This is an advantage for the manifold uses to which it can be put as well as for energy saving.

Important experience for planning of such spaces was gained: the results of measurements taken with the model and the results of measurements during the construction of the building were comparable and proved transferable.

Es handelt sich bei diesem Entwurf um ein Wettbewerbsprojekt. Es sollte ein Raum für kulturelle Veranstaltungen geschaffen werden, der nachts künstlich und am Tage natürlich belichtet werden kann. Aufgrund seiner Lage an einer stark befahrenen, lauten Hauptstraße, und der Anforderung, die Eingangshalle zur Landschaft hin zu öffnen, gab es keine andere Wahl, als den Tageslichteinfall vom Dach her zu konzipieren. Um eine gleichmäßige, freundliche Beleuchtung zu erzielen, wurde in Zusammenarbeit mit Christian Bartenbach ein sorgfältig durchdachtes System für Tageslichtlenkung und -verteilung entwickelt und eingebaut. Das führte dazu, daß die Halle sehr anpassungsfähig ist – ein Vorteil für die vielfältigen Nutzungen und auch für den Energiehaushalt. Wertvolle Erfahrungen für die Planung derartiger Räume wurden gewonnen: Meßtests am Modell und Messungen während der Bauzeit waren vergleichbar und konnten übertragen werden.

La concezione dell'edificio è scaturita da un concorso, nella partecipazione al quale è maturato l'obiettivo di creare uno spazio per eventi culturali che sarebbero stati illuminati artificialmente di notte e in maniera naturale durante il giorno. Posizionato a ridosso di una rumorosa strada ad alto scorrimento e dovendo esso rispettare l'esigenza di far aprire l'entrata principale della hall d'ingresso verso il paesaggio, non rimaneva altra scelta che quella di far penetrare la luce naturale dal tetto. Allo scopo d'infondere un livello d'illuminazione uniforme e vivace nella hall, il direzionamento e la distribuzione della luce diurna sono stati attentamente progettati ed eseguiti insieme a Christian Bartenbach. Ne è risultata una hall estremamente duttile, un vantaggio, questo, per un luogo che assolve a molte funzioni oltre a quella di contenere il consumo energetico.

Si è registrata un'importante esperienza per la progettazione di tali spazi: è stata infatti verificata la corrispondenza tra i risultati delle misurazioni effettuate sul modello e quelli presi durante la costruzione dell'edificio e, con questo, ne è stata comprovata la trasferibilità dalla teoria alla pratica.

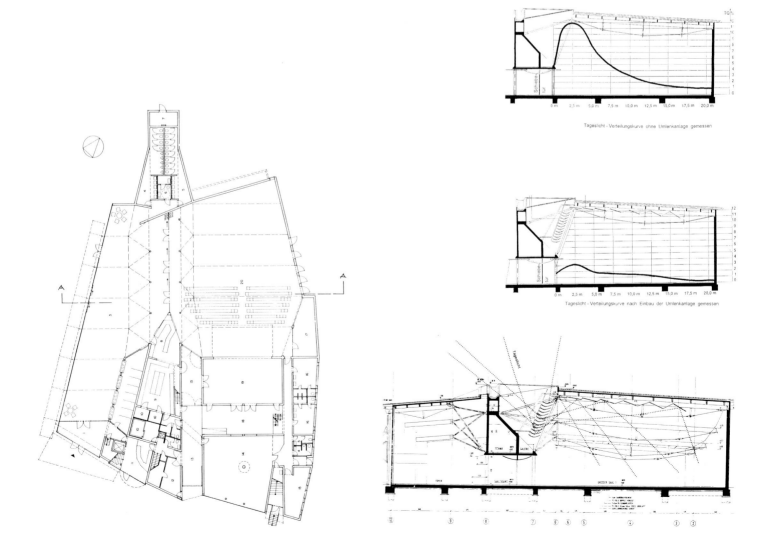

Tageslicht - Verteilungskurve ohne Umlenkanlage gemessen

Tageslicht - Verteilungskurve nach Einbau der Umlenkanlage gemessen

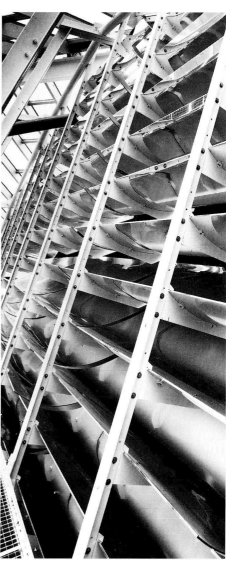

Cardiff Bay Opera House, Wales

Cardiff Bay Operngebäude
Opera, Cardiff

Architect: Manfredi Nicoletti, Rome
Competition: 1994

Collaborators: C. Tavani, P. Zucker, D. Sharp
Energy Study: Max Fordham
Acoustic Engineer: Y. Xu
Structural Engineers: RFR (Wave Roof);
Whitby & Bird
Services Engineers: M. Fordham & Partners,
Hoare Lea & Partners
Fire Prevention: Bickerdike Allen & Partners

Sea wave. Sound wave.

A landmark – a new covered piazza – a materialization of music and water.

The crystalline warped geometry of a huge glass "wave" envelops the entire "city of music." The interior atrium space spans from the ground to the rooftops of the auditorium, rehearsal rooms and other services, creating a series of piazzas at different levels. These are protected from external noise and pollution and the harsh seaside conditions.

This public space is never artificially heated or ventilated. In the warm season a natural ventilation system together with temporary sun shades, counteract the heat gain from solar radiaton. Comfortable conditions are ensured in winter by the green-house effect during the day time. At night the heat loss of the various buildings within the "city of music", requiring about 1.5 air changes/hour, is exploited. Their external skin surface is much greater than that of the glass wave envelope, which is a smooth device to preserve energy.

Meereswelle. Tonwelle.

Ein urbaner Ausnahmefall – ein neuer überdachter Platz – Verkörperung von Musik und Wasser. Die kristalline Geometrie einer riesigen gläsernen »Welle« umfaßt die gesamte »Musikstadt«. Das Gesamt-Interieur wird von der untersten Ebene bis zum Dach des Zuschauersaals in Probenräume und andere Funktionsbereiche aufgeteilt, es entstehen auf verschiedenen Ebenen eine Reihe von Plätzen, geschützt vor Straßenlärm, Schmutz und rauhem Seewetter.

Dieser öffentliche Raum wird weder künstlich beheizt noch gekühlt. Im Sommer verhindern eine Frischluftanlage und bewegliche Sonnenschutzvorrichtungen die Aufheizung durch Sonneneinstrahlung. Angenehme Temperaturen werden im Winter tagsüber durch den Gewächshauseffekt erzielt. Nachts wird die Abwärme der verschiedenen Baukörper der »Musikstadt« genutzt, was einen etwa 1,5-maligen Luftwechsel pro Stunde erfordert. Die Außenhautfläche aller Ein-Bauten der »Stadt« ist viel größer als diejenige der alles umhüllenden »gläsernen Welle«, einem eleganten Instrument zur Energiekonservierung.

Onda marina. Onda sonora.

Un'emergenza urbana – una nuova piazza coperta – materializzazione di musica e acqua. La cristallina e svergolata geometria di un'enorme «onda» di vetro avviluppa l'intera «Città della musica».

Il volume interno si dilata dal suolo alle coperture dell'auditorio, delle sale prova e degli altri spazi funzionali, creando una serie di piazze a differenti livelli protette dai rumori esterni, dall'inquinamento e dall'impervio clima del litorale. Questo spazio pubblico non è mai riscaldato e refrigerato artificialmente. Nella stagione estiva un sistema di ventilazione naturale abbinato a frangisole mobili, contrasta l'incremento della temperatura dovuto alla radiazione solare. In inverno, durante il giorno, l'effetto serra assicura condizioni confortevoli. Di notte, sono sfruttate le perdite caloriche dei vari edifici della «Città della musica», che richiedono circa 1,5 ricambi d'aria all'ora. La loro «epidermide» superficiale esterna è infatti di gran lunga maggiore di quella dell'«Onda di Cristallo», un elegante strumento di contenimento energetico.

CARDIFF BAY OPERA HOUSE TEMPERATURE PROFILE

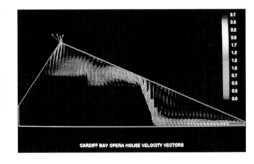

CARDIFF BAY OPERA HOUSE VELOCITY VECTORS

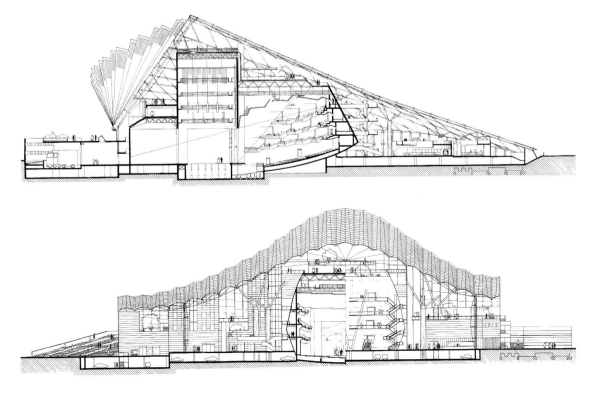

Museum of Natural History, Florence

Naturhistorisches Museum, Florenz
Museo di Scienze naturali, Firenze

Architects: Design team of the University of Florence
Planning and execution: 1993–

Design Team: Marco Sala, Alberto Breschi, Loris
G. Macci, Giuliano Maggiora
Collaborators: Antonella Cortesi, Marino Moretti

The object of the projected Museum of Natural History is the urban renewal of a former city abattoir. The bioclimatic aspect of this project is articulated in its two fundamental parts – the renovation of the existing buildings and the architectural interventions – by developing different energy strategies for each.

The eastern pavilion dedicated to the Natural History of Italy reveals its structure whilst taking advantage of solar energy: the twin glass walls form a green-house type space in which plants produce a humid climate. This mediates between the internal and external environment by air movement through small ventilation apertures. Brise-soleil regulate the direct solar radiation.

Bei dem Projekt handelt es sich um die städtebauliche Neugestaltung der ehemaligen städtischen Schlachthöfe. Die bioklimatischen Aspekte werden in den beiden wesentlichen Bestandteilen des Projekts – Renovierung der bestehenden Gebäude und Neubauten – berücksichtigt, indem unterschiedliche Energieversorgungsmodelle für beide entwickelt werden.

Der östlich gelagerte Pavillon, in dem die Naturgeschichte Italiens dargestellt wird, zeigt offen seine Tragwerksstrukturen und nutzt zugleich die Vorteile der Sonnenenergie: Doppelglaswände bilden eine Art Gewächshaus, in dem Pflanzen Luftfeuchtigkeit erzeugen. Dies und die Luftströme durch kleine Belüftungsöffnungen schaffen den Ausgleich zwischen Innen- und Außenklima »Brise-soleil« regulieren die direkte Sonneneinstrahlung.

La progettazione del Museo di Scienze naturali si è posta come obiettivo quello del rinnovamento urbano e del riuso dell'area che ospitava i vecchi macelli comunali. L'aspetto bioclimatico del progetto si è articolato in due temi fondamentali: la sua applicazione nel recupero degli edifici esistenti e quella nell'esecuzione delle nuove architetture, con lo sviluppo di differenti strategie energetiche.

Il padiglione orientale dedicato alla storia naturale italiana, rivela la sua novità costruttiva nello sfruttamento dell'energia solare: le doppie pareti vetrate contengono degli spazi-serra, nei quali la presenza di piante favorisce la formazione di un clima umido che interagisce sia con l'interno che con l'esterno, attraverso aperture munite di ventilatori tangenziali, mentre la regolazione della radiazione diretta è affidata a sistemi di frangisole.

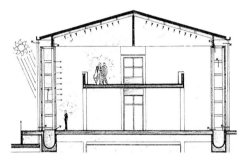

Natural light and "nervous system" of climate control

1   Upper ventilation system between interior/exterior
2   Circulation of upper air in the glazed double façade
3   Lower ventilation system between interior/exterior
4   Circulation of lower air in the glazed double façade
5   Heat transmitted through the glazed double façade
6   Air contitioning system

Tageslichtbeleuchtung und »neurales Steuerungssystem« für die Klimatisierung
1   Oberer Luftaustausch Innen/Außen
2   Luft strömt von oben in die doppelt verglaste Außenwand
3   Unterer Luftaustausch Innen/Außen
4   Luft strömt von unten in die doppelt verglaste Außenwand
5   Wärme gelangt durch die Doppelverglasung ins Innere
6   Klimaanlage

Luce naturale e Rete Neurale di Controllo dei sistemi di climatizzazione
1   Sistema di ventilazione superiore diretto interno-esterno
2   Sistema ricircolo aria superiore all'interno della doppia parete vetrata
3   Sistema di ventilazione inferiore diretto interno-esterno
4   Sistema ricircolo aria inferiore all'interno della doppia parete vetrata
5   Trasmissione del calore tramite le doppie pareti vetrate
6   Sistema di condizionamento

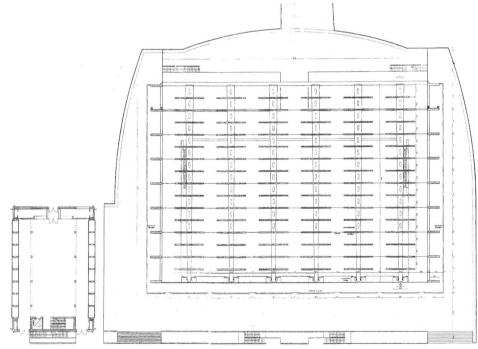

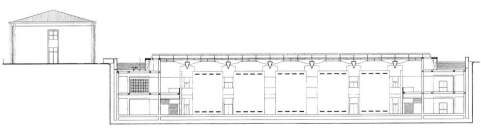

Exhibition Pavilion, Stuttgart

Ausstellungsgebäude Haus des Waldes, Stuttgart
Padiglione per esposizioni, Stoccarda

Architects: Jockers + Partner, Stuttgart
Planning and execution: 1993–1996

Structural Engineer: Rosemarie Wagner
Services Engineer: Zimmermann & Becker

Because it functions as an exhibition centre, the new building has an entirely transparent hall. Visitors are able to observe the sourrounding forest and study the influences of seasons and weather. An arched timber structure spans delicately over the exposition area, which can therefore be used in a very flexible way. All other funcitons are located in the two levels of the adjacent part of the building. The façade of these spaces is also articulated according to different needs. Strip windows alternate with bare wood panelling.
All rooms which call for lower ceiling heights are grouped together in the two-storey, highly insulated part of the building; whereas the transparent exposition hall is able to react to different seasons and weather conditions.
This contrast is the basis of a passive solar engergy concept. The heat of the sun is used directly to warm the air in the building and accounts for a large part of the annual power demand. All massive areas, especially those which are in contact with soil, help to store the gained solar energy. These two systems get support from a small air heating-unit, which reacts only to very extreme weather conditions. The 120 m² roof area is covered with photovoltaic cells. Thermal sun collectors heat the water supply of the whole complex.

Entsprechend seiner Funktion als Ausstellungsschwerpunkt erhält der Neubau einen rundum verglasten Hallenbereich zur Einbeziehung und Beobachtungsmöglichkeit des umliegenden Waldes und der Einflüsse aus Jahreszeit und Witterung. Eine filigrane Konstruktion aus Brettschichthölzern überspannt bogenförmig den flexibel nutzbaren Hallenbereich. Die Fassade ist entsprechend ihren jeweiligen Anforderungen in geschlossene, mit unbehandeltem Holz verschalte oder mit Fensterbändern versehene Teile gegliedert.
Die Raumgruppen, die eine geringere Zimmerhöhe erfordern, werden in einem kompakten, zweigeschossigen, hochwärmegedämmten Gebäudeteil zusammengefaßt. Das schafft zusammen mit der großzügig verglasten Ausstellungshalle die Grundlage für ein passives Solarenergiekonzept. Die einstrahlende Sonnenwärme wird zur Unterstützung der kleindimensionierten Gebäudeheizung eingesetzt und deckt so einen großen Teil des jährlichen Wärmebedarfs ab.
Ca. 120 m² Dachfläche wird mit Photovoltaikmodulen bestückt. Die Überschüsse der gewonnenen Elektrizität werden in das städtische Stromversorgungsnetz eingespeist.
Ca. 15 m² thermische Sonnenkollektoren heizen die für die Gesamtanlage (Bestand und Neubau) erforderliche Brauchwassermenge auf.

In qualità di centro espositivo il nuovo edificio ha una hall completamente trasparente, che pone i visitatori in condizione di osservare la foresta intorno e studiare le influenze dovute alle stagioni ed al tempo atmosferico. Una struttura in legno arcuata si estende delicatamente al di sopra dell'area espositiva, che, totalmente libera, può essere usata in maniera estremamente flessibile. Tutte le altre funzioni sono collocate su due livelli nella parte adiacente dell'edificio. La facciata di questi spazi inoltre è articolata in accordo con le differenti necessità, e in essa si alternano finestre a nastro con pannelli di legno grezzo.
Tutti gli ambienti che necessitano di un'altezza utile minore sono stati raggruppati su due piani, a costituire una porzione di edificio con un alto isolamento termico. Il calore del sole è usato in maniera diretta per riscaldare l'aria all'interno dell'edificio e risponde al fabbisogno annuo d'energia. Due sistemi sono supportati da una piccola unità per il riscaldamento dell'aria che viene messa in funzione soltanto in condizioni di tempo atmosferico sfavorevoli.
I 120 mq di superficie del tetto sono coperti con pannelli fotovoltaici e, con l'utilizzo di collettori solari, viene riscaldata l'acqua per le esigenze dell'intero complesso.

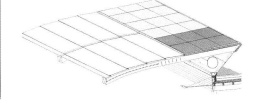

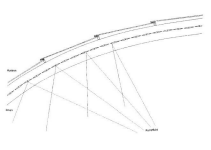

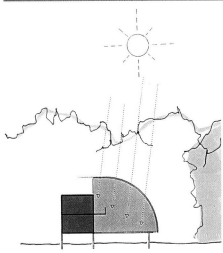

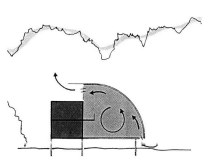

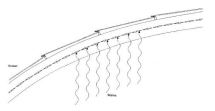

Cross-section
Natural light for the exhibition is only obtainable from above.

Querschnitt
Natürliches Licht für Ausstellung ist wegen der Lage im Wald nur von oben möglich.

Sezione trasversale
L'illuminazione naturale dello spazio espositivo, a causa del posizionamento nella foresta, è possibile solo dall'alto

Cross-section
Building form and section support natural ventilation because of the aerodynamically functioning envelope.

Querschnitt
Gebäudeform und Gebäudequerschnitt unterstützen die natürliche Luftbewegung durch aerodynamisch günstige Ausbildung der Hülle.

Sezione trasversale
Forma e sezione dell'edificio favoriscono una ventilazione naturale grazie all'involucro aerodinamico.

Lighting system (night):
Closed slats reflect the light from spotlights for a basic illumination in the hall of 250 Lux.
Closed slats keep the heat in the hall and reduce heat loss by 30%.

Lichtsystem (nachts):
Geschlossene Lamellen reflektieren das Licht der Strahler für eine Grundbeleuchtung der Halle mit 250 Lux.
Geschlossene Lamellen halten Wärme der Halle zurück reduzieren die Wärmeverluste um 30%.

Sistema di illuminazione (notturno):
Le lamelle chiuse riflettono la luce degli emettitori per ottenere un'illuminazione-base della sala con 250 lux.
Le lamelle chiuse trattengono il calore della sala, riducendo la dispersione del calore del 30 %.

151

New Acropolis Museum, Athens

Neues Akropolis-Museum, Athen
Nuovo Museo dell'Acropoli, Atene

Architects: Manfredi Nicoletti, Lucio Passarelli, Rome
Planning and execution: 1990–1996

Collaborators: P. Bisignani, P. Gandolfi
(Competition)
Solar Energy Study: Manfredi Nicoletti
(Coordinator), Raffaele De Angelis (Assistant),
Studio Nicoletti – Studio Passarelli (Laboratory),
Fraunhofer Institute for Solar Energy System
P. O. Braun, M. Goller, S. Herkel

An open eye on the Acropolis: immortal remains contemplating their own origin. The image of the Acropolis appears amongst the archaeological exhibits: this visual dialogue connects the unique quality of the theme with the place. At the foot of the Acropolis, the museum, collecting all archaeological elements of the Sacred Mound, will continue its rocky outline: an artificial geology respecting the incomparable environment.

The New Museum is a 40 % hypogeous structure protected by a roof-slab perforated by an eye oriented north – like the Parthenon – permitting the view of the Acropolis, but avoiding the penetration of harmful sun-light. A study has been performed so as to integrate natural cooling and lighting systems. The environmental conditions for visitors and works of art are optimized whilst energy is saved.

Die Akropolis mit offenen Augen sehen: unsterbliche Ruinen, die über den eigenen Ursprung nachsinnen. Das Abbild der Akropolis wird integraler Bestandteil der musealen Sammlungen: Dieser visuelle Dialog macht das Unverwechselbare aus, das die Besonderheit der Aufgabe und des Ortes definiert. Das Museum am Fuß der Akropolis versammelt alle archäologischen Funde der Tempelburg und setzt deren Felsenprofil fort: Es entsteht eine künstliche geologische Formation, die ihrem unvergleichlichen Standort Reverenz erweist.

Das Neue Museum ist zu 40 % unterirdisch angelegt, gedeckt von einer Steinplatte, in die eine – wie die Achse des Parthenon – nach Norden orientierte »Augenöffnung« eingeschnitten ist, von der man auf die Akropolis blickt, ohne daß direktes Sonnenlicht ins Innere dringt. Die Konstruktion integriert natürliche Systeme zur Kühlung und Beleuchtung, so daß das interne Mikroklima für Besucher wie Kunstwerke optimal ist und Strom gespart wird.

Un occhio aperto sull'Acropoli. Resti immortali che contemplano la loro stessa origine. L'immagine dell'Acropoli diviene parte integrante delle collezioni museali. Questo dialogo visivo è il carattere irripetibile che lega la specificità del tema e del luogo. Riunendo ogni reperto archeologico della Sacra Rocca, il Museo, ai piedi dell'Acropoli, ne continua il suo profilo roccioso: una geologia artificiale che rispetta un ambiente incomparabile.

Il nuovo museo è per il 40 % una struttura ipogea, protetta da una struttura a lastra perforata da un «occhio», orientato a Nord, come l'asse minore del Partenone. Da esso è possibile la vista dell'Acropoli evitando la penetrazione diretta dei raggi solari. La struttura integra sistemi naturali di refrigerazione e illuminazione per ottimizzare le condizioni microclimatiche interne per i visitatori e le opere d'arte, realizzando un risparmio energetico.

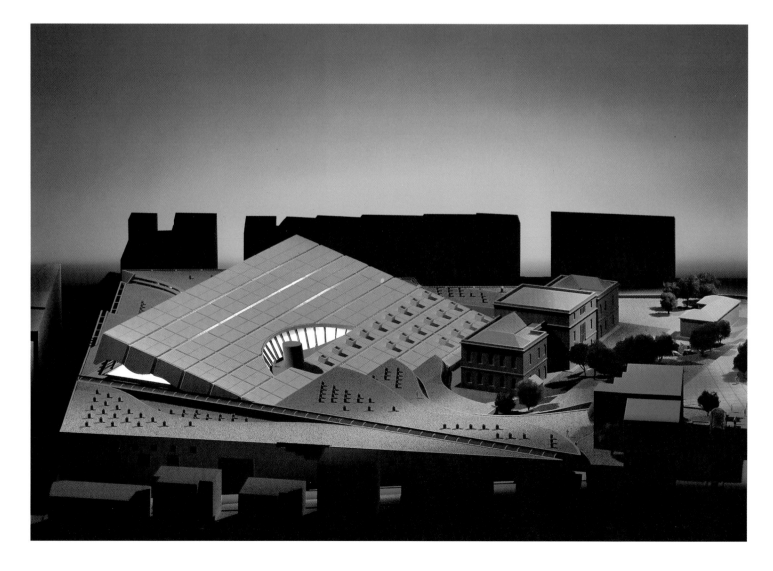

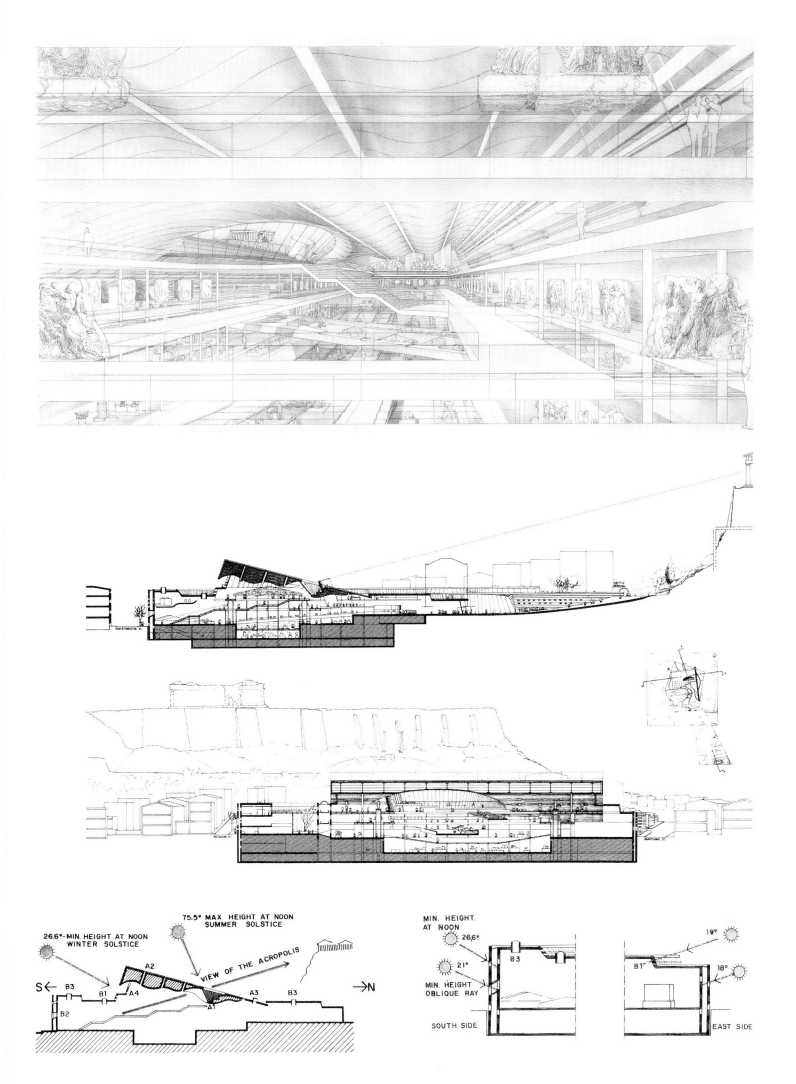

75.5° MAX HEIGHT AT NOON
SUMMER SOLSTICE

26.6°-MIN. HEIGHT AT NOON
WINTER SOLSTICE

VIEW OF THE ACROPOLIS

S ←

B3   B1   A4   A2   A3   B3

A1

→ N

MIN. HEIGHT.
AT NOON

26,6°

21°

B3

MIN. HEIGHT
OBLIQUE RAY

SOUTH SIDE

19°

B1

18°

EAST SIDE

Shelter for Archaeological Site, Santorini (Greece)

Schutz für eine archäologische Ausgrabungsstätte, Santorin
Sistema di protezione per un sito archeologico, Santorini

Architect: Nikos Fintikakis, Athens
Planning and execution: 1994–1996

Project Manager: Synthesis and Research Ltd;
G. Albanis, N. Fintikakis, M. Tzavelis, D. Mavrotas
Archaeological Consultant: Chr. Doumas
Mechanical Engineer: Talos Engineering SA;
N. Kouleimanis, A. Sgouropoulos
Civil Engineer: N. Papantoniou
Environmental Engineer: Norbert Kaiser

This project is part of a move to protect archaeological sites implementing renewable energy sources. The innovative protection of the Bronze Age City at Akrotiri, on the island of Santorini, employs the research and development of high solar technology.

The preservation of this historic monumental area of national heritage is from the damage occurring after the excavations and insufficient protection of the findings (frescoes, pottery etc.)

The replacement of the existing site roof by a new state-of-the-art envelope will filter out the ultraviolet radiation and control both visible and infrared sun radiation.

The environmental concept design for the whole excavation site also creates a large thematic museum.

A low energy-demand air-conditioning system has been designed for the internal parts of the site in order to achieve a good quality environment for visitors, archaeologists, and the exhibits, including an atmospheric control system with dehumidification and CO_2 absorption.

Dieses Pilot-Projekt gehört in eine Reihe von Bemühungen, Ausgrabungsorte zu schützen und zu konservieren, indem man erneuerbare Energiequellen einsetzt. In Akrotiri, auf der Insel Santorin, sollen die Reste der bronzezeitlichen Stadt konserviert werden, und das innovative Projekt beschäftigt sich mit der Erforschung und Entwicklung hochleistungs-fähiger Solartechnik. Der Erhalt dieser historischen Stätte, Teil des nationalen Kulturerbes, das nach Ausgrabungen und ungenügender Sicherung der Funde (Fresken, Töpferwaren etc.) schwer beschädigt worden ist, soll gewährleistet werden. Der Ersatz des bestehenden Schutzdaches über der Ausgrabungsstätte durch eine nach neuesten Erkenntnissen entwickelten Hülle, die ultraviolettes Licht herausfiltert und sowohl sichtbare als auch Infrarot-Sonneneinstrahlung steuern kann, ist vorgesehen. Ein umweltbiologisches Konzept für den gesamten Ausgrabungsort als Ausstellung sowie ein großes Museum zum Thema wurden ausgearbeitet.
Eine Klimaanlage mit Niedrigenergiebedarf zur Schaffung eines angenehmen Klimas im Innern für Besucher und Archäologen und in den Ausstellungsräumen wurde entwickelt. Die Anlage verfügt über einen Kontrollmechanismus, der die Luftqualität überwacht und Feuchtigkeit sowie Kohlendioxyd eliminiert.

Il progetto interessa parte di una zona archeologica che implementa le risorse di energia rinnovabile. L'innovativo sistema di protezione di Akrotiri, la città dell'età del bronzo nell'isola di Santorini, impiega infatti gli sviluppi delle ricerche in atto su alta tecnologia solare.

L'azione preservativa nei confronti di quest'area, monumento storico d'eredità nazionale, è operata in primo luogo nei confronti del danno che potrebbe essere arrecato, dopo gli scavi, dall'insufficiente protezione dei ritrovamenti archeologici (affreschi, ceramiche, etc.).

Il ripristino del tetto esistente inoltre verrà effettuato attraverso l'uso di una membrana state-of-the-art che filtrerà le radiazioni ultraviolette e controllerà le radiazioni solari sia visibili che infrarosse.

La progettazione di tipo bio-ambientale per l'intera area dello scavo, contribuisce anche a creare un'ampia tematica museale. E' stato ad esempio progettato un sistema di condizionamento d'aria a basso consumo per ottenere una buona qualità di comfort in tutti gli ambienti chiusi – quelli per il personale lavorativo come per i visitatori – con incluso un sistema di controllo atmosferico con deumidificazione e assorbimento di CO_2.

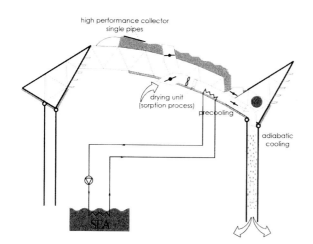

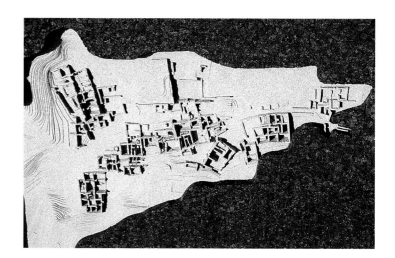

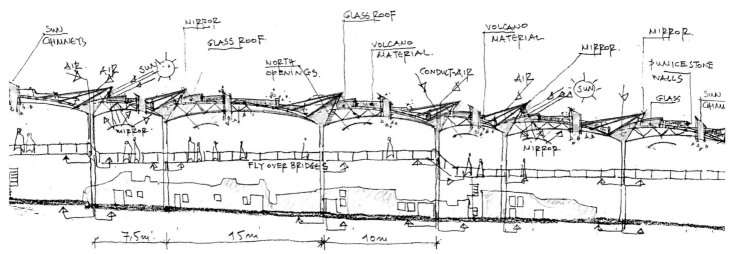

Restoration of Historic Baths, Rhodes (Greece)

Türkisches Bad, Restaurierung und Umbau, Rhodos
Restauro rigenerativo di un edificio termale, Rodi

Architects: A. Paraskevopoulou, N. Zarifis, A. Angelopoulos, Rhodes
Planning and execution: 1992–1994

Mechanical Engineer: M. Perros
Designers: M. Maria, F. Papadopoulou

The New Bath is the only Ottoman Bath still in use in the Old Town of Rhodes.

The proposed architectural interventions aim at restoration of the Bath, whilst keeping its original character.

Hot air instead of smoke will circulate in the hypocausts. Hot water will be provided by solar collectors. Wherever possible heat insulation is proposed. All water pipes and power lines will be replaced. Photovoltaic panels will serve the electricity demands of the building. Controlled mechanical ventilation will be achieved by transforming some light openings into air vents and by electrically operated windows.

Das neue Badehaus ist zugleich das einzige historische Türkische Bad, das in der Altstadt von Rhodos noch benutzt wird. Die architektonischen Eingriffe beim Wiederaufbau konzentrierten sich im Projekt auf die Restaurierung der Bäder, d.h. den Erhalt ihres ursprünglichen Charakters. Heißluft wird anstelle von Feuerrauch in den Hypokausten zirkulieren. Solarkollektoren erzeugen den Strom für die Wasseraufheizung. Wo immer möglich, ist Wärmedämmung vorgesehen. Sämtliche alten Wasserrohre und Stromleitungen wurden ersetzt. Über Photovoltaik-Felder gewonnene Elektrizität deckt den gesamten Strombedarf des Badehauses. Kontrollierte mechanische Belüftung erfolgt durch in Lüftungsöffnungen umgewandelte, ehemalige Oberlichter sowie durch Fenster, die elektrisch geöffnet werden können.

Le nuove terme sono le sole di epoca ottomana ancora in uso nella vecchia città di Rodi.

Gli interventi architettonici proposti come parte del progetto di ricostruzione hanno come scopo il restauro dell'edificio termale nel rispetto del suo carattere originale: nell'ipocausto si farà circolare aria calda anziché fumo; l'acqua calda sarà approvvigionata attraverso collettori solari; dove possibile è stato proposto l'isolamento termico; tutti i condotti d'acqua e le linee di corrente saranno ripristinati; pannelli fotovoltaici andranno a soddisfare il fabbisogno di elettricità dell'edificio, e per finire la ventilazione a controllo meccanico sarà ottenuta attraverso la trasformazione di alcuni lucernari in condotti per l'aria ed attraverso finestre a controllo elettrico.

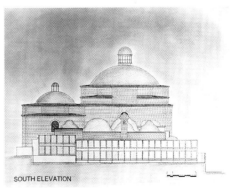

SOUTH ELEVATION

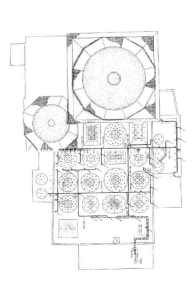

Youth Forum (JUFO), Möglingen (Germany)

Jugendforum JUFO, Möglingen
Centro sociale giovanile (JUFO), Möglingen

Architect: plus+, Peter Hübner, Neckartenzlingen
Planning and execution: 1991–1993

Project Leader: Siegfried Gaß
Structural Engineer: Schlaich, Bergermann und Partner

The youth forum in Möglingen, or JUFO, as it is known, symbolises a flying saucer. Beneath the sky of this artificial oasis, young people have erected a city of clay.

The revolving "solar eye" forms an ideal sun trap, its open face following the course of the sun in winter. The reflector cushion that forms the roof of the eye intensifies the energy gain. The heavy earth works inside the structure store this energy and thus help to stabilize the climate.

In summer, the eye turnes 180° away from the sun, so that only a relatively narrow slit of glass is exposed to solar radiation. Most of the sun's rays are reflected back to the sky from the outer face of the cushion, which is covered externally with stainless-steel foil.

The cushion itself is in a sandwich form of construction, consisting of two pneumatically stretched membranes, each only 0.23 mm thick, with a polystyrene-foam core. The technical perfection of the actual flying saucer with its spring-like legs, and the solar eye with its metallic appearance form a striking contrast to the city of clay, a structure of individual character, shaped by many hands. In conjunction with each other, both elements create a quite unique atmosphere, which is extremely popular with young people.

Das Jugendforum in Möglingen, genannt JUFO, stellt eine fliegende Untertasse dar, unter derem künstlichen Oasenhimmel die Jugendlichen eine Lehmstadt gebaut haben.

Das drehbare Sonnenauge ist eine optimierte Sonnenfalle, die im Winter dem Lauf der Sonne mit der geöffneten Seite folgt, wobei das Reflektorkissen, das das Dach des Auges bildet, die Energieausbeute verstärkt. Die schwere Lehmstadt im Inneren speichert die Energie und stabilisiert das Klima.

Im Sommerbetrieb wird das Auge um 180° verdreht gefahren, so daß nur ein relativ schmaler Glasspalt zur Sonne gerichtet ist und der größte Teil der Sonneneinstrahlung direkt in den Himmel reflektiert wird und zwar von der Außenseite des Kissens aus Edelstahlfolie.

Das Kissen selbst ist eine Sandwichkonstruktion, die aus zwei pneumatisch verformten Membranen von nur jeweils 0,23 mm Stärke und einem Kern aus Polystyrol-Hartschaum besteht.

Die technische Perfektion der eigentlichen fliegenden Untertasse mit ihren Federbeinen, dem Sonnenauge und ihrem metallischen Aussehen, steht in auffallendem Kontrast zu der Lehmstadt, die von vielen Händen geformt ist und eine ganz individuelle Ausstrahlung hat. Beides zusammen führt zu einer ganz eigenen Atmosphäre, die bei den Jugendlichen sehr beliebt ist.

Il centro giovanile a Möglingen, meglio noto col nome Jufo, è rappresentato simbolicamente da un disco volante. Sotto il cielo di questa oasi artificiale i giovani hanno innalzato una città di argilla.

L'«occhio solare» girevole rappresenta un'ideale trappola per i raggi solari, con la sua faccia aperta che segue il percorso solare in inverno. Il cuscino riflettore che il tetto dell'occhio viene a formare intensifica il guadagno energetico. La pesante struttura interna accumula questa energia e aiuta a stabilizzare il clima.

In estate l'occhio ruota di 180° rispetto al sole, cosicché solo una fenditura vetrata relativamente stretta è esposta all'irraggiamento solare. Molti raggi solari vengono riflessi all'indietro verso il cielo dalla faccia esterna del cuscino, che è ricoperto esternamente con un foglio di acciaio inossidabile. Il cuscino stesso è conformato a sandwich, essendo costituito da due membrane tirate pneumaticamente, ciascuna soltanto di 0.23 mm di spessore, con un nucleo di schiuma polistirolica. La perfezione tecnica dell'attuale disco volante, con le sue gambe a forma di molla e l'occhio solare con la sua forma in apparenza metallica, si pone in contrasto stridente con la sottostante città d'argilla, una struttura dal carattere individuale lavorata a mano.

In congiunzione con ciascun altro, entrambi gli elementi creano un'eccezionale atmosfera di calma, che è estremamente apprezzata tra i giovani.

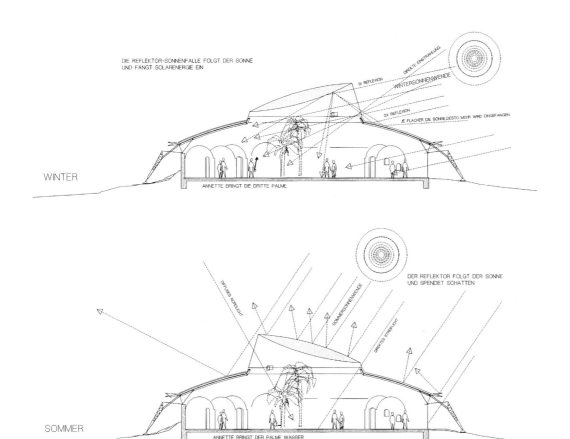

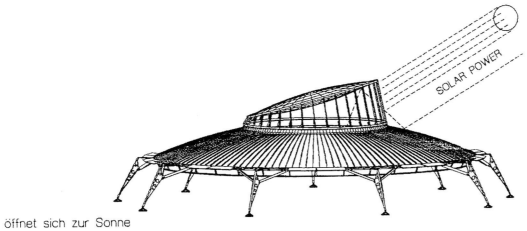

öffnet sich zur Sonne

Buddhist Retreat Centre, Holy Island, Scotland

Buddhistisches Meditationszentrum, Schottland
Centro per il ritiro spirituale, Scozia

Architects: Andrew Wright and Consultants, London
Planning and execution: 1994 –

Services Engineer: Battle McCarthy
Landscape & Water: Andrew Grant
Energy: ESD
Cost Analysis: Hanscomb

The Holy Island is a small mountainous island 20 km off the West Coast of Scotland. It was purchased six years ago by the Samye Ling Buddhist community in order to build a retreat complex.

The complex is divided into two separate buildings, one for male and one for female retreatants. The buildings are located on south facing spurs of land to make the most of passive solar gain.

The design team aimed to lay down a creative, integrated view of man living in harmony with nature.

The complex is targetted to be fully self-sufficient in terms of water, waste, food and energy. Below the two retreats cascading terraces are used to grow crops. Water is naturally collected and then distributed by gravity. Waste water is cleaned using reed beds.

The buildings are dug into the earth and designed to use very low levels of energy. At the moment modelling and calculations show consumption of about 32 % of a typical domestic building on such a site. All the remaining energy is produced by local wind generation.

Holy Island ist eine kleine, bergige Insel, 20 Kilometer vor der Westküste Schottlands. Vor sechs Jahren wurde sie von der buddhistischen Samye-Ling-Gemeinschaft gekauft, die darauf einen Ort der Besinnung errichten wollte.

Der Baukomplex gliedert sich in zwei separate Gebäude, eines für Männer, eines für Frauen. Beide stehen auf nach Süden weisenden Landzungen und nutzen so optimal die solare Einstrahlung aus.

Das Entwurfsteam hatte sich vorgenommen, eine kreative, integrierte Sicht des Lebens in und mit der Natur zu verwirklichen. Das Gebäude-Ensemble soll in Bezug auf Wasser-, Nahrungsmittel- und Stromversorgung sowie Abwasserentsorgung völlig autark sein. Unterhalb der Häuser wird auf den Hangterrassen Gemüse, Obst und Getreide angebaut. Wasser wird aus Bächen gewonnen und nach dem Prinzip der Schwerkraft verteilt. Abwasser wird in Reetfeldern geklärt. Die Gebäude sind am Hang eingegraben, und so gestaltet, daß sie möglichst wenig Energie verbrauchen. Im Modell und in den Vorberechnungen ergibt sich ein Energieverbrauch von 32 % eines typischen Wohnhauses auf einem solchen Grundstück. Zusätzlicher Strom wird je nach Bedarf vor Ort von Windmühlen erzeugt.

Holy Island è una piccola isola montuosa a 20 km dalla costa occidentale della Scozia, che fu acquistata sei anni fa dalla comunità buddista Samye Ling.

Il team progettuale ha puntato a realizzare quei propositi di fondo che vedevano la vita dell'uomo integrata armonicamente con la natura.

Il complesso consta di due edifici separati, uno per il ritiro spirituale degli uomini e l'altro per quello delle donne. L'insediamento, con le due costruzioni esposte a Sud, a simulare degli speroni di terra che sfruttano al meglio l'energia solare passiva, ha come obiettivo quello di essere interamente autosufficiente in termini di acqua, smaltimento rifiuti, cibo ed energia.

I terrazzamenti al di sotto dei due luoghi di ritiro sono sfruttati per far crescere le coltivazioni. Le acque piovane sono raccolte naturalmente e distribuite per gravità, mentre quelle sporche vengono purificate ed utilizzate per irrigare i canneti. Gli edifici sono scavati nella terra e progettati al fine di consumare una bassa quantità d'energia. Al momento la modellazione e il calcolo mostrano un consumo energetico intorno al 32 % di quello che normalmente occorrerebbe per un edificio ad uso residenziale in tale sito.

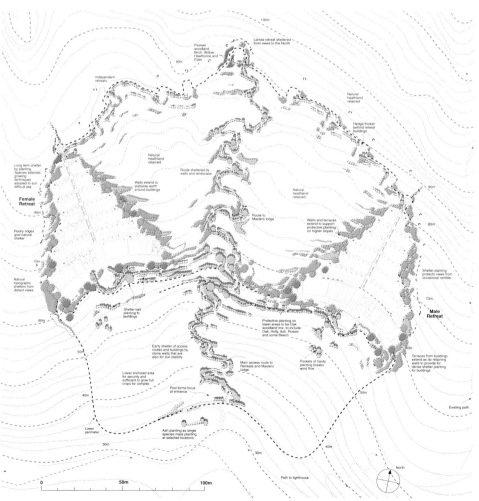

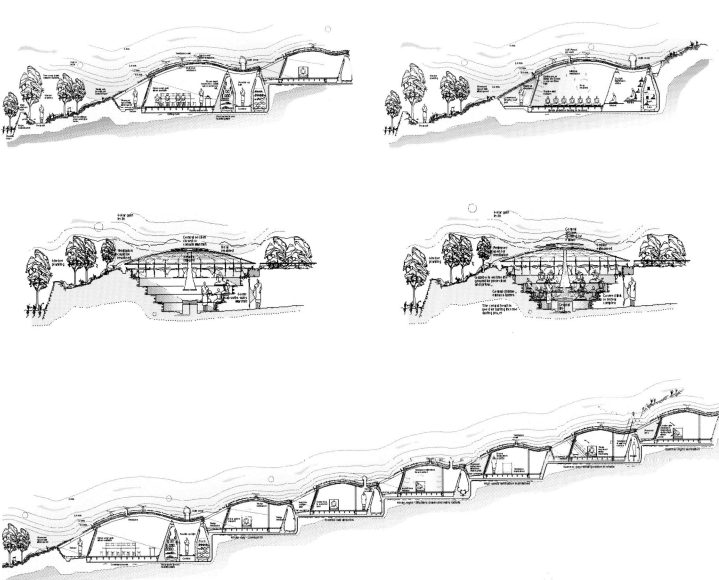

Jean-Marie Tjibaou Cultural Centre, Nouméa (New Caledonia)

Kulturzentrum Jean-Marie Tjibaou, Nouméa
Centro culturale Jean-Marie Tjibaou, Nouméa

Architects: Renzo Piano Building Workshop, Genoa/Paris
Planning and execution: 1990 –

An attempt was made in this project to unite modern technology with tradition and nature. An advanced yet "gentle" form of technology is used, allowing the design to complement traditional forms rather than opposing them.

The location is characterized by bold natural contrasts: rich vegetation, the tranquillity of the lagoon and the strong prevailing winds. Extensive wind-tunnel tests were carried out to determine the form of the building which would permit natural ventilation and an optimum saving of energy.

The shell-shape structures, set facing the prevailing winds, create a suction effect on the leeward side. This draws out the warm air that collects in the interior and ensures an adequate exchange of air.

The outer "shells" are of natural materials - mainly native timbers – thus creating a symbiosis of nature, kanakan tradition and modern architecture.

In diesem Projekt wird versucht, moderne Technologie mit Tradition und Natur zu vereinen. Durch eine fortschrittliche, aber »sanfte« Technologie nähert man sich den Traditionen, anstatt eine Gegenposition zu beziehen.

Der Ort wird geprägt von den Kontrasten der Natur: die intensive Vegetation, die Stille der Lagune und die dominierenden Winde.

Zur optimalen Energieeinsparung wurde die Gebäudeform nach Erkenntnissen umfangreicher Windkanaluntersuchungen zur natürlichen Be- und Entlüftung ausgearbeitet.

Durch die der Hauptwindrichtung zugewandten, schalenartige Ausformung der Gebäude entsteht Sog auf der windabgewandten Seite. Die Warmluft, die sich im Innern des Gebäudes sammelt, wird über die Sogwirkung nach außen abgezogen. Dadurch kann ein ausreichender Luftwechsel gewährleistet werden.

Die äußeren Schalen werden aus natürlichen Baustoffen, einheimischen Hölzern, erbaut. Es entsteht eine Symbiose von Natur, Tradition der Kanaken und moderner Architektur.

In questo progetto ci si è sforzati di unire la moderna tecnologia con tradizione e natura. E' stata pertanto impiegata una forma di tecnologia «avanzata» che permetta al progetto di essere di complemento a forme tradizionali piuttosto che opporsi ad esse.

Il luogo è caratterizzato da netti contrasti naturali: la vegetazione rigogliosa, la tranquillità della laguna ed il forte vento prevalente. Sono stati effettuati numerosi tests nel tunnel del vento per determinare la forma dell'edificio, il che potrà permettere una buona ventilazione naturale e un ottimo risparmio energetico.

Le strutture conformate a conchiglia, si affacciano ai venti prevalenti, e creano un effetto risucchio sul lato sottovento. Ciò innesca un processo d'estrazione di aria calda che nasce all'interno e assicura un adeguato scambio d'aria.

Le «conchiglie» sono all'esterno di materiale naturale – in gran parte di legno locale – ottenendo così una simbiosi tra natura, tradizione kanakan e architettura moderna.

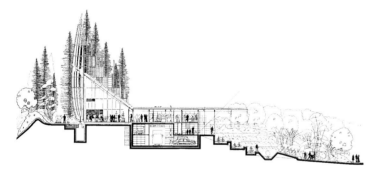

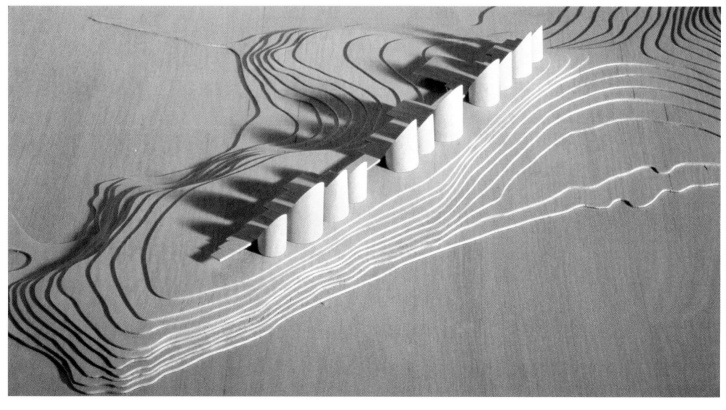

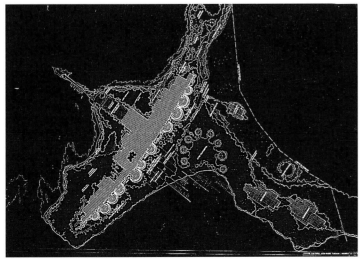

Transport Facilities

Verkehrsbauten
Edifici per trasporti

Motorway Service Station, Lechwiesen	D	Herzog + Partner, Thomas Herzog, Hanns Jörg Schrade, Munich
RAC Regional Centre, Bristol	GB	Nicholas Grimshaw and Partners, London
Bahnhof 2000, Station Roof, Berlin	D	von Gerkan, Marg + Partner, Hamburg

Motorway Service Station, Lechwiesen (Germany)

Tank- und Rastanlage, Lechwiesen
Stazione di servizio, Lechwiesen

Architects: Herzog + Partner, Thomas Herzog, Hanns Jörg Schrade, Munich
Competition: 1992; **planning and execution:** 1993–1996

Collaborators: A. Schankula, R. Geigl, D. Rieks, S. Weber
Structural Engineer: Sailer + Stepan
Mechanical Engineer: M. Bloos
Timber Technology: W. Winter

A new filling-station with restaurant and service facilities is under construction. It is a twin complex, either side of the Munich-Lindau Autobahn. The design was the winning-submission in an architectural competition. The brief called for a model complex that would take into account ecological constraints and would be constructed to conserve resources and allow the use of solar energy.

Filling-station and service-area developments are a building-type characaterized by the consumption of energy (petrol, diesel, lubricants). In this scheme the architectural expression was to be governed by the use of renewable forms of energy.

Particular attention was given to the natural ventilation scheme, with a specialized form of cross-section for the room, a heat regaining system, and a new system of unlaminated structural timbers which give architectonic quality to parts of the building. It is planned that active solar elements will be added.

The planners hope to set an example for future projects of this kind. The function of the complex and the large number of users give considerable social significance to the scheme.

Der Entwurf erhielt den ersten Preis in einem Architekten-wettbewerb für eine neue Tank- und Rastanlage auf beiden Seiten der Autobahn München – Lindau. Das Programm erforderte eine Modellanlage, welche ökologische Bindungen berücksichtigt und den Einsatz von Solarenergie und ressourcenschonenden Baustoffen forciert.

Tank- und Rastanlagen stellen einen Gebäudetyp dar, welcher durch den Verbrauch von Energie – Benzin, Diesel, Schmierstoffe – gekennzeichnet ist. Im vorliegenden Entwurf sollte der architektonische Ausdruck durch die Nutzung erneuerbarer Energien bestimmt werden.

Besondere Aufmerksamkeit erfuhr das Konzept für die freie Lüftung mit einer spezifischen Form des Raumquerschnitts, die Wärmerückgewinnung und neue Tragsysteme aus unverleimten Hölzern an architektonisch bedeutsamer Stelle. Aktive Solartechnik soll noch hinzukommen.

Man möchte damit ein Beispiel für zukünftige Projekte geben. Die Funktion dieser Anlage sowie die große Anzahl von Besuchern sichern ihr eine beträchtliche soziale Bedeutung.

Una nuova stazione di servizio con ristorante è al momento in costruzione su entrambi i lati dell'autostrada che congiunge Monaco a Lindau. Il progetto proposto è risultato vincitore del primo premio in un concorso di architettura, il cui programma chiamava ad osservare un modello complesso che doveva tener conto dei vincoli provenienti dalle problematiche ecologiche, e che doveva essere realizzato per salvaguardare le risorse ambientali e permettere l'impiego di energia solare.

Stazione ed area di servizio sono nella concezione canonica edifici-tipo caratterizzati dal consumo di energia (petrolio, diesel, lubrificanti). Coerentemente con questa logica l'espressione dell'architettura doveva essere improntata sulla tematica dell'impiego di fonti d'energia rinnovabile. Particolare attenzione ha guidato il concetto per l'areazione naturale, con una forma specifica della sezione nello spazio, il recupero di energia e il nuovo sistema portante di legno incollato, in un luogo architettonicamente significativo. La tecnica solare attiva deve ancora essere aggiunta.

Gli autori sperano di poter codificare per futuri progetti di questo tipo un modello paradigmatico, a cui inoltre la funzione del complesso e il gran numero di fruitori conferiscono un considerevole significato sociale.

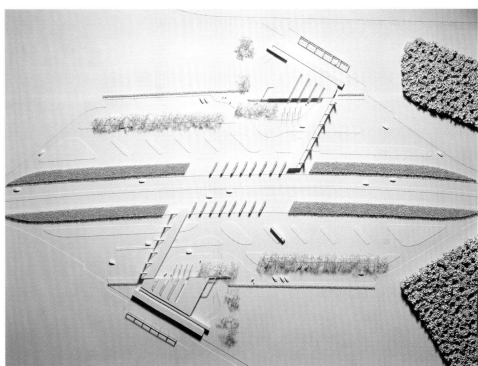

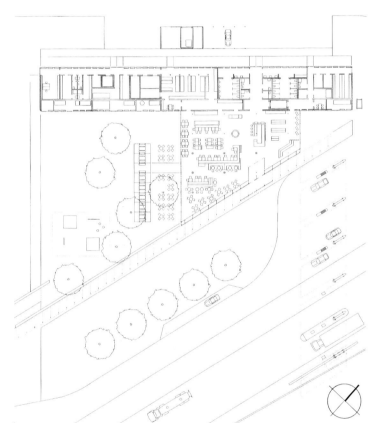

Winter – mechanical ventilation / Winter – mechanische Lüftung / Inverno – ventilazione meccanica

1 Air intake / Kanal Zuluft / Canale di immissione
2 Air outlet / Quellüftung / Sbocco dell'aria
3 Air jet / Weitwurfdüse Zuluft / Gettata d'aria
4 Thermal layering / Thermische Schichtung / Stratificazione termica
5 Air drawn off / Luftabsaugung / Deflusso dell'aria
6 Air expulsion / Kanal Abluft / Canale di espulsione

Summer – natural ventilation / Sommer – natürliche Lüftung / Estate – ventilazione naturale

1 Air intake from rear / rückwärtige Luftnachströmung / Immissione d'aria dal retro
2 Lateral air intake / seitliche Luftnachströmung / Immissione d'aria laterale
3 Air expulsion / Fortluft / Espulsione dell'aria
4 Heat buffer / Wärmepuffer / Cuscinetto termico

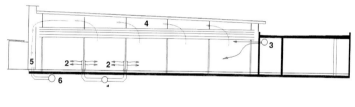

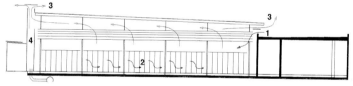

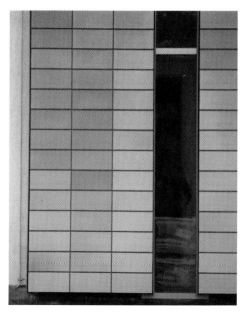

RAC Regional Centre, Bristol (Great Britain)

RAC-Regionalverwaltung (Royal Automobile Club), Bristol
Centro amministrativo regionale del RAC, Bristol

Architects: Nicholas Grimshaw and Partners, London
Planning and execution: 1992–1993

Sitting in a bowl that provides shelter from the motorway, the RAC Headquarters displays an environmentally sensitive response to a noisy and highly polluted site. Inside the building a quality working environment benefits from high levels of daylight. "State-of-the-art" measures have been introduced in order to mitigate glare. A sophisticated displacement ventilation system has been devised to control air quality, reduce the cooling demand and associated energy consumption of the building and constantly expose the occupants to fresh air. An avoidance of false ceilings means that the exposed thermal mass of the concrete floor slabs absorbs excess heat throughout the day.

Der RAC-Neubau liegt in einer Bodensenke, die Schutz vor dem Lärm der Autobahn bietet, und stellt eine, bezogen auf die Umwelt, sensible Baulösung für ein stark lärmbelastetes und hochgradig verseuchtes Gelände dar. Im Innern profitieren qualitätvolle Arbeitsbereiche von der hohen Tageslichtausnutzung. Die neuesten Blendschutzvorrichtungen wurden eingebaut. Eine raffinierte versetzbare Ventilationsanlage wurde entwickelt, die eine Kontrolle der Luftqualität ermöglicht, den Kühlenergiebedarf des Gebäudes reduziert und den Büros ständig Frischluft zuführt. Der Verzicht auf abgehängte, »falsche« Decken bedeutet, daß die thermische Speichermasse der Sichtbetondecken den ganzen Tag über Wärme absorbiert.

Collocato in una conca che funge da riparo dalla vicina autostrada, il quartier generale della RAC costituisce la risposta ai problemi ambientali, in un sito rumoroso e altamente inquinato. L'interno, caratterizzato da una struttura lavorativa di qualità, sfrutta un elevato grado di illuminazione naturale, e in esso sono state introdotte misure da «luogo dell'Arte», allo scopo di attenuarne l'abbagliamento. E' stato studiato un sofisticato sistema di ventilazione per il controllo della qualità dell'aria, per la riduzione del fabbisogno di refrigerazione dell'edificio e del consumo di energia a questa associato, per fornire costantemente agli utenti ricambio d'aria. L'eliminazione delle controsoffitture vuole favorire l'assorbimento dell'eccesso di calore prodotto durante la giornata da parte delle piastre in calcestruzzo esposte quali masse termiche.

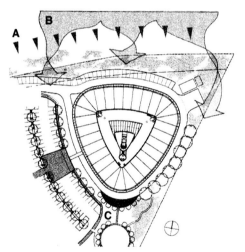

C1 RAC displacement system flow diagram
1 Air enters through plenum.
2 Adjustable floor inlets allow localized fresh air.
3 Perimeter inlets allow air to pass over glazing.
4 Perimeter inlets on second floor boost air buoyancy from first floor.
5 Air is extracted via a roof duct.

C1 Konvektions-Strömungsdiagramm für RAC
1 Luftzufuhr durch Luftkammer
2 Verstellbare Fußbodenöffnungen ermöglichen zonierte Frischluftzufuhr.
3 Öffnungen in der seitlichen Verglasung lassen Luft ein.
4 Öffnungen in der Verglasung im zweiten Stock fördern die Aufwärtsluftbewegung vom ersten Stock.
5 Luft wird über einen Dachabzug abgesaugt.

C1 Diagramma del sistema dei flussi convettivi nel RAC
1 L'aria entra attraverso il pavimento galleggiante.
2 Il pavimento regolabile permette l'immissione di ariab fresca localizzata.
3 Perimetralmente viene immessa aria che passa sopra la vetrata.
4 Perimetralmente viene immessa al secondo piano aria sospinta dal primo.
5 L'aria è estratta ed espulsa via in copertura.

C1

A Noise penetration from the motorways heavily influenced the form and orientation of the building.
B Exhaust emissions are also shielded from public landscaped areas.
C Heavy landscaping creates a south facing staff seating area.

A Die Lärmbelästigung von der Autobahn beeinflußte Form und Orientierung des Gebäudes ganz entscheidend.
B Landschaftsarchitektonisch gestaltete Freiflächen werden auch vor Abgasen abgeschirmt.
C Umfassende landschaftsgestalterische Erdarbeiten schufen einen nach Süden orientierten Park mit Sitzplätzen für die Angestellten.

A La penetrazione del rumore dall'autostrada influenza profondamente la forma e l'orientamento dell'edificio.
B L'ambiente naturale pubblico è protetto anche dalle emissioni di scarico.
C Una rigorosa progettazione degli esterni crea un'area pubblica con spazi di seduta per lo staff di fronte al lato Sud dell'edificio.

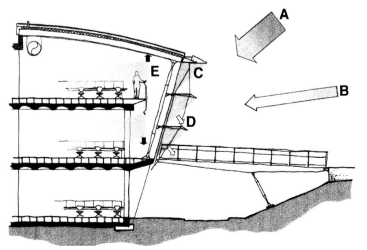

A Direct sunlight
B Low level sunlight
C Elevational overhang and horizontal aluminium 'sky limiters' reduce direct solar glare and heat gain.
D The glazing consists of grey-tinted toughened low-emissivity, double-glazed units, reducing sound penetration and heat gain.
E Roller blinds reduce low level sun glare on workstations.

A Direkte Sonneneinstrahlung
B Sonnenlicht mit flachem Einfallwinkel
C Dachüberhang und horizontale »Himmelsblocker« reduzieren Sonnenblendung und Wärmegewinn.
D Die Doppelverglasungsfelder bestehen aus graugetöntem, gehärtetem Glas mit niedriger Emissionskraft.
E Rolläden sorgen für Blendschutz der Arbeitsplätze vor Sonnenlicht mit flachem Einfallwinkel.

A Soleggiamento diretto
B Basso livello di soleggiamento
C Aggetti del tetto ed elementi «sky limiters» riducono l'abbagliamento del sole e l'assorbimento di calore.
D Per la facciata vengono usati elementi a doppi vetri tinti di grigio, temprati, a bassa emissività, dotati di potere fonoisolante e capaci di ridurre l'assorbimento termico.
E Gli avvolgibili provvedono a ridurre il livello di abbagliamento solare degli spazi di lavoro.

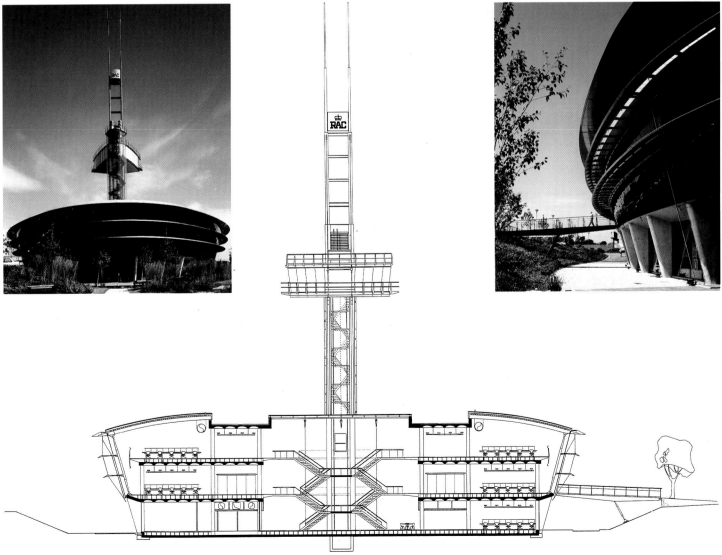

Bahnhof 2000, Station Roof, Berlin

Bahnhof 2000, Bahnsteigüberdachung, Berlin-Charlottenburg
Bahnhof 2000, copertura per banchine, Berlino

Architects: von Gerkan, Marg + Partner, Hamburg
Planning and execution: 1990–

Technical Planning: Atlantis Photovoltaik, Klaus Schlemper

Based on a study of the use of photovoltaic systems in station roofs in Berlin, a pilot project will be carried out at Berlin's Charlottenburg station. The combination of the newly designed "standard" roof and a well-integrated PV installation in a very public location will be an example for other stations in Germany and elsewhere.

Technical features: about 35 kWp, grid connected, roof integration with emphasis on architectural demands.

This project will be realized in association with the Deutsche Bahn AG.

Aufgrund einer Studie, in der das Potential von Bahnhofs-dachflächen der Berliner S-Bahn für die photovoltaische Nutzung untersucht wurde, soll eine vorbildliche Anlage auf dem Bahnhof Charlottenburg errichtet werden. Durch diese Kombination von Architektur und Photovoltaik entsteht ein neuartiger Dachtyp, der Vorbild für andere Standorte in Deutschland und darüber hinaus sein wird.

Technische Daten: ca. 35 kWp, netzgekoppelt, Dachintegration unter besonderer Beachtung des architektonischen Ergebnisses.

Dieses Projekt wird zusammen mit der Deutschen Bahn AG bearbeitet.

È stata programmata la realizzazione di un progetto pilota a Berlino Charlottenburg basato su uno studio dell'impiego dei sistemi fotovoltaici per le coperture delle stazioni a Berlino.

La combinazione di un nuovo progetto di copertura «standard» e un'istallazione di pannelli fotovoltaici ad essa integrati, sarà un modello di esempio per altre stazioni in Germania e altrove.

Le principali caratteristiche tecniche si segnalano in: circa 35 kWp; la presenza di una griglia di collegamento; l'integrazione delle coperture, con particolare attenzione alle esigenze architettoniche.

Il progetto è stato realizzato in collaborazione con la Deutsche Bahn AG.

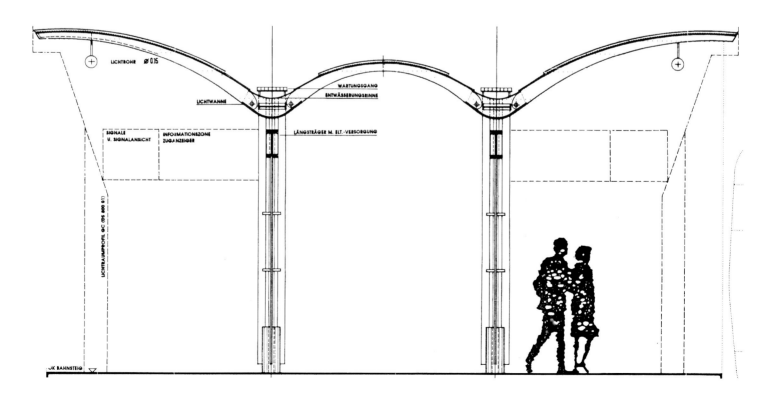

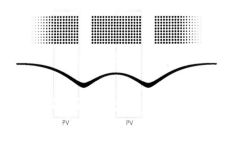

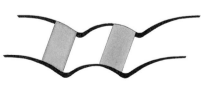

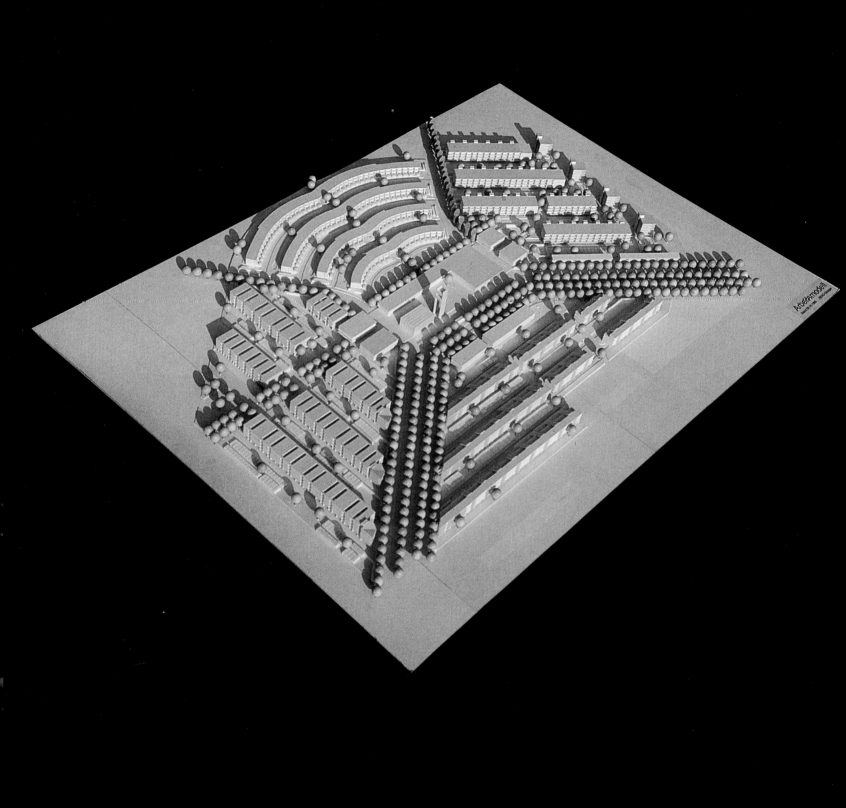

Urban Planning

Siedlungswesen/Städtebau
Pianificazione urbana

Urban Regeneration, Gas-Kerameikos, Athens	GR	Nikos Fintikakis, Yannis Polyzos, Athens
Urban Regeneration, Saline-Ostia Antica, Rome	I	Francesca Sartogo, Joachim Eble, Massimo Bastiani,
		Valerio Calderaro, Rome
Solar Village, ParcBIT, Majorca	E	Richard Rogers Partnership, London
Solar City, Linz-Pichling	A	Sir Norman Foster and Partners, London, Herzog + Partner, Munich,
		Richard Rogers Partnership, London

Urban Regeneration, Gas-Kerameikos, Athens

Stadtsanierungsprojekt Gas-Kerameikos, Athen
Riqualificazione urbana del Gas-Kerameikos, Atene

Architects: Nikos Fintikakis, Yannis Polyzos, Athens
Planning and execution: 1995–1996

Town Planners: Y. Polyzos, D. Karidis,
M. Mantouvalou, M. Mavridou, A. Sarigianni
Project Managers: Synthesis and Research Ltd;
G. Albanis, N. Fintikakis, D. Mavrotas, M. Tzaveli,
R. Rouggeri, K. Papadimitriou
Environmental Engineer: Norbert Kaiser
Mechanical Engineer: Talos Engineering SA;
N. Kouleimanis, A. Sgouropoulos

The core of the Gas-Kerameikos area originated in 1865, as a workers' settlement around the Gas-Works. Today it is a low-rise degraded area of mixed use (mainly residential with small scale manufacturing) close to the centre of Athens and the Acropolis. The aim is to refurbish the area, without major changes in its productive character and social structure, preserving its particular cultural identity.

The project is aiming at a "zero emission" town, by the extended use of renewable energies in buildings and public spaces and the removal of pollution from manufacturing. By using mainly non-polluting public transport, traffic emissions will be reduced.

In order to enhance the microclimate of the area, better cross-ventilation will be allowed through appropriate street and building design (as far as existing development permits). The unification of public and private open spaces with proper plant and water features will be used to create a breeze, through the alternation of hot and cool environments.

Der Kernbezirk von Gas-Kerameikos entstand 1865 als Arbeitersiedlung der Gaswerke. Heute ist es eine heruntergekommene Gegend niedriger Häuser mit Wohnungen und Handwerksbetrieben in der Nähe der Stadtmitte Athens und der Akropolis. Das Stadtgebiet soll unter Erhalt seiner besonderen kulturellen Identität saniert werden, ohne daß sein sozialer und kleinbetrieblicher Charakter wesentlich verändert wird. Ziel des Projekts ist die »Null-Emissions-Stadt« mittels weitgehender Nutzung erneuerbarer Energien sowohl in Gebäuden als auch in öffentlichen Räumen sowie der Eliminierung von umweltschädlichen Emissionen der herstellenden Betriebe. Außerdem sollen hauptsächlich umweltschonende öffentliche Transportmittel genutzt werden, was die Luftverschmutzung durch Auspuffgase verringert. Um das Mikroklima im Bezirk zu verbessern, soll durch die Art der Straßen- und Baugestaltung eine bessere Durchlüftung erzielt werden, soweit es der Bestand erlaubt. Öffentliche und private Freiplätze sollen mit Anpflanzungen und Wasserbecken ausgestattet werden. Durch den Wechsel zwischen warmen und kühlen Zonen wird daher eine kühlende Thermik entstehen

Quello che un tempo era il cuore del Gas-Kerameikos, un'area originata nel 1865 come colonia di lavoratori intorno al Gazometro, è oggi un sito dismesso low-rise, ad uso misto (maggiormente residenziale con servizi manifatturieri alla piccola scala) a ridosso del centro di Atene e dell' Acropoli. Lo scopo è rinnovare l'area, senza intaccarne il carattere industriale e la struttura sociale, preservandone piuttosto la peculiare identità culturale.

Il progetto è teso ad ottenere una città a «emissione zero» attraverso un uso estensivo di energia rinnovabile sia negli edifici che negli spazi pubblici e l'eliminazione dell'inquinamento dovuto ai servizi manifatturieri. Inoltre le emissioni dovute al traffico verranno ridotte grazie all'impiego di trasporti pubblici non inquinanti.

Per la valorizzazione del microclima dell'area sarà favorita la ventilazione trasversale con l'appropriata conformazione delle strade e degli edifici di progetto (per quanto lo sviluppo esistente lo permetta). L'unificazione degli spazi aperti pubblici e privati, con l'uso di appropriate piantumazioni e di specchi d'acqua, favorirà la formazione di una brezza nell'alternanza ambientale tra caldo e freddo.

Urban characteristics

The site is located next to the central area of Athens and the Acropolis, close to the traditional industrial area. The population is c. 4,000. The area is of mixed-use, mainly residential and small-scale manufacturing. 70% of the buildings are 1–2 floors, mostly old structures. Another 20% are 4–7 floors high. The area is situated between three major arteries, but traffic in the inner area is very low.
Though a deteriorated area, it has a strong historical character and a view of the Acropolis hill.

Städtebauliche Merkmale

Das Sanierungsgebiet grenzt an die Stadtmitte Athens und die Akropolis neben diesem alten Gewerbebezirk und hat etwa 4000 Bewohner. Die Häuser beherbergen vor allem Wohnungen sowie kleine Handwerksbetriebe. 70% der Häuser, vorwiegend Altbauten, haben ein bis zwei Geschosse, 20% sind vier bis sieben Stockwerke hoch. Der Stadtbezirk liegt zwischen drei Hauptstraßen, das Verkehrsaufkommen innerhalb des Gebiets ist jedoch gering.
Trotz seines heruntergekommenen Zustands ist Gas Kerameikos ein Bezirk mit starkem historischem Charakter und Sichtbezug zur Akropolis.

Caratteristiche urbane

Il sito è collocato in prossimità dell'area centrale di Atene e dell'Acropoli, vicino alla tradizionale area industriale, e ha una popolazione di circa 4000 abitanti. L'area è ad uso misto, principalmente residenziale ed industriale-manifatturiera alla piccola scala. Il 70 % delle costruzioni è a 1–2 piani, nella maggior parte vecchie strutture. Un altro 20 % si sviluppa su 4–7 piani di altezza. L'area è situata tra tre principali arterie di scorrimento, ma il livello del traffico al suo interno è molto basso.
Sebbene sia un'area dismessa, essa ha una connotazione fortemente storico e una vista sull'Acropoli.

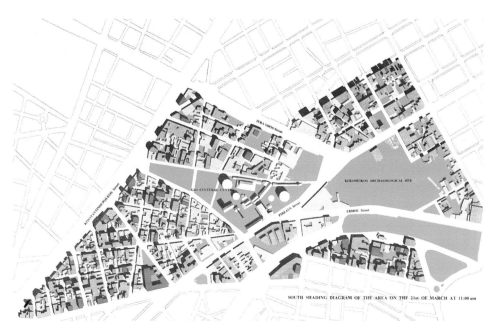

SOUTH SHADING DIAGRAM OF THE AREA ON THE 21st OF MARCH AT 11:00 am

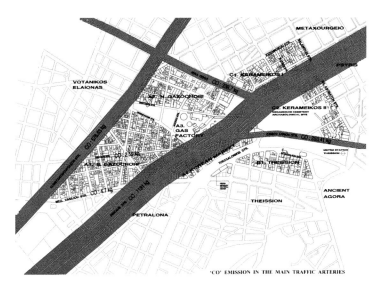

'CO' EMISSION IN THE MAIN TRAFFIC ARTERIES

PROPOSED USE OF AERODYNAMIC POTENTIAL OF INTERNAL COURTYARDS

Solar streets – solar open spaces – solar squares

Targets of environmental intervention:

reducing pollution caused by traffic with a system of absorbing and processing pollution through a green filter along the busy surrounding streets;
reducing pollution caused by the buildings through improvement of energy consumption;
improving ventilation by a better aerodynamic pattern of thermally induced airflow (temperature differences), and street management system in relation to the wind direction; improvement of insulation and shadowing of buildings, courtyards, streets and open spaces.

»Sonnenstraßen« – Besonnte Freiräume – Sonnenplätze

Umweltschützerische Zielsetzung der Sanierung:

Reduzierung von Luftverschmutzung durch Autoabgase mittels eines »Grünfilters« entlang der Umgehungsstraßen;
Reduzierung der von den Häusern verursachten Luftverschmutzung mittels verbesserter Energieausnutzung;
optimierte Ventilation mittels Nutzung eines aerodynamischen Konvektionsmodells (Temperaturunterschiede) und eines Windregulierungssystems für die Straßen, das auf Windrichtungen reagiert;
verbesserte Isolierung und Beschattung von Gebäuden, Höfen, Straßen und offenen Plätzen

Strade solari – spazi aperti solari – piazze solari

Obiettivi del risanamento ecologico:

riduzione della polluzione causata dai gas di scarico delle automobili «attraverso un filtro verde» posto lungo le strade principali di circonvallazione;
riduzione della polluzione causata dagli edifici attraverso un miglioramento del consumo energetico;
ottimizzazione della ventilazione tramite l'uso del modello di convezione aerodinamico (a differenti temperature) e un sistema di gestione stradale correlato alla direzione del vento;
ottimizzazione dell'isolamento ed ombreggiamento degli edifici, corti, strade e piazza aperte.

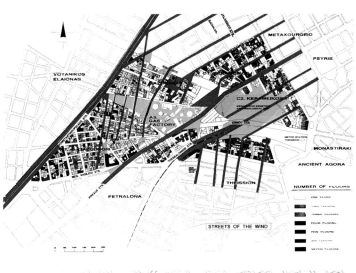

STREETS OF THE WIND

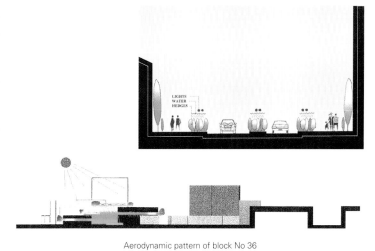

Aerodynamic pattern of block No 36

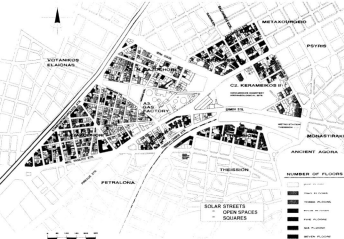

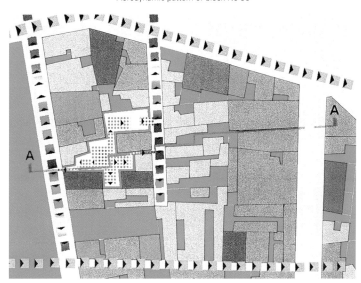

Urban Regeneration, Saline-Ostia Antica, Rome

Stadtsanierungsprojekt, Saline-Ostia Antica, Rom
Riqualificazione urbana di Saline-Ostia Antica, Roma

Architects: Francesca Sartogo, Joachim Eble, Massimo Bastiani, Valerio Calderaro, Rome
Planning: 1995

Scientific coordinator: PRAU srl Rome – Francesca Sartogo
Urban and environmental research: J. Eble, M. Bastiani, V. Calderaro, G. Bianchi, G. Gisotti, L. Venturi, K. Steemers
Energy consultant: W. Stahl
Municipality of Rome: D. Modigliani, A. Violo
Area: S. Bargiacchi, G. Noia

Saline-Ostia Antica represents an urban organism covering 900 ha on the outskirts of Rome, whose history has alternated between consolidation and cycles of decline. With the recent agricultural reclamation operation, it has regained its structure and identity. But today the agricultural crisis and the progression of the built city are compromising the morphological and structural continuity.

The project will reconstruct the relationship between built city, agriculture, and natural environment in a visibly global system. The organization of innovative technological elements such as the "Engergetic Power Ecostations" will re-establish the flow of circulation, infrastructure, and create new urban polarities.

Saline-Ostia Antica ist eine städtische Agglomeration auf 900 ha Land am Stadtrand von Rom, in deren Entwicklungsgeschichte sich Verdichtungs- und Verfallsperioden abgewechselt haben. Durch die vor nicht langer Zeit erfolgte Wiederurbarmachung erfuhr das Gebiet eine Neustrukturierung und Identität. Die Krise der Landwirtschaft und das Ausbreiten der Großstadt gefährden heute jedoch die morphologische und strukturelle Kontinuität seiner Entwicklung. Das Projekt will die Wechselbeziehungen zwischen gebauter Stadt, Landwirtschaft und Natur in einem sichtbar globalen System wiederherstellen, und zwar durch eine Reorganisation mittels innovativer Technologie wie der »Energetic Power Ecostation«, die in der Lage ist, die verschiedenen Kreisläufe, die Infrastrukturen sowie urbane Polaritäten neu aufzubauen.

Saline-Ostia Antica rappresenta un organismo urbano di 900 ha ai margini di Roma, che alterna la sua storia tra cicli di consolidamento e cicli di degrado. Con le recenti opere di bonifica agraria riacquista una strutturazione ed un'identità, ma la crisi dell'agricoltura e l'avanzamento della città costruita ne compromettono oggi la continuità morfologica e strutturale.

Il progetto vorrebbe ricomporre le interrelazioni tra città costruita, agricoltura e ambiente naturale in un sistema olistico globale, attraverso una organizzazione di elementi tecnologici innovativi quali le «Energetic Power Ecostation» capaci di ricostruire la circolarità dei flussi, le infrastrutture e le nuove polarità urbane.

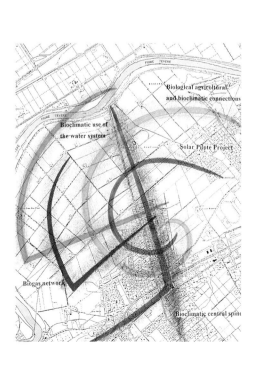

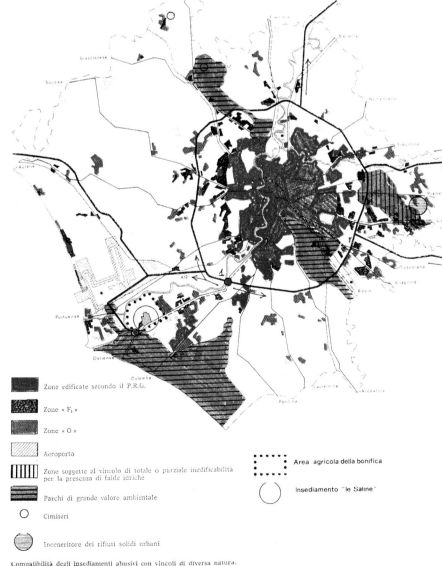

Zone edificate secondo il P.R.G.

Zone « F₄ »

Zone « O »

Aeroporto

Zone soggette al vincolo di totale o parziale inedificabilità per la presenza di falde idriche

Parchi di grande valore ambientale

Cimiteri

Inceneritore dei rifiuti solidi urbani

Compatibilità degli insediamenti abusivi con vincoli di diversa natura.

Area agricola della bonifica

Insediamento "le Saline"

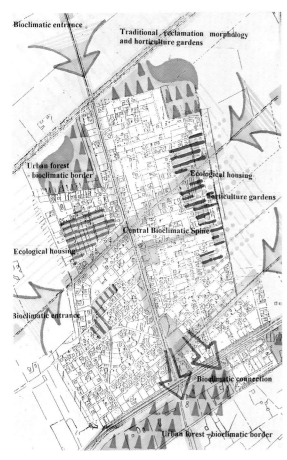

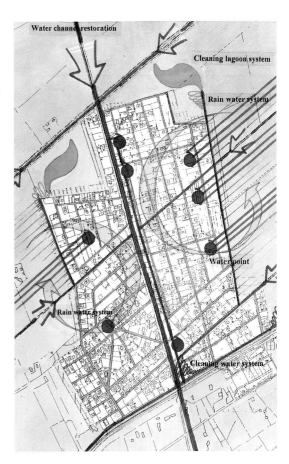

Water Concept
- Introduction of rain-, water channel, and water point systems.
- Support of bioclimatic urban vegetation by the water system.
- Cleaning lagoon system as new landscape.

Wasserkonzept
- Einführung eines Regenwasser-, Wasserrinnen- und Wassersammelstellensystems
- Unterstützung der bioklimatischen städtischen Vegetation durch das Wassersystem
- Bereinigung des Lagunensystems, um eine neue Landschaft zu bilden

Il ciclo dell'acqua
- Raccolta dell'acqua piovana
- Sistema bio-climatico garantito dal sistema urbano verde-acqua
- Sistema di depurazione acqua-vegetazione come bordo paesaggistico.

Urban vegetation and bioclimatic system
- Bioclimatic green central spine.
- Green belt against pollution and noise from the two roads.
- Inter-relation of specialized agricultural border gardens and the internal green space of the new solar buildings.
- Urban forest connecting the lagoon system and the green border.

Städtisches Vegetations- und bioklimatisches System
- Grüne bioklimatische Hauptachse
- Grüngürtel als Schutz gegen Umweltverschmutzung und Lärm von den zwei Straßen
- Wechselbeziehung zwischen den speziellen landwirtschaftlichen Randgärten und dem innenliegenden begrünten Raum der neuen Solargebäude
- Stadtwald verbindet das Lagunensystem mit dem grünen Rand

I sistema bioclimatico urbano
- Spina centrale bioclimatica
- Cintura verde contro l'inquinamento acustico ed atmosferico
- Interrelazione tra i margini ad agricoltura specializzata e gli spazi verdi interni dei nuovi compartimenti edilizi di completamento
- Bosco verde come connessione il sistema del lagunaggio e del verde dei margini.

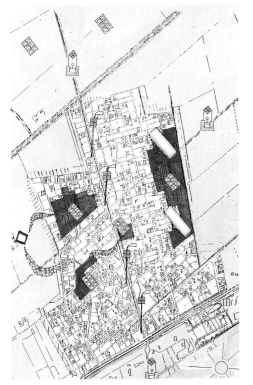

Ecological and Energy Concept
- Use of solar energy for water control (canals and ponds)
- Photovoltaic innovative technology for public lighting
- Ecostation, covered market, social and activity space, covered by photovoltaic panels producing energy.
- Biogas power station in the lagoon area generating from agricultural and organic waste.
- Mixed function district (with school, workshops, public offices, etc.) – Pilot project for an ecological bioclimatic school building.
- Solar district in the new built public and private area with CO_2 and neutral energy provision.
- Urban district energy network open to the neighbouring areas.
- Solar pilot project with example of a zero-energy building.
- Conversion from traditional agriculture to biological agriculture.
- Total unity of agricultural production, food production and marketing.

Obiettivi ecologici e la filosofia energetica
- Uso dell'energia solare come controllo dell'acqua canali e vasche di raccolta
- Illuminazione urbana fotovoltaica
- Ecostazione, mercato coperto, spazi coperti per attività sociali solarizzati ed usati per la produzione di energia
- Stazione di erogazione di Biogas
- Edifici multifunzionali a livello di distretto
- Progetto pilota di una scuola bioclimatica ed ecologica
- Comparti di completamento pubblici e privati nei margini come produttori di energia e ad emissione zero
- Sistema della rete infrastrutturale energetica dei distretti.
- Progetti pilota solari come nuovi edifici a basso consumo e ad emissione zero
- Unitarietà di conduzione nella produzione, commercializzazione e marketing agricolo.

Öko- und Energiekonzept
- Anwendung von Solarenergie für Wasserkontrolle/-regelung (Kanäle, Seen)
- Innovative PV-Technik für öffentliche Stadtbeleuchtung
- Ökostation, überdachter Markt und Raum für gesellschaftliche und andere Aktivitäten, von energieerzeugenden PV-Paneelen überdacht
- Biogas-Kraftwerk im Lagunenbereich, das Gas aus landwirtschaftlichem und organischem Abfall erzeugt.
- Gebiet mit Mischfunktionen (Schule, Werkstätten, öffentlichen Institutionen, etc.). Pilotprojekt für ein ökologisches bioklimatisches Schulgebäude
- Solarbereich im neugebauten öffentlichen und privaten Gebiet mit CO_2 und neutraler Energieversorgung
- Für die Nachbargebiete zugängliches Stadtbezirks-Energienetz
- Solar-Pilotprojekt mit Beispiel eines Nullenergie-Gebäudes
- Umstellung von traditioneller auf biologische Landwirtschaft
- Komplette Einheit der landwirtschaftlichen Produktion, Nahrungsproduktion und des Vertriebs

Solar Village, ParcBIT, Majorca

Solare Dorfanlage, Mallorca
Villaggio agricolo solare, Maiorca

Architects: Richard Rogers Partnership, London
Planning and execution: 1994–

Service Engineer: Battle McCarthy
Quantity Surveyor: Hanscomb International
Landscape Architect: Nicholas Pearson
Energy Consultant: Energy for Sustainable Development
Research: Cambridge Architectural Research

The Government of the Balearic Islands is interested in developing a pilot urban project 8 km north of Palma which would create a community for 7,000–8,000 people.
The aim of Richard Rogers Partnership is to create a vibrant community within an enriched rural landscape.
Public activities are concentrated at the centre of each of three villages and diffused out to residential areas on the periphery.
Water is collected in the wet winters to irrigate crops in summer. The water stimulates a rich landscape allowing crops to be diversified. The irrigation system allows energy crops to be grown to provide local power.
Emphasis is on a public tram system rather than the private car.

Die Regierung der Balearischen Inseln beabsichtigt die Entwicklung eines städtebaulichen Pilotprojekts 8 km nördlich von Palma, das für eine Gemeinde mit 7000–8000 Einwohnern ausgelegt ist.
Zur Schaffung einer lebendigen Gemeinde in einer abwechslungsreichen Landschaft, welche die vorhandenen Naturschätze optimal nutzt, wurden folgende Ziele berücksichtigt:
Die öffentlichen Nutzungen konzentrieren sich im Zentrum jedes der drei Dörfer, die Außenbereiche sind ruhigere Wohngebiete.
Das Wasser der winterlichen Regenfälle wird zur Bewässerung der Felder während des Sommers gesammelt.
Die Bewässerung erlaubt den Anbau von unterschiedlichen Früchten sowie Gemüse und Getreide und schafft somit eine abwechlungsreiche Landschaft. Gleichzeitig wird der Anbau von Pflanzen ermöglicht, die zur Energiegewinnung durch Biomasse genutzt werden können. Eine öffentliche Straßenbahn wird das Hauptverkehrsmittel sein.

Il governo delle isole Baleari si è interessato allo sviluppo di un progetto urbano pilota per realizzare l'insediamento a 8 km a Nord di Palma di una comunità di 7000–8000 persone.
Il principale obiettivo della Richard Rogers Partnership è quello di creare una comunità strutturata in maniera estremamente vitale, capace di apportare un arricchimento al paesaggio rurale. Pertanto le attività pubbliche sono condensate al centro di ciascuno dei tre villaggi e sono diffuse al di fuori delle aree residenziali verso la periferia.
L'acqua, raccolta durante gli inverni piovosi per irrigare i raccolti estivi, stimola la formazione di un paesaggio variato per ricchezza e differenziazione delle coltivazioni. Il sistema d'irrigazione assicura energia per far crescere i raccolti e per esaltare al massimo le potenzialità locali.
Viene privilegiato il sistema di trasporto pubblico a tram, piuttosto che quello privato dell'automobile.

Diagram illustrating transport links and comfortable walking distances

Graphische Darstellung der Verkehrsverbindungen und bequemen Fußgängerentfernungen

Diagramma che illustra i collegamenti tra mezzi di trasporto e distanze comode da percorrere a piedi

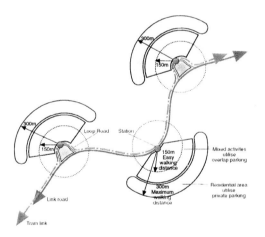

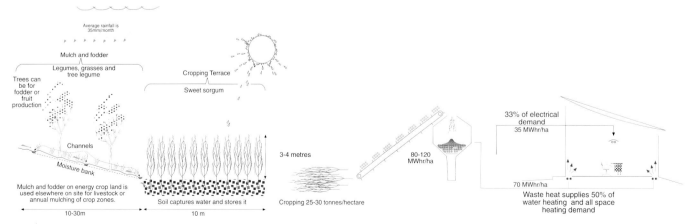

A Plan for Energy / Ein Energiekonzept / Un piano per l'energia

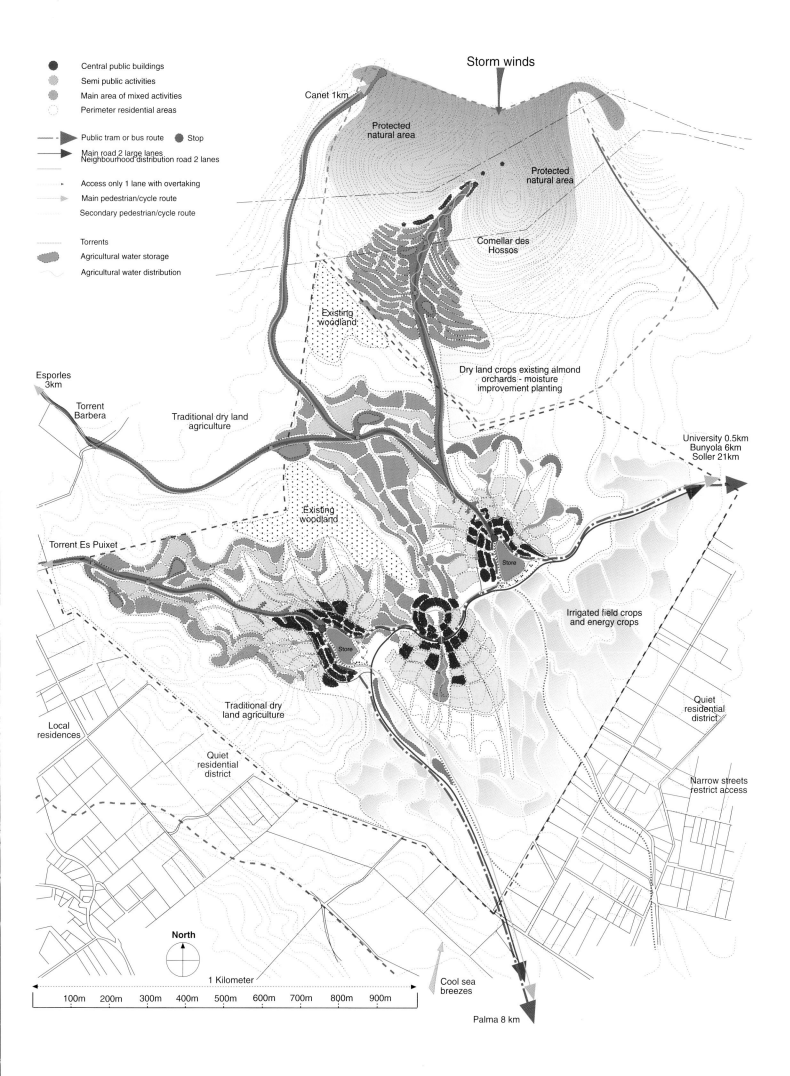

Central public buildings
Semi public activities
Main area of mixed activities
Perimeter residential areas

Public tram or bus route ● Stop
Main road 2 large lanes
Neighbourhood distribution road 2 lanes

Access only 1 lane with overtaking
Main pedestrian/cycle route
Secondary pedestrian/cycle route

Torrents
Agricultural water storage
Agricultural water distribution

Storm winds

Canet 1km

Protected
natural area

Protected
natural area

Comellar des
Hossos

Existing
woodland

Dry land crops existing almond
orchards - moisture
improvement planting

Esporles
3km

Torrent
Barbera

Traditional dry land
agriculture

University 0.5km
Bunyola 6km
Soller 21km

Existing
woodland

Torrent Es Puixet

Store

Irrigated field crops
and energy crops

Store

Quiet
residential
district

Traditional dry
land agriculture

Local
residences

Quiet
residential
district

Narrow streets
restrict access

North

1 Kilometer

100m   200m   300m   400m   500m   600m   700m   800m   900m

Cool sea
breezes

Palma 8 km

177

A Plan for Water

The climate is dry in summer and very wet in winter. Storm torrents are collected in reservoires for summer irrigation and drinking water. The main collection points create ornamental pools which are the social focus for the east and west villages.

Ein Wasserkonzept

Im Sommer ist das Klima trocken und im Winter sehr feucht. Nach Stürmen wird das in Sturzbächen geführte Wasser in Speichern zur Bewässerung der Felder im Sommer und für Trinkwasser gesammelt. Die Hauptsammelpunkte sind künstliche Seen, die die gesellschaftlichen Schwerpunkte der Ost- und Westdörfer bilden.

Un piano per l'acqua

Il clima è secco d'estate e molto umido d'inverno. I torrenti sono raccolti in riserve per l'irrigazione estiva e per l'acqua potabile. Nei maggiori punti di collegamento si vengono a creare specchi d'acqua ornamentali che sono il fulcro sociale dei villaggi orientali ed occidentali.

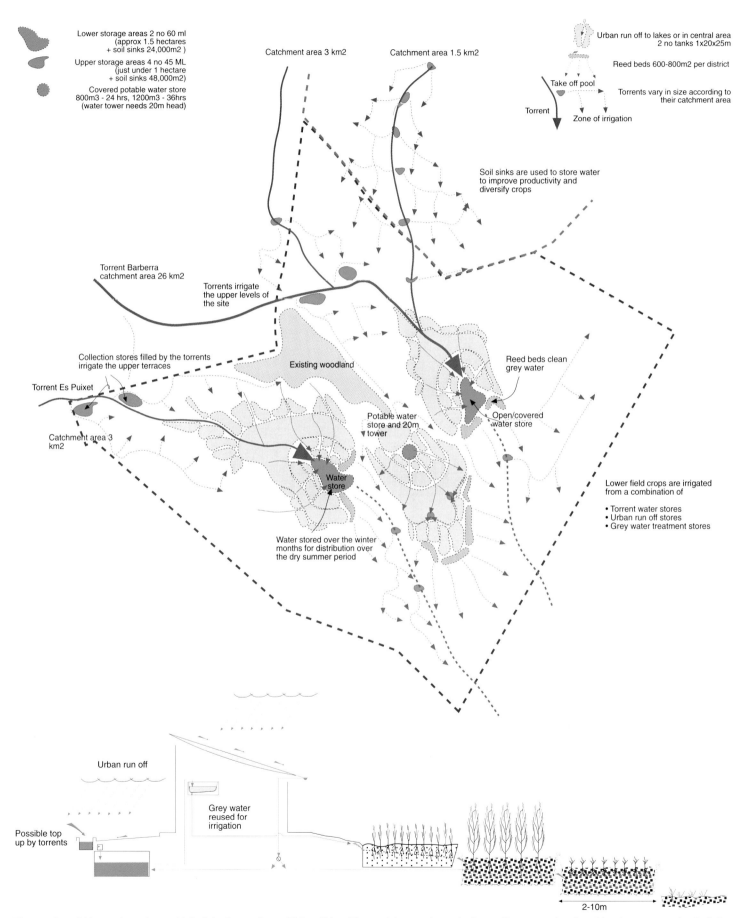

Lower storage areas 2 no 60 ml
(approx 1.5 hectares
+ soil sinks 24,000m2)

Upper storage areas 4 no 45 ML
(just under 1 hectare
+ soil sinks 48,000m2)

Covered potable water store
800m3 - 24 hrs, 1200m3 - 36hrs
(water tower needs 20m head)

Catchment area 3 km2

Catchment area 1.5 km2

Urban run off to lakes or in central area
2 no tanks 1x20x25m

Reed beds 600-800m2 per district

Take off pool

Torrent

Zone of irrigation

Torrents vary in size according to their catchment area

Soil sinks are used to store water to improve productivity and diversify crops

Torrent Barberra catchment area 26 km2

Torrents irrigate the upper levels of the site

Collection stores filled by the torrents irrigate the upper terraces

Torrent Es Puixet

Existing woodland

Reed beds clean grey water

Catchment area 3 km2

Potable water store and 20m tower

Open/covered water store

Water store

Lower field crops are irrigated from a combination of

• Torrent water stores
• Urban run off stores
• Grey water treatment stores

Water stored over the winter months for distribution over the dry summer period

Urban run off

Grey water reused for irrigation

Possible top up by torrents

2-10m

The naturally available water is used to provide fertile land and irrigate crops.

Das natürlich verfügbare Wasser wird verwendet, um fruchtbares Land zu gewinnen und Feldfrüchte zu bewässern.

L'acqua naturale a disposizione è usata per rendere fertile la terra ed irrigare i raccolti.

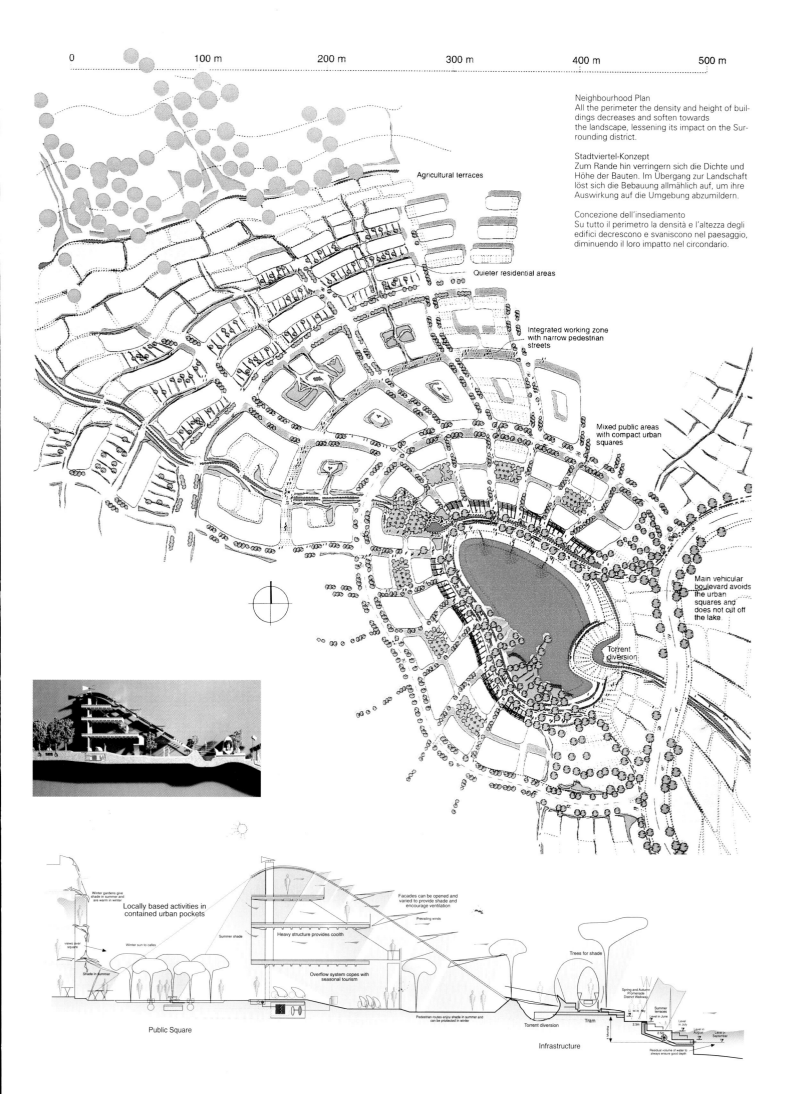

0   100 m   200 m   300 m   400 m   500 m

Agricultural terraces

Quieter residential areas

Integrated working zone
with narrow pedestrian
streets

Mixed public areas
with compact urban
squares

Main vehicular
boulevard avoids
the urban
squares and
does not cut off
the lake

Torrent
diversion

Neighbourhood Plan
All the perimeter the density and height of buildings decreases and soften towards
the landscape, lessening its impact on the Surrounding district.

Stadtviertel-Konzept
Zum Rande hin verringern sich die Dichte und
Höhe der Bauten. Im Übergang zur Landschaft
löst sich die Bebauung allmählich auf, um ihre
Auswirkung auf die Umgebung abzumildern.

Concezione dell'insediamento
Su tutto il perimetro la densità e l'altezza degli
edifici decrescono e svaniscono nel paesaggio,
diminuendo il loro impatto nel circondario.

Winter gardens give
shade in summer and
are warm in winter

Locally based activities in
contained urban pockets

Facades can be opened and
varied to provide shade and
encourage ventilation

Prevailing winds

views over
square

Winter sun to cafes

Summer shade

Heavy structure provides coolth

Trees for shade

Shade in summer

Overflow system copes with
seasonal tourism

Spring and Autumn
Promenade
District Walkway

Summer
terraces

Level in June

Pedestrian routes enjoy shade in summer and
can be protected in winter

Torrent diversion

Tram

Level in July

2.5m

Level in
August

Level in
September

Residual volume of water to
always ensure good depth

Public Square

Infrastructure

179

Solar City, Linz-Pichling (Austria)

Solarstadt, Linz-Pichling
Città solare, Linz-Pichling

Architects: Sir Norman Foster and Partners, Herzog + Partner, Richard Rogers Partnership
Planning: 1995 –

Environmental Engineer: Norbert Kaiser
Landscape Architect: Latz + Partner
Visiting Critic: Renzo Piano Building Workshop
Clients: The City of Linz, ESG, SBL
Housing Trusts: GWG, NH, WAG, WSG
Local Coordination: Heinz Stögmüller
Documentation: TU München, Lehrstuhl
Professor Th. Herzog, J. Höpfner

The north Austrian provincial capital of Linz is planning to build a new urban district for some 25,000 inhabitants, incorporating extensive use of solar energy. The architectural practices involved have developed the overall concept and worked in detail on the first housing units, due to be built in the near future. The maximum allowable density and variety of options for mixed use and subsidized (social) housing have to be realised on a very limited budget. Solar means of energy generation should be integrated in technically functional and socially effective ways.

Development is distributed in a series of compact urban nodes of mixed use. The extent of each node is defined by ease of walking distance around a central square, which acts a social magnet to generate urban quality. Convenient public transport from the centre of each node, reached by pedestrian routes, is thereby made more attractive to residents than the use of cars.

In order to create a variety of new situations, or otherwise to respond to the differnent existing conditions a diversified range of building types has been developed, which broadens the scope of currently accepted architectural solutions to the use of solar energy.

The seperate building plots within the open spaces are highly individuated and broken up into a small areas by allotments, quiet zones, children's play areas and places for communal activities.

The fact that transport networks and energy-supply can be defined from the outset gives the development an economic advantage. Surplus electricity produced locally by means of co-generation, can be supplied to the urban grid.

Die oberösterreichische Landeshauptstadt Linz plant die Errichtung eines neuen Stadtteils für rund 25 000 Einwohner, dessen Versorgung weitgehend solare Energie einbezieht. Die planenden Büros entwickelten ein Gesamtkonzept und im Detail die erste Siedlungseinheit als »Starterprojekt«, die demnächst gebaut werden soll. Maximal zulässige Dichte, Vielfalt, Möglichkeiten zur Mischnutzung und geförderter ›sozialer‹ Wohnungsbau zu sehr geringen Gesamtkosten sind zu realisieren. Es sollen technisch-funktionale und soziale Wirkungen von solarer Energie implementiert werden.

Die Siedlung als Ganzes erhält eine Reihe verdichteter Stadtknoten mit Mischnutzung. Die Ausdehnung jedes dieser Knotenpunkte orientiert sich daran, wie bequem der zentrale Platz – als Sozialmagnet mit städtischer Qualität – zu Fuß erreichbar ist. So soll die Benutzung von öffentlichen Verkehrsmitteln vom Zentrum jedes Quartiers aus, das leicht zu Fuß erreicht werden kann, für die Bewohner attraktiver werden als das Auto.

Um unterschiedliche Situationen neu gestalten bzw. auf unterschiedliche Gegebenheiten reagieren zu können, wurde ein differenziertes Repertoire von Gebäudetypen entwickelt, das die bisher üblichen architektonischen Lösungsansätze zur Nutzung solarer Energie erweitert.

Die einzelnen Baufelder werden in den Freiräumen durch Mietergärten, Ruhezonen, Kinderspielplätze, Orte gemeinsamer Aktivitäten, kleinmaßstäblich gegliedert und vielfach individualisiert.

Daß das Verkehrsnetz und die Stromversorgung von Anfang an festgelegt werden konnten, bietet wirtschaftliche Vorteile für das Projekt. Überschüssige Elektrizität, die vor Ort erzeugt wird, kann ins städtische Stromnetz eingespeist werden.

La capitale di provincia dell'Austria settentrionale, Linz, sta progettando di costruire un nuovo distretto urbano per circa 25 000 abitanti, che includa un impiego intensivo di energia solare. Gli Studi di architettura coinvolti hanno sviluppato un concetto generale e hanno lavorato fino al dettaglio sulle prime unità di abitazione, quale «progetto di partenza» da costruire nel prossimo futuro. Sono state realizzate la massima densità raggiungibile e una grande varietà di opzioni per uso misto e case sovvenzionate (sociali) su un budget molto limitato. Gli impianti solari per la produzione dell'energia dovranno essere integrati in maniera tecnicamente funzionale che sia socialmente efficace.

Il complesso è stato distribuito in una serie di nodi urbani compatti ad uso misto. Il limite di lunghezza di ciascun nodo è stato definito da una comoda distanza di cammino a piedi intorno ad una piazza centrale, che dovrebbe giocare un ruolo di magnete sociale e generare qualità urbana.

Un opportuno sistema di trasporto pubblico dal centro di ciascun nodo, raggiungibile con percorsi pedonali, è stato pensato per rendere più attraente, per i residenti, l'uso dei mezzi pubblici anziché delle macchine.

Per rispondere alle differenti situazioni urbane è stato progettato un differenziato repertorio di tipi edilizi, che amplia le finora usuali soluzioni architettoniche per l'impiego di energia solare.

I singoli lotti costruiti vengono disposti e spesso caratterizzati negli spazi aperti attraverso giardini in affitto, zone tranquille, piazze per il gioco dei bambini, spazi per le attività sociali.

Il fatto che i mezzi di trasporto e gli approvvigionamenti energetici possano essere definiti dall'esterno, permette lo sviluppo di un considerevole vantaggio economico. Surplus di elettricità prodotti localmente attraverso mezzi di cogenerazione, potrebbero essere forniti alla rete urbana.

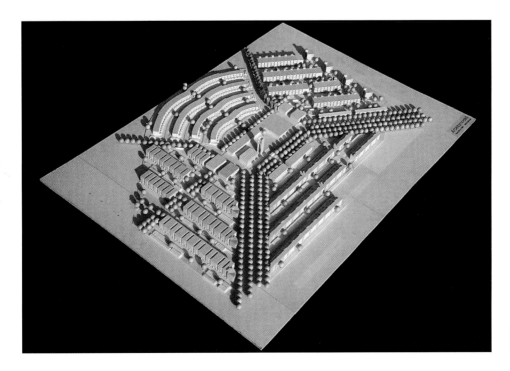

Working model
Arbeitsmodell
Modello di lavoro

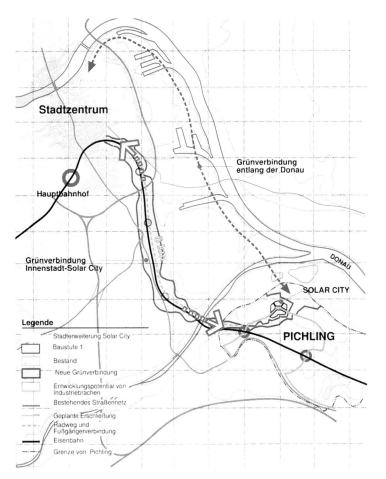

Stadtzentrum

Hauptbahnhof

Grünverbindung
entlang der Donau

Grünverbindung
Innenstadt-Solar City

DONAU

SOLAR CITY

PICHLING

Legende

- Stadterweiterung Solar City
- Baustufe 1
- Bestand
- Neue Grünverbindung
- Entwicklungspotential von Industriebrachen
- Bestehendes Straßennetz
- Geplante Erschließung
- Radweg und Fußgängerverbindung
- Eisenbahn
- Grenze von Pichling

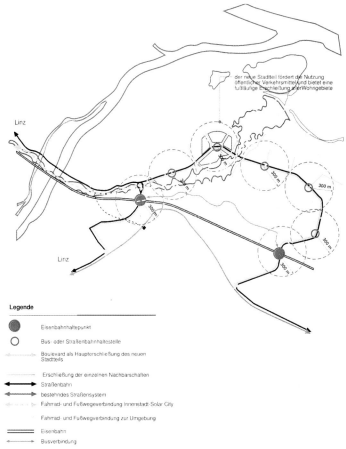

der neue Stadtteil fördert die Nutzung öffentlicher Verkehrsmittel und bietet eine fußläufige Erschließung der Wohngebiete

Linz

Linz

Legende

- Eisenbahnhaltepunkt
- Bus- oder Straßenbahnhaltestelle
- Boulevard als Haupterschließung des neuen Stadtteils
- Erschließung der einzelnen Nachbarschaften
- Straßenbahn
- bestehndes Straßensystem
- Fahrrad- und Fußwegverbindung Innenstadt-Solar City
- Fahrrad- und Fußwegverbindung zur Umgebung
- Eisenbahn
- Busverbindung

Integrated Urban Plan – new connection to the city centre by a green zone

Städtebauliche Integration – neue Grünverbindung zur Innenstadt

Piano urbano integrato – nuova connessione al centro cittadino con la zona a verde

Integrated Transport System
5,000 inhabitants is the minimum size to allow a sensible co-ordination of the infrastructure, services, traffic/public transport and to create urban quality. Public transport is of essential importance and has to be made attractive by keeping the maximum walking distance at 350 m.

Integriertes Verkehrssystem
5000 Bewohner umfaßt die kleinste Siedlungseinheit, damit eine vernünftige Koordination von Infrastruktur, Dienstleistungen, Straßenverkehr/öffentlichen Verkehrsmitteln möglich ist und Stadtqualität entsteht. Die öffentliche Verkehrsanbindung ist von wesentlicher Bedeutung und wird dadurch attraktiv, daß alle Fußwegstrecken maximal 350 m lang sind.

Sistema di circolazione
5.000 abitanti sono la dimensione minima per permettere una sensibile coordinazione tra le infrastrutture, i servizi, il trasporto traffico/pubblico e creare una qualità urbana.
Il trasporto pubblico è di importanza essenziale e deve essere raggiunto con una distanza percorribile a piedi di un massimo di 350 m.

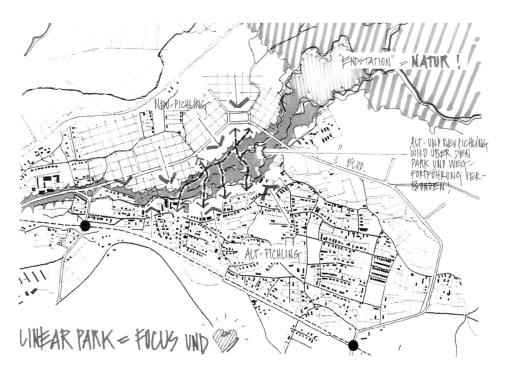

"ENDSTATION" = NATUR !

NEU-PICHLING

ALT- UND NEU PICHLING WIRD ÜBER DEN PARK UND WEG-FORTFÜHRUNG VERBUNDEN,

BLVD.

ALT-PICHLING

LINEAR PARK = FOCUS UND ♡

This project is a realistic approach towards the thorough integration of solar energy on an urban level, based on the conditions of local policies and economy, with all the accompanying constraints regarding political, legal and economic decisions, (such as land-ownership, acceptance of the design by neighbourhood inhabitants, dependence on local politicians and changes due to elections and political forces).

Dieses Projekt stellt einen realistischen Ansatz zur gründlichen Integration von Solarenergie auf städtischem Niveau dar, und zwar auf der Basis von lokalpolitischen und wirtschaftlichen Gegebenheiten vor Ort, mit allen Begleitzwängen aufgrund politischer, juristischer und ökonomischer Entscheidungen (z. B. betreffs Grundbesitz, Akzeptanz des Entwurfs durch Anwohner, Abhängigkeit von Lokalpolitikern und Veränderungen aufgrund von Wahlen und Einfluß von Machtgruppen).

Il progetto costituisce un realistico approccio verso la completa integrazione dell'energia solare a livello urbano, basato sulle situazioni politiche ed economiche locali, con tutti i vincoli correlati alle decisioni politiche, giuridiche ed economiche (come proprietà fondiaria, accettazione del progetto da parte degli abitanti, dipendenza dagli amministratori locali, cambiamenti dovuti ad elezioni, influsso di gruppi di potere).

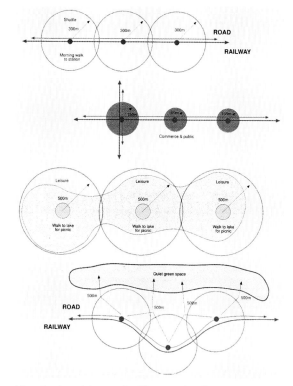

Hierarchy of travel distances for different modes of transport

Fußläufige Distanzen bezogen auf unterschiedliche Verkehrsmittel

Gerarchia delle distanze di spostamento per differenti modalità di trasporto

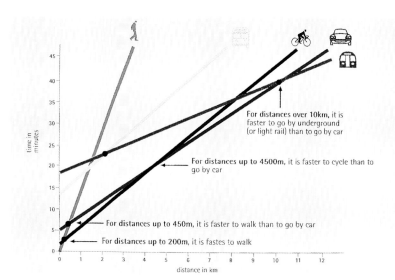

For distances over 10km, it is faster to go by underground (or light rail) than to go by car

For distances up to 4500m, it is faster to cycle than to go by car

For distances up to 450m, it is faster to walk than to go by car

For distances up to 200m, it is fastes to walk

Travel times for different modes of transport in urban areas, from door to door*

Wegzeiten im städtischen Raum für verschiedene Arten des Transports von Tür zu Tür

Fasce orarie di spostamento per differenti modalità di trasporto in aree urbane, da porta a porta

Pedestrian
0.0 M2 Required for a speed of 5km/hour

Bicycle
3 M2 required for a speed of 10 km/h

Light rail or underground one third fullL
6.9 M2 Required for a speed of 30 km/hour

Bus one third full
28.1 M2 Required for a speed of 30 km/hour

Car with driver only
46 M2 required for a speed of 30 km/h

Space required by one person using different modes of transport at different speeds*

Vergleich des Platzbedarfs pro Person bei unterschiedlichen Verkehrsmitteln und verschiedener Geschwindigkeit

Spazio richiesto da una persona che usufruisce di differenti modalità di trasporto a differenti velocità

Public transportation is one of the most important issues in defining the pattern of urban developments and their use of energy.

A traditional masterplan would have given primary importance to the private car as a means of transport. This would have undermined the entire project, because even when only used minimally (c. 10,000 km per annum) the enrgy consumed by modern cars exceeds any potential enrgy savings made on the site.

Die öffentliche Verkehrsanbindung ist einer der wichtigsten Faktoren in der Gestaltung von städtischen Siedlungen und deren Energieverbrauch.

Ein heute üblicher Masterplan sieht i. d. R. zunächst das Auto als wichtigstes Verkehrsmittel vor. Dies hätte das gesamte Projekt in Frage gestellt, denn der Energieverbrauch moderner Autos übersteigt sogar bei minimaler Nutzung (etwa 10 000 km/Jahr) bereits die möglichen Energieeinsparungen der Siedlung.

Il trasporto pubblico è uno dei più importanti fattori nella definizione degli insediamenti urbani e del loro impiego d'energia.

Una tradizionale pianificazione avrebbe attribuito primaria importanza all'auto privata quale mezzo di trasporto. Ciò avrebbe minato alla base l'intero progetto, perchè anche se usate al minimo (circa 10.000 km all'anno), l'energia consumata dalle moderne automobili avrebbe ecceduto su ogni potenziale risparmio energetico realizzabile nell'insediamento.

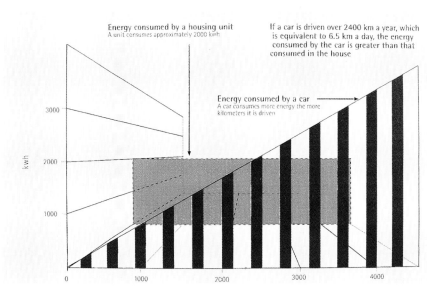

Energy consumed by a housing unit
A unit consumes approximately 2000 kwh

If a car is driven over 2400 km a year, which is equivalent to 6.5 km a day, the energy consumed by the car is greater than that consumed in the house

Energy consumed by a car
A car consumes more energy the more kilometers it is driven

Comparison of energy consumption of housing and cars*

Vergleich des Energieverbrauchs von Wohnungen und PKWs

Comparazione di consumo energetico di abitazioni e automobili

* (Source: Prof. J. Whitelegg, *Transport for a Sustainable Future – The case for Europe*)

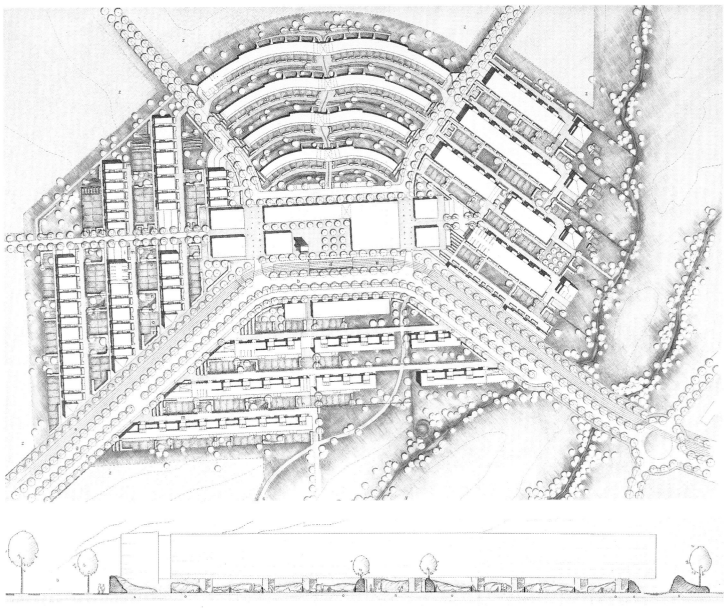

a) Solar Square / Solarer Platz / Piazza solare
b) Boulevard or "Neu-Pichlinger Hauptstraße" / »Neu-Pich-linger Hauptstraße« oder Boulevard oder Promenade / Strada principale della nuova- Pichling
c) Former Weikerlseestraße as pedestrian and cycle path / ehem. Weikerlseestraße als Rad- und Fußweg / Precedente Weikerlseestrasse percorso pedonale e ciclabile
d) Tram stop / Stadtbahnhaltestelle / Fermata del tram
e) Tram track / Stadtbahntrasse / Percorso del tram
f) Suspended lighting / Beleuchtung abgespannt / Luci appese
g) Vehicle lane / Fahrspur / Corsia veicolare
h) Side access lane (one way) / Nebenfahrbahn (Eisenbahn) / Strada secondaria (a senso unico)
i) Parking spaces for visitors / Besucherparkplätze / Spazio di parcheggio per i visitatori
j) Footpath / Fußgänger / Percorsi pedonali
k) Pedestrian and cycle path / Fußgänger und Radfahrer im Mischverkehr / Percorsi pedonali e ciclabili
l) Cycle path / Radfahrer / Piste ciclabili
m) Pedestrian, delivery, refuse and emergency access / Fußgängererschließung, notbefahrbar für Ver- und

Entsorgung / Chiusura dei percorsi pedonali, accesso per la raccolta dei rifiuti e per le emergenze
n) Neighbourhood square / Quartiersplatz / Piazza di quartiere
o) Allotments / Mietergärten / Giardini da affittare
p) Private front garden / private Vorgärten / Giardini privati
q) Green /allotments / Gemeinschaftswiese wahlweise Mietergärten / Prati comuni, giardini da affittare a scelta
r) Recycling collection point – garbage, compost / Recy-cling-Sammelstelle, Müll, Kompost / Punto di raccolta per il riciclaggio di spazzatura e rifiuti organici
s) Formal and informal hedges of varying heights and widths / Form- und freiwachsende Hecken in unter-schiedlicher Höhe und Breite / Angoli formali ed informali di varia altezza e profondità
t) Open rainwater gully / Regenwasserrinnen / Condotto di scolo delle acque a cielo aperto
u) Storage pond / Retentionsmulden / Stagno accumulatore
v) Filter and drainage pond / Reinigungsfilter, Sickermulden / Stagno filtro drenante
w) Clumps of ash, elder and willow / Eschen-, Erlen-, Weidenhain / Frassino, sambuco, salice

x) Restored stream / reaktivierter Bach / Ruscello ripristi-nato
y) Meadows / Parkwiesen / Prati
z) Sites for future development / Bauvorhalteflächen / Spazi per futuri insediamenti

Landscape architect: Latz + Partner

Density is one of the main criteria for keeping the overall energy consumption of buildings and traffic at the lowest level possible.

Bebauungsdichte ist ein Hauptkriterium für die Reduzierung des Gesamtenergieverbrauchs auf ein möglichst niedriges Niveau.

La densità è uno dei criteri principali per mantenere al livello più basso possibile il consumo totale di energia.

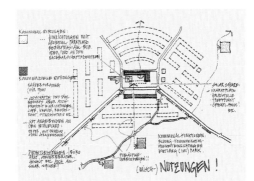

A mix of uses and different sizes of housing units are crucial for the creation of an urban life and the reduction of traffic movement. The correct balance will have a positive influence on the social structure of a community.

Eine Mischung von Geschäften und Wohnungen sowie verschieden großen Wohnhäusern sind wesentlich für die Entstehung eines städtischen Lebens und die Reduzierung von Verkehrsaufkommen. Das richtige Gleichgewicht wird sich positiv auf die Sozialstruktur des Gebiets auswirken.

Usi misti e differenti tagli di abitazioni sono cruciali per la creazione di un sistema di vita urbano e la riduzione del movimento di traffico. Il corretto equilibrio avrà un'influenza positiva sulla struttura sociale di una comunità.

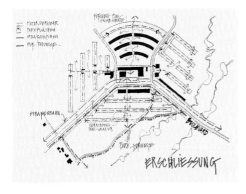

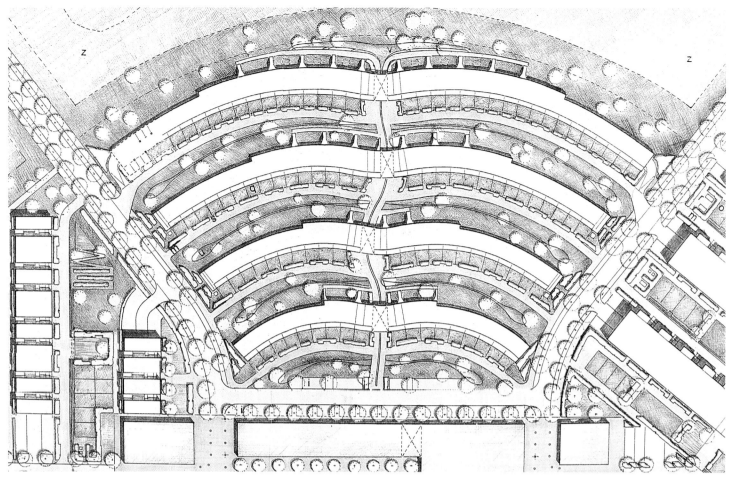

Architect: Richard Rogers Partnership in association with Future Systems
Environmental Engineer: Battle McCarthy
Housing Trust: WSG

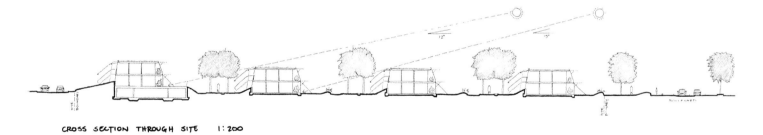

CROSS SECTION THROUGH SITE   1:200

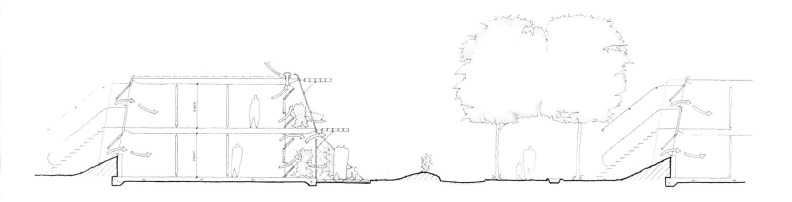

SITE SECTION THROUGH 1-BED FLATS

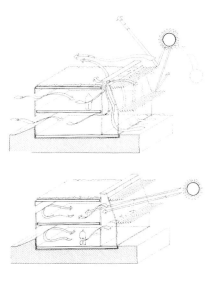

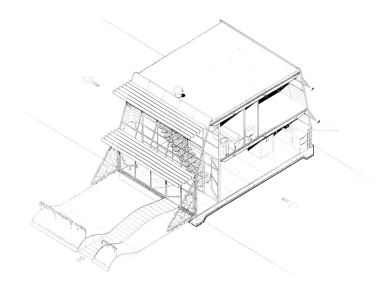

N

FIRST FLOOR

TYPE A - 1 BED FLAT

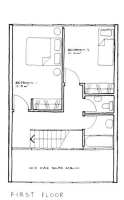

FIRST FLOOR

TYPE B - 2 BED HOUSE

FIRST FLOOR

TYPE C - 3 BED HOUSE

GROUND FLOOR

TYPE A - 1 BED FLAT

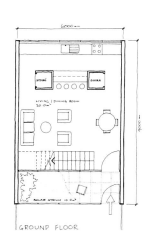

GROUND FLOOR

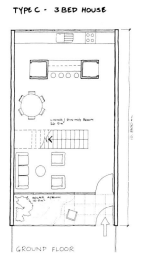

GROUND FLOOR

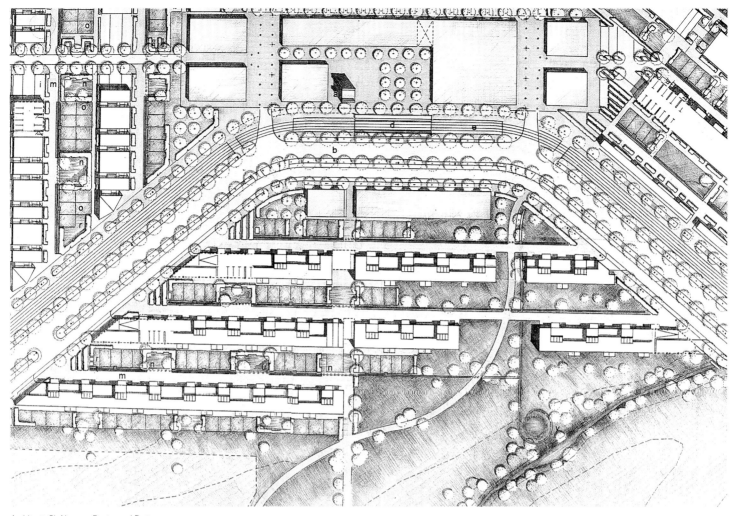

Architect: Sir Norman Foster and Partners
Environmental Engineer: Atelier 10
Housing Trust: Neue Heimat

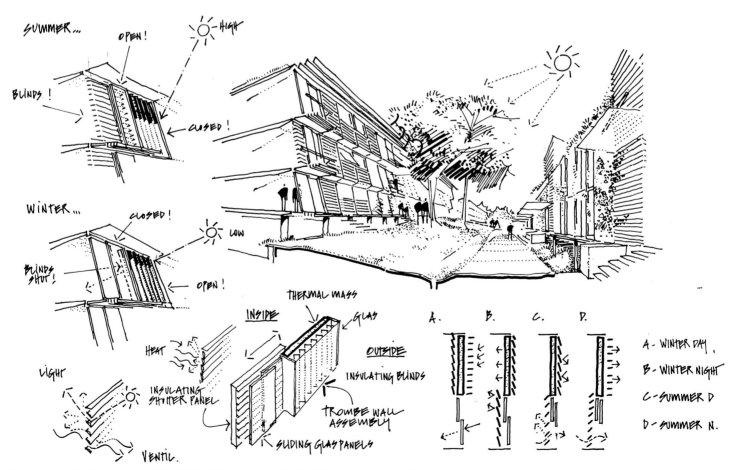

Envelope study with Trombe Façade; Gebäudehülle mit Trombe-Fassade; Studio dell'involucro con Facciata-Trombe

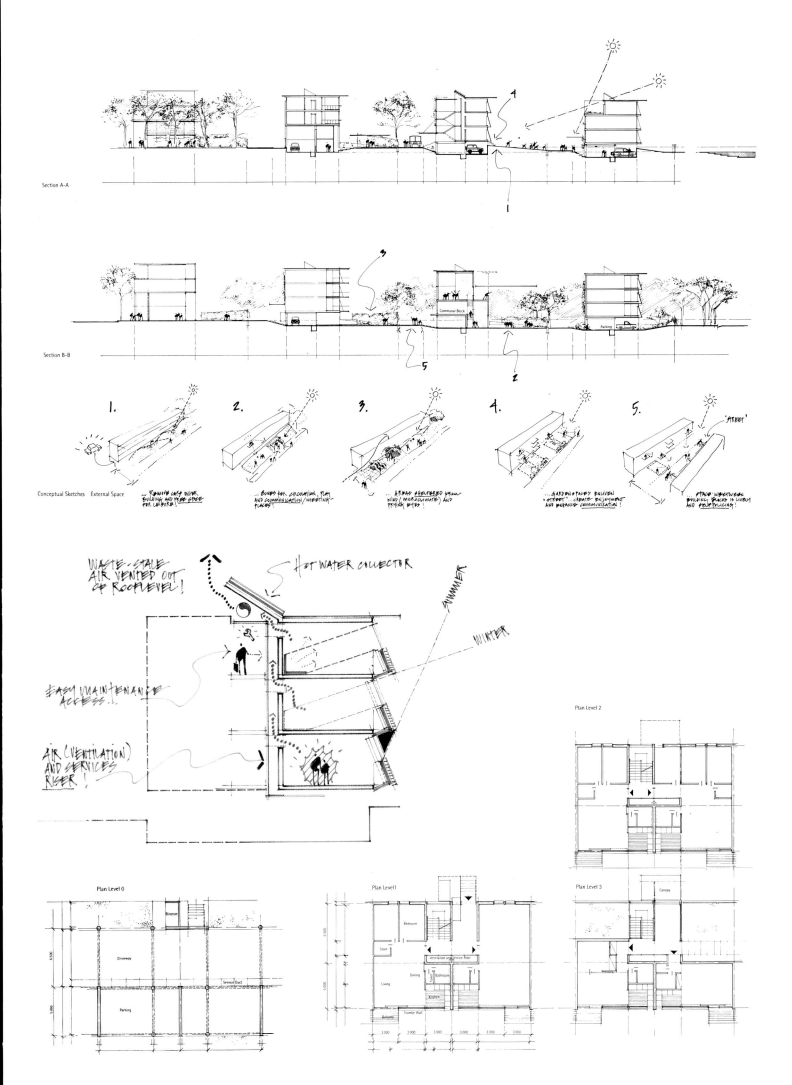

Section A-A

Section B-B

Conceptual Sketches   External Space

1. ... RAINWATER CARS UNDER BUILDING AND PROPER SPACE FOR LEISURE!

2. ... BUNDS FOR CIRCULATION, PLAY AND COMMUNICATION/MEETING PLACES!

3. ... AREAS SHELTERED FROM WIND (MICROCLIMATE) AND TRYING BYES!

4. ... GARDEN & PLACES ENLIVEN "STREET" - CREATE ENJOYMENT AND ENHANCE COMMUNICATION!

5. ... SPACE INBETWEEN BUILDING BLOCKS IS LIVELY AND SELF POLICING!

WASTE-STALE AIR VENTED OUT OF ROOFLEVEL!

HOT WATER COLLECTOR

SUMMER

WINTER

EASY MAINTENANCE ACCESS!

AIR (VENTILATION) AND SERVICES RISER!

Plan Level 2

Plan Level 0

Plan Level 1

Plan Level 3

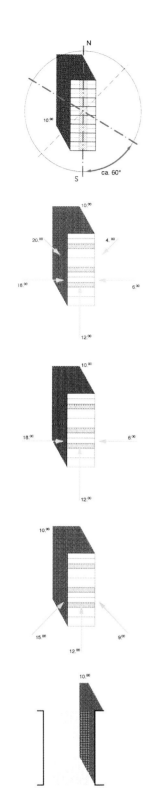

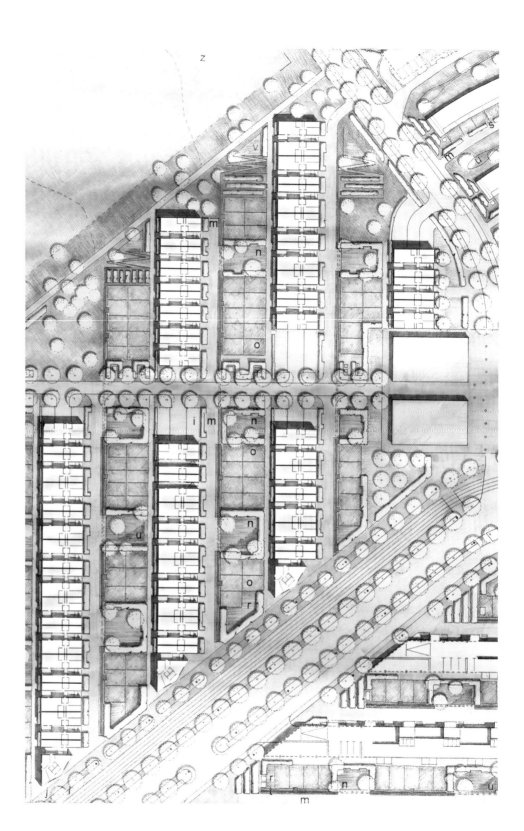

Architect: Herzog + Partner
Environmental Engineer: N. Kaiser
Housing Trust: GWG

East-west oriented linear block housing

3-storey double-span flats of compact construction with minimal surface area; 16m deep 2- and 4-room flats. In the buffer zone between each unit is a naturally lit interior space, with covered balconies on the west side, and lobbies and staircases on the east.

Parking and access roads are beneath the housing, so as to maximise use of green space (allotments, play areas, quiet zones, sun traps and shaded places...)

Centralized servicing, in vertical cores, with integrated heat recovery.

Optimal alignment of open space to the sun because of the north-south alignment of the blocks. Effective wind protection for the exterior space from west and east wind.

O-W-orientierte Zeilenbebauung

3-geschossige Zweispänner, kompakte Bauweise mit geringer Oberfläche, 16 m tiefe 2- bis 4-Zimmer-Wohnungen über zwischenliegende Pufferzonen natürlich belichtete Innenräume, westseitige Loggien, ostseitige Wohnungsvorräume und Treppenhäuser

Stellplätze und Fahrstraße unter den Häusern, Maximierung nutzbarer Grünbereiche (Mietergärten, Spiel- und Ruhebereiche, Sonnen- und Schattenplätze...)

zentral angeordnete Gebäudetechnik, Vertikalstrang mit integrierter Wärmerückgewinnung.

optimale Ausrichtung der Freiräume zur Sonne infolge der Nord-Süd-Ausrichtung der Bebauung.

Bebauung als wirksamer Windschutz des Außenraums vor West- und Ostwinden.

Blocco lineare di residenze orientato Est-Ovest

Appartamenti a 3 piani e a doppia campata di costruzione compatta con superficie minimale; 16 m di profondità, per appartamenti di 2 e 4 camere. Nella zona di cuscinetto termico tra ogni unità, vi è uno spazio interno illuminato naturalmente, con logge nel lato Ovest, e corridoi e scale ad Est.

Parcheggio e strade di accesso sono sotto le residenze, così da ottimizzare l'uso di spazi verdi (giardini da affittare, aree di gioco, zone di relax, zone di sole e di ombra...).

Impianti centralizzati, ordinati in fasci verticali, con recupero di calore integrato.

Ottimale esposizione al sole degli spazi aperti, grazie all'allineamento Nord-Sud della costruzione, che costituisce un'efficace protezione per gli spazi esterni dal vento proveniente da Ovest e da Est.

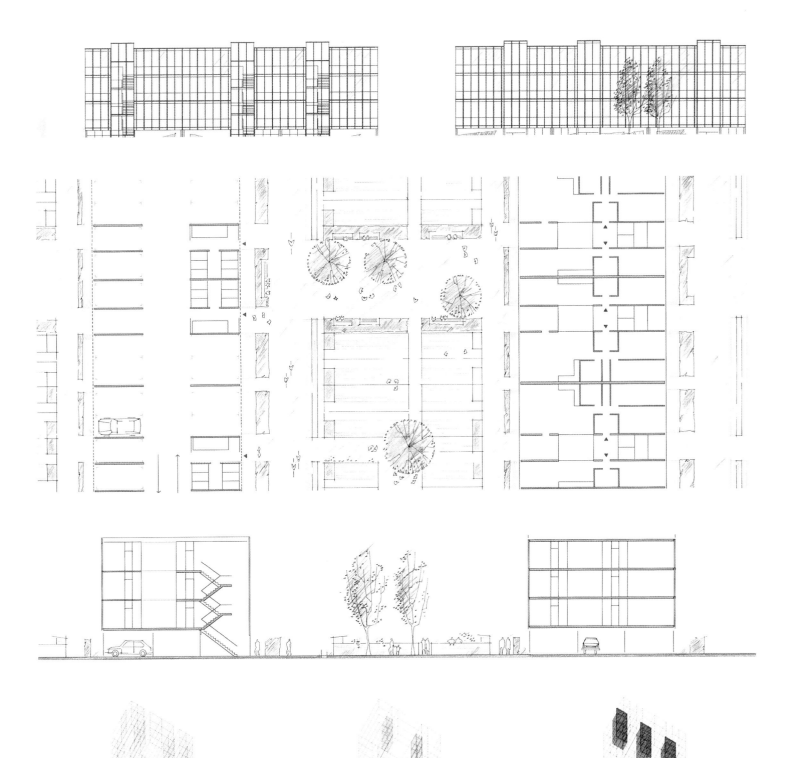

Natural Lighting

The deep plan receives light from the East and West through the extensively glazed façade. All apartments look out on both sides. In the central area are the kitchens and dining areas naturally lit from the bufferzone.

Natürliche Belichtung

tiefe Wohnungsgrundrisse erhalten durch großflächig verglaste Fassaden Licht von Osten und Westen; keine einhüftigen Wohnungen; im zentralen Bereich Küche und Eßplatz. Auch diese sind über die Zwischenzonen natürlich belichtet.

Illuminazione naturale

Le profonde abitazioni ricevono luce da Est e da Ovest attraverso l'ampia facciata vetrata. Tutti gli appartamenti si affacciano su entrambi i lati. Nello spazio centrale vi sono le cucine e le zone pranzo illuminate naturalmente dalla zona di cuscinetto termico.

Thermal Buffer Zone

Glazed atria that act as thermal buffer zones between the housing units are used for: 1. staircases and lobbies to the flats; 2. protected green courtyards and play areas for small children; 3. hanging balconies.

Zwischentemperaturbereiche

überglaste Erschließungs- und thermische Pufferzone zwischen den Wohneinheiten; Nutzung: 1. Treppenhaus mit Vorplatz zur Wohnung; 2. wettergeschüzter Grünhof auch als Spielflächen für Kleinkinder nutzbar; 3. eingehängte Loggien.

Zona di cuscinetto termico

Gli atri vetrati che fungono da zona di cuscinetto termico tra le unità d'abitazione sono usati per: 1. scale e corridoi per gli appartamenti; 2. corti di verde protette ed aree di gioco per bambini piccoli; 3. logge appese.

Sanitary core with central shaft

for servicing. Heat from waste water and exhaust air should be processed by heat exchange and heat pump for heating and domestic water preheating. Extensive prefabrication and preinstallation possible: short cabling, good access for maintenance.

Sanitärkerne mit zentralem Schacht

für die Haustechnik. Abwärme aus Abwasser und Abluft soll über Wärmetauscher und Wärmepumpen für Heizung und Brauchwasservorerwärmung genutzt werden; weitgehende Vorfertigung und Vorinstallation möglich: kurze Leitungslängen; gute Wartungsmöglichkeit.

Nucleo dei sanitari con pozzo centrale

per gli impianti. Il calore contenuto nelle acque di scarico e nell'aria in uscita dagli impianti di ventilazione dovrebbe, attraverso pompe e scambiatori di calore, essere riutilizzato per il riscaldamento domestico e il preriscaldamento dell'acqua corrente. Possibile prefabbricazione estensiva e premontaggio: cablatura ridotta, buona accessibilità per manutenzione.

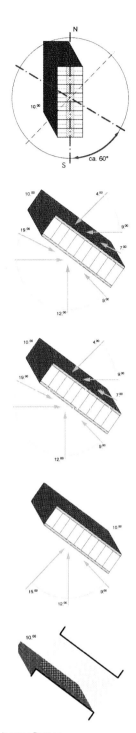

Architect: Herzog + Partner
Environmental Engineer: N. Kaiser
Housing trust: WAG

Northwest-southeast oriented linear blocks

3-storey double-span flats of compact construction with minimal surface area; 15m deep 3-room flats with conservatories or covered balconies at the front. The façades have mobile blinds to protect against solar gain and heat loss. Parking is under the building.

Centralized servicing, in vertical cores, with integrated heat recovery.

Favourable sun-aspect of open spaces as a result of the northwest-southeast alignment of the buildings.

Slender block on the street

Small apartments, of which the focus is a central glazed hall to the south-west. The front elevations enjoy an optimal level of sunshine.

Point blocks

4-storey, double span apartments, facing south-east and south-west; parking below; south-facing conservatories. Compact building form with favourable orientation for absorbing solar energy during the heating period.

NW-SO-orientierte Zeilenbebauung

3-geschossige Zweispänner, kompakte Bauweise mit geringer Oberfläche, 15 m tiefe 3-Zimmer-Wohnungen mit vorgelagerter Wintergärten bezw. Loggien
Fassaden mit temporärem Sonnen- und Wärmeschutz
Stellplätze unter dem Haus
zentral angeordnete Gebäudetechnik, Vertikalstrang mit integrierter Wärmerückgewinnung
günstige Besonnung der Freiräume infolge
der Nordwest-Südost-Ausrichtung der Bebauung

Schmales Haus an der Straße

kleine Wohnungen, deren Zentrum eine zentrale, nach SW verglaste Wohndiele ist. Fassadenfront mit optimaler Besonnungsmöglichkeit.

Punkthäuser

4 geschossige Zweispänner, unterparkt, mit Wohnungen, die sich nach SO und SW öffnen. Im Süden Wintergärten. Kompakte Baukörper mit günstiger Orientierung zur Gewinnung solarer Energie in der Heizperiode.

Blocchi lineari orientati NordOvest-SudEst

Appartamenti a 3 piani su doppia campata di costruzione compatta con superficie minimale; 15 m di profondità per appartamenti a 3 camere con serre o balconi coperti sul fronte. Le facciate hanno persiane mobili per la protezione dal sole e dal caldo. Il parcheggio è sottostante l'edificio. Impiantistica centralizzata, ordinata in fasci verticali, con recupero integrato di calore.
Buon soleggiamento degli spazi aperti come risultato dell'allineamento degli edifici in direzione NordOvest-SudEst.

Blocco stretto sulla strada

Piccoli appartamenti, il fulcro dei quali è un atrio centrale vetrato a Sud-Ovest.
I fronti godono di un ottimo livello di soleggiamento.

Blocchi singoli

Appartamenti a 4 piani, su doppia campata, con affaccio a Sud-Est e a Sud-Ovest; parcheggio sottostante; serre esposte a Sud. Edifici di forma compatta con orientamento favorevole all'assorbimento di energia solare durante il periodo di riscaldamento.

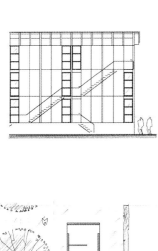
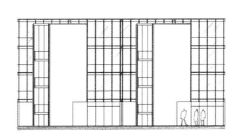
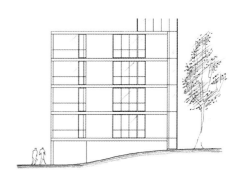

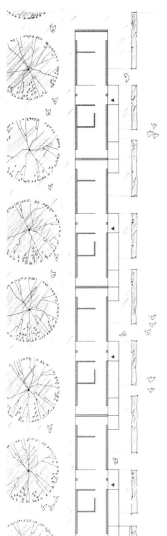
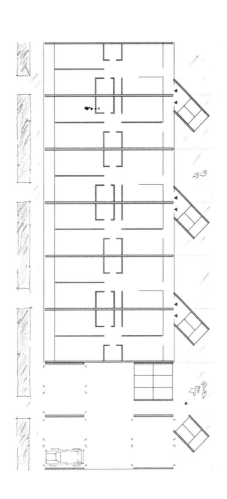
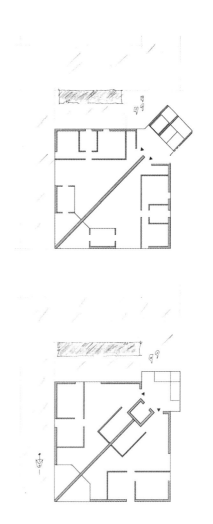

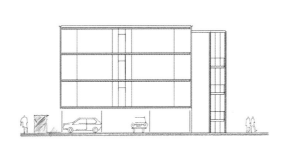
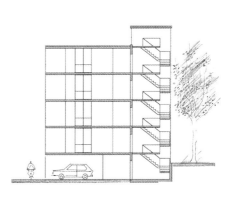

Slender block along the street
Schmales Haus an der Straße
Blocco stretto lungo la strada

Linear Block
Zeilenbebauung
Blocco lineare

Point Blocks
Punkthäuser
Blocchi singoli

191

Options for supply of electricity and heat

Varianten Strom-Wärmeversorgung
Varianti opzionali per l'approvvigionamento di elettricità e di calore

Environmental Engineer: Norbert Kaiser

Supply of electricity from gas and steam (GuD Süd) power plant with electricity and district heating in a combined cycle, with complementary photovoltaic (PV) electricity generation.

Versorgung über GuD Süd (Gas- und Dampfturbine) mit Strom und Fernwärme, zusätzlich PV (Photovoltaik)-Anteil

Approvvigionamento di elettricità e calore dall'impianto a gas e vapore GuD Süd; completamento del fabbisogno con energia fotovoltaica.

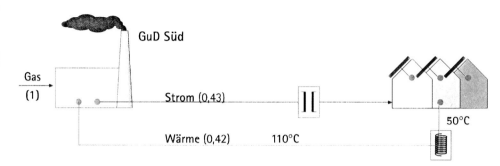

Supply of electricity from GuD Süd power plant, heated by electric heat pumps using excess heat from building exhaust and waste water with complementary PV electricity generation.

Ausschließlich Strom vom GuD Süd, Wärme 100 % von elektrisch betriebener Wärmepumpe mit Abwärmenutzung aus Abluft und Abwasser des Gebäudes, zusätzlich PV-Anteil

Approvvigionamento di elettricità dall'impianto di energia GuD Süd; riscaldamento operato da pompe elettriche, che recuperano il calore in uscita dalle abitazioni e dalle acque di scarico; completamento del fabbisogno con energia fotovoltaica.

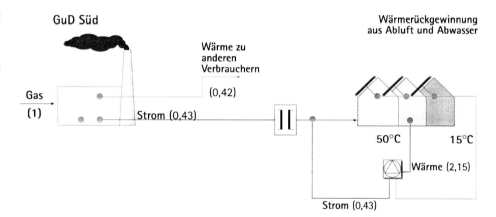

Supply of electricity from GuD power plant and installation of a Combined Heat and Power Plant (CHP) in Pichling fired by gas from the sewage plant (Asten), using the heat for the buildings and returning the generated electricity to Asten, with complementary PV electricity generation.

Ausschließlich Strom vom GuD Süd, Abwärmenutzung aus deponiegasgefeuertem Motor-Heiz-Kraftwerk (MHKW) in Pichling, Rückführung des erzeugten Stroms zur Deponie Asten, zusätzlich PV-Anteil

Approvvigionamento di elettricità dall'impianto GuD Süd e installazione di un impianto a Calore Combinato e di un impianto d'energia (CHP) a Pichling alimentato da gas di recupero dalla depurazione delle acque di scarico (Asten); usando il calore per le abitazioni e rimandando l'energia elettrica generata ad Asten.Completamento del fabbisogno con energia fotovoltaica.

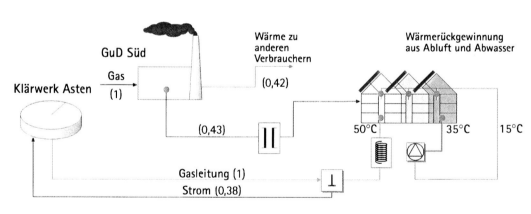

CHP (natural oil fired) generation of electricity and heat, generation of heat peaks using electric heat pumps and excess heat from buildings and waste water, with complementary PV electricity generation.

Pflanzenölbetriebenes MHKW, Abwärmenutzung , Spitzenwärmebedarf mit elektrischer Wärmepumpe und Nutzung der Abwärme aus Abluft und Abwasser, zusätzlich PV-Anteil

Generazione di elettricità e di calore da impianto CHP (alimentato ad olio vegetale). Supporto del fabbisogno invernale tramite pompe elettriche che recuperano calore dalle abitazioni e dalle acque di scarico. Energia fotovoltaica di completamento.

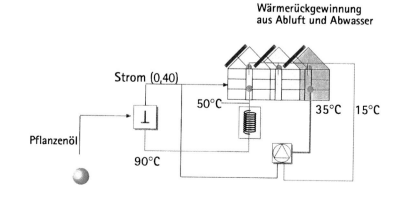

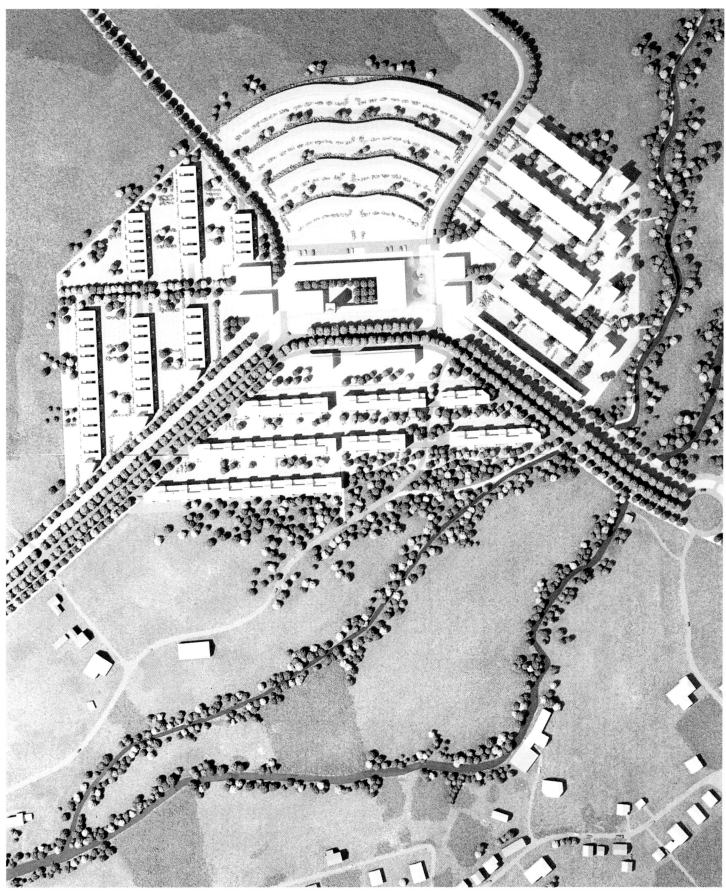

Overall model Autumn 1995
Gesamtmodell Herbst 1995
Modello generale Autunno 1995

Materials, Products, Systems

Materialien, Produkte, Systeme
Materiali, Prodotti, Sistemi

Double Glazing K-PLUS	FLACHGLAS AG, Gelsenkirchen
Micro-Sun Shielding Louvre	SITECO Beleuchtungstechnik GmbH, Traunreut
Translucent Heat Insulation	Glaswerke Arnold GmbH & Co. KG, Merkendorf
made from Glass – HELIORAN™	
Translucent Thermal Insulation Façade Systems	Okalux Kapillarglas GmbH, Marktheidenfeld-Altfeld
KAPIPANE, KAPILUX	
Solar Façade Element SolFas	Ernst Schweizer AG, Hedingen
Façade-Integrated Solar-Air Systems	GRAMMER KG Solar-Luft-Technik, Amberg
Membrane Structures	Koch Membrane Structures GmbH, Rimsting/Chiemsee
System Control	LUXMATE Controls GmbH, Dornbirn

Double Glazing K-PLUS

Isolierglas K-PLUS
Vetro isolante K-PLUS

FLACHGLAS AG

Haydnstraße 19
D-45884 Gelsenkirchen
Phone +49/209/168-0
Fax +49/209/1682053

Even prior to the introduction of the new code for thermal insulation in Germany, which came into force in 1995, there were good reasons for creating south-facing areas of fenestration when planning new buildings. The ingress of natural light through transparent forms of construction is a means of improving habitable quality. With the introduction of the new code for thermal insulation, this form of construction was given statutory support in a number of respects. Windows were no longer regarded merely as elements of a building that result in heat losses. Their ability to exploit solar energy was also recognized.

Since heat losses have to be reduced even further, one can, in effect, use only double or multiple forms of glazing with a thermally insulating coating. At the same time, one must be aware that coatings of this kind, which result in particularly low k-values for the glazing, may also cause a considerable reduction of the total energy transmittance (diathermancy or g-value) of the glass. Effective solar architecture, therefore, requires the use of thermally insulating glazing with a better energy balance, i.e. with a higher g-value. K-PLUS, the energy-saving glass manufactured by FLACHGLAS AG, offers ideal qualities. It has a good u-value (1.6 W/m^{2}K) and an outstanding g-value of 71 per cent.

Bereits vor Einführung der neuen Wärmeschutzverordnung 1995 bestanden gute Gründe, bei der Planung von Gebäuden die Ausrichtung der Fensterflächen nach Süden anzustreben, denn das Einfließen natürlichen Lichts durch transparente Bauweise schafft Lebensqualität. Im Zuge der neuen Wärmeschutzverordnung wird diese Bauweise durch gesetzliche Vorgaben mehrfach unterstützt. Das Fenster wird jetzt nicht mehr allein als Bauteil angesehen, das Wärmeverluste hervorruft, sondern ebenfalls als Element, das Sonnenenergie nutzen kann.

Weil Wärmeverluste auch weiterhin minimiert werden sollen, können praktisch nur noch Isoliergläser mit Wärmeschutzbeschichtung eingesetzt werden. Jedoch muß beachtet werden, daß solche Beschichtungen mit besonders niedrigen k-Werten der Verglasung auch die Gesamtenergiedurchlässigkeit des Glases erheblich reduzieren können. Unter solararchitektonischen Gesichtspunkten sollten demnach Wärmeschutzgläser mit ausgewogener Energiebilanz, d.h. auch mit hoher Gesamtenergiedurchlässigkeit, gewählt werden. Ideale Voraussetzungen dafür bietet z.B. K-PLUS, das Energiegewinnglas der FLACHGLAS AG, mit seinem guten k-Wert von 1,6 W/m^{2}K und seinem hervorragenden g-Wert von 71 %.

Già prima dell'introduzione della nuova disposizione sulla salvaguardia del calore, buoni principi nella progettazione degli edifici tendevano all'orientamento delle superfici vetrate verso Sud, poiché il confluire di luce naturale, attraverso la trasparenza con cui si costruisce, crea qualità della vita.

Sulla scia della recente disposizione sulla salvaguardia del calore, questa nuova maniera di costruire viene ultimamente appoggiata da varie direttive di legge. La finestra ora viene vista non più soltanto come un componente della costruzione che causa perdite di calore, ma parimenti come elemento che può sfruttare l'energia solare.

Poiché le perdite di calore dovrebbero essere minimizzate anche in futuro, si potrebbero montare inoltre vetri isolanti con rivestimento a protezione del calore. Si deve però tener conto che tali rivestimenti, soprattutto con un basso valore k della vetratura, possono ridurre notevolmente la permeabilità totale di energia g del vetro. Dal punto di vista architettonico, si dovrebbero di conseguenza scegliere vetri isolanti termicamente con un adeguato bilancio energetico, ossia con una più alta permeabilità totale di energia.

Ad esempio presenta a questo fine presupposti ideali K-PLUS, il vetro a guadagno energetico della FLACHGLAS AG, con il suo buon valore – k di 1.6 W/m^{2}K ed il suo straordinario valore g pari al 71 %.

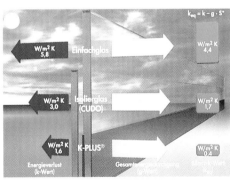

The illustration shows on the one hand how heat loss can be reduced, and on the other how free energy can be obtained from the sun.

Die Graphik verdeutlicht, wie einerseits Wärmeverluste verringert und andererseits kostenlose Energie aus der Sonnenstrahlung gewonnen werden.

Lo schema spiega come da un lato si diminuiscono le perdite di calore e dall'altro lato si guadagna energia dalla radiazione solare.

K-Plus – energy-saving glass as the ideal way to combine solar exploitation and thermal insulation.

K-Plus – das Energiegewinnglas als ideale Verbindung aus solarem Nutzen und Wärmedämmung.

K-Plus – il vetro di guadagno energetico: una combinazione ideale tra l'uso della energia solare e la salvaguardia del calore.

Micro Sun Shielding Louvre

Micro-Sonnenschutzraster
Microreticolo per protezione solare

SITECO Beleuchtungstechnik GmbH

Ohmstraße 50
D-83301 Traunreut
Phone +49/8669/33-591
Fax +49/8669/33-443
Contact person: Herr Buntkiel-Kuck

The micro-sunscreen grid, integrated in a double-glazing unit, helps to create bright, transparent internal spaces with pleasantly cool temperature conditions even at the height of summer.
The special louvre construction of the micro-sunscreen system consists of a directional grid with blocking and non-blocking zones.
"Hot", direct sunlight is reflected away from the building.
"Cool", diffuse daylight is admitted.

Design:
- special sunscreen grid between panes of cavity-sealed double glazing
- vapour-blasted grid elements for light deflection
- orientation within the glazing panel depending on the position of the building in relation to the sun

Lighting technology:
- special louvre profile grid with partial permeability
- sunlight and daylight deflection
- built-in computer layer – depending on roof pitch and relative position to sun
- a U-value of 1.6 W/m^{2}K is attainable
- G-value below 0.2

Application:
- glass roofs of all kinds, including lantern lights, etc.
- congress and sports halls
- in all situations where diffused daylight is required and direct solar radiation is to be avoided

Das in eine Isolierglasscheibe integrierte Micro-Sonnenschutzraster schafft helle, transparente Innenräume, die selbst im Hochsommer angenehm kühle Temperaturen aufweisen.
Die spezielle Lamellenstruktur des Micro-Sonnenschutzrasters besitzt einen richtungsabhängigen Sperr- und Durchlaßbereich.
Das »heiße« direkte Sonnenlicht wird reflektiert – das »kühle«, diffuse Tageslicht wird durchgelassen.

Design:
- Spezielle Sonnenschutzraster in Isolierglasscheibe
- Bedampfte Rasterelemente zur Lichtlenkung
- Orientierung in der Scheibe je nach Lage der Gebäude zur Sonne

Lichttechnik:
- spezielle teildurchlässige Lamellenkontourraster
- Sonnen- und Tageslichtlenkung
- Computerberechnete Einbaulage, je nach Dachneigung und Relation zur Sonne
- k-Wert von 1,6 W/m^{2}K erreichbar
- g-Wert unter 0,2

Anwendung:
- Glasdächer aller Art, auch Lichtkuppeln
- Kongress- und Sporthallen
- Überall dort wo diffuses Tageslicht gewünscht wird und direkt Sonneneinstrahlung vermieden werden soll

Il microreticolo per protezione solare integrato in un lastra di vetro isolante produce ambienti interni luminosi e trasparenti, che perfino in piena estate presentano una piacevole bassa temperatura.
La speciale struttura a lamelle del microreticolo a protezione solare possiede un campo di barriera e di passaggio a direzione regolabile.
La «calda» luce solare diretta viene riflessa, la «fredda» luce diffusa del giorno viene lasciata passare.

Design:
- Speciale reticolo di schermatura solare in lastre di vetro isolante
- Elementi di reticolo attenuanti per guidare la luce
- L' orientamento degli elementi all'interno del vetro dipende dalla posizione dell'edificio rispetto al sole

Tecnologia della luce:
- Speciale reticolo di profili di lamelle parzialmente permeabile
- Pilotaggio della luce solare giornaliera
- Simulazione al computer della posizione degli elementi, secondo l'inclinazione del tetto ed in relazione al sole
- Valore k ottenibile 1.6 W/m^{2}K
- Valore g inferiore a 0.2

Impiego:
- Tetti vetrati di ogni tipo, anche cupole a lucernario
- Sale da congresso e palestre
- Soprattutto ambienti dove viene richiesta una luce naturale diffusa e dove va evitato un irraggiamento diretto

Funktionsprinzip
Principle

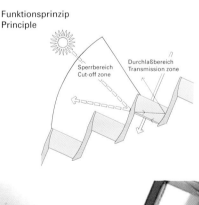

Sperrbereich
Cut-off zone

Durchlaßbereich
Transmission zone

Translucent Heat Insulation made from Glass – HELIORAN™

Transluzente Wärmedämmung aus Glas – HELIORAN™
Isolante termico traslucente in vetro – HELIORAN™

Glaswerke Arnold GmbH & Co. KG

Werk Merkendorf
Neuseser Straße 1
D-91732 Merkendorf
Phone +49/9826/656-0
Fax +49/9826/656-490

In solar architecture, modern developments have paved the way towards multi-functional façade systems. This regulates the flow of solar energy into the building, thus guaranteeing a pleasant room temperature and daylight conditions for the user. Schott developed a new translucent heating insulation system made from glass tubes (HELIORAN™).
HELIORAN can be used as daylighting or as a solar wall for saving heating energy.

Daylighting with HELIORAN™
As a daylight element, HELIORAN is not only an ideal heat insulating material but also an excellent element for design with glass and natural light. Through the light guiding effect of HELIORAN darker parts of the room can be brightened up with daylight. Through this an even distribution of the light in the rooms is achieved.

The Solar Wall with HELIORAN™
The solar wall with HELIORAN makes use of solar energy in order to heat interior rooms. With their high degree of transmission and their good heat insulating properties, a solar wall with HELIORAN leads to savings in heat energy of up to 200 kWh/m² per year.
HELIORAN is an ideal material for attractive energy façades as it is thermally stable, colour-fast, resistant to UV radiation and not inflammable.
HELIORAN is still at the development stage and is being prepared for the market in the course of a promotion project of the BMBF (Federal Ministry for Culture, Science, Research and Technology). Initial pilot projects have already beer successfully carried out.

In der Solararchitektur führen die modernen Entwicklungen hin zu einer intelligenten, multifunktionalen Fassade. Diese regelt den solaren Energieeintrag ins Gebäude, so daß für die Benutzer angenehme Raumtemperatur und Tageslicht-verhältnisse gewährleistet werden. Schott entwickelte hierzu eine neuartige Transluzente Wärmedämmung aus Glasröhr-chen (HELIORAN™).
HELIORAN kann als Daylighting oder als Solarwand zur Heizenergieeinsparung eingesetzt werden:

Daylighting mit HELIORAN™
Als Tageslichtelement ist HELIORAN nicht nur ein ideales Wärmedämm-Material, sondern auch ein hervorragendes Gestaltungselement. Durch die lichtlenkende Wirkung von HELIORAN werden auch tiefere Raumbereiche mit Tageslicht erhellt. Dadurch wird eine gleichmäßigere Ausleuchtung der Räume erreicht.

Die Solarwand mit HELIORAN™
Die Solarwand mit HELIORAN nutzt die Sonnenenergie, um die Innenräume zu heizen: Mit ihrem hohen Transmissions-grad und ihrer guten Wärmedämmeigenschaft führt eine Solarwand mit HELIORAN zu Heizenergieeinsparungen von bis zu 200 kWh/m² pro Jahr.
Thermisch stabil, farb- und alterungsbeständig gegen UV-Strahlung und nicht brennbar ist HELIORAN ein ideales Material für attraktive Energiefassaden.
HELIORAN befindet sich noch in der Entwicklung und wird im Rahmen eines Förderprojektes vom BMBF zur Marktreife geführt. Erste Pilotprojekte wurden bereits mit Erfolg durch-geführt.

Nell'architettura solare, sviluppi moderni si sono fatti strada verso sistemi di facciata multifunzionali. Ciò regola il flusso dell'energia solare nell'edificio, garantendo per l'utente una piacevole temperatura-ambiente e condizioni di illumina-zione naturale. Schott ha pertanto elaborato un nuovo sistema di isolamento termico traslucente composto di tubi in vetro (HELIORAN™).
HELIORAN può essere usato come sistema di illuminazione naturale oppure come parete solare per accumulo di energia di riscaldamento.

Illuminazione naturale con HELIORAN™
Come elemento per l'illuminazione, HELIORAN non è sol-tanto un materiale isolante ideale, ma anche un eccellente elemento per progettare con vetro e luce naturale
Attraverso l'effetto di pilotaggio della luce operato dal-l'HELIORAN, le zone più scure possono essere ravvivate dalla luce del sole. Si riesce così a raggiungere una distri-buzione di luce regolata negli ambienti.

La parete solare con HELIORAN™.
La parete solare con HELIORAN fa uso dell'energia solare per riscaldare gli ambienti interni.
Con il suo alto grado di trasmissione e le sue proprietà di isolamento termico, una parete solare con HELIORAN pro-duce un risparmio energetico di 299 kWh/mq l'anno.
Termicamente stabile, con colori duraturi, resistente alle radiazioni UV e non infiammabile, HELIORAN è il materiale ideale per facciate attrattive di energia.
HELIORAN è ancora allo stadio di sviluppo e sta per essere immesso sul mercato nell'ambito di un progetto promozio-nale del BMBF (Ministero Federale della Cultura, Scienza, Ricerca e Tecnologia).
I progetti-pilota iniziali sono già stati portati avanti con successo.

Translucent Thermal Insulation Façade Systems KAPIPANE, KAPILUX

TWD-Fassadensysteme KAPIPANE, KAPILUX
Sistema di facciata con isolante traslucido KAPIPANE, KAPILUX

Okalux Kapillarglas GmbH

D-97828 Marktheidenfeld-Altfeld
Phone +49/9391/900-0
Fax +49/9391/900-100
Contact person: Dr. Alexander Link

Principle (Fig. 3)

Translucent thermal insulation is based on a simple functional principle. Solar radiation passing through the panel strikes a black-painted wall, which absorbs the energy and emits heat after an interval of time into the space on the other side. In this way, external walls can be transformed from heat-loss to heat-gain surfaces.

Material – KAPIPANE

The capillary structure of KAPIPANE (Fig. 1) is ideally suited to the principle of translucent thermal insulation, It combines maximum transmittance of solar radiation with excellent thermal insulation properties. KAPIPANE capillary-structure transparent thermal insulation consists of a mass of thin-walled, fine tubes set at right angles to the surface of the panel. The diameter of the tubes is approx. 3.5 mm. This capillary sheet is used throughout the world in the manufacture of all kinds of translucent thermal insulation systems (panels with float or textured glass, composite thermal insulation systems, storage collectors, etc.).
The reflective properties of the walls of the tubes deflect light falling on them. Where there is no absorption wall at the rear, the light will be deflected in diffused form far into the space beyond, thus achieving a considerable improvement in the lighting in the depth of the room. (Fig. 4)

Panel – KAPILUX-H (Fig. 2)

KAPILUX-H is a hermetically sealed glass panel consisting of toughened safety glass on both faces as weatherproofing, with KAPIPANE in the cavity between. The filling is thus permanently protected against soiling. The element is roughly 50 per cent thinner than conventional panels and possesses a k-value of 0.8 W/m²k and a total energy transmittance value of 80 per cent.

Das Prinzip (Abb. 3)

Das Funktionsprinzip der Transluzenten Wärmedämmung (TWD) ist einfach. Solarstrahlung trifft durch die TWD auf eine schwarz gestrichene Absorberwand, die Wand erwärmt sich und gibt die entstehende Wärme gepuffert an die dahinter liegenden Räume ab. Auf diese Weise wandelt sich die Außenwand von einer Wärmeverlustfläche in eine Gewinnfläche.

Das Material – KAPIPANE

Optimal auf das Prinzip der Transluzenten Wärmedämmung abgestimmt ist die Kapillarstruktur KAPIPANE (Abb. 1). Sie vereinigt die Eigenschaften maximaler Durchlässigkeit für die Solarstrahlung mit ausgezeichneter Wärmedämmung. KAPIPANE kapillarstrukturierte transparente Wärmedämmung besteht aus einer Vielzahl senkrecht zur Oberfläche orientierter dünnwandiger Röhrchen mit einem Durchmesser von ca. 3,5 mm. Diese Kapillarplatte dient weltweit zur Herstellung der verschiedensten TWD-Systeme (Glaspaneele aus Flach- und Profilglas, Wärmedämmverbundsysteme, Speicherkollektoren, etc.)
Durch die Reflexion an den Röhrchenwänden wird das Licht umgelenkt und bei Anwendungen ohne Absorberwand tief in den Raum gestreut und somit die Raumtiefenausleuchtung wesentlich verbessert. (Abb.4)

Das Panel – KAPILUX-H (Abb. 2)

KAPILUX-H ist ein hermetisch geschlossenes Glaspaneel, bestehend aus beidseitig Einscheibensicherheitsglas als Wetterschutz und KAPIPANE im Scheibenzwischenraum, die somit dauerhaft vor Verschmutzung geschützt ist. Das Element weist, gegenüber herkömmlichen Paneelen, eine um ca. 50 % reduzierte Dicke auf und besitzt einen k-Wert von 0,8 W/m²K bei einem Gesamtenergietransmissionsgrad von 80 %.

Il principio (Fig. 3)

Il principio funzionale per il materiale di isolamento termico traslucente è semplice. Il raggio del sole colpisce il materiale traslucente su di una parete assorbente dipinta di nero, la parete si scalda e trasmette il calore derivante contenuto nella zona cuscinetto agli ambienti retrostanti. In questo modo il muro esterno si trasforma da superficie che disperde calore in superficie che guadagna calore.

Il materiale – KAPIPANE

La struttura capillare KAPIPANE (Fig. 1) si accorda in maniera ottimale al principio dell'isolamento del calore traslucente. Essa riunisce le caratteristiche di massima permeabilità all'irraggiamento solare con un ottimo isolamento termico.
Il KAPIPANE, una trasparente barriera al calore strutturata in maniera capillare, consiste in una grande quantità di tubicini di sottile pellicola orientata perpendicolarmente alla superficie di 3.5 mm di diametro. Questa lastra capillare è usata internazionalmente nella produzione di differenti sistemi di materiale isolante traslucente (pannelli vetrati in lastre o profili vetrati, sistemi di isolamento termico, collettori di accumulo, etc.).
Attraverso la riflessione sulla parete dei tubicini la luce viene deviata e, nell'uso senza lastra assorbente, viene trasmessa profondamente all'ambiente così da migliorare notevolmente l'intensità di illuminazione dello spazio. (Fig.4)

Il pannello – KAPILUX-H (Fig. 2)

KAPILUX-H è un pannello vetrato a chiusura ermetica, costituito da una lastra di vetro di sicurezza da ambo i lati quale barriera agli agenti atmosferici, e KAPIPANE in lastre con spazio intermedio, in modo da essere protetto costantemente dall'inquinamento.
L'elemento mostrato, rispetto ai pannelli tradizionali, ha uno spessore ridotto di circa il 50 % e possiede un valore k pari a 0.8 W/mqK per un grado totale di trasmissione di energia dell'80 %.

1

2

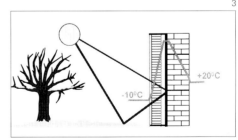
3

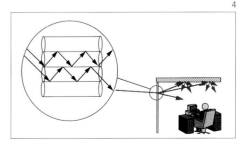
4

Solar Façade Element SolFas

Solar-Fassadenelement SolFas
Elemento di facciata solare SolFas

Ernst Schweizer AG

Metallbau
CH-8908 Hedingen
Phone +41/1/7636111
Fax +41/1/7618851
e-mail info@eschweizer.ch

Translucent thermal insulation has three main uses: the passive exploitation of solar energy; as an insulated light source; and for heating hot-water collectors. The core material looks like a mass of drinking straws glued together. It consists of polymethylmetacrylat (PMMA), a plastic substance with a fine tubular structure, which has two properties. It allows light to pass through, and it transforms light into heat. The plastic tubes are fixed between a sheet of glass and an absorption sheet, which are held in position by a frame.

The SolFas solar façade element transforms sunlight into heat, thereby reducing heating energy requirements. Additionally, the higher temperature of the inner surface of the wall increases comfort in the home.

Light is converted directly into heat according to the principle of translucent thermal insulation. Sunlight penetrates the membrane of solar glass and is converted into heat on the Pelicolor (absorber) sheet. This sheet transmits the heat in the form of radiation to the outer wall of the building, in which it is stored. The external wall therefore functions as a large-area heating unit. In summer, the translucent thermal insulation should be screened from direct solar radiation by a shading device.

Es gibt drei Anwendungen der transluzenten Wärmedämmung: passive Sonnenenergie nutzen, Einsatz als gedämmte Lichtquelle und Heizen von Warmwasserkollektoren. Ihr Kernmaterial sieht aus wie zusammengepappte Trinkhalme. Der Kunststoff (PMMA Polymethylmetakrylat) in Röhrchenform kann zwei Dinge: Er läßt das Licht durch und verwandelt Licht in Wärme. Die Kunststoffröhrchen werden zwischen einer Glasscheibe und einer Absorberplatte montiert und in einem Montagerahmen gefaßt.

Das Solar-Fassadenelement SolFas wandelt Sonnenlicht in Wärme um und reduziert damit den Heizenergiebedarf. Zusätzlich steigert die höhere Temperatur der Innenwandoberfläche den Wohnkomfort.

Das Licht wird nach dem Prinzip der transluzenten Wärmedämmung direkt in Wärme umgewandelt. Sonnenlicht durchdringt die Membrane (Solarglas) und wird auf der Pelicolor-Platte (Absorber) in Wärme transformiert. Die Pelicolor-Platte überträgt die Wärme in Form von Strahlung auf die Gebäudeaußenwand, wo sie gespeichert wird. Die Außenwand wird dadurch zum großflächigen Wandheizkörper. Im Sommer ist die transluzente Wärmedämmung mit einer Beschattungsvorrichtung vor direkter Sonnenbestrahlung zu schützen.

Vi sono tre applicazioni del sistema traslucente con qualità di isolamento termico: uso dell'energia solare, impiego quale isolata sorgente di luce e riscaldamento dei collettori d'acqua calda. Il materiale sintetico (PMMA Polimetilmetacrilico) in forma tubolare può due cose: lascia passare la luce attraverso e la trasforma in calore. I tubolari di materiale sintetico sono montati tra una lastra di vetro e un piano di assorbimento e contenuti in un telaio di montaggio.

L'elemento di facciata solare Solfas trasforma la luce solare in calore e con questo riduce il bisogno di energia per il riscaldamento. Inoltre la più alta temperatura della parete interna aumenta il comfort dell'abitazione.

La luce, secondo il principio del materiale traslucente con qualità di isolamento termico, viene trasformata direttamente in calore. La luce solare penetra attraverso la membrana (vetro solare) e viene trasformata in calore sull'elemento piano Pelicolor (assorbente). La lastra Pelicolor cede il calore in forma di radiazione alla parte esterna dell'edificio, dove esso viene accumulato. La parete esterna viene così trasformata in un accumulatore termico.

In estate il materiale traslucente con qualità di isolamento termico è da proteggere dal diretto irraggiamento solare tramite dispositivo per l'ombreggiamento.

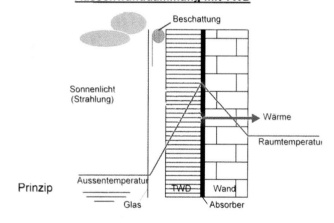

Façade-Integrated Solar-Air Systems

Fassadenintegrierte Solar-Luft-Systeme
Facciate integrate sistema solare aria

GRAMMER KG Solar-Luft-Technik

Wernher-von-Braun-Straße 6
D-92224 Amberg
Phone + 49 / 96 21 / 60 11 51
Fax + 49 / 96 21 / 60 12 60
Contact person: Siegfried Schröpf

Beginnend mit der Applikation konventioneller Kollektoren an die Außenfassade über Komplettverglasungen des Daches, steht heute mit der Integration von Solar-Luft-Absorberelementen in hochwertige Pfosten-Riegel-Konstruktionen eine Technik zur Verfügung, die andere teure Fassadenelemente, wie Spiegelglas oder Marmor ersetzt und damit auch wirtschaftlicher wird.

Gelöst wurde damit insbesondere das Problem der Luftdurchführung durch die Pfostenelemente, wobei die Verbindung zwischen den einzelnen Kollektoren mit Hilfe von speziellen Muffen und Steckhülsen erfolgt. Durch diese patentierte Verbindung der einzelnen Kollektoren ist auch ein hoher Vorfertigungsgrad für die Fassade möglich, so daß die Montagezeiten vor Ort minimiert werden können.

Avendo cominciato con la convenzionale applicazione di collettori sulle facciate esterne e sulla vetratura completa del tetto, oggi con l'integrazione di elementi di assorbimento-solari ad aria c'è a disposizione una tecnica di alta qualità per le costruzioni-montanti-seriali, che viene a sostituire gli altri costosi elementi di facciata, come il vetro specchiato oppure il marmo, risultando con ciò anche economico. E' stato così risolto soprattutto il problema dell'incanalamento dell'aria attraverso gli elementi montanti, avendo luogo il collegamento tra singoli collettori con l'ausilio di speciali valvole avvitate e valvole a pressione. Attraverso questi collegamenti brevettati dei singoli collettori è possibile anche un più alto grado di prefabbricazione per la facciata, in modo che i tempi di montaggio sul posto vengano minimizzati.

The integration of solar-air absorber elements in a high-quality post and rail form of construction provides a modern, economic alternative to expensive façade elements such as mirror glass or marble panels. The application of these elements ranges from conventional collectors in the external skins of buildings to fully glazed roofs.

The solar-air system solves the problem of the passage of air by conducting it through the posts. The connections between the individual collectors are in the form of special socketed joints. This patented connection between collectors also facilitates a high degree of prefabrication of the façade elements, so that assembly times on site can be reduced to a minimum.

Membrane Structures

Konstruktive Membranen
Membrane costruttive

Koch Membrane Structures GmbH

Nordstraße 1
D-83253 Rimsting/Chiemsee
Phone +49/8051/688-0
Fax +49/8051/968762 und 688-240

Buildings with high tension, flexible plastic material in conjunction with construction create new horizons for architecture. Our team looks after engineering, manufacture, installation and maintenance.

Plastic is a unique building material with technical and ecological advantages. It is extremely heat and cold resistant and has exciting engineering possibilities. The light spectrum ranges from opaque to fully transparent. If required the material is available in inflammable, light resistant and 'easy care' forms. It is durable and easily replaceable without interference to building structure, which makes it economically efficient. Recycling poses no problems – another positive aspect in comparison with other building materials. Our range of uses includes:
– Extensive surface areas
– 'Intelligent' cladding for buildings
– Interior design

Das Bauen mit hochfesten, flexiblen Kunststoffen im Zusammenhang mit Konstruktionen eröffnet der Architektur neue Perspektiven. Unser Team leistet Engineering, Fertigung, Montage und Maintenance.

Kunststoff ist ein einzigartiger Baustoff mit technischen und ökologischen Vorteilen. Er ist extrem hitze- und kältebeständig und hat überzeugende bauphysikalische Eigenschaften. Das Lichtspektrum reicht von opaque bis völlig transparent. Je nach Anforderung ist er sogar unbrennbar, lichtbeständig und »pflegeleicht« lieferbar. Seine Langlebigkeit und die problemlose Austauschbarkeit ohne Eingriff in die Bausubstanz schlagen sich positiv bei der Wirtschaftlichkeit nieder. Die Recycling-Frage ist geklärt – ein weiteres Plus gegenüber manch anderen Baustoffen. Unser Anwendungsspektrum:
– Weitgespannte Flächen
– Intelligente Gebäudehüllen
– Innenraumgestaltung

Costruire con materiali artificiali altamente resistenti e flessibili in armonia con gli edifici apre nuove prospettive all'architettura. Il nostro team si occupa di ingegneria, produzione, montaggio e manutenzione. La plastica è un materiale da costruzione unico con vantaggi tecnici ed ecologici. Essa è fortemente resistente al caldo estremo ed al freddo e possiede qualità fisico-costruttive convincenti. Lo spettro luminoso varia dall'opaco al totalmente trasparente. Se richiesto, il materiale è disponibile nella forma ininfiammabile, resistente alla luce e «che necessita di poche cure». La sua durabilità ed intercambiabilità senza problemi, senza inficiare la struttura dell'edificio lo rendono efficiente anche dal lato economico. Sono contemplate le possibilità di riciclaggio – un vantaggio in più rispetto agli altri materiali da costruzione. La nostra gamma include:
– superfici estese
– ›involucri intelligenti‹
– architettura d'interni

System Control

Systemsteuerung
Comando del sistema

LUXMATE Controls GmbH

Höchster Straße 8
A-6850 Dornbirn
Tel. +43/5572/390-1554
Fax +43/5572/390-699
e-Mail: luxmate@luxmate.co.at
http://www.luxmate.com

Because daylight feels good.
Because daylight is for free.

Daylight is rarely used to its fullest potential. However, daylight could be utilized for enormous energy savings. Daylight is the ideal basis for a well-functioning energy management system.

With LUXMATE all measures regarding daylight, such as shading, sun protection, darkening and level of daylight, are integrated into the artificial light system.

The external daylight sensor registers intensity, direction and beam angle of the sunlight or cloud cover, while the daylight processor processes the data. The data is calculated separately for each individual room in a building. Artificial light and blinds are controlled differently, but with equally high precision in each room. If there is enough light in a room due to a great amount of daylight, the "superfluous" light is dimmed in a manner unperceivable to anyone in the room. According to the type of blinds, an exact blade control, dependent on the position of the sun, is possible.

Each room has its own control unit, additionally influencing light and blinds. This allows for more or less light, thus more or less sun – this is always the user's personal choice.

Weil Tageslicht gut tut.
Weil Tageslicht gratis ist.

Tageslicht wird leider noch immer zu selten optimal genutzt. Tageslicht könnte einen enormen Teil zur Energieeinsparung und zur Motivation beitragen. Tageslicht ist die ideale Basis für ein funktionierendes Energiemanagement-System.

Mit LUXMATE werden alle tageslichtbezogenen Maßnahmen wie Abschattung, Sonnenschutz, Verdunkelung und Tageslichtniveau in das Kunstlichtangebot integriert. Intensität, Richtung, Einstrahlwinkel des Sonnenlichts oder bedeckende Wolken werden vom Tageslichtmeßkopf zentral erfaßt und im Tageslichtrechner verarbeitet. Die Daten werden für jeden Raum des Gebäudes individuell berechnet. Kunstlicht und Jalousien werden für jeden Raum unterschiedlich, aber mit gleichbleibend hoher Präzision gesteuert. Ist durch hohe Tageslichteinstrahlung genügend Licht in einem Raum vorhanden, so wird »überflüssiges« Licht behutsam und vom Raumnutzer unbemerkt ausgedimmt. Je nach Jalousietyp ist exakte, sonnenstandsabhängige Lamellensteuerung möglich.

Jeder Raum verfügt über sein Bediengerät, das Licht und Jalousien zusätzlich beeinflußt. Mehr oder weniger Licht, mehr oder weniger Sonne bleiben zu jeder Zeit dem einzelnen Anwender überlassen.

Perché la luce diurna è efficace.
Perché la luce diurna non costa.

Purtroppo la luce diurna non viene utilizzata ancora in maniera ottimale.

La luce diurna potrebbe essere giustificata e avere un grande ruolo nell'ambito del risparmio di energia. La luce diurna è la base ideale per validi sistemi di management energetico.

Con LUXMATE si realizza l'integrazione di tutti componenti relativi a luce diurna come ombreggiatura, protezione solare, oscuramento e livello.

I fattori come intensità, direzione, angolo di irradiazione di luce diurna o nuvole che coprono il cielo, vengono rilevati centralmente dall'apparecchio misuratore ed elaborati poi dal calcolatore.

I dati vengono calcolati singolarmente per ogni stanza. La luce artificiale e le gelosie sono differenti per ogni stanza, ma vengono comandati con la stessa grande precisione. Se, grazie a molta irradiazione di luce diurna, la stanza è sufficientemente illuminata, allora la luce »in eccedenza« viene cautamente diminuita da chi usa la stanza. Per ogni tipo di gelosie, è possibile agire sulle alette in relazione all'altezza del sole.

Ogni stanza dispone di un proprio dispositivo di comando, influiscono in più la luce e le gelosie. In ogni caso, chi usa la stanza decide quando avere più o meno luce, più o meno sole.

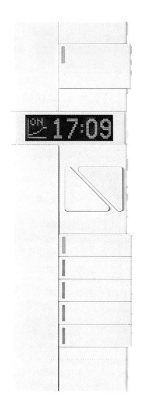

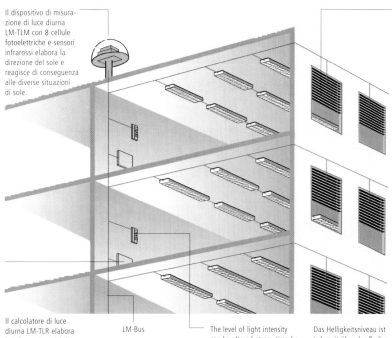

The external daylight sensor LM-TLM with eight photocells and infrared sensor measures the intensity of the daylight, registers the direction of the sun and responds to weather conditions.

Der Tageslichtmeßkopf LM-TLM mit acht Fotozellen und Infrarotsensorik mißt die Intensität des Tageslichts, erfaßt die Sonnenrichtung und reagiert auf Wettersituationen.

The daylight processor LM-TLR processes the information of the external sensor and regulates the blinds and light in every room.

Der Tageslichtrechner LM-TLR verarbeitet die Informationen des Meßkopfes und steuert Raum für Raum alle Leuchten und Jalousien.

Il dispositivo di misurazione di luce diurna LM-TLM con 8 cellule fotoelettriche e sensori infrarossi elabora la direzione del sole e reagisce di conseguenza alle diverse situazioni di sole.

Il calcolatore di luce diurna LM-TLR elabora le informazioni del dispositivo di misurazione e agisce stanza per stanza su tutte le luci e le gelosie.

LM-Bus

The level of light intensity can be altered at any time by the control unit. Automatic and static room scenarios can be retrieved at the touch of a momentary action switch.

Das Helligkeitsniveau ist jederzeit über das Bediengerät veränderbar. Automatische und statische Raumszenarien sind auf Tastendruck abrufbar.

Il livello di illuminazione può essere cambiato in ogni momento in connessione al dispositivo d'uso. Gli ambienti automatici e statici sono da inserire tramite interruttore.

Blinds are moved automatically according to need. That way one can avoid reflexes on the screen and maintain a relation to the outside.

Jalousien werden bei Bedarf automatisch gefahren. Reflexe am Bildschirm werden vermieden, der Bezug nach draußen bleibt bestehen.

Le gelosie vengono adoperate automaticamente secondo necessità. Si evitano riflessi sullo scermo, il collegamento rivolto all'esterno non viene interrotto.

Appendix

Anhang
Appendice

Building with regenerable raw materials such as wood

Bauen mit nachwachsenden Rohstoffen am Beispiel Holz
Costruire con materie prime rigenerabili ad esempio il legno

Michael Volz

A quantity of energy equivalent to roughly half that consumed for heating during the entire lifetime of a building is additionally contained in the construction and materials that go to make it up. For that reason, it will be necessary in future to take account of the intensity of energy involved in any decisions relating to choices of materials or forms of construction.

An important normative instrument for gauging the significance of products and services is soon to be introduced by the International Standardization Organization (ISO); and in October 1995, a collection of data compiled for the building sector in Switzerland was published by the Swiss Association of Engineers and Architects (SIA) with the title "Hochbaukonstruktionen unter ökologischen Gesichtspunkten – D 0123". What these two documents have in common is their attempt to arrive at a balance of the quantities of the resources used and consumed, also taking into account the effects of their use. The method, which is as elaborate as it is efficient (as far as one can tell today), is particularly impressive in view of the fact that, after the introduction of the German code for thermal insulation, nearly two decades passed before it was recognized that quantitative ratios play a major role in the overall energy balance of buildings.

"Life-cycle assessment" is the theme of the moment. It involves life-cycle inventory analysis, life-cycle impact assessment and a process of classification, evaluation and interpretation (life-cycle interpretation). Life-cycle inventory analysis represents a quantification of the input and output (in connection with a product, for example) and of the life cycles of the materials related to this – in particular, the consumption of energy and raw materials. Based on the results of the life-cycle inventory analysis, the life-cycle impact assessment seeks to provide an answer to the question of environmental influences. The third stage – the interpretation – is concerned with setting the results of the life-cycle impact assessment in their proper context and formulating guidelines for the decision-making process.

As a result, the manufacturers of building materials and components are called upon not only to provide the performance data of their products, but to clarify and state their sources and details of their disposal (waste management). One may only hope that this will lead to a proper assessment of decisions affecting the use of materials and processes and the effects they have on the future of our world. In the paper industry, it is already common practice to consider life-cycle assessment data when making purchase decisions. This is also an issue of current concern in the furniture industry. In the building sector, glass and window manufacturers have taken the lead in this respect.

Taking wood as an example of a universal building material, an attempt has been made in the following pages to show the energy input and output in relation to its evolution, production, use and disposal in comparison with other materials.

Etwa die Hälfte der Energiemenge, die im Laufe der gesamten Nutzungsdauer für das Heizen von Bauten verbraucht wird, steckt zusätzlich in der Konstruktion und in den Materialien dieser Bauten. Deshalb muß es künftig auch darum gehen, Konstruktions- und Materialentscheidungen mit Rücksicht auf die Energieintensität zu treffen.

Ein Beurteilungs-Instrument mit übergeordneter Bedeutung für alle Produkte und Dienstleistungen wird demnächst im Rahmen der internationalen Normengebung ISO (International Standartization Organization) eingeführt werden. Eine für die in der Schweiz im Bauwesen Tätigen geschaffene Datensammlung ist im Oktober 1995 vom SIA (Schweizerischer Ingenieur- und Architekten-Verein) unter dem Titel »Hochbaukonstruktionen unter ökologischen Gesichtspunkten – D 0123« veröffentlicht worden. Gemeinsam ist den vorgenannten Arbeiten der Versuch, die Mengen der jeweils verwendeten und verbrauchten Stoffe einschließlich der damit verbundenen Auswirkungen zu bilanzieren. Diese gleichermaßen aufwendige wie – soweit heute abschätzbar – effiziente Methode beeindruckt besonders, wenn man bedenkt, daß bei der deutschen Wärmeschutzverordnung fast 2 Jahrzehnte vergingen, bis berücksichtigt wurde, daß die Mengenverhältnisse eine ausschlaggebende Rolle im Gesamtenergiehaushalt von Bauten spielen.

Ökobilanz (life cycle assessment) ist der aktuelle Begriff. Dabei geht es um die Sachbilanz (life cycle inventory analysis), um die Wirkungsbilanz oder Wirkungsabschätzung (life cycle impact assessment) und um die Klassifizierung, Bewertung und Interpretation (life cycle interpretation). Die Sachbilanz ist eine Quantifizierung von In- und Output. Die Wirkungsbilanz soll eine Antwort auf die Frage nach den Umweltbeeinflussungen auf der Basis des Sachbilanz-Resultates geben. Im dritten Schritt, der Interpretation, wird es darum gehen, die Ergebnisse der Wirkungsbilanz in den richtigen Zusammenhang zu stellen und Entscheidungshilfen zu formulieren.

Die Hersteller von Baumaterial und Bauteilen werden so veranlaßt, neben den Leistungsmerkmalen ihrer Produkte auch deren Herkunft und deren Entsorgung zu klären und offenzulegen. Es bleibt zu hoffen, daß damit die Voraussetzungen für die zutreffende Beurteilung von Material- und Prozeß-Entscheidungen hinsichtlich ihrer Auswirkungen auf die Zukunft unserer Welt geschaffen werden. Im Papiersektor ist die Einbeziehung der Ökobilanzdaten in die Kaufentscheidung bereits weit verbreitet. Auch die Möbelindustrie bemüht sich aktuell um dieses Thema. Im Bausektor gehören die Glasindustrie und Fensterhersteller zu den Vorreitern. Einen Eindruck von der Bedeutung dieses Themas sollen die im Folgenden dargestellten Inhalte vermitteln. Es wurde versucht, am Beispiel des Universalbaustoffs Holz im Vergleich mit anderen Materialien, Input und Output bei der Entstehung, Verwendung und Entsorgung aufzuzeigen.

Una quantità di energia pari all'incirca a metà del totale impiegato per il riscaldamento di un edificio durante l'arco della sua vita, è addizionalmente contenuta nella costruzione e nei materiali che la costituiscono. Per questa ragione, sarebbe necessario tener conto in futuro dell'intensità di energia implicata in ogni decisione relativa alla scelta dei materiali e alla forme della costruzione.

E' stato pertanto introdotto dall'Organizzazione Internazionale per le Standardizzazioni (ISO) un importante strumento normativo per valutare il significato di tutti i prodotti e le loro prestazioni di servizio; e nell'ottobre 1995 in Svizzera è stata pubblicata dall'Associazione Internazionale di Ingegneri ed Architetti (SIA) una raccolta di dati riguardanti il settore dell'edilizia con il titolo «Hochbaukonstruktionen unter okologischen Gesichtpunkten – D 0123». Questi due documenti hanno in comune la tensione nell'arrivare ad un equilibrio delle quantità e delle risorse usate e consumate, tenendo anche conto degli effetti del loro impiego. Il metodo tanto elaborarato quanto – per ciò che è valutabile oggi – efficiente, impressiona soprattutto se si pensa che quasi due decenni sono passati prima di riconoscere che le quantità relazionate avessero un – forse proprio «il» – ruolo decisivo nel bilancio energetico globale degli edifici.

Il bilancio ecologico (life cycle assessment) è il tema del momento. Si va pertanto verso il blancio degli elementi (life cycle inventory analysis), degli effetti o valutazione degli effetti (life cycle impact assessment), e verso un processo di classificazione, valutazione e interpretazione (lyfe cycle interpretation). Il bilancio degli elementi è una quantificazione delle entrate e delle uscite. Basata sui risultati del bilancio degli elementi, la valutazione degli effetti tenta di dare una risposta alla domanda proveniente dagli influssi ambientali. Il terzo passo, l'interpretazione, consiste nel delineare il processo decisionale in relazione con i risultati del bilancio degli effetti nel loro contesto, e formularne le linee guida.

Come risultato, le fabbriche di materiali da costruzione e componenti sono chiamate non solo a dichiararne i dati di prestazione, ma anche a chiarirne le modalità di provenienza ed i dettagli del loro processo di smaltimento.

Si può soltanto sperare che ciò condurrà ad una più adeguata valutazione delle decisioni che riguardano l'uso dei materiali ed i processi e gli effetti che essi producono sul futuro del nostro mondo. Nel settore della carta è ormai pratica comune considerare il bilancio ecologico quando si effettuano le decisioni di acquisto. Anche l'industria dei mobili è attualmente impegnata su questo tema. Nel settore edile l'industria del vetro ed i costruttori di finestre sono all'avanguardia rispetto a ciò.

Il contenuto del seguente catalogo dovrebbe dare un'idea del significato della tematica in oggetto. Si dovrebbe prendere il legno come esempio di materiale da costruzione universale, e mostrare in relazione agli altri materiali i suoi input ed output nel suo intero arco di vita dalla nascita, all'uso, fino allo smaltimento.

Resources
Bestand
Risorse

World Forests
Waldfläche der Welt / Superficie boschiva nel mondo

Forests in Waldfläche in Superficie boschiva	Mio. ha Mio. ha Mio. ha	% of land cover % der Landfläche % di superficie terrestre	ha/1.000 person ha/1.000 Ew. ha/1.000 ab.
North / Central America	531	25	1.240
Canada	247	27	9.278
USA	209	23	839
Mexico	47	25	548
Nicaragua	6	51	1.553
South America	898	51	3.027
Brazil	561	66	3.732
Peru	68	53	3.151
Columbia	54	52	1.639
Bolivia	49	45	6.743
Argentina	45	16	1.395
Venezuela	45	52	2.315
Europe	140	30	280
Sweden	25	59	2.853
Finland	20	66	4.037
France	13	24	232
Germany	10	30	140
Norway	9	28	2.050
Poland	9	28	227
Africa	536	19	835
Zaire	113	50	3.185
Sudan	43	18	1.705

Forests in Waldfläche in Superficie boschiva	Mio. ha Mio. ha Mio. ha	% of land cover % der Landfläche % di superficie terrestre	ha/1.000 person ha/1.000 Ew. ha/1.000 ab.
Tanzania	34	38	1.228
Zambia	32	44	3.822
Central African Republic	31	49	10.057
Angola	23	19	2.303
Cameroon	20	43	1.720
Congo	20	58	8.748
Asia	463	18	149
China	128	14	112
Indonesia	110	60	594
India	52	17	61
Burma	29	44	692
Japan	24	64	196
Laos	13	57	983
Malaysia	18	54	3.183
Thailand	13	25	229
Cambodia	12	69	1.475
Turkey	9	11	159
Ociania	88	10	3.287
Australia	40	5	2.332
Papua New Guinea	36	80	9.292
Former USSR	755	34	2.609
World	3.411	26	644

German Forests
Waldfläche Deutschlands / Superficie boschiva in Germania

Bundesland	Waldfläche (1.000 ha)	% von Gesamt- waldfläche	Bewaldungs- prozent
Baden-Württemberg	1.353	12	38
Bayern	2.526	23	36
Berlin	15	0,1	16
Brandenburg	1.071	10	37
Bremen	0	0	0
Hamburg	3	0	4
Hessen	870	8	41
Mecklenburg- Vorpommern	505	5	21
Niedersachsen	1.068	10	23
Nordrhein-Westfalen	873	8	26
Rheinland-Pfalz	813	7	41
Saarland	90	1	35
Sachsen	496	5	27
Sachsen-Anhalt	474	4	23
Schleswig-Holstein	155	1	10
Thüringen	532	5	33
Total / Gesamt / Totale	**10.844**	**100**	**30**

Source / Quelle / Fonte:
FAO Forestry Statistics Today for Tomorrow, Roma 1993

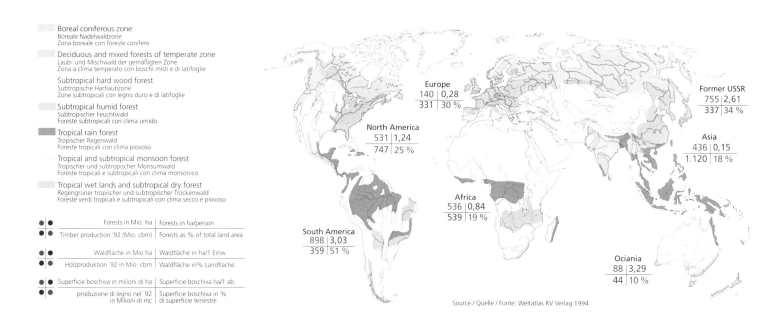

Boreal coniferous zone
Boreale Nadelwaldzone
Zona boreale con foreste conifere

Deciduous and mixed forests of temperate zone
Laub- und Mischwald der gemäßigten Zone
Zona a clima temperato con boschi misti e di latifoglie

Subtropical hard wood forest
Subtropische Hartlaubzone
Zone subtropicali con legno duro e di latifoglie

Subtropical humid forest
Subtropischer Feuchtwald
Foreste subtropicali con clima umido

Tropical rain forest
Tropischer Regenwald
Foreste tropicali con clima piovoso

Tropical and subtropical monsoon forest
Tropischer und subtropischer Monsunwald
Foreste tropicali e subtropicali con clima monsonico

Tropical wet lands and subtropical dry forest
Regengrüner tropischer und subtropischer Trockenwald
Foreste verdi tropicali e subtropicali con clima secco e piovoso

Forests in Mio. ha | Forests in ha/person
Timber production '92 (Mio. cbm) | Forests as % of total land area

Waldfläche in Mio ha | Waldfläche in ha/1 Einw.
Holzproduktion '92 in Mio. cbm | Waldfläche in% Landfläche

Superficie boschiva in milioni di ha | Superficie boschiva ha/1 ab.
produzione di legno nel '92 | Superficie boschiva in %
in Milioni di mc | di superficie terrestre

Europe
140 | 0,28
331 | 30 %

Former USSR
755 | 2,61
337 | 34 %

North America
531 | 1,24
747 | 25 %

Asia
436 | 0,15
1.120 | 18 %

Africa
536 | 0,84
539 | 19 %

South America
898 | 3,03
359 | 51 %

Ociania
88 | 3,29
44 | 10 %

Source / Quelle / Fonte: Weltatlas RV Verlag 1994

World Timber Production (1.000 cbm)
Weltholzproduktion (1.000 cbm)
Produzione di legno nel mondo (1.000 cbm)

	Firewood and charcoal Brennholz und Holzkohle Legna da ardere e carbone di legna	Round timber total Rundholz gesamt Totale legna in tronchi	Coniferous round timber Nadel- rundholz Legno in tronchi di conifere	Deciduous round timber Laub- rundholz Legno in tronchi di latifoglie	Sawn timber total Schnittholz gesamt Totale legno segato	Coniferous sawn timber Nadel- schnittholz Legno segato di conifera	Deciduous sawn timber Laub- schnittholz Legno segato di latifoglie
Africa	480.313	539.350	16.819	455.343	8.179	2.417	5.762
North & Central America	153.737	746.637	498.525	242.652	167.630	139.330	28.300
South America	242.143	358.813	69.643	244.628	26.272	11.815	14.457
Asia	854.304	1.119.713	194.399	903.471	97.346	46.272	51.074
Europe	52.983	331.434	219.081	110.053	79.674	65.045	14.629
Ociania	8.750	43.660	22.636	20.826	5.800	4.107	1.693
Former USSR	81.100	337.100	277.800	59.300	65.000	52.000	13.000
World / Welt / Nel mondo	**1.873.330**	**3.476.707**	**1.298.903**	**2.036.273**	**449.901**	**320.986**	**128.915**
Industrialized countries / Industrieländer / Paesi industrializzati	244.583	1.432.729	1.019.832	407.093	343.285	283.594	59.691
Developing countries / Entwicklungsländer / Paesi in via di sviluppo	1.628.747	2.043.977	279.072	1.629.180	106.616	37.392	69.224

Source / Quelle / Fonte: FAO Forestry Statistics Today for Tomorrow, Roma 1993

Functions
Funktionen
Funzioni

Protection of water
Wasserschutz / Difesa dell'acqua
The forest keeps ground and surface water clear (water quality) and regulate their expenditure.

Protection of earth
Bodenschutz / Protezione del suolo
The forest protects itself and beneath its protection the earth is safe from wind erosion, shrinkage, loss of earth and landslide.

Protection against climate
Klimaschutz / Difesa climatica
The forest protects against frost damage and the negative influences of wind. This improves the climate of nearby housing and open spaces with air exchange (regional climate).

Protection against pollution
Immissionsschutz / Difesa dall'inquinamento ambientale
The forest moderates the bad effects and contamination of noise, dust, aerosol, gas and radiation. It protects areas for living, working and recreation, guarding its own surroundings and others from pollution.

Space to live
Lebensraum / Spazio vitale
The forest is the home to animals and vegetation.

Protection of Roads
Straßenschutz / Protezione stradale
The forest is good for protecting the traffic against the influences of weather and affords a pleasant landscape to the side of the road.

Protection against Landslide
Lawinenschutz / Protezione dalle valanghe
The forest can prevent the development of landslides and avalanches of snow and can divert them or halt them.

Recreation areas
Erholungsraum / Spazio di riposo
The forest cares for physical and psychological well-being, giving visitors a unique experience of nature.

Visual protection
Sichtschutz / Protezione della vista
The forest gives structure to the landscape and protects buildings and factories with a visual screen which integrates them into the landscape.

Ecology
Ökologie
Ecologia

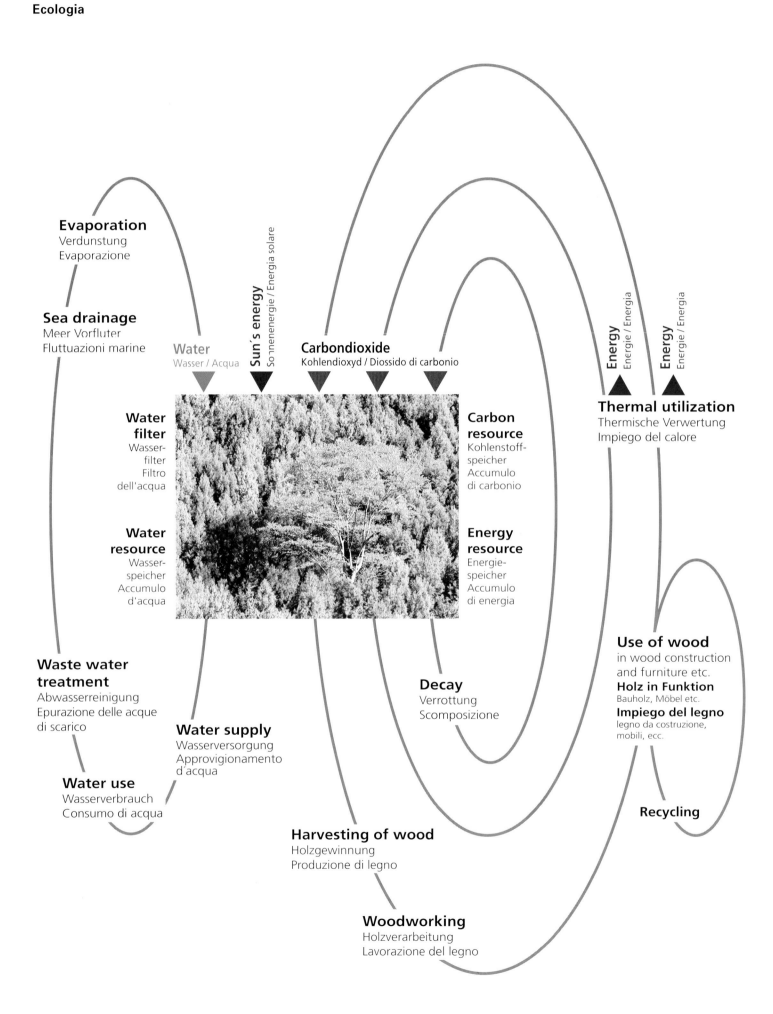

Evaporation
Verdunstung
Evaporazione

Sea drainage
Meer Vorfluter
Fluttuazioni marine

Water
Wasser / Acqua

Sun´s energy
Sonnenenergie / Energia solare

Carbondioxide
Kohlendioxyd / Diossido di carbonio

Energy
Energie / Energia

Energy
Energie / Energia

**Water
filter**
Wasser-
filter
Filtro
dell'acqua

**Water
resource**
Wasser-
speicher
Accumulo
d'acqua

**Carbon
resource**
Kohlenstoff-
speicher
Accumulo
di carbonio

**Energy
resource**
Energie-
speicher
Accumulo
di energia

Thermal utilization
Thermische Verwertung
Impiego del calore

**Waste water
treatment**
Abwasserreinigung
Epurazione delle acque
di scarico

Water supply
Wasserversorgung
Approvigionamento
d´acqua

Decay
Verrottung
Scomposizione

Use of wood
in wood construction
and furniture etc.
Holz in Funktion
Bauholz, Möbel etc.
Impiego del legno
legno da costruzione,
mobili, ecc.

Water use
Wasserverbrauch
Consumo di acqua

Harvesting of wood
Holzgewinnung
Produzione di legno

Recycling

Woodworking
Holzverarbeitung
Lavorazione del legno

Energy
Energie
Energia

Embodied energy for different building materials / Herstellungsenergiebedarf verschiedener Baustoffe / Quantitativo energetico per i differenti materiali da costruzione

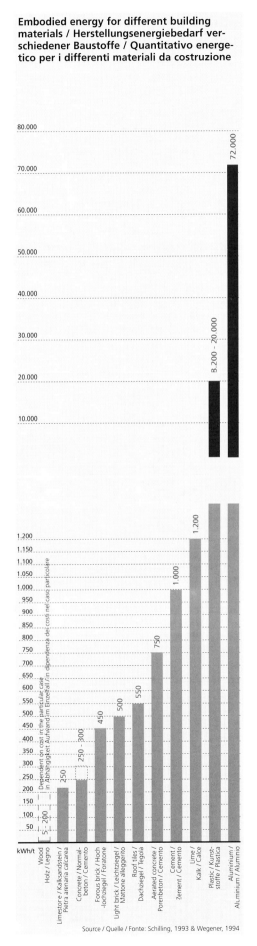

Source / Quelle / Fonte: Schilling, 1993 & Wegener, 1994

Sample Calculations / Modellrechnungen / Elaborazione del modello

Energy balance in the production of composite wooden panels / Energiebilanz von Brettschichtholz / Bilancio energetico dei prodotti di legno multistrato

Input

Timber production / Holzproduktion / Produzione di legno	62
Transport (1) / Transport (1) / Trasporto (1)	250
Sawn timber production (2) / Schnittholzherstellung (2) / Produzione di legno segato (2)	220
BSH production (3) / Brettschichtholzherstellung (3) / Produzione di legno multistrato (3)	1.800
BSH transportation (4) / Brettschichtholztransport (4) / Trasporto di legno multistrato (4)	105
Total / Summe / Somma	**2.437**

Output

Energy content (5) of BSH (3) / Energieinhalt (5) Brettschichtholz (3) / Tenore energetico(5) Legno multistrato(3)	3.300
Waste (off-cuts) for production of BSH / Reststoffe bei BSH-Herstellung / Elementi di risulta della produzione di multistrato	1.400
and sawn timber / und Schnittholzherstellung / e della produzione di legno segato	3.100
Total / Summe / Somma	**7.800**
Balance / Bilanz / Bilancio	**+ 5363**

Unit: cbm round timber, (MJ/cbm) / Zahlenbasis: cbm Rundholz, (MJ/cbm) / Unità di misura: mc di legno in tronchi, (MJ/cbm)
(1) Range 100 km; (2) Yield 60%; (3) Yield 70% in relation to cut timber; (4) Range 200 km; (5)17,5 MJ/kg air-dry, density 450 kg/cbm
(1) Entfernung 100 km; (2) Ausbeute 60%; (3) Ausbeute 70% bezogen auf Schnittholz; (4) Entfernung 200 km; (5)17,5 MJ/kg lufttrocken, Dichte 450 kg/cbm
(1) Distanza 100 km; (2) Prodotto utile 60%; (3) Prodotto del 70% riferito quantità di legno segato; (4) Distanza 200 km; (5)17,5 MJ/kg Aria secca, Densità 450 kg/cbm

Source / Quelle / Fonte: Wegener 1994

Energy required for production, use and dismantling of a warehouse in wood, steel and reinforced concrete (MWh) / Energieaufwand für Herstellung, Betrieb und Abbau von Lagerhallen aus Holz, Stahl und Stahlbeton (MWh) / Impiego di energia per produzione, esercizio e smantellamento di magazzini di legno, acciaio e cemento armato (MWh)

Activity Verwendungsbereich / Attività	Wood Holz / Legno	Steel Stahlbau / Acciaio	Reinforced concrete Stahlbeton / Cemento armato
Production of building materials / Baustoffproduktion / Produzione	330	630	826
Transportation / Transporte / Trasporto	60	60	121
Use (20 years) / Betrieb (20 Jahre) / Esercizio (20 anni)	1.000	1.075	1.139
Dismantling / Abbruch / Demolizione	90	62	137
Total / Summe / Somma	**1.480**	**1.827**	**2.223**

Source / Quelle / Fonte: Baier 1982

Use of energy in building an apartment / Energieaufwand zum Bau einer Wohnung / Impiego di energia per la costruzione di un´abitazione

Type of construction Bauweise / Tipi di costruzione	Bricks Ziegel / Mattoni	Aerated concrete Porenbeton / Cemento alveolare	Wooden plank Holztafelbau / Tavole di legno
Shell/ Rohbau / Costruzione al grezzo	151.757	123.219	98.336
Completion / Ausbau / Completamento e finiture	40.388	32.263	28.670
Total / Summe / Somma	**192.145**	**155.482**	**127.006**

Living area 100 qm, Energy use kWh / Wohnfläche 100 qm, Energieaufwand in kWh / Superficie abitabile 100 mq, Impiego di energia in kWh

Source / Quelle / Fonte: Weller und Rehberg 1989

Energy used in production of a beam / Energieaufwand bei der Herstellung eines Einfeld-Trägers / Impiego di energia nella produzione di un´ architrave

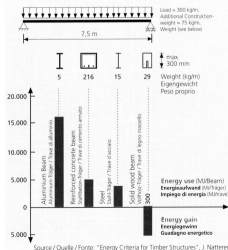

Source / Quelle / Fonte: "Energy Criteria for Timber Structures", J. Natterer

Energy used for production of a window with 2.6 sqm area / Energieaufwand zur Herstellung eines Fensters mit 2,6 qm Fläche / Impiego di energia per la produzione di una finestra con una superficie di 2,6 mq

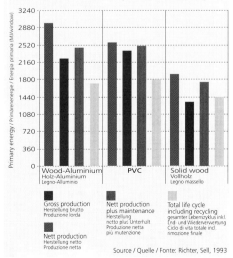

Source / Quelle / Fonte: Richter, Sell, 1993

Climate
Klima
Clima

· CO_2 emissions are the main cause of the green-house effect.
· The world-wide resources of wood amount to 400 Mrd. cbm (or c. 250 Mrd tonnes).

· In this is contained c. 125 Mrd. tonnes of Carbon (CO_2 equivalent = c. 450 Mrd. tonnes.)

· The world-wide CO_2 emission currently amounts to 22 Mrd. tonnes per annum.
· The technical use of wood in construction and products with long life is more important than ever today.
· By using low grade wood as a thermal medium one can reduce the consumption of other fossil fuels.
· Thus there is an improvement in the CO_2 balance, because the inevitable decomposition of this wood gives an emission of CO_2 comparable to combustion.

· Kohlendioxid (CO_2) - Emissionen sind hauptver-antwortlich für den Treibhauseffekt.
· Der weltweite Holzvorrat beträgt 400 Mrd. cbm (entspricht ca. 250 Mrd. Tonnen).

· Darin sind ca. 125 Mrd. Tonnen Kohlenstoff ent-halten (CO_2 -Äquivalent = ca. 450 Mrd. Tonnen).

· Die weltweite CO_2 - Emission beträgt zur Zeit jährlich 22 Mrd. Tonnen.
· Die technische Nutzung von Holz für die langfri-stig in Gebrauch befindlichen Konstruktionen und Produkte ist wichtiger und aktueller denn je.
· Durch die thermische Verwertung von Rest- und Abfallholz kann der Verbrauch anderer fossiler Energieträger reduziert werden.
· Der Effekt wäre eine Verbesserung der CO_2 - Bilanz, da beim Verzicht auf die Verbrennung zwangsläufig die Verrottung dieses Holzes folgt und dabei eine mit der Verbrennung vergleichba-re Menge CO_2 entsteht.

· Le emissioni di CO_2 sono i principali responsabili dell'effetto-serra.
· La provvista di legno mondiale ammonta a 400 Miliardi di mc (corrispondenti a circa 250 Miliardi di Tonnellate).
· In questa sono contenute circa 125 Tonnellate di Carbonio (CO_2-equivalente = circa 450 Miliardi di Tonnelate).
· L'emissione mondiale di CO_2 ammonta per il momento a 22 Miliardi di Tonnellate annue
· L'utilizzazione tecnica del legno, in prima linea per le costruzioni ed i prodotti che si trovano da lungo tempo in uso, è più importante che mai.
· Attraverso l'impiego del legno di più scarsa qua-lità come mezzo isolante si può ridurre il consu-mo dello sfruttamento di altre energie fossili.
· Da ciò risulta un miglioramento nel bilancio di CO_2, dal momento che dall'imputridimento che inevitabilmente avverrà di questo legno si spri gionerà una quantità di CO_2 paragonabile a quella che normalmente viene sprigionata per combustione.

Comparison of carbon emissions
for heating systems using wood and oil.

Fuel	Wood	Oil
Fuel quantity	1.000 kg	229 kg
Power	11,9 MJ/kg	42,7 MJ/kg
Efficiency	70 %	85 %
Process	Wood harvesting, sawing	Extraction, refining
Energy used by the process	0,34 MJ/kg	10,9 MJ/kg
Nett carbon deposit	0 kg from wood 18.1 kg from processing	213.6 kg from oil 65.6 kg from processing
Total C-emission	18,1 kg	279,2 kg
Total CO_2 emission	66,4 kg	1.023 kg

Vergleich der Kohlenstoffemission
bei der Heizung mit Holz und mit Heizöl (1t Holz bzw. 229 kg Heizöl)

Brennstoff	Holz	Heizöl
Brennstoffmenge	1.000 kg	229 kg
Heizwert	11,9 MJ/kg	42,7 MJ/kg
Wirkungsgrad	70 %	85 %
Aufbereitung	Holzernte, -transport, Hacken	Förderung, Transport, Raffinerie
Energieaufwand bei der Aufbereitung	0,34 MJ/kg	10,9 MJ/kg
Netto-C-Freisetzung	0 kg aus Holz 18,1 kg aus Aufbereitung	213,6 kg aus Heizöl 65,6 kg aus Aufbereitung
Gesamte C-Emission	18,1 kg	279,2 kg
CO_2-Gesamtemission	66,4 kg	1.023 kg

Confronto dell'emissione di Carbonio

Combustibile	Legno	Olio combustibile
Quantità di combustibile	1.000 kg	229 kg
Potere calorifero	11,9 MJ/kg	42,7 MJ/kg
Efficienza	70 %	85 %
Trattamento	Coltivazione, trasporto, taglio	Estrazione, trasporto, raffinazione
Impiego di energia per il trattamento	0,34 MJ/kg	10,9 MJ/kg
Netto-Quantità di C-Depositata	0 Kg di legno 18.1 Kg di trattamento	213.6 Kg di olio 65.6 Kg di trattamento
Emissione totale di C	18,1 kg	279,2 kg
Emissione totale di CO_2	66,4 kg	1.023 kg

CO_2 accumulated in untreated timber
(round wood with diameter > 7cm)
CO_2 Speicher im Derbholz
(Rundholz mit d > 7cm)
Accumulo di CO_2 nel legno grezzo
(tronchi di legno con d > 7cm)

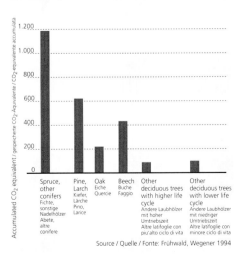

Accumulated CO_2 equivalent / gespeichertes CO_2-Äquivalente / CO_2-equivalente accumulata

Spruce, other conifers / Fichte, sonstige Nadelhölzer / Abete, altre conifere
Pine, Larch / Kiefer, Lärche / Pino, Larice
Oak / Eiche / Quercie
Beech / Buche / Faggio
Other deciduous trees with higher life cycle / Andere Laubhölzer mit hoher Umtriebszeit / Altre latifoglie con più'alto ciclo di vita
Other deciduous trees with lower life cycle / Andere Laubhölzer mit niedriger Umtriebszeit / Altre latifoglie con minore ciclo di vita

Source / Quelle / Fonte: Frühwald, Wegener 1994

CO_2 balance for the production of a beam
CO_2 Bilanz bei der Herstellung eines Einfeld-Trägers
Bilancio di CO_2 nella produzione di un'architrave

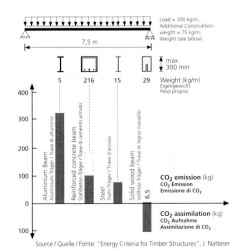

Load = 300 kg/m, Additional Construktion-weight = 75 kg/m, Weight (see below)
7,5 m
max. 300 mm

| 5 | 216 | 15 | 29 | Weight (kg/m) Eigengewicht Peso proprio |

Aluminium Beam / Aluminium-Träger / Trave di alluminio
Reinforced concrete beam / Stahlbeton-Träger / Trave di cemento armato
Steel / Stahl-Träger / Trave di acciaio
Solid wood beam / Vollholz-Träger / Trave di legno massello 6,5

CO_2 emission (kg) CO_2 Emission Emissione di CO_2

CO_2 assimilation (kg) CO_2 Aufnahme Assimilazione di CO_2

Source / Quelle / Fonte: "Energy Criteria for Timber Structures", J. Natterer

In a wood house of 50 cbm of wood there are stored 12,5 t of carbon with a CO_2 equivalent of 45 t / In einem Holzhaus mit 50 cbm Holz sind 12,5 t Kohlenstoff mit einem CO_2-Äquivalent von 45 t gespeichert. / In una casa di legno ci sono 12,5 t di Carbonio con una CO_2-equivalente di 45 t accumulata.

Wohnhaus in Pullach, Arch. Herzog und Volz mit Streib

Future
Zukunft
Futuro

Wood is
not only produced
under the
unique ecological
conditions of the forest,
which
themselves bring
about a wealth
of special benefits, but may
also respond
to a demand for
materials which constitute a
renewable and cyclical economic system. The role of wood in such a system is ecological and cost effective, and manifests a CO_2 balance. The proper use and cultivation of our forests and an increased use of wood are coming to play a key role in a society which today behaves in such a way that future generations can also fulfil their essential needs. Forests and wood can only play this role if all the responsible authorities are prepared to dedicate their creativity and economic resources
to concerted
action.
Wegener 1994

Holz wird
nicht nur unter
einmalig
ökologischen Bedingungen
produziert,
wobei die
Wälder einzigartige
und vielfältige Wohlfahrtswirkungen
erbringen, sondern
es kann sich
den kritischen Anforderungen einer ökologisch und ökonomisch ausgerichteten Kreislaufwirtschaft stellen, was CO_2-Energiebilanzen deutlich machen. Einer ordnungsgemäßen Erhaltung und Bewirtschaftung unserer Wälder, sowie einer verstärkten Holznutzung kommen daher eine Schlüsselrolle zu in einer Gesellschaft, die heute so handelt, daß auch nachkommenden Generationen die Erfüllung ihrer wesentlichen Bedürfnisse möglich ist. Diese Rolle können Wald und Holz auf verantwortlichen
Kräfte mit außergewöhnlichen
Engagement,
Kreativität, ökonomischem
Aufwand, und
Risiko zu gemeinsamem
Handeln finden.
Wegener 1994

La produzione del legno non
riguarda solo
l'ambito
ecologicole
foreste forniscono infatti effetti benefici molteplici e straordinari- ma può anche essere vista in chiave critica a favore di un sistema economico ciclico orientato in modo ecologico e teso al risparmio, modello la cui validità è mostrata chiaramente dai bilanci energetici della CO_2. È possibile che un mantenimento e anzi uno sviluppo delle nostre foreste, nonche' un incremento dell'impiego del legno, vengano a giocare un ruolo chiave, in una società quale è la nostra al momento, tale che anche le generazioni a venire possano godere
dei loro
sostanziali benefici. Legno
e foresta possono
adempiere a
questo compito solo
a lungc termine, quando tutte le forze
responsabili si
trovino ad operare insieme
con straordinario
impegno, creatività,
dispendio economico e rischio.
Wegener 1994

Index of Names

Namenregister
Indice dei nomi

Photo Credits

Unless otherwise listed below, all illustrations and photographs are the property of the corresponding architects or architectural offices.

Atlantis 169
Peter Bartenbach 145 centre left
Peter Bonfig 67 lower right
Balthasar Burkhard 48, 49
Peter Cook 107
N. Daniilidis 103 centre, and lower
Richard Davis 109 upper, 133
Michel Denancé 110, 111, 160, 161
F. Döring 180
Energy Research Group ERG 56, 57
Mischa Erben 59, 81 centre
Wolfgang Feil 50, 51
Georges Fessey 87, 88, 89
Foto Archivio Comunale di Perugia (Tomas Clocchiatti) 116 right
Foto Gramigni 150
Foto Mattei 150
Foto Teia Cusachs 140, 141 centre left, 141 right
Fregoso/Basalto 120
Verena von Gagern 94, 95
Dennis Gilbert 83 lower
Gubli Foto 121 upper
Robert Häusser 147
Elmar Hahn Sudios 203
Jochen Helle 99 upper
Verena Herzog-Loibl 66, 122, 141 upper left
Holger Knauf 127 upper right
Ferit Kuyas 52, 53
Werner Lang 164, 165
Dieter Leistner 67 upper, and lower left, 145 upper, and centre right, and lower
Battle McCarthy 105
Sigrid Neubert 69
Eamonn O'Mahony 113, 119, 127 lower right, 158, 159, 176, 179
Pilkington 196
Karsten Rabas 196
Paul Raftery 83 centre
Ralph Richter 99 lower, 200
Schlosser GmbH 205
Manfred Seidl 80
Stringer 135
Transsolar 85
TU München 50, 51 centre